The Precautionary Principle in the 20th Century

The Precautionary Principle in the 20th Century

Late Lessons from Early Warnings

Edited by
Poul Harremoës
David Gee
Malcolm MacGarvin
Andy Stirling
Jane Keys
Brian Wynne
Sofia Guedes Vaz

European Environment Agency

Earthscan Publications Ltd
London • Sterling, VA

First published in the UK and USA in 2002
by Earthscan Publications Ltd

ISBN: 1 85383 893 4 paperback
       1 85383 892 6 hardback

DISCLAIMER
The contents of this publication do not necessarily reflect the official opinions of the European Commission or other European Communities institutions. Neither the European Environment Agency (EEA) nor any person or company acting on the behalf of the Agency is responsible for the use that may be made of the information contained in this publication

Typesetting by PCS Mapping & DTP, Gateshead
Printed and bound in the UK by Creative Print and Design Wales, Ebbw Vale
Cover design by Susanne Harris

For a full list of publications please contact:

Earthscan Publications Ltd
120 Pentonville Road, London, N1 9JN, UK
Tel: +44 (0)20 7278 0433
Fax: +44 (0)20 7278 1142
Email: earthinfo@earthscan.co.uk
Web: **www.earthscan.co.uk**

22883 Quicksilver Drive, Sterling, VA 20166-2012, USA

Earthscan is an editorially independent subsidary of Kogan Page Ltd and publishes in association with WWF-UK and the International Institute for Environment and Development

A catalogue record for this book is available from the British Library

Library of Congress Cataloging-in-Publication Data

The precautionary principle in the 20th century : late lessons from early warnings / edited by Poul Harremoèes ... [et al.].
    p. cm.
  Includes bibliographical references and index.
  ISBN 1-85383-893-4 (pbk.) — ISBN 1-85383-892-6 (hard)
  1. Environmental risk assessment. 2. Economic development—Environmental aspects. 3. Sustainable development. I. Title: Precautionary principle in the twentieth century. II. Harremoèes, Poul

GE145.P74 2002
333.7'14—dc21

                                                                2002002436

This book is printed on elemental chlorine free paper

Contents

List of figures, tables and boxes

Figures

Tables

Boxes

Foreword

A decade ago, precaution was a dirty word. It was treated with great suspicion by the UK government, because it was regarded as a cost-raising, time-delaying and benefits-reducing measure. The Royal Society tended to regard it as beyond science and not helpful in dealing with unpredictability. It took a year of discussion before a version of precaution appeared in the Rio Declaration of 1992. Even then, the line was to encourage action rather than inaction only when there was substantial evidence of irreversible harm. In a nutshell, precaution was regarded with suspicion in official scientific and governmental circles, and a Trojan horse for all manner of meddling and mischief by single-minded lobbies of protest and reform.

This volume is resplendent with case studies and analysis as to why precaution can provide a many-splendoured approach to better decision-making over the long sweep of a contested event. The strength of this volume lies in the meticulous research on each of the selected topics by sympathetic and knowledgeable insiders. The text as a whole is wonderfully framed by opening and concluding chapters by the editorial team. The members of this group are not iconoclasts. They have looked at precaution from all angles and weighed the evidence in its favour and to its potential discredit. The last two chapters provide the most authoritative summary of the evolving role of the precautionary principle in science policy and sustainable development that I have seen in print.

Yet early warnings are still being ignored. In Scotland, salmon farming is tainted with scandal. Organic compounds appear in feed, and toxic pesticides are used without full regulatory surveillance in the heaving biomass caged in tight areas. The western Scottish lochs are full of contaminated sediment, and the wild salmon stocks are threatened with genetic transfer, sea-lice transmission and altered chemical habitats. Yet the two main Scottish custodial agencies, Scottish Natural Heritage and the Scottish Environmental Protection Agency, cannot manage to persuade the Scottish executive to hold a full inquiry into the industry and the consequences of non-sustainable development. This is in spite of the fact that a Scottish parliamentary committee is also pressing for the same outcome. For salmon farming in Scotland, early warnings will inevitably still provide lessons too late.

Precaution is now a fully politicised phenomenon. It is as much a function of styles of government, patterns of power, and changing interpretations of participation and value in a complex world and changing society as it is about taking awkward decisions in states of uncertainty and ignorance. We are moving to a more multi-centred approach to governance. This is a fascinating arena in which networks adapt by foreseeing and including, while many actors in the public, private and voluntary sectors join to share decisions and subsequent actions. Under this emerging pattern of shared responsibility, precaution becomes an ingredient in negotiated partnerships, in listening and responding, and in declaring more firmly that sustainability is the ultimate objective.

The Scottish story can be replicated elsewhere. Precaution is at its most interactive as a process in a form of governing that is participatory, adaptive and sensitive to a variety of outlooks and framing values. This is not yet a pattern of governance that is common, so precaution remains a piece of grit in the lubricating oil of conventional governance. Therefore it is always being 'put in its place', namely being kept manageable as a process of enquiry and exploration. This is why precaution will always be a troublesome concept and process for government. I am not sure that even an open, networked and adaptive method of governance can fully handle precaution. It is also a vision that needs examination and analysis, so we are still in transition. There will still be many late lessons and ignored early warnings. However, the reformist tides are washing away some of the worst of the old attitudes and institutional failures. This volume straddles the old order and senses the vistas of emerging new methods of governance. Precaution is both a catalyst and an outcome of these healthy but painful shifts in governing styles and views on science generally. That is why this is such an important book.

The authors are all associated with the European Environment Agency. It is a fine institution but it lacks the mandate to promote the very lessons that the editors advocate. The alternative lesson is that all our forms of regulatory arrangements need to evolve further, or be granted the freedom to do so, before the precautionary principle is awarded its rightful place in the transition to sustainability.

Tim O'Riordan
Associate Director, Centre for Social and Economic Research on
the Global Environment (CSERGE), University of East Anglia, Norwich

Preface

To know and not to know?
To act or not to act?

The task of the European Environment Agency (EEA) is to provide information of direct use for improving decision-making and public participation. We often provide information in situations of scientific uncertainty, in which the precautionary principle, enshrined in the Maastricht Treaty on European Union, is increasingly relevant. The growing innovative powers of science seem to be outstripping its ability to predict the consequences of its applications, whilst the scale of human interventions in nature increases the chances that any hazardous impacts may be serious and global. It is therefore important to take stock of past experiences, and learn how we can adapt to these changing circumstances and improve our work, particularly in relation to the provision of information and the identification of early warnings.

The Precautionary Principle in the 20th Century is about the gathering of information on the hazards of human economic activities and its use in taking action to protect both the environment and the health of the species and ecosystems that are dependent on it, and then living with the consequences.

The book is based on case studies. The authors of the case studies, all experts in their particular field of environmental, occupational and consumer hazards, were asked to identify the dates of early warnings, to analyse how this information was used, or not used, in reducing hazards, and to describe the resulting costs, benefits and lessons for the future.

The lessons they drew from their histories were then distilled into twelve 'late lessons' by the editorial team, under the guidance of the EEA Scientific Committee. In a separate EEA publication, some implications of the late lessons for the policy process and associated information flows will be further explored (EEA, forthcoming 2002).

The precautionary principle is not just an issue for the European Union (EU): its potential impact on trade means that its application can have global repercussions. The current dialogue between the EU and the US on the use and application of precaution is partly affected by confusion about the meaning of terms used in the debate. This volume should contribute to a greater shared understanding about past decisions on hazardous technologies and therefore, we hope, to improved transatlantic agreement about future decisions. It may also help the dialogue *within* both the EU and the US, where there are healthy debates about the pros and cons of applying the precautionary principle.

That we have all acted too late in many areas is now well known. Over the next 50 years we will see some thousands of extra skin cancers as today's children grow up exposed to the higher levels of ultraviolet radiation penetrating the normally protective ozone layer through the 'hole' created by chlorofluorocarbons (CFCs) and other synthetic chemicals. Over the same period many thousands of Europeans will die from one of the most painful and terminal of cancers, mesothelioma, caused by the inhalation of asbestos dust. In both cases we were taken by surprise: the hazards of these beneficial technologies were not 'known about' until it was too late to stop irreversible impacts. Both phenomena had such long latent periods between first exposures and late effects that 'pipelines' of unstoppable consequences, decades long, were set in place before actions could be taken to stop further exposures.

The first reports of injuries from radiation were made as early as 1896. The first clear and credible early warning about asbestos came two years later in 1898. A similar signal for action on CFCs came in 1974, though some may argue that important clues were missed earlier. Eleven other well-known hazards are dealt with in this book. We invite the reader to judge whether, as in the cases of radiation, asbestos and CFCs, the early warnings could have led to earlier actions to reduce hazards, at a lower overall cost to society.

The costs of preventive actions are usually tangible, clearly allocated and often short term, whereas the costs of failing to act are less tangible, less clearly distributed and usually longer term, posing particular problems of governance. Weighing up the overall pros and cons of action, or inaction, is therefore very difficult, involving ethical as well as economic considerations, as the case studies illustrate.

A key question arising from the case studies is how to acknowledge and respond not only to scientific uncertainty but also to ignorance, a state of not knowing from which springs both scientific discoveries and unpleasant 'surprises', such as ozone holes and rare cancers. Socrates had a response to this when he acknowledged ignorance as a source of wisdom. *The Precautionary Principle in the 20th Century* shows that this is a lesson from history that many people have forgotten. Misplaced 'certainty' about the absence of harm played a key role in delaying preventive actions in most of the case studies. However, there is clearly nothing scientific about the pretence of knowledge. Such 'certainty' does little to reduce ignorance, which requires more scientific research and long-term monitoring in order to identify the unintended impacts of human activities.

Could we have known about, or anticipated, the hazards any earlier? Are there ways of 'knowing more' or 'knowing better' that could help justify our self-awarded title of *Homo sapiens* – the 'wise ones'?

Readers of the case studies may conclude that we have a long way to go. Some possible directions are indicated in Chapter 16, 'Twelve late lessons', derived from the case studies.

A phenomenon that Socrates probably did not know about, but may have suspected, is that 'everything connects' – or at least, so many things do react with each other that the simple science of linear, mechanistic propositions needs to be supplemented with the dynamic and emergent properties of systems science. The potential systemic instabilities of such complex phenomena as climate change or brain-cell behaviour may be critical yet unpredictable determinants of our fate, whether they be systems that govern the stability of the Gulf Stream or that generate the 'genomic instabilities' of irradiated cells.

Compartmentalised science, no matter how erudite, is an insufficient base for knowing enough to anticipate or mitigate the impacts of such complex systems; integrated and synthesised knowledge, which pools the wisdom from many natural and social sciences, is a necessary condition for being *Homo sapiens*. But just knowing enough is not of itself sufficient: acting wisely, and in good time, is also necessary. It is part of the EEA's task to help expand the knowledge base through integrated assessments, thereby assisting decision-makers to foresee the possible consequences of regulatory and stakeholder actions and inactions.

Knowing enough, and acting wisely enough, across the full range of environmental and related health issues seems daunting. The interconnections between issues, the pace of technological change, our limited understanding and the 'time to harm and then to heal' of the ecological and biological systems that can be perturbed over decades by our technologies together present an unforgiving context. Some people fear or imagine that a more precautionary approach to forestalling potentially irreversible hazards will stifle innovation or compromise science. However, there are immense challenges and opportunities in understanding complex and emergent systems while meeting human needs with lower health and ecological costs. Many of the case studies suggest that wider use of the precautionary principle can help stimulate both innovation and science, replacing the 19th-century technologies and simple science of the first industrial revolution with the 'eco-efficient' technologies and systems science of the third.

One final and obvious question arises from the case studies: why were not only the early warnings but also the 'loud and late' warnings often ignored for so long? This question we largely leave to the reader, whilst noting that the absence of political will to take action to reduce hazards, in the face of conflicting costs and benefits, seems to be an even more important factor in these histories than is the availability of trusted information. However, as Aristotle observed, the way we perceive the world determines in large part how we act, and information plays a critical role in how we see the world. But whose information is received? Is it 'true, fair and independent'? And is it understandable to the politicians and business people who are rarely experts but nevertheless have to make the difficult decisions?

This book notes the importance of trusted and shared information for effective policy-making and stakeholder participation in decision-making, especially in the context of complexity, ignorance, high stakes and the need for 'collective learning'. We must not forget that EU product legislation defines as 'safe' any product that does not present 'unacceptable risks' under normal or foreseeable conditions of use. Public acceptance of risks requires public participation in the decisions that create and manage such risks, including the consideration of values, attitudes and overall benefits. Sound public policy-making on issues involving science therefore requires more than good science: ethical as well as economic choices are at stake. Such matters concern not only the experts and the politicians but all of us.

It is my hope that this book contributes to more effective stakeholder participation in the governance of economic activity so as to help minimise environmental and health costs and maximise innovation.

Decision-makers need not only to have more and better quality information, but also to act wisely more often so as to achieve a better balance between the benefits of innovations and their hazards. Learning and applying these late lessons from the last century's early warnings could help all of us to achieve this better balance during this century.

I would like to thank the editorial team and the authors who took up the challenge of making this book, as well as the peer reviewers and members of the EEA Scientific Committee, who also played an important role.

Finally, I would like to thank David Gee, who initiated this publication, and the many EEA staff whose contributions made it possible.

Domingo Jiménez Beltrán
Executive Director, European Environment Agency (EEA), Copenhagen

Acknowledgements

Thanks are given to the editorial team for their invaluable help and assistance in producing this book: Poul Harremoës (Chairman), Malcolm MacGarvin (executive editor), Andy Stirling (editor), Brian Wynne (editor), Jane Keys (editor), David Gee and Sofia Guedes Vaz (EEA editors).

Thanks are also given to the authors and the peer reviewers, as follows.

Authors: Malcolm MacGarvin, Barrie Lambert, Peter Infante, Morris Greenberg, David Gee, Janna G Koppe, Jane Keys, Joe Farman, Dolores Ibarreta, Shanna H Swan, Lars-Erik Edqvist, Knud Børge Pedersen, Arne Semb, Martin Krayer von Krauss, Poul Harremoës, Michael Gilbertson, David Santillo, Paul Johnston, William J Langston, Jim W Bridges, Olga Bridges, Patrick van Zwanenberg and Erik Millstone.

Peer reviewers: Joel Tickner, Richard Young, Wolfgang Witte, Stuart Levy, Henk Aarts, Jacques Nouws, Michael Skou Andersen, Anthony Seaton, Harry Aiking, Leonard Levy, Ron Hoogenboom, Glen Fox, Andrew Watterson, Arturo Keller, Finn Bro Rasmussen, Sandrine Dixson-Decleve, Hilkka Vahervuori, Grete Østergaard, Erik Arvin, Eberhard Morgenroth, Guus Velders, Madhava Sarna, Tom Webster, Niklas Johansson, Ernst Boersma , Nigel Bell, Beldrich Moldan, John Seager, Kees van Leeuwen, Mark Montforts and Robert Luttik.

Finally, thanks are also given to members of the EEA Scientific Committee, Philippe Bourdeau, Eileen Buttle, Robert Kroes, Bo Jansson and Poul Harremoës, the Chair of the editorial team.

List of acronyms and abbreviations

AAOE	Airborne Antarctic Ozone Experiment (US)
ACGIH	American Conference of Governmental Industrial Hygienists
API	American Petroleum Institute
BBC	British Broadcasting Corporation
B_{lim}	biomass lower limit
B_{pa}	biomass precautionary-approach target (level appropriate for the ICES-defined precautionary approach)
BSE	bovine spongiform encephalopathy
CAD	Canadian dollars
CAPM	Chinese Academy of Preventative Medicine
CC	cubic centimetre
CFC	chlorofluorocarbon
CJD	Creutzfeldt-Jakob disease
CLRTAP	Convention on Long-range Transboundary Air Pollution
CMO	Chief Medical Officer (UK)
CO	carbon monoxide
CRF	Federation of Swedish Farmers
CTA	constructive technology assessment
DDT	dichlorodiphenyltrichloroethane
DEFRA	Department for Environment, Food and Rural Affairs (UK) (*formerly* MAFF)
DES	diethylstilboestrol
DFO	Department of Fisheries and Oceans (Canada)
DG III	*former abbreviation for* Enterprise Directorate-General (European Commission)
DG VI	*former abbreviation for* Agriculture Directorate-General (European Commission)
DG XXIV	*former abbreviation for* Health and Consumer Protection Directorate-General (*also known as* DG SANCO) (European Commission)
DIPE	di-isopropyl ether
ECE	Economic Commission for Europe
EEA	European Environment Agency
EPA	Environmental Protection Agency
EQS	environmental quality standards
ESTO	European Scientific Technology Observatory
ETBE	ethyl tert-butyl ether
ETS	emergency temporary standard
EU	European Union
FAO	Food and Agriculture Organization of the United Nations

FDA	Food and Drug Administration (US)
F_{lim}	fishing mortality lower limit (level at which the risk of stock collapse becomes substantial)
F_{pa}	fishing mortality precautionary-approach target (level appropriate for the ICES-defined precautionary approach)
GDI	gasoline direct injection
GDR	German Democratic Republic
GMO	genetically modified organism
HCFC	hydrochlorofluorocarbon
HFC	hydrofluorocarbon
HIV	human immunodeficiency virus
IAEA	International Atomic Energy Agency
IARC	International Agency for Research on Cancer (WHO)
ICES	International Council for the Exploration of the Sea
ICNAF	International Commission for the Northwest Atlantic Fisheries
ICPS	International Programme on Chemical Safety
ICRP	International Commission on Radiological Protection
IEA	integrated environmental assessment
IEHO	Institute of Environmental Health Officers
IJC	International Joint Commission
IMO	International Maritime Organization
IXRPC	International X-ray and Radium Protection Committee (now ICRP)
JECFA	Joint FAO/WHO Expert Committee on Food Additives
LCA	life cycle analysis
m^3	cubic metres
MAFF	Ministry of Agriculture, Fisheries and Food (UK) (now DEFRA)
MBAL	minimum biologically acceptable level
MCM	multi-criteria mapping
MEPC	Marine Environment Protection Committee
MFMP	Multilateral Fund for the Implementation of the Montreal Protocol
mg/l	milligrams per litre
MRM	mechanically recovered meat
MSY	maximum sustainable yield
MTBE	methyl tert-butyl ether
NACA	National Agricultural Chemicals Association (US)
NAFO	Northwest Atlantic Fisheries Organization
NASA	North American Space Agency
NCI	National Cancer Institute (US)
ng/l	nanograms per litre
NGO	non-governmental organisation
NILU	Norwegian Institute for Air Research
NIOSH	National Institute for Occupational Safety and Health
NLG	Netherlands guilders
NOAA	National Oceanic and Atmospheric Administration (US)
NO_x	nitrogen oxide
NRC	National Research Council (US)

NRPB	National Radiological Protection Board (UK)
NRC	National Research Council (US)
NTP	National Toxicology Program (US)
ODS	ozone depleting substance
OECD	Organisation for Economic Co-operation and Development
OSHA	Occupational Safety and Health Administration (US Department of Labor)
OSPAR	Convention for the Protection of the Marine Environment of the North-East Atlantic
PARCOM	Paris Commission
PCB	polychlorinated biphenyl
PFC	perfluorocarbons
pg	picogram
pg/ml	picograms per millilitre
PHLS	Public Health Laboratory Service (UK)
POP	persistent organic pollutant
ppb	parts per billion
ppbv	parts per billion by volume
ppm	parts per million
ppt	parts per trillion
pptv	parts per trillion by volume
RCEP	Royal Commission on Environmental Pollution (UK)
RFG	reformulated gasoline
SBO	specified bovine offal
SCAN	Scientific Committee on Animal Nutrition (EU)
SEAC	Spongiform Encephalopathy Advisory Committee
SED	skin erythema dose
SSC	Scientific Steering Committee (EU)
SST	supersonic stratospheric transport (aircraft)
TAC	total allowable catch
TAME	tert-amyl methyl ether
TBT	tributyltin
TCDD	tetrachlorodibenzoparadioxin
TEF	toxic equivalent factor
TEQ	toxic equivalent
TLV	threshold limit value
TOA	technological options analysis
TSE	transmissible spongiform encephalopathy
μg/l	micrograms per litre
UK	United Kingdom
UNEP	United Nations Environment Programme
US	United States
USSR	Union of Soviet Socialist Republics (until 1991)
vCJD	variant CJD
VOC	volatile organic compound
WBGU	German Advisory Council on Global Change
WHO	World Health Organization
WMO	World Meteorological Organization
WTO	World Trade Organization

1

Introduction

Late lessons from early warnings: an approach to learning from history

In 1898, Lucy Deane, a United Kingdom (UK) factory inspector, observed:

> *'The evil effects of asbestos dust have also instigated a microscopic examination of the mineral dust by HM Medical Inspector. Clearly revealed was the sharp glass-like jagged nature of the particles, and where they are allowed to rise and to remain suspended in the air of the room in any quantity, the effects have been found to be injurious as might have been expected' (Deane, 1898)*

One hundred years later, in 1998, the UK government decided to ban 'white' asbestos, a decision that was echoed by the European Union (EU) the following year. The current asbestos-induced death rate in the UK is about 3000 deaths per year, and some 250,000–400,000 asbestos cancers are expected in Western Europe over the next 35 years, due to past exposures (Peto, 1999).

The hundred years between the 1890s and 1990s is the main focus of this detailed review of the use, neglect and possible misuse of the concept of precaution in dealing with a selection of occupational, public and environmental hazards. The costs and benefits of the actions or inactions of governments and others in responding to 'early warnings' about hazards provide us with its content. The aim of this volume is to see if something can be learnt from these histories that can help us prevent, or at least minimise, future impacts of other agents that may turn out to be harmful, and to do so without stifling innovation or compromising science.

The book is an example of the information needed to help the EU and European Environment Agency (EEA) member countries to frame and identify sound and effective policies that protect the environment and contribute to sustainable development. Providing such information is the regulatory duty of the EEA, an independent agency of the European community established in 1993 to provide objective information to the policy-making bodies of the EU and its Member States (Council Regulations, 1210/90 and 993/99).

In trying to reduce current and future risks the lessons of history have rarely been used. The histories of a selection of hazards is therefore the subject matter of *The Precautionary Principle in the 20th Century*. Fourteen case studies (arranged chronologically according to the first date of early warning) have been chosen from a range of well-known hazards to workers, the public and the environment, where enough is now known about their impacts to enable conclusions to be drawn about how well they were dealt with by governments and civil society. Such conclusions should be based on 'the spirit of the times' and not on the luxury of hindsight. There are other public health effects and environmental disasters that have not been looked at, such as thalidomide (James, 1965), lead (Millstone, 1997) and the Aral Sea (Small, 2001) These provide additional information about unintended consequences, and the conflict between economic and social interests, from which additional lessons from history can be drawn.

The authors of the case studies were asked to structure their chapters around four key questions:

1 When was the first credible scientific 'early warning' of potential harm?
2 When and what were the main actions or inactions on risk reduction taken by regulatory authorities and others?
3 What were the resulting costs and benefits of the actions or inactions, including their distribution between groups and across time?
4 What lessons can be drawn that may help future decision-making?

The case studies and authors have also been chosen with a transatlantic audience in mind. Three chapters are focused either on North American issues (eg, pollution of the Great Lakes) or primarily on the North American handling of issues that are also directly relevant to Europe (benzene, and diethylstilboestrol (DES) administered in pregnancy) and are authored by scientists from North America (Gilbertson, Infante and co-author Swann, respectively). Three chapters cover issues of some conflict between North America and Europe (hormones as growth promoters, asbestos and methyl tert-butyl (MTBE) in petrol); all the other chapters are as relevant to North Americans, their public health and their environments as they are to Europeans.

It is sometimes said that the United States (US) does not use the precautionary principle, but it is worth noting (see Table 1.1) that the US has helped to promote what could be called 'precautionary prevention', without necessarily calling it 'the precautionary principle'.

The precautionary principle has become controversial, not least because of the disputes between the EU and the US over hormones in beef, genetically modified organisms (GMOs), global warming and other issues in which precautionary approaches have been invoked. There is now considerable debate (not to say terminological confusion, particularly between politicians on different sides of the Atlantic) as to what the precautionary principle means, and how it can be implemented. One aim of this book is to try to improve transatlantic understanding on the use of precaution in policy-making.

The authors of the case studies, who provided their services *pro bono*, were asked to keep their contributions brief, which obviously inhibits detailed treatment of the issues. However, we wanted to elicit key conclusions from the

Table 1.1 *Some examples of 'precautionary prevention' in the US*

Issue	Precautionary prevention
Food safety (carcinogenic additives)	The Delaney Clause in the Food, Drug and Cosmetics Act, 1957–96, which banned animal carcinogens from the human food chain
Food safety (bovine spongiform encephalopathy, BSE)	A ban on the use of scrapie-infected sheep and goat meat in the animal and human food chain in the early 1970s, which may have helped the US to avoid BSE
Environmental safety (chlorofluorocarbons, CFCs)	A ban on the use of CFCs in aerosols in 1977, several years before similar action in most of Europe
Public health (DES)	A ban on the use of DES as a growth promoter in beef, 1972–79, nearly ten years before the EU ban in 1987

Source: EEA

histories and not the detailed post mortems that others have produced: these can be accessed via the references for each chapter.

It has been pointed out that the case study authors are not without strong views, being for the most part active participants in the process of making the histories that are summarised in each chapter. Joe Farman, the author of the chapter on halocarbons, for example, discovered the 'hole' in the stratospheric ozone layer; Morris Greenberg helped to set up the first asbestos mesothelioma register; Michael Gilbertson has spent most of his professional life researching Great Lakes pollution and advocating its clean-up; and Peter Infante did the first cohort epidemiological study of benzene-exposed workers, and has worked for many years in the US Health and Safety Department to reduce workers' exposure to benzene and other pollutants. All other authors, to varying degrees, have had significant involvement in the subject of their chapters: indeed, they would not have been approached if they had not already extensively studied the case that they were asked to write about. All of them, as respected scientists in their fields, were expected to be as objective as possible in answering the four questions put to them. This involvement of the authors in the histories of their case studies is therefore brought to the attention of readers.

The case studies are all about 'false negatives' in the sense that they are agents or activities that were regarded at one time as harmless by governments and others, at prevailing levels of exposure and 'control', until evidence about their harmful effects emerged. But are there no 'false positives', where action was taken on the basis of a precautionary approach that turned out to be unnecessary? It was felt necessary to include such examples, but despite inviting some industry representatives to submit them, and discussing these in some detail, no suitable examples emerged. Attention was drawn to a US publication, *Facts Versus Fears* (Lieberman and Kwon, 1998), which attempted to provide some 25 examples of 'false positives'. However, on closer examination these turned out not to be robust enough for those who recommended them to accept our invitation to use the strongest half dozen in this book. The challenge of demonstrating 'false positives' remains: possible candidates that have been mentioned include the ban on dumping sewage sludge in the North Sea, and the 'Y2K millennium bug'.

What is the 'precautionary principle'?

Albert Schweitzer (1875–1965) may have been pessimistic when he said 'Man has lost the capacity to foresee and forestall... he will end up destroying the earth'. However, being wise before it is too late is not easy, especially when the environmental or health impacts may be far into the future and the real, or perceived, costs of averting them are large and immediate. Forestalling disasters usually requires acting before there is strong proof of harm, particularly if the harm may be delayed and irreversible, an approach to scientific evidence and policy-making which is part of what is now called the precautionary principle.

Precautionary prevention has often been used in medicine and public health, where the benefit of doubt about a diagnosis is usually given to the patient ('better safe than sorry'). However, the precautionary principle and its application to environmental hazards and their uncertainties only began to emerge as an explicit and coherent concept within environmental science in the 1970s, when German scientists and policy-makers were trying to deal with 'forest death' (*Waldsterben*) and its possible causes, including air pollution.

The main element of the precautionary principle they developed was a general rule of public policy action to be used in situations of potentially serious or irreversible threats to health or the environment, where there is a need to act to reduce potential hazards *before* there is strong proof of harm, taking into account the likely costs and benefits of action and inaction. A precautionary approach, however, requires much more than establishing the level of proof needed to justify action to reduce hazards (the 'trigger' for action). The *Vorsorgeprinzip* ('foresight' or 'precautionary' principle), in the German Clean Air Act of 1974, as elaborated in the 1985 report on the Clean Air Act (Boehmer-Christiansen, 1994) also included elements such as:

- research and monitoring for the early detection of hazards;
- a general reduction of environmental burdens;
- the promotion of 'clean production' and innovation;
- the proportionality principle, which states that the costs of actions to prevent hazards should not be disproportionate to the likely benefits;
- a cooperative approach between stakeholders to solving common problems via integrated policy measures that aim to improve the environment, competitiveness and employment; and
- action to reduce risks before full 'proof' of harm is available if impacts could be serious or irreversible.

Since the 1970s, the precautionary principle has risen rapidly in the political agenda, and has been incorporated into many international agreements, particularly in the marine environment, where an abundance of ecological data on pollution yielded little understanding but much concern: 'huge amounts of data are available, but despite these data... we have reached a sort of plateau in our understanding of what that information is for... This is what led to the precautionary principle' (*Marine Pollution Bulletin*, 1997). More generally, Principle 15 of the UN Rio Declaration on Environment and Development 1992 (see Table 1.2) extended the idea to the whole environment.

The use of different terms in these treaties and agreements such as 'precautionary principle', 'precautionary approach' and 'precautionary measures' can cause difficulties for communication and dialogue on how best to deal with scientific uncertainties and potential hazards. The concluding chapters of this book attempt to clarify some of these ambiguities.

In Europe, the most significant support for the precautionary principle has come from the European Commission's *Communication on the Precautionary Principle* (European Commission, 2000) and the Council of Ministers' Nice Decision, both in 2000. They have made significant contributions to the practical implementation of the precautionary principle, especially concerning stakeholder involvement and the avoidance of trade disputes. Some of the main issues raised by the case studies and by the European Commission's Communication are elaborated in the concluding chapters.

An early use of the precautionary principle: London, 1854

The use of precautionary approaches to hazards began well before the 1970s, particularly in the field of public health. One early application in Europe was by Dr John Snow, who in 1854 recommended removing the handle from the Broad Street water pump in an attempt to stop the cholera epidemic that was then ravaging central London. Some evidence for a correlation between the polluted water and cholera had been published five years earlier by Snow himself (Snow, 1849). This evidence was not 'proof beyond reasonable doubt'. However, it was proof enough for Snow to recommend the necessary public health action, where the likely costs of inaction would have been far greater than the possible costs of action (see Box 1.1).

The costs of Snow being wrong in getting the pump handle removed would essentially have been angry and inconvenienced citizens who nevertheless wanted cholera stopped. These costs were small in relation to the cost of being wrong in *not* removing the pump handle, once the evidence of the link between the Broad Street pump water and the cholera was available. His evidence that there seemed to be a link was reliable enough to help make a public policy decision that proved correct: the cholera was being caused by sewage-contaminated water and removing exposure helped to remove the risk.

Table 1.2 *The 'precautionary principle' in some international treaties and agreements*

Montreal Protocol on Substances that Deplete the Ozone Layer, 1987
'Parties to this protocol... determined to protect the ozone layer by taking precautionary measures to control equitably total global emissions of substances that deplete it...'

Third North Sea Conference, 1990
'The participants... will continue to apply the precautionary principle, that is to take action to avoid potentially damaging impacts of substances that are persistent, toxic and liable to bioaccumulate even where there is no scientific evidence to prove a causal link between emissions and effects.'

The Rio Declaration on Environment and Development, 1992
'In order to protect the environment the Precautionary Approach shall be widely applied by states according to their capabilities. Where there are threats of serious or irreversible damage, lack of full scientific certainty shall not be used as a reason for postponing cost-effective measures to prevent environmental degradation.'

Framework Convention on Climate Change, 1992
'The Parties should take precautionary measures to anticipate, prevent or minimise the causes of climate change and mitigate its adverse effects. Where there are threats of serious or irreversible damage, lack of full scientific certainty should not be used as a reason for postponing such measures, taking into account that policies and measures to deal with climate change should be cost-effective so as to ensure global benefits at the lowest possible cost.'

Treaty on European Union (Maastricht Treaty), 1992
'Community policy on the environment... shall be based on the precautionary principle and on the principles that preventive actions should be taken, that the environmental damage should as a priority be rectified at source and that the polluter should pay.'

Cartagena Protocol on Biosafety, 2000
'In accordance with the precautionary approach the objective of this Protocol is to contribute to ensuring an adequate level of protection in the field of the safe transfer, handling and use of living modified organisms resulting from modern biotechnology that may have adverse effects on the conservation and sustainable use of biological diversity, taking also into account risks to human health, and specifically focusing on transboundary movements.'

Stockholm Convention on Persistent Organic Pollutants (POPs), 2001
Precaution, including transparency and public participation, is operationalised throughout the treaty, with explicit references in the preamble, objective, provisions for adding POPs and determination of best available technologies. The objective states: 'Mindful of the Precautionary Approach as set forth in Principle 15 of the Rio Declaration on Environment and Development, the objective of this Convention is to protect human health and the environment from persistent organic pollutants.'

Source: EEA

Box 1.1 John Snow's 'precautionary prevention'

In a ten-day period from 31 August to 9 September 1854, there were about 500 deaths from cholera in the parish of St James, which included the Golden Square area of Central London. John Snow, a London physician, investigated the outbreak, having previously written *The Mode of Communication of Cholera*, a pamphlet of 30 pages which he published at his own expense in 1849. Prior to the Golden Square outbreak, Snow was studying cholera and the water supplies from two different water companies in South London: one 'clean', and the other 'polluted' with sewage. This incomplete study was already producing data that supported his theory that cholera was caused by contaminated water when he went to investigate the Golden Square outbreak.

A short investigation revealed that virtually all of the 83 people who had died in the Golden Square area between 31 August and 5 September had drawn water from the popular Broad Street water pump, rather than from the available, and cleaner yet less popular, piped water supplies. On 7 September, Snow recommended the removal of the Broad Street water pump on the grounds that there was 'no ... Cholera ... except amongst persons who were in the habit of drinking the water of the (Broad Street) water pump'. The authorities removed the pump handle the next day, thereby helping to speed up the decline of the cholera outbreak and preventing further infection from that source.

Snow later produced one of the first epidemiological maps of disease and possible causes at a presentation to the Epidemiological Society of London on 4 December 1854, which included a map of cholera deaths and the wells nearest to Broad Street.

Snow's views on cholera causation were not shared by the majority of relevant scientists. The Royal College of Physicians' inquiry into the earlier 1853–54 cholera outbreak had considered Snow's thesis and rejected it as 'untenable', as had the General Board of Health in 1854: 'we see no reason to adopt this belief'. They believed that cholera was caused by airborne contamination.

The biological mechanism underlying the link between polluted water and cholera was unknown at the time of this successful 'precautionary prevention' in 1854: that came 30 years later, in 1884, when Koch announced his discovery of the cholera vibrio in Germany.

Source: EEA, based on Brody et al, 2000

The story of John Snow and cholera has sometimes been misinterpreted as an example of how very strong evidence of harm and its causes can be used in a relatively uncontroversial way. However, it was a classic case of precautionary prevention, containing several of the key elements of an approach to scientific uncertainty, ignorance and policy-making. These elements include the difference between 'knowing' about a hazard and its likely causes and 'understanding' the chemical and biological or other processes underlying the link; a focus on the potential costs of being wrong; and the use of minority scientific opinions in public policy-making. These issues are taken up in the concluding chapters of this book.

There are many differences between cholera, asbestos (which came into use at about the time of Snow's action) and the other harmful agents in the case studies, not least the time lag between exposure to the harmful agent and the health damage, which was hours in the case of cholera but decades in the case of asbestos and most of the other agents studied. Yet had governments adopted a similar approach to precautionary prevention as Dr Snow once the early warnings on asbestos had been published, much of the tragedy and the huge costs of asbestos exposure could have been averted.

Forestalling disasters: integrating science and public policy

Snow was working, both as a scientist and policy-maker, in the conditions of scientific uncertainty and political stress shared by all who are charged with responsibilities for protecting the public and the environment from potentially harmful economic activity. Politicians today are working in similar conditions of scientific uncertainty and stress as Dr Snow, made more difficult by the higher risks and uncertainties (economic, health and ecological) of larger-scale activities (Beck, 1992) and by greater pressure from the mass media (Smith, 2000). They also work with more democratic institutions, and are accountable to a better-educated and more involved citizenry, which can have good access to information from the Internet. Globalisation and free trade issues add further complications, as does the emerging science of complexity and chaos, which can require more humility and less hubris in science. It is in these circumstances of trying to prevent potentially serious and irreversible effects, without disproportionate costs, that the precautionary principle can be useful. It helps policy-makers and politicians in circumstances in which waiting for very strong evidence of harm before taking precautionary action may seriously compromise public health or the environment, or both.

Achieving consensus on the history of accepted hazards, such as asbestos, CFCs and the other case studies, is not easy, but it is easier than achieving consensus on how to deal with current controversies such as climate change, mobile phones or GMOs. There are some well-established criteria for helping scientists to move from 'association' to 'causation' in health hazard identification (Hill, 1965), but there are no generally accepted criteria for helping politicians to make sound public policy decisions in the face of scientific uncertainty, despite several good proposals (Raffensperger and Tickner, 1999; Gee, 1997).

There is already a large amount of literature on risk assessment and hazard reduction, which can assist decision-makers in certain circumstances, but a historical perspective might also help. There is a rich history of hazards covered in this book, from which something of value can be learnt. In Chapter 16 lessons are drawn that can help frame and identify sound and effective public policy measures. These may help minimise the future costs of being wrong about environmental and health risks. There is particular concern to see fewer 'false negatives' in the future, but the late lessons should also help to reduce the smaller but commonly-feared risk of 'false positives'.

Public trust in the politicians and scientists who are trying to protect people and the planet from hazards is very low, especially in Europe, where BSE in the UK and elsewhere, dioxins in Belgium, and the human immunodeficiency virus (HIV)-contaminated blood transfusion affair in France have contributed to a general sense of malaise. Governments are aware of this and are developing responses, such as the EU White Paper on European Governance (July 2001). This includes recommendations for improving public participation in managing the inter-reactions between science, technologies and society. This book aims to contribute to the debate on the emerging issue of democratising scientific expertise.

2

Fisheries: taking stock

Malcolm MacGarvin

Fisheries have had to deal with uncertainties – with attempts made to manage them – for centuries. The topic is therefore doubly challenging as, while the underlying precautionary principle is the same as for pollutants, the practical approach to implementation is necessarily very different.

'Late lessons' is certainly an appropriate topic for marine capture fisheries. Awareness of events such as those described here – from the Middle Ages through to 19th-century Scottish fisheries, the mid-20th century Californian sardine fishery crash and the collapse of Canadian northern cod stocks in the 1990s – provide a sometimes gloomy awareness of history repeating itself. But there are also positive things to learn from the past. The need for an explicitly precautionary approach has been increasingly recognised in the last decade. In areas such as the North Atlantic, the principal problem now is finding a means to allow fishers to turn theory into practice, against the backdrop of short-term economic pressures.

Early warnings

The relationships between precautionary attitudes, cultural perspectives, techno-logical ability, and risks and benefits, are complex. In a sense there is nothing new in varying degrees of precautionary management, and warnings of the risk of overexploitation. There is some evidence that certain Native North American communities may have died out because they overexploited marine resources. Others, however, circumscribed their catches by rights and taboo, re-enforced by knowledge of fish ecology. They maintained substantial catches for centuries, for example of salmon, in contrast to the commercial fishers who displaced them and extinguished the stocks (McEvoy, 1986).

In medieval Europe people were also aware that fish could be overexploited. An early call for precautionary action comes from 1376–77 (March, 1953). A petition was presented to the English parliament calling for the prohibition of a net 'of so small a mesh, no manner of fish, however small, entering within it can pass out and is compelled to remain therein and be taken... by means of which instrument the fishermen aforesaid take so great an abundance of small fish aforesaid, that they know not what to do with them, but feed and fatten pigs with them, to the great damage of the whole commons of the kingdom, and the destruction of the fisheries in like places, for which they pray remedy.' The response to this assertion was to set up a commission 'by qualified persons to inquire and certify on the truth of this allegation, and thereon let right be done'. Between then and the late 19th century there were numerous attempts in England (as elsewhere) to regulate fishing by still familiar means (such as, in 1716, a minimum mesh size, a ban on circumvention by placing one net within another, and minimum fish-landing sizes).

19th-century British fisheries

In the 19th century British fisheries, as elsewhere, grew rapidly. Uncertainty about the consequences for the valuable herring fishery, and the expansion of trawling for other species (recently unearthed by a 'lay' Wick inhabitant, historian Ian Sutherland (Sutherland, n.d.)) provoked, among other events, a series of official enquiries between 1866 and 1893 (Report, 1866; Report, 1885).

Scottish herring fishery

Many marine fish species markedly fluctuate in abundance as a result of natural causes. In this, herring and its relatives, such as sardine, can show extreme changes over tens of years. Given this context, it took a long time for it to be accepted that fisheries could exacerbate such natural cycles. In 1865 the prescient James Bertram (Bertram, 1865, pp277–82) documented inshore Scottish herring catches between 1818 and 1863, when the area of drift nets carried per boat grew from 4500 to 16,800 square yards, yet the catch fell from 125 to 82 crans (barrels). Such figures spoke too plainly to him to 'expend further argument'. He wrote 'I have always been slow to believe in the inexhaustibility of the shoals, and can easily imagine that overfishing, which some people pooh-pooh so glibly, could easily be possible... As it is, I fear the great Wick fishery must come some day to an end. When (it) first began the fisherman could carry in a creel on his back the nets he required; now he requires a cart and a good strong horse.'

Subsequent action or inaction
Bertram's words proved prophetic. Yet several decades later Thomas Huxley, President of the Royal Society and Inspector of Fisheries (no fool, yet now infamous for his comment that 'marine fisheries are inexhaustible' (Huxley, 1883)), could still maintain for British herring in general 'nothing to show, so far as I am aware, that, taking an average of years, they were ever either more or less numerous than they are at present' (Huxley, 1881), while in 1893 a parliamentary committee also saw 'no indication of any falling off in the numbers of

herrings to be found off our coast'. Presumably landings were equated with stock size, without allowing for increasing effort, area covered and length of season.

In the 1890s the German Heincke established, contrary to general belief, that herring existed as isolated races, implying management at this level. But by then the innermost shoals of Wick and the Moray Firth were gone. The fishing moved further offshore and, overall, North Sea herring landings fluctuated without trend during the first half of the 20th century. This was not so much due to lessons learnt and action taken, but to turmoil in the continental European markets that restrained the technological potential of the new motorised drifters. When an 'industrial' fishery for fishmeal and oil subsequently developed in the second half of the 20th century, both the new technology and the necessary safety margins were underestimated. This brought the North Sea herring to the brink of collapse by the 1970s, forcing a moratorium on the fishery. The stocks did recover, and the industrial fishery upon herring was subsequently restricted when fishing resumed; nevertheless the pressure from 'human consumption' fisheries remained so great that, by the mid-1990s, further emergency measures had to be imposed, until once more the stocks recovered. Although we appear to have learnt enough by the late 1990s to stave off total collapse, it was hardly a model of effective management.

The advent of steam trawlers

Another major development of the late 19th century was steam-powered trawling for 'demersal' fish (such as cod, haddock, whiting and flatfish). This allowed access to areas too dangerous or inaccessible for sail or oar (a natural equivalent of modern 'no-take' zones), and increased the ability to drag and haul nets, resulting in much bigger catches. Trawling divided scientists and fishers alike. The principal complaints were that trawling destroyed spawn on the seabed; caught immature fish; resulted in wastage through damaged fish; interfered with other fishers; and that trawlermen – mobile outsiders – depleted the traditional grounds of others. Interestingly, in 1883 trawlermen based in Yarmouth themselves voluntarily agreed not to work certain offshore grounds at certain seasons to avoid catching immature fish, although this was undermined by other trawlermen and abandoned.

Subsequent action or inaction
In 1865 Bertram raised such accusations against trawling, although he also thought it was, used wisely, the best tool for certain fisheries (Bertram, 1865, p308). By 1883 another parliamentary enquiry had commissioned research which concluded that the immature catch from trawling was insignificant (less than by traditional multiple hook and line 'long-lining'); that most fish caught were undamaged for sale; and that, of the commercial species, only herring spawn lay on the seabed, and even here it was questionable whether injury would occur. But regarding the effects of trawling within the most accessible inshore waters, McIntosh – the research's author – stated that these 'could very easily be trawled out' and that the suspension of trawling 'would be a very valuable exper-

iment. It would set at rest all sorts of notions, and it is upon safe lines, and does no harm to anyone'. This was supported by Scottish fisheries officers, other scientists, some trawlermen and evidence from neighbouring countries and the US. However the enquiry concluded that, although fishers tended to blame each other for any decline, natural fluctuations 'largely influence the supply of fish'. They could not justify prohibition unless experimental evidence 'decisively settled' the issue, because of the loss of valuable catches.

This was controversial. In Scotland (only), despite the enquiry, a political decision was made to ban trawling in inshore waters, including the Moray and other firths. This continued until the 1920s when fishers, under pressure from the failing herring market and searching for alternatives, started dragging their 'seine' nets, effectively using these as a trawl. The initially large landings of codfish and flatfish suggested that the previous policy had successfully nurtured stocks.

Costs and benefits

It is possible to give some qualitative statements about the immediate costs and benefits of actions taken in the 19th century regarding British herring fishing and trawling (MacGarvin and Jones, 2000). Scottish towns such as Wick, heavily dependent on local herring fisheries, went into decline. The centralisation that accompanied trawling contributed to an increase in the prosperity of larger centres, such as Fraserburgh, Peterhead and Aberdeen, at the expense of smaller communities. The same expansion was true of the home ports of widely ranging trawler fleets south of the Anglo-Scottish border, such as Grimsby, Hull, Newlyn, Fleetwood and Swansea.

Over the longer term, the 19th century set in train events that can be traced through to the present day. Concentrating on Scotland, landings and boat tonnage (including both the herring and dermersal fleet) stayed remarkably constant between 1898 and 1998, at around 333,000 tonnes and 109,000 tonnes respectively (Scottish Office, 1898 to present). But the number of boats fell from 11,536 to 2661, and the number of fishers from 36,161 to 7771. Sail and oar boats fell from 11,383 to nil, and fossil fuel use increased enormously. Prosperity fluctuated widely, but overall was not maintained. By the late 1990s the average net profit on capital invested for the Scottish demersal fleet was just 0.1% per annum, according to the 2001 European Commission Fisheries Green Paper (European Commission, 2001b).

One can question just what had been gained by this investment in technology. But on the benefits side, one change has been a marked fall in deaths at sea (although fishing remains dangerous). In the good years, it may also have provided some individuals with a means of acquiring significant capital in a relatively remote area with few economic opportunities. This could then be invested in other activities, or elsewhere, resulting in higher returns. In such circumstances there is no particular interest in maintaining a sustainable fishery. But for others (probably the majority) it was and is a way of life, with a deeply ingrained wish to maintain this for future generations, and a sense of being forced down a track whose direction they do not control.

The changing catch composition for Scotland was broadly similar to that for the North Sea as a whole during this period of over a century. First, overall in the North Sea, herring caught for human consumption become less important. Demersal catches increased and then declined in turn, being supplanted by 'industrial' catches (initially for herring, sprats and mackerel, and later for species such as sand-eels) which grew explosively from the 1950s. These peaked, for the North Sea as a whole, in the 1970s at 2.2 of the 3.5 million tonne total catch. This reflects a global pattern of 'fishing down the food web' (Pauly et al, 1998), proceeding from (potentially) high-value species to industrial stocks lower in the food web, and of lower unit value. One can surmise that the vast removal of biomass by the fisheries will also have had an impact on other species, but comprehensive data are scarce.

Californian sardine fishery, 1920s to 1942

By the 1920s both exploitation strategies and scientific and managerial arrangements were beginning to take their current form. In this the Californian sardine fishery was precocious. The fish were originally canned for human consumption, but similar market conditions to those faced by the British herring fishers meant that their reduction to fishmeal and oil became far more important, driving the economics.

At this time there were no catch limits. Californian state scientists, involved in overseeing the fishery, were by the mid-1920s emphasising what was clearly precautionary action: 'Unnecessary drain upon the supply should be avoided until research has shown that it is possible to detect overfishing in time' (McEvoy, 1986, pp160–1). It was the function of government 'not only to aid in the greatest possible use, but to ensure its continuance because it is the only agency uniting all factions and successive generations' (McEvoy, 1986, p159). As in Scotland decades earlier, the catch was no longer increasing in proportion to the increasing effort; the average age of the fish was falling, and ships had to travel further and fish longer – classic signs of overfishing. A limit was recommended. While there were uncertainties, the State Fisheries Laboratory concluded that the growing intensity of the fishery was 'fact enough to make us sure that we are headed for destruction and a great loss'.

Subsequent action or inaction

The federal authority, the US Bureau of Fisheries, took a different view. While acknowledging that the evidence of depletion was strong, there was 'no clear-cut or convincing evidence that will satisfy everyone' that the sardines were overexploited. Its view ran thus: 'to us conservation means wise use. We do not believe in hoarding our fisheries resources'. Rather, 'We believe very firmly that restrictions that are unnecessary hamper or restrict legitimate business enterprise' (McEvoy, 1986, pp162–6).

The fishers were divided. Those disadvantaged by the developments saw depletion as inevitable. Those behind the expansion saw a plot to 'impoverish one of the few successful enterprises in the Depression'; they believed that any changes could be attributed to environmental fluctuations, and that in any case sardines were so fecund they would soon grow back. To simply discount their testimony that the sardines were abundant was 'brutal... medieval scholasticism'.

The dispute rumbled on unresolved until, in 1939, the new Californian governor replaced the state experts with 'emergency' appointees, and the tone of the reports changed from 'unmistakable' signs of depletion and an 'imperative' need to reduce the catches (1938) to 'no reason to be concerned' (1942). It was then agreed to increase the catch (to 'assist the war-effort'), but in that year the sardine stock collapsed. It only began to show signs of a recovery in the mid-1980s (San Diego Natural History Museum, 2000).

Costs and benefits

There are similar imponderables regarding the impact on other species as for the British fisheries. Regarding the economics, the rate of return on processing fishmeal and oil prior to the collapse was extraordinary, with many plants in the 1930s recovering the entire investment in one season (McEvoy, 1986, p145).

So far as the processing companies such as Starkist and Van Camp were concerned, it could be argued that they had followed an optimum economic strategy, effectively 'mining' the fish in a seller's market as quickly as possible, and then shifting equipment and operations down to South America, with heavy involvement in opening the Peruvian anchoveta fishery, whose exploitation followed the Californian model, and which collapsed in the early 1970s (McEvoy, 1986, p155).

Newfoundland cod

Soon after the Californian experience, managers turned to increasingly complex mathematics in an attempt to squeeze more from the limited information on stock sizes, and the effect of fishing intensity. This was assisted by ever increasing computational powers. By the 1970s there was optimism that past mistakes could be avoided.

Nowhere was this more applicable than for the Newfoundland 'northern cod' stock. This, historically the largest cod stock in the world, had been exploited by European fishers since the 16th century (DFO, 2000). However, fishing intensity grew dramatically in the 1960s with a peak catch of 800,000 tonnes in 1968, after which it dropped well below those actually authorised by the international regulatory body. This, the International Commission for the Northwest Atlantic Fisheries (ICNAF), was regarded by many Canadians as ineffective (O'Reilly Hinds, 1995), which was also true of its successor, the Northwest Atlantic Fisheries Organization (NAFO) (Day, 1995).

In the late 1970s, using the-then novel UN Convention on the Law of the Sea, Canada extended its jurisdiction from 12 to 200 nautical miles, one intention being to bring much of this stock under its control. Its goal was to impose what many would even now consider as precautionary measures, setting 'deliberately conservative' restrictions on catches, aiming to limit these to around 20% of the stock, with the intention of rebuilding. The Department of Fisheries and Ocean's calculations indicated that this was happening, and offshore catches by Canadian trawlers increased. In 1988 the Department of Fisheries and Oceans (DFO) claimed a 'five-fold increase in northern cod since 1976', and it was held in wide regard as an example of how cautious, science-driven management could turn around a seemingly hopeless situation.

Subsequent action or inaction

The only dissenting group were inshore fishers, who (unlike those offshore) had generally not upgraded their technology, and who could not reconcile their falling catches with this supposed increase. Their protests disregarded, they commissioned what became the Keats Report, published in 1986. Keats highlighted the DFO's own (downplayed) retrospective analyses that indicated consistent and severe underestimation of the fishing pressure on the stock since the imposition of Canadian control, with 'the result that we have consistently taken from 1.5–3 times the (20% of stock) catch since 1977' (Keats et al, 1986). The DFO dismissed this 'as biased pseudoscience written to support a political agenda' (Finlayson, 1994). Keats nevertheless gained media attention, forcing the commissioning, by the federal fisheries minister, of an official report.

This 1988 Alverson Report had authority, in official eyes, because it was prepared by fisheries scientists. In the body of the report they concluded that the stock had increased since 1977, although after 1982 it increased 'probably only very slowly'. But they too stated that the 'fishing mortality actually exerted has been considerably in excess of target mortality' because of the 'consistent overestimation of the current stock size'. The problem was that, for any year, some five subsequent years' data were required before the estimated fishing mortality and biomass estimates for the original year 'effectively converged to the correct answer'. The shorter this period the more it simply reflected the assumed level of fishing mortality. This is a critical flaw where a stock becomes so depleted that it depends on the last few years' breeding success (now commonplace for many stocks). Moreover, if a stock goes through a period of sharp decline, the method instils a false sense of assurance. Alverson demon-strated how sensitive conclusions about stock size were to the wide range of fishing mortality estimates that might be implied by the data. However in the executive summary this was turned on its head, it being stating that the DFO calculations of fishing mortality fell 'within the range of estimates supported by the data', albeit at the lower end.

The DFO had responsibility for the management of the release of the Alverson Report. Publicly Alverson noted that 'it's rather amazing that we are as close to each other as we are'. The DFO in its response emphasised that 'the difference in numbers overall was about 4 to 5% ... the conclusions... are quite similar (with respect to stock size and cause of the decline in inshore fisheries)... the credibility of DFO science was not questioned'. Privately the Alverson team were less sanguine and there was an internal reappraisal of DFO methodology. The 1989 assessment assumed that fishing mortality was higher, concluded that the stock was not growing, and recommended that the offshore catch be virtually halved.

This reappraisal was seen as an admission that the DFO had got it wrong all along. This caused serious problems for the administration, as they depended on the 'science' touchstone as an arbiter of conflicting claims to resources. Now the offshore fishers were complaining bitterly that there was no evidence that stocks had fallen. The fisheries minister called a new enquiry, the 1990 Harris Report, this time fully independent of DFO control. Harris also concluded that, prior to 1989, fishing mortality was probably more than double that intended, and the stock little more than half the assumed size, with the result that the stock had been fished at levels that pointed towards commercial extinction – a conclusion widely reported by the media.

The Harris Report cautiously concluded that the revised DFO 1989 assessment was a better approximation of reality. But also, over many pages, it pointed to major issues, not easily resolved, at every conceivable level. 'We acted in substantial ignorance of the animals in which we were principally interested and in almost total ignorance of the dynamics of the ecosystems in which they existed.' 'We continued for too long to wear rose-tinted glasses and to interpret all data in the manner best calculated to support and confirm the model of growth upon which our hearts had been set.' What were (and often still are) 'believed to be the best available management theory, data and assessment methodologies will legitimately support claims of stock status ranging from sustainable growth to dangerous decline' (Harris, 1990).

Costs and benefits

Harris estimated that the total allowable catch (TAC) would have be reduced from 235,000 tonnes in 1989 to around 125,000 in 1990 to bring this into line with the goal of no more that 20% stock removal, but that this 'would precipitate social and economic repercussions of a particularly drastic nature'. Instead Harris suggested a TAC of 190,000 tonnes (around 30% removal), although cautioning that 'this may contribute to further decline'. Yet this was done, at a loss of 26 million Canadian dollars (CAD) (around 21 million) of landings, CAD 66.6 million (53 million) processed product and the equivalent of some 1000 jobs. Similar limits were set for 1991–92. But during the 1992 fishing season it became apparent that there was little left to catch. The situation was far worse than even the most pessimistic projections. An emergency moratorium was imposed in July 1992, initially for two years. But the stock failed to rebound, and it was not until 1999 that an inshore fishery of just 9000 tonnes was permitted. The financial cost during the 1990s, including lost sales, unemployment benefit and financial assistance, was in excess of several billion Canadian dollars (MacGarvin, 2001a).

Somewhat depressingly, the 2000 DFO assessment concluded that 1999 catch was already in excess of the 20% reference level, something 'unacceptable under a precautionary approach', and that the stock remained so weak that even an index fishery (for monitoring the state of the stock) 'may be associated with an increased risk of the inshore (stock) declining and the offshore not recovering'.

The 2000 DFO assessment also makes it clear just how little is understood about this most studied stock – why it collapsed, why it has failed to recover, what proportion is being taken by predators and other fishing activities – and of the poor status of capelin, small fish that are important prey for the northern cod. Even the linkage between inshore stocks and those offshore – the source of the original controversy – is now open to question. There is also growing awareness that the 'stock' is made up of more or less discrete local populations (cf Heincke's conclusions about herring in the 19th century), and this has considerable implications for recovery programmes (Kent Smedbol and Wroblewski, 2000). On the positive side, the assessments are freely available and the uncertainties clearly set out; attempts are being made to incorporate 'lay' assessments of stock strength made by fishers (DFO, 2000); a constructive debate has been initiated concerning the future of the fisheries (Atlantic Fisheries Policy Review, 2000); and management methods, such as no-take zones, that are not so dependent on the accuracy or theory of stock assessments are being evaluated (Guénette et al, 2000).

The human dimension

As described so far, the demise of the northern cod is already a remarkable event, one that challenges the likely success of precautionary approaches, still advocated, based on setting a limit on calculated fishing mortality as part of an intensive reliance on stock modelling and prediction (see below). Yet there is more. *Fishing for Truth* (Finlayson, 1994), a remarkable sociological study completed just before the final collapse, contains many illuminating interviews with key participants detailing the human dimension.

According to the views quoted there, DFO scientists warned of the uncertainties at an early stage of Canadian management, but in the event not loudly enough (ibid, p136). Pleas that the information demanded (for long-term forecasts) was impossible to provide were over-ridden, and they apparently took seriously the threat that if they did not do the job, then economists would do it for them (ibid, p135). There was a double pressure to downplay the uncertainty; the politicians pleaded for constancy and certainty to aid them resolve disputes (ibid, pp132–3, p142). The scientists – believing that, given a range of estimates, the highest catch would always be taken – also tended towards lower (and, they believed, precautionary) estimates, and with a greater assertion of precision than their internal assessments suggested (ibid, p141). Ultimately this public overemphasis of confidence hoist them on their own petard, when even their most pessimistic view turned out to be based on underestimates of the historic level of fishing mortality.

Moreover, the scientists were aware of wider shortcomings regarding biological and physical parameters (ibid), fundamental sampling problems (ibid, pp73–4), and the often dubious nature of scientific advice hammered out each year for the many stocks in a few weeks of intensive meetings (ibid, p79). Harris likened fisheries science to the Ptolemaic model of the solar system (which placed Earth at the centre of the universe): when observations did not fit the theory, an additional layer of complexity was added, rather than questioning the basic theory (ibid, p69). This accorded with strong criticism, at that time, from related but separate disciplines, such as theoretical ecology (Peters, 1991).

However, none of this happened because the participants were stupid, careless or lacking in intent to restore the stock. It was a systems failure that prevented fishers, scientists and politicians from responding to existing information or extracting themselves from the situation.

Precaution becomes explicit

By the early 1990s precaution had become explicit, due both to disasters such as northern cod, and to its increasing prominence in other fields. The most significant global development was the negotiation of two related documents in 1995: the Code of Conduct for Responsible Fisheries published by the Food and Agriculture Organization of the United Nations (FAO) (FAO, 1995) and the UN Agreement on Straddling Fish Stocks and Highly Migratory Fish Stocks (UN, 1995).

The FAO code applies a 'precautionary approach' to fisheries. The adoption of this terminology initially arose from a nervousness amongst the fishing industry and managers that the precautionary 'principle' was a concept captured by environmental NGOs, which might unjustifiably use it as a weapon to substantially reduce or even halt fishing. Their use of 'approach' is therefore probably best seen as an initial statement about ownership of the process, rather than any close analysis, or fundamental difference of outcome, arising from this choice of terminology. However, as described in the opening paragraph, there are advantages in maintaining a distinction between a universally applicable principle and the detailed approach to implementation, which will differ from field to field, although this was not a distinction made by those who negotiated the Code.

'Precaution' in the Code covers uncertainties relating to individual stocks, other affected species, and environmental and socio-economic conditions. However, the aspect emphasised is the mechanism for taking account of uncertainties in stock assessment models, namely to determine 'stock-specific target reference points (ie, the "positive" goal of optimum stock size), and at the same time, the action to be taken if they are exceeded' and 'limit reference points (the negative goal of the lowest acceptable stock size), and at the same time, the action to be taken if they are exceeded; when a limit reference point is approached measures should be taken to ensure that it will not be exceeded'. The explicit reference to targets, limits and predetermination were novel developments.

The UN agreement provides details, notably that 'the fishing mortality rate that generates maximum sustainable yield (MSY) should be regarded as a minimum standard for limit reference points (ie the "negative" goal)'. It is a minimum because the old concept of MSY (although it is a widely used method of calculation) is known to overestimate sustainable yields. The implications are profound, because many stocks are depleted well beyond formal MSY. It continues, 'For stocks which are not overfished, fisheries management strategies shall ensure that fishing mortality does not exceed that which corresponds to maximum sustainable yield, and that the biomass does not fall below a predefined threshold'. For overfished stocks 'the biomass which would produce maximum sustainable yield can serve as a rebuilding target'. The possible contradiction here may well be the result of a negotiated compromise: it can be a mistake to try to interpret such documents as the product of a single consistent mind.

Nevertheless, overall the UN agreement and, indirectly, the FAO code emphasise precaution at the level of maximising long-term yields.

Subsequent action or inaction

US federal guidelines (Restrepo et al, 1998) recognise that stocks should be managed in a manner consistent with the UN agreement and FAO code.[1] The Canadian position (Richards and Schnute, 2000) is that stocks must be equal to or greater than, and fishing mortality less than, that resulting from MSY, or for equivalent proxies to be used where MSY is inappropriate or inapplicable.

Unlike the US and Canada, fisheries responsibilities within the seas under EU Member State control are split. The International Council for the Exploration of the Sea (ICES) is responsible for technical advice, but the respon-sibility for management, including the setting of targets, resides with the European Commission and Member States. This causes complications. Currently ICES advice centres around B_{lim} (biomass lower limit) and a larger 'precaution-ary approach' target fish stock biomass, B_{pa}, at least according to interpretations arising from within the FAO (Garcia, 2000). Two equivalent levels of fishing mortality believed to achieve these reference points are also used: F_{lim} and F_{pa}. Blim is set not to MSY but to a level where, if depleted further, a stock 'is in immediate danger of collapse' (Garcia, 2000, p22). B_{pa} is set inconsistently, depending on the state of the stock. For those in a poor state, such as North Sea cod, haddock and plaice, it is set at or close to the minimum biologically accept-able level (MBAL), below which there is judged to be unacceptable risk that it could reach Blim. Unfortunately many stocks are judged by ICES to be below B_{pa}, even close to B_{lim} (cf ICES' advice on North Sea cod in 2000 (ACFM ICES, 2000a)). This emphasis and interpretation of reference points has been seen as conflicting with the FAO/UN approach, resulting in peer-group criticism from within the FAO (Garcia, 2000, p23), the US (Restrepo et al, 1998, p24) and Canada (Richards and Schnute, 2000, p7). In effect the earlier management regime (a goal of maintaining stocks above MBAL) often remained unchanged, although the language has been given a precautionary gloss.

ICES may concur, noting that this use of limit reference points 'is a needlessly restricted interpretation of a concept' and – obliquely – that 'the

---

1   The US position and technical guidance is of interest beyond fisheries. It requires the implementation of protective measures 'even in the absence of scientific certainty that stocks are being exploited'. Prior to this approach there was a 'perceived... inabil-ity to implement timely conservation measures without scientific proof of overfishing. Thus, the precautionary approach is essentially a reversal of the "burden of proof."'

adoption of precautionary reference points requires discussion with fisheries management agencies' (ACFM ICES, 2000b, p55). This illustrates the tensions that arise from split responsibility. ICES itself does not refer to B_{pa} as a 'target' reference point, but as a 'buffer' or a 'precautionary reference point' (ACFM ICES, 2000b, p2), presumably because setting a 'target' is seen as impinging on the responsibilities of the Commission and Member States. The 1995 criticism by the Commission's Scientific, Technical and Economic Committee (European Commission, 1995) of a management system 'at ease with crisis management or an unwillingness or inability to state specifically a more positive goal aimed at enhancing the productivity of fisheries in either a biological, economic or social sense' still appears valid. As yet, Member States appear unwilling, or unable, to fund the short-term investment involved in restoring stocks to optimal levels. The European Commission's 2000 communication on the application of the precautionary principle (European Commission, 2000) argues that the reason why ICES does not refer to MSY is twofold: namely that for 'a number of stocks' the conditions whereby sustainable yields can be obtained are 'difficult, if not impossible' to define, and that fishing pressure on many EU stocks is 'well above that which would correspond to the maximising of yield'. A likely response is that establishing maximum yields is no more or less certain than establishing the level at which stocks will collapse, while high fishing pressure is the reason why the code is necessary, not a reason why it should not be applied.

The relationship between EU policy and the FAO code and UN agreement certainly has the potential to become a highly contentious issue. However, the Commission's 2001 Green Paper on the Future of the Common Fisheries Policy (European Commission, 2001a), while general in scope, contains a frank identification of the problems as well providing a constructive basis for discussing the way forward. Concentrating on the future rather than dwelling overmuch on the past may be the most constructive way forward.

Turning back to the code and agreement in general, one problem remains unchanged: the quality of the data. For Canadian northern cod the underestimation of a vital statistic, fishing mortality, was a key factor. Yet a retrospective analysis in 1999 of fishing mortality rates of major North Sea stocks for which the best data were available (cod, haddock, whiting, plaice and sole) found the same fundamental problems (van Beek and Pastoors, 1999; ACFM ICES, 1999, p12). For cod, haddock and whiting, mortality was much higher than originally stated; for plaice there was no correlation; and for sole there was a possible negative correlation. This also noted that underestimating fishing mortality is associated with an overestimate of stock size. Moreover, this problem had been identified as early as 1977. The parallels are startling. One conclusion drawn is that northeast Atlantic cod can survive higher levels of mortality that the northern cod, but this seems to be based on the circular argument that they have not yet crashed. Northern cod also survived periods of intense fishing pressure beyond that prevalent at the time of the crash.

Indeed the goal that the Canadians adopted after taking over control of northern cod management was identical to that now advocated under the precautionary approach: to severely curtail fishing effort and to build up the stock to a level above that predicted for optimum economic yields. Yet still it crashed. So it is legitimate to ask whether the change – as yet – is sufficient.

The ecosystem approach

Another criticism of the UN/FAO approach is that while it nominally requires precaution at the ecosystem level, the practical emphasis remains on single stock management. Moreover, one's value judgement might be to target precaution not at avoiding stock collapses (cf ICES/EU), or even ensuring that stocks are maintained above MSY (UN/FAO), but at preventing adverse effects on other species dependent on the fish. Greenpeace was an early advocate of this in its 1994 precautionary approach (Earl, 1994), although since then others have also argued that catches, in order to be sustainable, should be reduced in the same order of magnitude as other predators (Fowler, 1999). There is thus no one 'correct' precautionary approach; it depends on the objectives set (MacGarvin, 2001b). Even between different fisheries in the same area, judgements will necessarily differ as to the costs and benefits, and the acceptable risks, of different elements of a precautionary response, depending on how these impinge on activities and interests.

Indeed, stocks cannot be treated in isolation from one another, because many of them are major predators on each other (Swain et al, 2000). Fishing one stock has implications for the others. An attempt is sometimes made to allow for this in the single species models, but it falls far short of the evident complexity. Indeed, the gulf between the disciplines of fisheries science and theoretical or community ecology is remarkable. In the early 1990s prominent ecologists commented that fisheries management was, for example, a field 'so accustomed to inaccuracy in its basic models that striking differences between model and observation are scarcely noted... Nevertheless fisheries biologists fit data to models that are clearly inaccurate and make decisions on that basis'.

Nevertheless there are signs of change, with a new emphasis by regulators on the need to adopt an 'ecosystem approach'. Notably in the US (Ecosystems Principles Advisory Panel, 1998) but also within ICES's Advisory Committee on the Marine Environment (ACME ICES, 2000) and in Canada (Murphy and O'Boyle, 2000) there is an increasing involvement of theoretical and community ecologists and concepts. The US report (Ecosystems Principles Advisory Panel, 1998) notes the role of chaotic population dynamics that may make systems fundamentally unpredictable. Indeed, an earlier study of interactions between fish species on the Canadian Grand Banks suggests that the more realism that is incorporated into the models, the more unpredictable the effects of a change in any one species become – in effect, the system may work as a gigantic random number generator (Gomes, 1993).

However, the US report also emphasises that we do know that ecosystems have limits which, when exceeded, can result in irreversible changes; that diversity is important; that systems operate at multiple scales; and that boundaries, to the great inconvenience of managers, are indistinct. 'There is simply not enough money, time or talent to develop a synthetic and completely informed view of how fisheries operate in an ecosystem context. There will always be unmeasured entities, random effects, and substantial uncertainties, but these are not acceptable excuses to delay implementing an ecosystem-based management strategy.' Similar conclusions have been drawn by European experts (Daan, 1998). For example, we have been unable to fill a crucial gap identified as long ago as 1914 (Hjort, 1914): that of being able to predict, from the number of eggs laid, the number of fish that will subsequently mature to appear in the stocks. However, according to the US approach, we know enough about ecosystem functioning to do a better job of management than in the past. Whilst in 1919 a Californian fisheries regulator required that 'proof that seeks to change the ways of commerce and sport must be overwhelming' (Thompson, 1919), now the burden of proof is on fisheries to take account of uncertainty regarding ecosystem effects. At an operational level, stakeholder involvement is essential. What might be called a 'second generation' precautionary approach, less centred on stock assessment models (even with their precautionary attempts to incorporate error), and including error-resilient concepts such as no-take zones, appears to be producing results for finfish and shellfish on the US Georges Bank (Murawski et al, 2000).

The Canadian approach in particular highlights the active involvement of fishers, and the stock assessments now attempt to incorporate their knowledge (for example, DFO, 2000), while in northern Europe considerable attention has been devoted to the policy implications of ecosystem management (Norwegian Ministry of the Environment, 1997; Nordic Council of Ministers, 1998). While at an early stage, and as yet without overall consensus, taken together they provide the elements of a new approach, incorporating precaution, which has considerable potential if implemented.

Late lessons

Fisheries provide a rich seam of lessons regarding the precautionary approach, of wider interest than to fisheries alone. These include:

- the distinction between the precautionary principle and precautionary approaches (logical distinction between a simple 'principle' and differing practical implementation in different fields; also a 'political' distinction as in the FAO Code);
- appropriate levels of proof (19th-century Scottish fishery, 1920s Californian state scientists, 1990s US ecosystem approach);
- distinguishing between uncertainty and ignorance (Harris Report, uncertainties attached to estimates, ignorance regarding ecology);
- unrealistic expectations (or incredible claims) as to the 'soundness' of scientific conclusions (specifically northern cod, but a general feature);
- drawing upon historical knowledge (Heincke's importance of sub-stocks, Scottish natural no-take zones, success of areas protected from trawling);
- not brushing 'blind spots' under the carpet (Harris Report, rose-tinted spectacles);

Table 2.1 *Fisheries: early warnings and actions*

Early fisheries in the UK

1376–77	Setting up a committee is the answer of the English parliament to a call for precautionary actions in fishing by controlling the mesh of the nets
1866–93	Following uncertainty about the consequences of fisheries growth official enquiries take place, but no action is taken

Sardine fisheries in California

Mid-1920s	Californian sardine fisheries scientists call for precaution and research
1942	Continuous inaction leads to the collapse of the sardine stock (signs of recovery only in mid-1980s)

Northern cod fisheries in Canada

Late 1970s	Canada starts managing the northern cod fisheries up to 200 nautical miles, claiming it is doing so on a precautionary basis
1986	Keats Report commissioned by inshore fishers indicates severe underestimation of the fishing pressure
1988	Alverson Report, prepared by fishery scientists, states that consistent overestimation of the stock size leads to overfishing
1989	A new government assessment recommends that the offshore catch should be halved
1990	A new independent assessment, the Harris Report, confirms overfishing
1992	The stock collapses and a moratorium is imposed
1999	Resumption of the northern cod fisheries at low levels, but dissidents state it is not low enough

General fisheries

1990s	The ecosystem approach slowly settles in fisheries management procedures
1995	FAO Code of Conduct for Responsible Fisheries and the UN Agreement on Straddling Fish Stocks and Highly Migratory Fish Stocks are negotiated and published
2001	European Commission Green Paper on the future of the Common Fisheries Policy
2001	Positive changes are occurring, but are they happening fast enough to avoid further collapses?

Source: EEA

- avoiding dominance by any one discipline or sub-discipline (the general dominance of stock modellers);
- accounting for 'real-world' conditions (underestimation of real fishing mortality and technologies);
- taking full account of the pros and cons of any one approach (stock assessment versus wider approaches);
- using lay knowledge (Native American, Scottish 19th-century fishers, Canadian inshore fishers);

- taking account of wider social perspectives, acknowledging the importance of value judgements and evaluating all the options available (different interpretations of precautionary approach);
- avoiding reliance on ever more elaborate models to explain away predictive failures (Harris, Ptolemaic astronomers and analytical fisheries science);
- dealing with institutional obstacles and regulatory independence (reluctance to address fundamental economic issues, blurred independence of technical advisers and policy-makers from Californian sardines to the present); and
- maintaining due humility ('biased pseudoscience' 1986 response of DFO to criticism).

Positive changes of attitude are occurring. The question is whether they are happening fast enough to stave off further collapses. While there will be some interest groups who see it as being in their interests to pursue a short-term strategy, the need for precaution is generally not something that should need to be laboured within the fishing industry. Not cutting stocks so 'close to the bone' not only takes us into areas of greater certainty regarding the maintenance of stocks, but will also greatly increase the economic returns (Whitmarsh et al, 2000). The problem is that the natural capital has been run down so far that industry in many cases cannot absorb the short-term hit necessary to rebuild the stocks. Interest groups need to redirect their attention from arguing with each other and instead learn the language of, and engage with, the economic ministries who – not surprisingly given the history of inappropriate subsidy – have a highly jaundiced view of the merits of investing in recovery programmes.

Radiation: early warnings, late effects

Barrie Lambert

Since the discovery of ionising radiation just over 100 years ago, it has been appreciated that injudicious exposure could produce harmful effects, even death. However, the general excitement in the scientific community and the – often inappropriate – publicity which followed these discoveries ensured that the damage to health, particularly in the long term, was not given any prominence. The undoubted medical diagnostic and therapeutic value of X-rays and radioisotopes meant that caution tended to be thrown away and it was several decades before control over exposure of the public and workers was put in place. This control has slowly evolved as more knowledge of the processes of interaction between radiation and biological tissue has accrued, but it has often lagged behind clear evidence of effect. Changes over the last 70 years to recommendations governing radiation exposure have usually been more restrictive; even over the last 20 years we have perceived that the risk is about four to five times larger than hitherto thought. However, the controls have not always managed to adequately balance risk and benefit. To understand and analyse the development of radiation protection it is necessary to go back more than 100 years.

X-rays

Wilhelm Conrad Roentgen is credited with the discovery of X-rays at the University of Wurtzburg in 1895, but there is reasonable evidence that a number of other physicists, notably Goodspeed in 1890, had produced similar penetrating radiations without appreciating their significance. Roentgen was the first to publish an account of the production of X-rays (Roentgen, 1895) and immediately recognised their value to medical diagnosis – in fact he publicised his work by sending an X-ray of his wife's hand to prominent scientists. There was an immediate worldwide interest in this tool for medical diagnosis, and because of the cavalier approach generally adopted by physicians it was inevitable that X-ray injuries would soon appear. The scientific and lay worlds were captivated by the new phenomenon, which could penetrate human tissues and reveal bony structures. Despite the occasional ominous warning to the contrary (Thompson, 1898), the general consensus was that X-rays, used judiciously, were without adverse effects. Simplistically it was assumed that harm could not result from an agent that could not be appreciated by the senses – ironically, this is the very reason given, nowadays, for the unreasonable fear of radiation.

There were reports of injuries as early as 1896 – for instance, Thomas Edison, Tesla and Grubbe noted eye and skin injuries and the former, particularly, cautioned about excessive exposure to X-rays (Edison, 1896). Unfortunately, this was too late for Edison's assistant, Clarence Dally, who suffered from severe radiodermatitis resulting in the amputation of his arm and his subsequent death in 1904. By the late 1890s there were numerous reports of radiation skin burns and loss of hair (epilation) in the scientific literature bearing testimony to the apparent cavalier attitudes and the size of the doses which were being experienced. One of the more absurd actions was that of the well-known American physicist Elihu Thomson, who purposely exposed the little finger of his left hand to the direct beam of an X-ray tube over a period of several days. The inevitable severe damage to his finger made him caution against overexposure '...or there may be cause for regret when too late' (Thomson, 1896). Ironically, because of the increasing number of reports of radiation injury, some physicians recognised the possible therapeutic value of the rays and the first 'treatment' was reported in 1896 (Stone, 1946) when a woman with advanced carcinoma of the left breast was treated in Chicago. At about this time there was some pressure in the media. John Dennis, a New York journalist, who could possibly be considered the first radiation 'whistle blower', campaigned for controls on radiologists and radiographers by licence issued by the state, and suggested that injury to a patient was a criminal act (Dennis, 1899). It was many decades before this was acted upon.

Despite the reports and cautions of adverse effects, and even the use of X-rays for therapy, a degree of overconfidence existed in the medical fraternity regarding the use of X-rays. The theories were that the effects were not caused by the interactions of the X-rays themselves but by static electricity or individual sensitivity – there was even total denial of the existence of X-ray effects (Scott, 1897).

Perhaps the first and most important person in the role of radiation protection pioneer was a Boston dentist, William Rollins. Rollins, who was a Harvard graduate in dentistry and medicine, was the first to suggest a 'tolerance' dose or exposure for X-rays and also the first to recommend ways of shielding and collimating X-ray tubes. His criterion or standard was to expose a photographic plate outside the tube; if the plate did not fog in seven minutes the shielding was adequate. During the period 1900–04 he published more than 200 papers urging physicians to use the minimum possible exposure, and he made many suggestions on how to reduce the exposure of both radiologist and patient (Rollins, 1904). This latter point has only recently been addressed again by the UK's National Radiological Protection Board (NRPB, which advises the government). Rollins also recognised the potential for the induction of cataract and he carried out some animal experiments that showed, amongst other effects, the possibility of acute (teratological) damage to the foetus. He was the first to warn of the risks in the X-ray of women for the diagnosis of pregnancy (pelvimetry). However, his cautions often went unheeded – his warnings about pelvimetry were only revisited, albeit with reference to late effects, by Alice Stewart, the British epidemiologist, about 40 years later (Stewart et al, 1958). It is noteworthy that her work was also at first rejected by the medical authorities (see below).

It would be reasonable to assume that, once it had been identified that excessive X-ray exposure produced tissue damage, care would be exercised. This was not so – even in 1903, Albers-Schönberg (1903), who produced a set of rules for the use of radiologists in protecting themselves, suggested that the regularly used technique of testing the 'hardness' of the X-ray tube by placing the hand between the tube and fluorescent screen was dangerous. It must be said that, in this period, the absence of an agreed unit of radiation exposure or dose was a problem to those who wanted to establish effective standards of protection; this had to wait until the adoption of the roentgen as the unit of exposure in 1928. However, notwithstanding the absence of units, the first set of published rules of radiation protection was produced by the German Radiological Society in 1913 (Taylor, 1979). Shortly after this, also in 1913, Coolidge invented the hot-cathode, tungsten-target X-ray tube, which contributed immeasurably to lower doses to both patients and radiographers (for instance, with early tubes operating at low voltages, exposures of more than an hour were common).

Radioactivity and radioactive materials

Unfortunately, another hazard became apparent very soon after Roentgen's work because within weeks Henri Becquerel had discovered radioactivity and then, in 1898, Marie and Pierre Curie reported the discovery of radium. The extent of the hazard of radioactivity was no more recognised than that of X-rays and both Becquerel and Pierre Curie suffered skin erythemas from carrying samples of radioactive materials in their pockets. Although it was soon realised that radium could be used therapeutically, for example for killing malignant cells, for some reason the public became besotted with the idea of radium (and radium-emanation, radon) being a general panacea.

The precautionary principle seemed to act even more slowly in this field, because not until about 1920 was it realised that controls were necessary. This was initiated at least partly by the use of radium in luminous paint that was used extensively in the First World War. The radium-activated paint was applied by brush and the painters, mostly young women (in New Jersey and elsewhere), found they could work faster and earn more by tipping their brushes with their lips – in this way they ingested considerable quantities of radium. Very little attention was paid to industrial hygiene and the workers were irradiated internally from the radium they had taken in, and externally from accumulations of the paint which contaminated their workplaces and from the inhalation of radon. The hazard of this work was not at first recognised, but in 1924 a New York dentist, Theodore Blum, published a paper that identified a new disease which he called 'radium jaw' (sometimes known as 'phossy jaw') which he had seen in his patients who were ex-dial painters. He attributed the condition to the toxicity of phosphorus. However, a local New Jersey pathologist, Harrison Martland, recognised the bone lesions as being caused by radium and in 1925 started a study that unearthed the whole sorry story (Martland and Humphries, 1929). The first bone sarcoma was recorded in this group of women in 1923 and there have been 55 such cancers studied in a population of nearly 3000 women (Rowland et al, 1983) – altogether about one third have died of various malignancies (including leukaemia and breast cancer). The data derived from the experiences of these women did eventually set the standard for the intake of radioactive material for many years: this was the so-called radium standard. This standard was set at the amount of radium in the body which apparently produced no effect. There was then an assumption of a threshold for the effects but this was in accord with the general attitude in the years up to 1930 of setting a 'tolerance' dose. The radium standard was set at a level of radioactivity of 0.1 microcuries (3.7 kilobecquerels) of radium which would deliver a radiation dose of 150 millisieverts to the bone.

In a somewhat bizarre way, in the 1920s radium was looked upon as a source of health and healing. This cumulated in many potions being sold containing radium, the most famous being Radiothor. Four hundred thousand bottles of this quack nostrum, which was said to cure a range of maladies from stomach ulcers to impotence, were sold between 1925 and 1930. The more dangerous aspects of this were highlighted when a famous US golfer, industrialist and millionaire, Eben Byers, died from radiation-induced disease after consuming about 1000 bottles over a long period of time (Macklis, 1993). This case did quite a lot to encourage a more restrictive approach to the use of radium, as did the death of Marie Curie in 1934 from (probably) aplastic anaemia (which was at the time attributed to the effects of radium). Nevertheless, such use of radium and radon has lasted to this day in the form of, for instance, 'emantoria' where radon is breathed for (presumed) beneficial purposes, for example in Salzburg.

Early moves towards control of exposure

During the 1920s the concept of radiation dose was not defined but there were a number of reports aimed at restricting exposure. These often quoted a level which could be 'tolerated'. One of these was a fraction of the skin erythema dose (SED) which was suggested by an American physicist, Arthur Mutscheller (Mutscheller, 1925). His proposal was one hundredth of the SED in a month. This would be very roughly equivalent to an annual dose limit of about 700 millisieverts (the contemporary dose limit for workers is now 20 millisieverts per year). It is noteworthy that during this period the emphasis was on limits driven by a desire to control the immediate effects of radiation. There seemed to be no realisation that cancer would follow after a long lag, or latent, period.

Clearly there was some pressure from within part of the scientific community for control of the use of radiation and with the establishment of the International X-ray and Radium Protection Committee (IXRPC) at the second International Congress of Radiology in 1928 the setting of standards became more regularised. However, comments on the misuse of radiation were often missing. For some reason in the early pontifications of the IXRPC emphasis was placed on leisure activities for radiographers (Desjardins, 1923). For example, 'The cultivation of an outdoor hobby is of special importance to all persons exposed to radiation.' The IXRPC eventually metamorphosed in 1950 into the International Commission on Radiological Protection (ICRP) but again it was some time before this advisory body began to recommend dose limits without connotation of a dose threshold. All this was against a background of reports of more than 200 radiologists who had died of what were thought to be radiation-induced malignant diseases (Colwell and Russ, 1934), particularly the pioneering British radiologist Ironside-Bruce in March 1921. As a result of his death there were several press articles commenting on the adequacy of shielding of X-ray tubes which prompted the Roentgen Society ('Editorial', 1921) to state 'the scientific competency of the press is less than its ability to write lurid journalise'.

The post-war watershed: justification, optimisation, limitation

The essential change in radiation protection philosophy came at a meeting in Canada in 1949 (National Bureau of Standards, 1954) when it was concluded that, 'there may be some degree of risk at any level of exposure' and 'the risk to the individual is not precisely determinable but however small is believed not to be zero'. The additional philosophy from this meeting, which is of great importance, was that 'radiation exposures from whatever sources should be as low as practicable'. This is what is now known as the optimisation principle. The risk versus benefit (justification) principle, which is probably unique to radiation as a pollutant, was also introduced.

The ICRP was set up to do no more than make 'recommendations' which, presumably, could have been accepted or rejected by national governments, but from its inception its role has been criticised. For example, it took no stand about the testing of nuclear weapons in the atmosphere which produced worldwide fallout. In addition it has generally been the work of individuals, rather than the ICRP, which has prevented the misuse of radiation. There are numerous examples of the ill-conceived use of radiation, including:

- the widespread use of pedascopes for fitting children's shoes. These X-ray fluoroscopy devices were in nearly every shoe store in the 1940s and 1950s and could produce reported dose rates of 1 roentgen per minute. They did no more than keep children amused whilst their parents selected shoes and thus the radiation doses received by children and shop staff were totally unnecessary.
- Children who had ringworm were treated with X-rays to produce epilation but many subsequently developed cancer (see, for example, Ron et al, 1989).
- Patients with psychological disorders were 'treated' with radium in the 1930s.

- X-rays were used for the removal of unwanted hair in beauty shops in the 1930s and 1940s.

These misuses of radiation were largely uncontrolled because there were, at that time, no specific legal regulations governing radiation safety, only recommendations. In the UK legal regulation was first encapsulated in the Ionising Radiations Regulations (1961), and later separately for medical radiations (POPUMET, 1988).

Following the Second World War there was a rush to develop both nuclear power and nuclear weapons. The radiation protection community was faced with the problem of setting dose limits that did not appear to restrict the expansion of these industries: politics entered the scene. At first the public were beguiled by the promise of endless cheap nuclear power but demonstrations of nuclear weapons produced a different reaction. Gradually people began to have less and less confidence in, and more suspicion of, the motives of governments, particularly with regard to bland reassurances about the effects of radioactive contamination of the environment. This apprehension was fuelled by the rise of the 'green movement' and was to a certain extent justified – it is only surprising that it took so long to develop. This was maybe because the early uses of radiation had to a large extent been in medicine and the public had a trust of doctors. However, the motives of the nuclear industry were seen as less likely to be for the good of the individual. Even confidence in medical radiology received a jolt in the late 1950s when a well-known public health epidemiologist, Alice Stewart, carried out some studies which linked radiology during pregnancy (pelvimetry) with leukaemia in children (Stewart et al, 1958). This finding was at first controversial and disbelieved but, after being repeated by others, it is now accepted that there is a significant risk of leukaemia from even small radiation doses received by the embryo or foetus. Nowadays it is recommended (RCR, 1993) that no obstetrician should consider the use of X-rays if some other diagnostic tool is available. It has been estimated (Doll, 1989) that about 5% of all cases of childhood cancer were caused by pelvimetry, which in the UK was about 75 cases each year and in the US about 300. In could be claimed that these numbers of leukaemias would have been prevented had the work of Stewart et al been acted on earlier. A similar and contemporary story may be unfolding in relation to the childhood leukaemia risk in proximity to overhead power lines in the US.

Contemporary risk estimates for radiation are probably more quantified and more soundly based than risks from any other environmental pollutant. However, there are problems with even these estimates because they are derived almost exclusively from the health records of the survivors of the atomic bombings in Japan in 1945, that is at high dose and dose rate. A conservative linear dose–effect relationship is assumed and it is therefore appreciated that there is a risk at all doses. Exposures to radiation are therefore associated with a certain acceptance of risk. For this reason the ICRP have based their philosophy (ICRP, 1977) around three tenets.

1   Justification – all uses of radiation have to be justified so that the detriment is offset by some net benefit.

2   Optimisation – all exposures must be kept as low as reasonably achievable, social and economic factors being taken into account.

3   Limitation – all exposures must be below the appropriate dose limit.

It is of interest to examine the first and second of these tenets to see what progress has been made in the 100 years of radiation use, using medical radiology as an example.

In medical radiation exposure it is intended that there should be some benefit to the patient. Although this is usually true there are an increasing number of occasions when it is doubtful, for example the use of X-rays as part of health monitoring for job selection, or some screening procedures. The NRPB has estimated (NRPB, 1990) that about 20% of all X-rays carried out in the UK are clinically unhelpful. Thus it has been stated in guidance principles given to radiographers that 'there should be a valid clinical indication for all examinations of patients where ionising radiation is used.' This constitutes 'justification' and is a major step forward compared to the radiology of, say, even 40 years ago, particularly as it refers to the patient and not just the radiologist. In addition to this criterion, the dose received by the patient should be optimised, and here progress is not so good. The NRPB has estimated (NRPB, 1990) that the total annual collective dose from medical examinations in the UK is about 16,000 man-sieverts. It also suggests a number of patient dose reduction methods which should result in a reduction in this collective dose of about 7500 man-sieverts, that is to say nearly 50%. It has also been shown, more recently, that the variation in the dose received at different hospitals for the same examination can be more than an order of magnitude (Wall and Hart, 1997). Thus, although the individual radiation dose is now maybe two orders of magnitude lower than 60 years ago, the problem of optimisation of that dose still exists.

Conclusions

Overall it can be concluded that radiation protection standards have slowly evolved as the perception of radiation effects has developed. However, there have also been some people, maybe ahead of their time, who warned of impending doom. Thus, there have always been periods when changes in limits have lagged some years behind clear evidence of harm to human health. There are now substantial lobbies for changes which include both re-introducing the concept of thresholds and considerations of hormesis (small doses which are thought to do some good); these have been resisted by the ICRP.

Radiation protection is now firmly established in legislation both in the EU (by directives) and, internationally, in the Basic Safety Standards of the International Atomic Energy Agency (IAEA). All of these use the recommendations of the ICRP as their basis. In the UK the most recent legislation which covers workers and members of the public is the Ionising Radiations Regulations of 1999. These are intended to implement EU Directive 96/29 (laying down basic safety standards for the protection of the health of workers

Table 3.1 *Radiation: early warnings and actions*

1896	Injuries from exposure to X-rays noted by Edison, Tesla and Grubbe.
1899	John Dennis, New York journalist, campaigns for licensing of radiologists and warns of harm from X-rays.
1904	Death of Edison's assistant from complications arising from severe X-ray radiodermatitis.
1904	William Rollins, Harvard dentist/doctor, publishes many warnings on X-ray hazards, and recommendations on prevention for radiologists and patients, including pregnant women.
1913	First published rules of voluntary radiological protection by German Radiological Society.
1924	New York dentist, Theodore Blum, identifies 'radium jaw' in radium dial painters, but wrongly attributes this to phosphorous.
1925–29	Harrison Martland, New Jersey pathologist, identifies radium as the cause of the jawbone cancers in the dial painters studied.
1928	Establishment of the International X-ray and Radium Protection Committee, which later became the International Commission on Radiological Protection (ICRP).
1934	Reports by Colwell and Russ on the death of more than 200 radiologists from radiation-induced cancers.
1949	ICRP concludes that there is no dose threshold for radiation-induced cancer and optimisation of all exposures is crucial.
1958	Alice Stewart reports that 'low dose' X-rays to pregnant women can cause leukaemia in their children. Not generally accepted until the 1970s.
1961	UK publishes regulations covering the use of radioactive substances.
1977	ICRP updates its radiation protection recommendations and links dose limits to risk.
1988	Regulations covering radiation doses to patients produced in the UK
1990–97	NRPB reports 20% of medical X-rays are probably clinically unhelpful; that 50% of the collective dose to patients could be avoided; and that individual doses for the same X-ray vary by an order of magnitude (10x) between hospitals.
1990	ICRP concludes in Publication 60 that the risk of radiation-induced cancer is 4–5 times greater than estimated in 1977, and reduces the occupational dose limit to 20 million sieverts per year.
1996	EU Directive on Ionising Radiations, based on ICRP 60, which will be mandatory on Member States.

Source: EEA

and the general public against the dangers arising from ionising radiation). This directive will (eventually) be implemented throughout Europe, and similar regulations from the IAEA should apply in other countries. There are now, also, regulations which cover the use of radiation in medicine and the limitation of doses to patients. However, it has been found difficult to ensure that radiation protection legislation is implemented uniformly and there continue to be examples of careless or irresponsible attitudes towards radiation sources and waste which have resulted in horrendous injuries and death, such as the caesium-137 incident at Goiania (Rosenthal et al, 1991).

Historically, less stringent dose limits have also given rise to claims from workers for compensation for cancer allegedly caused by radiation exposure. In this context, the issue of liability for radiation injury has some lessons for other 'long latent period' hazardous agents. In the UK liability in the nuclear industry was originally state funded (Nuclear Installations Act 1965) but the Radiation Workers Compensation Scheme, which is run jointly by trades unions and the nuclear industry, has been extremely successful in providing an alternative to litigation.

Thus, although we have learnt much about the risks of radiation exposure in the last 100 years (probably more than about any other environmental pollutant) we are still constantly having to react to new knowledge. For instance, the risk rate for radiation-induced cancer was perceived (by ICRP) as four to five times higher in 1990 as compared to 1977. This resulted in changes in dose limits but was a belated response to mounting incontrovertible evidence, a situation which has been a recurring theme in the history of radiation protection, where precaution has sometimes been lacking despite the clear warnings given from the discovery of radiation to the present day. Thus it must be concluded that the precautionary principle suggests that epidemiological databases of long-term effects must be funded and maintained for the future even when an immediate need is not perceived.

Benzene: a historical perspective on the American and European occupational setting

Peter F Infante

Early warnings

Since the 1897 report of Santessen, who observed aplastic anaemia among young women engaged in the manufacture of bicycle tyres in Sweden, and the report in the same year by LeNoir and Claude, who observed haemorrhaging in a young man engaged in a dry-cleaning operation in France, benzene has been known to be a powerful bone marrow poison. Similar reports of workers developing benzene-related diseases of the bone marrow increased dramatically through the first half of the 20th century.

Between 1910 and 1914, the first major use of benzene as a solvent in the rubber industry took place. Production of benzene was also stimulated greatly by the demand for toluene in the manufacture of explosives during the First World War. Expanded use of benzene in industry after the war led to an increased use of benzene as a solvent in the artificial leather industry, rubber goods, glue manufacturing, hat manufacturing, rotogravure printing, paint, adhesives, coatings, dry cleaning, car manufacturing, tin-can assembly, as a starting material in organic synthesis, in petroleum products and in the blending of motor fuels.

This expansion in the industrial uses of benzene was accompanied by a vast increase in the numbers of reported cases of aplastic anaemia, generally referred to as 'benzene poisoning'. Some individuals were diagnosed with benzene poisoning within a few weeks of initial employment and some died within a few months of beginning their jobs (Hogan and Schrader, 1923). These poisonings were associated with benzene levels ranging mostly between 200 ppm (parts per million) and 1000 ppm. Greenburg (1926) and colleagues made a survey of 12 plants in the US that used benzene and observed that 32% of the workers had

---

Box 4.1 Glossary

Leukaemia: a progressive cancer of the blood. It can be classified clinically by duration of the disease (acute or chronic), and by character of the disease, including myelogenous (myeloid cells in excess); lymphatic (lymphoid cells in excess); monocytic (monocytes in excess).

Aplastic anaemia: a condition whereby the bone marrow fails to produce enough red blood cells, white blood cells and platelets. Therefore the individual is usually tired because there are not enough red blood cells available, is susceptible to infection because there are not enough white blood cells present, and bleeds easily because there are not enough blood platelets available.

Benzene poisoning: usually refers to aplastic anaemia.

Hypersusceptibility: a condition of increased susceptibility to toxic exposures in relation to the average person.

Haemopathy: an abnormality of the blood.

Multiple myeloma: a cancer of the lymphatic system.

---

abnormally low white blood cell counts (below 5500 per cubic centimetre (cc)), and 12% had below 4000 per cc. The benzene exposure levels associated with this extremely high prevalence of abnormal white blood cell counts were 90 ppm and higher. Greenburg (1926) recommended medical removal if an employee developed clinical symptoms of poisoning, or if blood values for individual workers dropped 25% or more.

First report of benzene-induced leukaemia

In 1928, Dolore and Borgomano published the first case of benzene-induced leukaemia. This case of acute lymphatic leukaemia was identified in a pharmaceutical worker who had a job considered dangerous because of high benzene exposure levels. Another worker at the same plant died of aplastic anaemia and the authors were of the opinion that some previous cases of aplastic anaemia reported in association with benzene exposure may also have been leukaemia. The company's means of dealing with the high exposure levels that caused these blood diseases was to rotate the workers out of the specific job every month.

Actions and inactions

Exposure recommendations

By 1939, the vast number of benzene poisonings among workers in all parts of the world led to the recommendation for the substitution of benzene with other solvents by a number of investigators (Greenburg, 1926; Erf and Rhoads, 1939; Mallory et al, 1939). In 1939 Hunter, and Mallory et al, reported 89 cases of 'poisoning' and three cases of leukaemia among workers exposed to benzene in a variety of occupations. Two of the 'poisonings' were associated with benzene levels of less than 25 ppm and 10 ppm.

Yet, in 1946, the American Conference of Governmental Industrial Hygienists (ACGIH) recommended a limit of 100 ppm for benzene exposure in the workplace (ACGIH, 1946). Subsequently, the recommended value was reduced to 50 ppm in 1947 and to 35 ppm in 1948 (ACGIH, 1948). Because of evidence of 'hypersusceptibility' to the bone marrow suppressing effects of benzene, a document published in 1948 by the American Petroleum Institute (API) concluded that the only absolutely safe level from exposure to benzene was zero (API, 1948). This opinion was based on observations of some workers developing various blood diseases indicative of bone marrow depression who had worked alongside other workers whose blood counts were in the normal range. The API then proceeded to recommend a limit of 50 ppm or less. In 1957, the ACGIH lowered its recommended eight-hour time-weighted average exposure limit to 25 ppm for benzene (ACGIH, 1957).

Disregard for recommendations

In spite of the recommendations mentioned above, cases of aplastic anaemia, and central nervous system toxicity manifested by headache, nausea, giddiness, staggering gait, paralysis and unconsciousness (leading to death in 13 cases in the UK) continued to be reported in the 1940s and 1950s (Browning, 1965). These symptoms of the central nervous system are thought to be associated with benzene exposures ranging from 3000 ppm to 20,000 ppm (Flury, 1928) – levels 200 to 800 times higher than the limits recommended in the 1940s and 1950s and 2000 times higher than the 10 ppm level already associated with aplastic anaemia by Hunter and by Mallory et al (1939).

In the 1950s and 1960s, an obvious lack of precaution for workers exposed to benzene was taking place in many parts of the world, including France, Italy, Turkey, the UK, the US, the former Union of Soviet Socialist Republics (USSR) and other countries, as documented by the publication of case reports of blood diseases as a result of benzene exposures well above levels known to be toxic to the bone marrow and central nervous system of workers. For example, Vigliani and Saita, in 1964, reported that the risk of acute leukaemia among workers 'heavily exposed to benzene' in the rotogravure and shoe industries in the Italian provinces of Milano and Pavia was at least 20 times higher than for the general population. Vigliani (1976) reported that over 200 cases of benzene haemopathy, including 34 cases of acute leukaemia, had been treated at the institutes of Milano and Pavia between 1942 and 1965. These workers were exposed to benzene levels ranging mostly from 200 to 500 ppm, with occasional peaks above these levels. In 1967, Goguel et al reported 44 cases of benzene-induced leukaemia, mostly chronic forms, having occurred in the Paris region of France between 1950 and 1965.

Blood poisonings among workers exposed to benzene were being documented in other parts of Europe as well. As stated by Aksoy (1977), because 'benzene containing glue adhesives were extremely practical and cheaper in the market, they replaced their customary petroleum containing adhesives with the new product' in the shoe and slipper industry in Turkey in 1961. Benzene exposures experienced by these workers were reported to have been between 150 ppm and 650 ppm (Aksoy, 1978). By the mid-1970s, an epidemic of aplastic anaemia and leukaemia among Turkish shoe workers began to unfold as reported by Aksoy (Aksoy et al, 1971; Aksoy 1977 and 1978). The majority of the individuals who were identified in the reports from these European countries as dying from leukaemia as well as other benzene-related blood diseases were exposed to levels shown decades earlier to cause benzene poisoning. (For a review of case reports of benzene-related blood diseases associated with the countries mentioned above, see IARC, 1974.)

Epidemiological evidence for leukaemia

Beginning in the early 1970s, the University of North Carolina in the US published a series of epidemiological studies demonstrating significant excesses of leukaemia, mostly chronic forms, among workers exposed to presumably low atmospheric levels of benzene (McMichael et al, 1975). The benzene exposure resulted primarily from the use of rubber solvents such as petroleum naphtha, toluene, mineral spirits, etc, that were contaminated with benzene ranging in volume from about 1–5% in the 1940s to about 0.5% for petroleum naphtha in the 1970s.

In 1977, Infante et al published the results of the first cohort study of workers exposed specifically to benzene. The workers were engaged in the manufacture of a rubberised food wrap called Pliofilm. The study demonstrated a five- to ten-fold risk of leukaemia among workers exposed to technical-grade benzene at levels that were generally considered within the various limits recommended over the time period 1940–71, that is a 10 ppm time-weighted average to a maximum limit of 100 ppm (Infante et al, 1977a). Until this time, benzene was considered a cause of leukaemia based not upon epidemiological studies, but rather upon case reports of leukaemia and the clinical observation that individuals with benzene-induced aplastic anaemia and other blood diseases transformed into acute leukaemia.

US attempt to control occupational exposure

In 1977, on the basis of the Infante et al (1977a) study results supplemented by the world literature on benzene and leukaemia, the US Department of Labor (OSHA, 1977a) issued an emergency temporary standard (ETS) that would have reduced the occupational benzene exposure limit in workplace air to 1 ppm as an eight-hour time-weighted average. The 1 ppm exposure limit was based on the Occupational Safety and Health Administration (OSHA)'s policy at the time that exposure to carcinogens in the workplace should be lowered to the lowest feasible limit. Such feasibility analyses take into consideration both technological and economic feasibility.

The new OSHA ETS was stayed in 1977, however, in response to a challenge in the US Court of Appeals by the API, who in essence argued that there was no increased risk of developing leukaemia as a result of benzene exposures below the old limit of 10 ppm. Then OSHA proposed a permanent standard, requested comments and held a public hearing (OSHA, 1977b). In 1978, OSHA issued a final standard (OSHA, 1978) that included a 1 ppm atmospheric exposure limit. This standard was challenged by the API on the same grounds. The US Court of Appeals again vacated the final standard, and that decision was appealed to the Supreme Court. In an unrelated development, benzene was voluntarily withdrawn from consumer products in the US after it was shown that use of a paint stripper in the home could generate atmospheric levels up to 200 ppm in a short period of time (Young et al, 1978).

The US Benzene Decision and dose–response analyses

In July 1980, the US Supreme Court (IUD, 1980) issued what has become known as the Benzene Decision. This decision has had a major impact on OSHA's ability to control exposures to benzene and other toxic substances in the workplace. The court stated that before OSHA can promulgate any permanent health standard, the Secretary of Labor is required to make a threshold finding that a place of employment is unsafe in the sense that significant risks are present and can be eliminated, or lessened, by a change in practices. Although the Benzene Decision recognised the uncertainties involved, it indicated that the determination of 'significant risk' should, if at all possible, be established on the basis of an analysis of the best available evidence through such means as quantitative risk assessments. The Supreme Court in its general guidance for future OSHA rule-making noted that the requirement that a significant risk be identified is not a mathematical straitjacket and that it is the OSHA's responsibility to determine what it considers to be a significant risk based largely on policy considerations. In the only concrete example of significant risk, the court stated that if, for example, the odds are one in a million that a person will die from cancer by taking a drink of chlorinated water, the risk clearly could not be considered significant. On the other hand, if the odds are one in 1000 that regular inhalation of petrol vapours that are 2% benzene will be fatal, a reasonable person might well consider the risk significant and take appropriate steps to decrease or eliminate it.

Since the Benzene Decision, OSHA has considered an occupational lifetime risk (over a 45-year period) of one extra case of cancer, or other material impairment of health consequence, per 1000 workers to be 'significant'. It has not yet considered the other end of the range – what it considers to be a nonsignificant risk – because all the health standards that OSHA has promulgated since the Benzene Decision, with the exception of perhaps formaldehyde, have resulted in estimates of excess risk that are greater than one per 1000 over an occupational lifetime. (For quantitative estimates of risk for health standards promulgated by OSHA since the Benzene Decision, see Infante, 1995b.)

A straitjacket, however, appropriately describes the risk analyses that OSHA currently engages in prior to proposing any regulatory action. The long delay recognised in OSHA promulgating standards before 1980 has now been superseded by additional detailed analyses of risk related to exposure. While on the surface such analyses may seem appropriate, they have become encumbered by additional analyses that take into account the mechanism by which the substances being regulated may cause cancer. Since the exact mechanism by which any substance causes cancer (including benzene which has been studied for decades) has not been identified, speculation and argument about various unproven hypotheses for cancer causation are time consuming. Many other issues also have been added to the debate on risk assessment procedures such as whether the mouse, the hamster or the rat is the most appropriate species to use when human data are not available. Since the OSHA is required to review and comment on all possible cancer mechanisms, appropriateness of species, etc, the entire 'risk assessment' process has created additional years of delay in standard-setting. Instead of reasonable precautions being promulgated by government and employers, years pass as analyses are performed to determine the dose response between exposure and risk of disease. These analyses can also include incorporation of speculative mechanistic data that have not been validated.

Cost in lives of the prolonged regulatory process

Eleven years after the OSHA promulgation of an ETS for benzene, a new benzene standard that included a 1 ppm eight-hour time-weighted average exposure limit was finally issued (OSHA, 1987). The new limit was based on 'economic feasibility', not elimination of 'significant risk', as an occupational lifetime risk of ten extra leukaemia deaths per 1000 workers was associated with the 1 ppm limit. Other estimates of leukaemia risk, limited to the cohort data from the National Institute for Occupational Safety and Health (NIOSH) (as updated by Paxton et al, 1994) and to deaths from acute myelogenous and monocytic leukaemias only, indicate a range of 0.02 to 5.1 per 1000 excess deaths depending upon the estimates of benzene exposure and the model chosen (Crump, 1994). However, these later analyses are based on a follow-up period of the NIOSH cohort that results in selection bias for the reasons described below. Based on OSHA's final quantitative risk assessment for benzene and estimates of extra benzene exposure among the US workforce during the ten years that it took to complete the benzene standard, it has been estimated that an extra 198 deaths from leukaemia and 77 extra deaths from multiple myeloma will eventually develop among US workers as a result of the ten-year delay – deaths that could have been prevented (Infante and DiStasio, 1988). This estimate of preventable deaths from benzene exposure did not include blood diseases other than leukaemia, which were known at the time to be caused by benzene exposure, the reason being that there were no dose–response data available for the other blood diseases.

Expansion of lymphohaematopoietic diseases

The quantitative estimate of extra deaths from benzene exposure indicated above did not include non-Hodgkin's lymphoma, which has been shown more recently to be associated with occupational exposure to very low levels of benzene (Hayes et al, 1997). Quantitative risk assessment (Infante, 1997) based on the 1996 Hayes et al study results suggests an extra risk of 54 deaths from leukaemia/lymphoma per 1000 workers exposed over an occupational lifetime (45 years). This risk is 54 times greater than a level considered significant by OSHA. The 1997 Hayes et al study results and dose–response analyses based upon those data clearly demonstrate the inadequacy of the 1 ppm exposure limit for benzene based on cancer risk alone. Fortunately, most occupational settings in the US are able to achieve benzene exposure levels in the range of 0.2–0.3 ppm, or lower. Additionally, the US standard includes provisions ancillary to the exposure limit such as exposure monitoring, medical surveillance and hazard training – all of which should presumably further reduce the risk of benzene exposure and related diseases. In addition to quantitative risk assessment, direct observation of data from the 1997 Hayes et al study demonstrates significantly elevated relative risks for all lympho-haematopoietic cancers combined, and for acute non-lymphocytic leukaemia and myelodysplastic syndrome combined, among the group of workers exposed to a constant average benzene level of only 1.2 ppm for 5.5 years for a total cumulative dose of 6.7 ppm-years (Hayes, pers comm., 1999), which is a much lower cumulative dose than that allowed by a limit of 1 ppm over an occupational lifetime of 45 years (45 ppm-years of cumulative dose). Some individuals within the benzene cohorts who have died from leukaemia or lymphoma experienced estimated benzene exposures of 0.5–2 ppm for only one to two years or less (Infante, 1992).

By the 1990s, toxicologic research demonstrated the multiple-site carcinogenicity of benzene in experimental animals, and additional epidemiological studies and case reports of exposed workers expanded the carcinogenicity of benzene to all major forms of leukaemia in the aggregate (Savitz and Andrews, 1997; Infante, 1995a; Wong, 1987b) and specifically acute myelogenous leukaemia and its variants (Hayes et al, 1997; Browning, 1965; Rinsky et al, 1987; Bond et al, 1986; DeCoufle et al, 1983), acute lymphatic leukaemia (Hernberg et al, 1966; Shu et al, 1988), chronic lymphatic leukaemia (McMichael et al, 1975), chronic myelogenous leukaemia (Browning, 1965; Goguel et al, 1967; Tareeff et al, 1963; Infante, 1995a; Wong, 1987b) and some minor forms such as hairy cell leukaemia (Aksoy, 1987; Flandrin and Collado, 1987), myelodysplastic syndrome (Hayes et al, 1997), myeloproliferative disorders (Rawson et al, 1941; Tondel et al, 1995) as well as non-Hodgkin's lymphoma (Hayes et al, 1997), including multiple myeloma (DeCoufle et al, 1983; Rinsky et al, 1987; Ireland et al, 1997; Goldstein, 1990). An 'updated' analysis of the NIOSH benzene cohort (Infante et al, 1977a; Rinsky et al, 1987) by Wong (1995) concluded that the excess of multiple myeloma in the NIOSH cohort was no longer statistically significant. Wong (1995), however, changed the beginning date of follow-up from 1950 to 1940. In doing so, he introduced selection bias into his analysis because the company removed records for individuals who died at one of the study locations for several of the years prior to 1950. Thus, analyses of the NIOSH cohort by Wong (1995) that begin follow-up prior to 1950 cannot be relied upon for estimating risk of death from multiple myeloma, or any other cause of death.

Discussion

The response to information on the toxicity of benzene has at times demonstrated concern by some in the field of occupational health, particularly in the earlier years when large numbers of workers in various sectors and jobs were being surveyed to determine the extent of their blood diseases. Nevertheless, even during this period, benzene exposure levels were not reduced to levels commensurate with the toxicity data available at the time, and the epidemic of poisonings and leukaemia among benzene-exposed workers continued through the first six decades of the 20th century. Various reasons for the limited public health response and subsequent overexposure and disease in light of the knowledge of benzene toxicity are apparent.

Some reasons for lack of precaution

Lack of knowledge

The lack of precaution about exposure to benzene has been attributed in part to lack of knowledge of its toxicity during the first four decades of the 20th century. For example, even though Santessen (1897) reported four cases of aplastic anaemia among women manufacturing raincoats in Sweden in 1897, exposures were not lowered enough and Helmer (1944) reported 60 cases of benzene poisoning (58 were women) at a single raincoat manufacturing facility in the same country in 1940 and 1941. The epidemic of benzene poisoning in Sweden was ascribed in part to a lack of knowledge of the toxicity of benzene by plant management and workers (Helmer, 1944).

Cost of solvents

Several investigators who surveyed workforces and identified workers with various benzene-induced blood diseases, namely Greenburg and colleagues in 1926, Erf and Rhoads in 1939 and Mallory et al in 1939, recommended the substitution of benzene with other solvents. Yet, worldwide consumption of benzene in the marketplace continued to expand after the Second World War. One of the reasons for expanded use of benzene in the synthetic rubber industry is that it was such a good rubber solvent. Another reason, as expressed by Aksoy (1977), is that benzene was cheaper than other solvents used in the shoe and slipper industry in Turkey. Thus, economic consequences led to other solvents being replaced with benzene in the Turkish shoe manufacturing industry as late as 1961. This substitution with benzene led to high-level workplace atmospheric benzene concentrations and to the epidemic of leukaemia, preleukaemia, pancytopenia and other blood diseases as reported by Aksoy (Aksoy et al, 1971; Aksoy, 1977 and 1978). Thus, economic considerations in the 1960s (Aksoy, 1977) further contributed to the overexposure and subsequent benzene-related diseases.

Consensus recommendations and corporate influence

The 1939 reports by Hunter and Mallory et al indicated that some cases of benzene poisoning were associated with levels of 25 ppm and 10 ppm. Yet, in 1946, the ACGIH recommended a limit of 100 ppm. Although the ACGIH recommendation for benzene was lowered to 35 ppm in 1948, this level was still higher than the levels reported in association with benzene poisonings. From my personal experience over the years, it is apparent that one of the problems being faced in the occupational health community for benzene (as well as for other toxic substances) is that consensus organisations usually base their recommended exposure levels on what is easily achievable in the workplace. Data related to level of exposure and toxicity are reviewed, but are not translated into health-based exposure-limit recommendations. Castleman and Ziem (1988) investigated this behaviour by the ACGIH and concluded that the ACGIH threshold limit values (TLVs) were based heavily on corporate influence. Thus, consensus recommendations were inadequate and corporate influence may have played a role in these recommendations and in the resultant proliferation of benzene-induced diseases in the workplace. Castleman and Ziem (1988) were of the opinion that an international effort was needed 'to develop scientifically based guidelines to replace TLVs in a climate of openness and without manipulation by invested interests'. To date, this goal has not been achieved (Castleman and Ziem, 1994).

Anti-public health attitude (call for scientific certainty)

In the 1970s, benzene manufacturers and users began a new approach for conveying knowledge about the toxicity of benzene to the public in general, and to workers and plant managers specifically, which contributed to a continuation of overexposure to benzene. This is the period when manufacturers began to hire consultants to downplay the importance of the scientific observations related to the toxicity of benzene and to introduce unresolvable arguments about dose–response analyses, which had an impact in delaying much needed government regulations that sought to reduce benzene exposure in the workplace. Economic considerations were again being given a higher priority than concerns for public health, but this time the economic concerns appeared to be based on the cost of lowering exposures (OSHA, 1987), and perhaps on the increasing cost of litigation and liability related to workers contracting benzene-related diseases on the job. This era has fostered the development of arguments that seek to minimise or misrepresent study results. In my opinion, it is part of a new anti public health approach that calls for scientific certainty in terms of causality for every specific lymphohaematopoietic disease related to benzene by exposure level. As a result, workers employed worldwide in benzene exposure operations today may not be afforded the appropriate protection to the extent feasible in order to reduce their risk of haematopoietic diseases and many of those who develop benzene-related diseases may receive little or no compensation.

For example, during the OSHA rule-making hearings held in 1977, it was argued that the benzene cohort study conducted by NIOSH, which demonstrated a five to ten-fold elevated risk of leukaemia (Infante et al, 1977a), was meaningless in terms of public health intervention to reduce exposures in the workplace. Although not persuasive, one of the arguments raised by consultants to the industry was that the study had simply identified a random leukaemia cluster, and since clusters of leukaemia are known to occur in time and space, this cluster of leukaemia just happened to be identified among a cohort of benzene-exposed workers (Tabershaw and Lamm, 1977). (See Tabershaw and Lamm, 1977, and Infante et al, 1977b, for a series of arguments and rebuttal of the study findings.) It was further argued that benzene could not cause leukaemia in workers because there was no evidence that benzene caused cancer in experimental animals (Olson, 1977). This argument was clearly fictitious given the overwhelming evidence of carcinogenicity provided by the study of humans. In any case, shortly thereafter the evidence of carcinogenicity of benzene in experimental animals became available (Maltoni and Scarnato, 1979; NTP, 1986).

In the 1980s, when OSHA again published a new benzene proposal taking into consideration the guidance offered by the Supreme Court's Benzene Decision on determination of the significance of health risk, attention during the rule-making focused on the dose–response analyses prepared by OSHA and its consultants in support of its new standard (OSHA, 1987). Most of the argument addressed the benzene exposure assessment portion of the risk assessment, with new estimates of exposure among the benzene cohort members being provided for time periods in which there were no exposure data available. These 'educated' guesses by the various parties involved in the rule-making could not be confirmed. Proposed government regulation of benzene, however, resulted in a number of new dose-response analyses and a protracted debate about which exposure assessment was the most appropriate for use in the quantitative risk assessment – the resolution of which can never be determined with scientific certainty. Argument about the type of dose-response model that was most appropriate for benzene exposure and risk of leukaemia was also raised. While nobody would object to debate on these issues, the continuation of the arguments for protracted periods of time resulted in workers and the public in general being unnecessarily exposed to benzene levels that could have otherwise been reduced through a shorter regulatory process. Studying a subject to death often results in the death of those we are trying to protect (Infante, 1987).

In the 1990s, the US National Cancer Institute (NCI), in collaboration with the Chinese Academy of Preventive Medicine (CAPM), published a series of ongoing studies of Chinese workers exposed to benzene. These studies (Hayes et al, 1997 and 1996; Dosemeci et al, 1996) demonstrate a dose response for exposure to benzene and leukaemia, lymphoma, myelodysplastic syndrome and aplastic anaemia. They also demonstrate, through direct observation, high relative risks for leukaemia, myelodysplastic syndrome and non-Hodgkin's lymphoma as a result of very low average benzene exposures, such as around 1 ppm. Since the results of these well-conducted studies may be used in the future by governments in Europe, the US and other countries for estimating benzene-related diseases from low-level exposure to the general population, the findings have broad implications for public health intervention. In response to the publication of these studies, consultants to the chemical industry have published critiques of both the health findings and the benzene exposure estimates related to those findings (Wong, 1998 and 1999; Budinsky et al, 1999), which in the opinion of some misrepresent the data on health effects as well as the benzene exposure estimates made by the NCI/CAPM investigators (Hayes et al, 1998; Hayes, personal communication). Some of these same consultants have also expressed surprising views about the more general findings related to benzene exposure and disease (Wong, 1995 and 1996; Bergsagel et al, 1999). For example, based on his analysis of data from the NIOSH benzene cohort study, one author concluded that benzene can only cause acute myelogenous leukaemia, in contrast to other types of leukaemia, and that the threshold is between 370 and 530 ppm-years of exposure (Wong, 1995). In this publication, he failed to include data from his own benzene study whereby he reported a statistically significant dose response for benzene exposure and leukaemia among workers whose cumulative benzene exposures ranged from less than 15 ppm-years to more than 60 ppm-years (Wong, 1987a and b). Furthermore, in the latter study, none of the leukaemia deaths were from acute myelogenous leukaemia. Thus, the findings and conclusions he drew from his own study contradict his opinion that benzene causes only acute myelogenous leukaemia and that the cumulative exposure threshold is between 370 and 530 ppm-years.

Wong (1995) further concluded that there is no evidence that benzene exposure was associated with multiple myeloma in the NIOSH study because he could not identify a dose response based on four cases of multiple myeloma in the study population. Lack of ability to observe a dose–response relationship based on four deaths from multiple myeloma is essentially meaningless, because four cases are too few to allow enough statistical power to observe a dose response if in fact one were present. In any case, Rinsky et al (1987) of NIOSH had previously demonstrated a significant excess of death from multiple myeloma among the benzene cohort members and concluded that low-level benzene exposure was related to multiple myeloma. Wong (1995) has also argued that benzene in general is not associated with multiple myeloma and, contrary to the findings in the NCI/CAPM study, he has argued that there is no evidence that benzene is associated with non-Hodgkin's lymphoma (Wong, 1998) – conclusions that appear to be at odds with the views of others on benzene toxicity (Goldstein and Shalat, 2000; Goldstein, 1990; Rinsky et al, 1987; DeCoufle et al, 1983; Infante, 1995a; Savitz and Andrews, 1996 and 1997; Hayes et al, 1998 and 2001).

The arguments about the NCI/CAPM study seem reminiscent of the protracted debate and delay in necessary government action that took place after release of the NIOSH benzene study in 1977 (Infante et al, 1977a). It will be unfortunate if more precaution is taken with the use of data from the NCI/CAPM study than with the protection of populations exposed to levels of benzene that can be reduced with technology currently available. Scientific certainty is difficult to achieve, but stressing the uncertainty does not do justice to the data on benzene exposure and related diseases. In the case of benzene historically, taking precaution to maintain exposure levels in the workplace in accordance with the scientific data available at the time would have eliminated much needless suffering and death among the workers. In my opinion, the protracted argument about the dose response for benzene-related diseases among exposed workers and denial about the lymphohaematopoietic diseases most likely associated with benzene exposure is counterproductive to efforts to provide a workplace relatively free of harm. While the continuation of this debate may be interesting from an academic viewpoint, it also raises the question of whether it may be more a reflection of economic concerns and potential liability on the part of companies than a concern for the public's health based on a reasonable interpretation of available scientific data.

Benzene in petrol a continuing hazard

Most consumers and many medical personnel are not aware of the fact that petrol contains benzene. In the US, petrol has contained an average of about 1.5% benzene for the past two decades, but may reach 5% by volume (Infante et al, 1990). Historically, petrol in most European countries has contained more benzene than US varieties and the trend apparently still existed through 1994 (Deschamps, 1995), but the benzene content has supposedly been reduced more recently. Not surprisingly, epidemiological studies, analyses and case reports have demonstrated an association between petrol exposure and leukaemia (Schwartz, 1987; Jakobsson et al, 1993; Infante et al, 1990), other blood diseases (Infante et al, 1990; Lumley et al, 1990; Naizi and Fleming, 1989), chromosomal defects (Lumley et al, 1990; Hogstedt et al, 1991) and other manifestations of genetic damage (Nilsson et al, 1996). Yet, petrol station pumps do not provide adequate information on the cancers known to be associated with benzene exposure. Nor do the material safety data sheets for petrol provide the available evidence on chromosomal or genetic damage.

Because of this lack of candour about the hazards of benzene in petrol, garage mechanics and highway maintenance workers take unnecessary risks by using petrol as a solvent in cleaning car parts (Infante, 1993), and consumers take unnecessary risks by using petrol as a solvent and fail to take the necessary precautions when using petrol in various home appliances such as lawn mowers, weed trimming devices, power saws, etc. In addition, a study of roadside vendors who sold re-packaged petrol in Nigeria has demonstrated that 26% had neutropenia as compared to 2–10% in controls, a significant difference (Naizi and Fleming, 1989). The hazards of benzene in petrol have been recognised since at least 1928, when Askey (1928) reported a case of aplastic anaemia in a US worker exposed to petrol, and more recently by the report of a case of myelofibrosis in a Swedish petrol station attendant (Tondel et al, 1995) and a case of aplastic anaemia in a US roofer who used petrol to clean seams before fitting rubberised roofing material (Infante et al, 1990). Despite the overwhelming literature on the hazards of benzene in petrol, the public health community and safety officials, including those employed by industry, have yet to come to grips with the task of adequately informing workers and consumers about this hazard.

Conclusions and lessons for the future

The available knowledge on the toxicity of benzene and the failure to take precautions to protect workers (and the public in general) in light of this knowledge over the past century is cause for concern. The inaction or inadequate actions by consensus organisations and governments alike throw into question the ability of these organisations to protect the health of the public. In the case of benzene exposure in the workplace, the precautionary principle is not relevant. Recommendations made in the US and the UK in the 1920s for the substitution of benzene with other solvents known to be less toxic to bone marrow went unheeded for decades even though high percentages of workers being surveyed demonstrated blood disorders. Furthermore, benzene was not withdrawn from consumer products in the US until 1978 and this was done by manufacturers on a voluntary basis, and it has never been adequately validated.

It is also difficult to accept the claimed ignorance of the toxicity of benzene in the raincoat manufacturing industry in Sweden in the 1940s when 60 cases of blood poisoning in a single factory were reported. Forty years earlier (in 1897) published case reports of aplastic anaemia among women employed in this same industry in Sweden appeared in the literature. The claim that management was unaware of the hazards of benzene exposure in such a small industry in a country known for its humanitarian concerns is incomprehensible. In the 1940s and 1950s, 13 deaths from the neurotoxic effects of benzene were reported to have occurred in the UK. The benzene exposure levels associated with these acute deaths were most likely more than 200 to 800 times the occupational exposure levels recommended at the time. Clearly, this situation could, and should, have been avoided had there been any serious concern for worker health.

With the knowledge available at the time, it is also difficult to understand how benzene was substituted for other petroleum solvents in the shoe industry in Turkey in 1961. Aksoy states that the substitution was made because benzene was cheaper than the other solvents. Data on the costs of benzene and the other solvents in Turkey in the 1960s are not available, but it is unlikely that the difference could have been more than a few cents a gallon. Yet, the epidemic of leukaemia and other fatal blood diseases that followed this substitution had to have been very costly in terms of the workers' diseases, the associated expenses for health care and the loss of wages, etc. This is simply a case, as in other instances, of the cost of production being more important to the manufacturers than the cost of human life.

Even though numerous case reports (in the thousands) of benzene-related blood diseases, including leukaemia, were reported in the literature, precautionary measures to reduce exposure levels below those known, or reasonably anticipated, to cause blood diseases were not taken, and recommended exposure limits by consensus organisations like the ACGIH were based on those that were easily achievable in the workplace. According to Castleman and Zeim, such recommendations stemmed from the participation of scientists employed by various corporations on the Threshold Limit Value Committee that made the exposure recommendations. Thus, one of the lessons to be learned, if not already obvious, is that consensus organisations in the process of developing exposure limits for chemicals should maintain distance from the producers of the chemicals and their 'consultants' when evaluating evidence for the diseases of concern.

Finally, affixing a warning label on petrol pumps that includes the cancers and other diseases known, or likely to be caused by benzene exposure, may serve to reduce unnecessary benzene exposure to garage mechanics, petrol service station attendants, road maintenance workers and consumers who fill their own petrol tanks, but who more unknowingly use the petrol in consumer products at home, and not infrequently use petrol as a solvent at home without full knowledge of its cancer and non-cancer disease risks. Failure adequately to inform the public of the cancers, bone marrow proliferative diseases and genetic hazards associated with benzene in petrol is to repeat our failures of the 20th century in the 21st century and to make a mockery of public health education.

Table 4.1 *Benzene: early warnings and actions*

1897	Santessen report on observed aplastic anaemia in Sweden and other reports show that benzene is a powerful bone marrow poison
1926	Greenburg and colleagues observe abnormally low white blood cell counts in benzene workers
1928	Dolore and Borgomano publish the first case of benzene-induced leukaemia
1939	A number of investigators recommend the substitution of benzene with other solvents, but this was not implemented
1946	American Conference of Governmental Industrial Hygienists (ACGIH) recommends a limit of 100 ppm for benzene exposure, even though some cases of benzene poisoning were associated with levels of 25 ppm and 10 ppm
1947	Recommended value reduced to 50 ppm
1948	Further reduced to 35 ppm
1948	American Petroleum Institute (API) concludes that the only absolutely safe level is zero, but recommends 50 ppm or less
1957	ACGIH lowers recommended exposure to 25 ppm
1950s–60s	Obvious lack of precaution for workers exposed to benzene in many parts of the world with fatal consequences
1977	Infante et al publish the first cohort study of workers linking benzene exposure directly to leukaemia
1977	Based on these results, the US Department of Labor wants to reduce exposure to 1 ppm, but is challenged in the courts by API
1978	Benzene was voluntarily withdrawn from consumer products in the US
1980	US Supreme Court issues the Benzene Decision severely limiting regulatory actions
1987	New benzene standard of 1 ppm. This ten-year delay caused more than 200 deaths in the US
1996	Studies showing benzene-related diseases from 1 ppm level of exposure
2001	Petrol contains benzene, giving public exposure risk

Source: EEA

Asbestos: from 'magic' to malevolent mineral

David Gee and Morris Greenberg

'Looking back in the light of present knowledge, it is impossible not to feel that opportunities for discovery and prevention of asbestos disease were badly missed'
Thomas Legge, ex Chief Medical Inspector of Factories, in *Industrial Maladies*, 1934

Introduction

On 20 May 2000, the family of a senior UK hospital surgeon was awarded £1.15 million in compensation for his death, at 47, from the asbestos cancer, mesothelioma. The disease was caused by exposure to 'blue' asbestos dust from damaged pipe insulation which was present in the communication tunnels under Middlesex Hospital, London, where the surgeon worked for four years as a student and trainee, during the period 1966–73 (*British Medical Journal*, 2000). The main cause of mesothelioma is asbestos. It is now estimated that some 250,000 cases of mesothelioma, which is normally fatal within one year, will occur in the EU over the next 35 years (Peto, 1999). As asbestos is also a cause of lung cancer, the total disease burden could be around 250,000–400,000 deaths, including cases of the lung disease, asbestosis, which was the first disease to be associated with asbestos exposure. Figure 5.1. shows the peak of asbestos imports into the UK being followed some 50–60 years later by the estimated peak of mesotheliomas.

Ninety years before this environmental exposure in the London hospital occurred, a new global public health hazard was born when mining for chrysotile ('white') asbestos began in Thetford, Canada, in 1879. Some years later, two other types of asbestos, 'blue' (crocidolite) and 'brown' (amosite) came to be mined in Australia, South Africa, the former USSR and other countries, and the

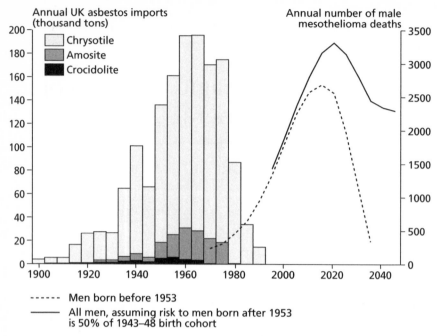

Annual UK asbestos imports (thousand tons)

Annual number of male mesothelioma deaths

----- Men born before 1953

——— All men, assuming risk to men born after 1953 is 50% of 1943–48 birth cohort

Source: Peto, 1999

Figure 5.1 *UK asbestos imports and predicted mesothelioma deaths*

annual production of all types of asbestos worldwide grew to 2 million tonnes in 1998. Imports into the EU peaked in the mid-1970s and remained above 800,000 tonnes a year until 1980, falling to 100,000 tonnes in 1993.

Today, a substantial legacy of health and contamination costs has been left for both mining and user countries, and asbestos use is continuing, now largely in developing countries.

The focus of this chapter is primarily on the UK but the histories of asbestos have been similar in France, Germany, Italy, Scandinavia and the US (Castleman, 1996), as well as in the main mining countries of Australia, Canada, South Africa and the former USSR. These histories are now being repeated, albeit with some differences, in Asia, Africa and South America.

The first 'early warnings' of asbestosis and some responses

Within 20 years of the start-up of asbestos mining, over 100 products made from the 'magic mineral' had been developed, but reports of serious disease had also begun to appear.

The earliest account of the health hazard of working with asbestos was provided by Lucy Deane, one of the first Women Inspectors of Factories in the UK. Writing in 1898, Deane included asbestos work as one of the four dusty occupations which came under observation that year, 'on account of their easily demonstrated danger to the health of workers and because of ascertained cases of injury to bronchial tubes and lungs medically attributed to the employment of the sufferer'.

She went on to observe that: 'the evil effects of asbestos dust have also instigated a microscopic examination of the mineral dust by HM Medical Inspector. Clearly revealed was the sharp glass-like jagged nature of the particles, and where they are allowed to rise and to remain suspended in the air of the room in any quantity, the effects have been found to be injurious as might have been expected.' (Deane, 1898)

Two similar observations by women inspectors followed in 1909 and 1910. They appeared in the annual reports of HM Chief Inspector of Factories, which were widely circulated amongst policy-makers and politicians.

The observations of these laywomen might not have been categorised as 'expert opinion' but they were competent observers whose discussion of occupational disease would have done credit to a medical scientist. Their reports were not refuted but simply ignored.

One year after Lucy Deane's report, Dr Montague Murray of Charing Cross Hospital, London, saw the first reported case of lung disease attributed to inhaled asbestos dust in a 33-year-old man. In Murray's words: 'He had been at work some fourteen years, the first ten of which he was in what was called the carding room, which he said was the most risky part of the work. He volunteered the statement that of the ten people who were working in the room when he went into it, he was the only survivor. I have no evidence except his word for that. He said they all died somewhere about thirty years of age.' (Murray, 1906)

This observation was brought to the attention of the UK government inquiry into compensation for industrial diseases in 1906. In the same year, a French Factory Inspector reported some 50 deaths amongst female asbestos textile workers (Auribault, 1906). This report dealt with the nature of asbestos, its processing and uses, safety and health hazards in the spinning and weaving processes, and designs for apparatus to capture dust at source. It too was largely ignored, but it was the French ban on asbestos, some 90 years later, which led to the high-profile case at the World Trade Organization (WTO) in 1999, discussed below.

The French report provided confirmation of the earlier observations of the British Women Inspectors. However, the 1906 British government inquiry did not include asbestos as a cause of industrial disease. Dr Murray had stated in evidence: 'one hears, generally speaking, that considerable trouble is now taken to prevent the inhalation of the dust, so that the disease is not so likely to occur as heretofore.' (Murray, 1906)

This may have influenced the committee. However, no attempt was made to check on the truth of Dr Murray's patient's claim about the deaths of nine fellow workers. Nor were the surviving workers at that factory investigated, despite the proposals from Lucy Deane about the kinds of mortality statistics that would be helpful.

Dr Murray's view that 'no evidence of harm' is the same as, 'there is evidence of no harm', is an early example of a common fallacy that has inhibited the identification of many dangerous substances which were initially considered to be harmless ('false negatives').

Other evidence about the hazards of asbestos was noted in workers in 1910 (Collis, 1911) and in pioneering dust experiments with rats in 1911 (Merewether and Price, 1930), and this was later considered to have been 'reasonable grounds for suspicion that the inhalation of much asbestos dust was to some extent harmful', such that the Factory Department pressed for the installation of exhaust ventilation in the dusty processes (Merewether, 1933). However, subsequent Factory Department inquiries in 1912 and 1917 found insufficient evidence to justify further action. Meanwhile in the US and Canada, insurance companies had seen enough proof of asbestos disease by 1918 to decline insurance cover for asbestos workers 'due to the assumed injurious conditions in the industry' (Hoffman, 1918). Unfortunately, this early precautionary action was later forgotten, such that asbestos costs to US insurers became hugely damaging in the 1990s.

In 1924 in Rochdale, home of the Turner Brothers asbestos factory since 1880, was the first inquest and pathological examination of an asbestos worker. Nellie Kershaw was diagnosed as having died of asbestos poisoning by her local doctor, Dr Joss, who observed that he saw 10–12 such cases a year. His view was corroborated by pathologist Dr W Cooke, who wrote the case up in the medical literature (Cooke, 1924 and 1927). In Leeds, where another Turner Brothers factory was situated, a local doctor had found enough asbestos cases to produce a doctoral thesis (Grieve, 1927). By 1930 there had been at least 12 deaths amongst workers from these two factories with asbestosis cited as the cause or partial cause (Tweedale, 2000). In some cases tuberculosis, heart failure and pneumonia complicated the diagnosis, as they did for the next few decades.

However, the combination of at least some of this evidence with two other reports in the medical literature in 1928 (Simpson, 1928; Seiler, 1928), including four cases from South Africa, was sufficient to prompt a major government inquiry into the effects of asbestos dust by Dr Merewether, Medical Inspector of Factories, and C W Price, a factory inspector and pioneer of dust monitoring and control. It included the first health study of asbestos workers and found that 66% of those employed for 20 years or more suffered from asbestosis, compared to none of those employed for less than four years, with an average of 25% for the 363 workers studied (Merewether and Price, 1930). This was probably an underestimate, as only current workers were examined, excluding those who had left employment through ill health. However, these results led, in 1931, to the first asbestos dust control regulations, medical surveillance and compensation arrangements in the world. These remained largely unaltered (but also unenforced) until 1969, when new asbestos regulations were introduced in the UK.

Early warnings on asbestos cancers

In 1932 in a report to the Trades Union Congress (TUC), a freelance investigator, Ronald Tage, drew attention to three asbestosis cases from the Cape Asbestos Company in Barking, London, that were complicated by cancer (Greenberg, 1993). Reports of lung cancers being associated with asbestos appeared in the US, German and UK medical literature in the 1930s and 1940s (Lynch and Smith, 1935; Gloyne, 1935; Wedler, 1943; Heuper, 1942) including the 1938 Report of the Chief Inspector of Factories. In 1938, when lung cancer was generally much less prevalent, the German authorities were persuaded that the association was causal, and asbestos lung cancer was made a compensatable industrial disease in 1943. (Decades later the complication of smoking-induced lung cancer made the link with asbestos that much harder to prove.)

A high rate of lung cancer found at autopsy in asbestosis cases was reported in the Chief Inspector of Factories' Annual Report in 1949 and industry had two unpublished US reports of an excess of respiratory cancers in mice (Scheper, 1995). Three in-house investigations of cancer mortality in the Rochdale district had failed to find evidence of lung cancer in asbestos workers (Knox, 1952 and 1964), but the company doctor admitted that his knowledge of statistics was 'nil' (Tweedale, 2000, p148). In 1953, Turner Brothers asked Richard Doll, an independent epidemiologist, to study the mortality of Rochdale asbestos workers. He found a lung cancer risk in those who had been exposed to asbestos for 20 years or more which was ten times that expected in the general population. Despite attempts by the Turner directors to suppress these findings they were published in the medical literature (Doll, 1955). However, it was to be another 30 years before the government accepted lung cancer from asbestos as a compensatable industrial disease, and then only if it was accompanied by asbestosis. This was partly because future studies were to be increasingly complicated by the rising trends of lung cancer caused by smoking, which Doll had also discovered in a study of British doctors in 1955.

Later studies of asbestos workers showed that the combination of the two carcinogens, cigarette smoke and asbestos, multiplied the risks of lung cancer. Asbestos alone increased the lung cancer risk five-fold, and smoking alone increased the risk ten-fold, but the two together produced not 15 times the risk (an additive effect) but over 50 times the risk, a multiplicative or synergistic effect. (Hammond, 1979). Smoking and radiation from uranium and other mining has a similarly synergistic effect in radiation exposed workers (Archer, 1973).

As with all other human studies of asbestos exposure, there was only a relatively small number of workers who had been working in the 'new conditions' of improved dust control for the 20–25 years before lung cancer could appear, so it was not possible to say what the risks were in 1955 until many more years had passed, when again, in conditions of improving dust control, it was impossible to know what the risks could be. This problem, which might be called the 'latency lacuna', characteristic of all long-latent-period hazards under conditions of technological change, is a major reason why preventative action is often too late.

Early, devastating warnings about mesothelioma cancer

Cases of mesothelioma, a normally very rare cancer of the lining of the chest or abdomen, had been observed in association with asbestos exposure in the 1940s and 1950s, but it was not until 1955 that Dr Sleggs, a local doctor in South Africa, noted a number of these unusual cancers at the centre of the asbestos mining areas and sent some to a pathologist, Dr Wagner. The association with asbestos was made and they toured the mining areas trying to reconstruct the history of asbestos exposure of those who had died by talking to colleagues and families. Out of 47 cases of mesothelioma, they found earlier asbestos exposure in all but two, and many of them were environmental cases including children exposed when playing on waste dumps. They published their findings in 1960 (Wagner et al, 1960).

This was devastating news because the exposure needed to cause mesothelioma seemed to be a matter of months only. In contrast, most lung cancer and asbestosis cases seem to need ten or more years of exposure to asbestos dust. The average latent period between first exposure and the mesothelioma cancer appearing was about 40 years, in contrast to the 20–25 years for lung cancer.

Wagner's paper provided evidence of a very strong association between asbestos and mesothelioma, but by 1964 most experts accepted that the relationship was causal, based mainly on the studies of Dr Selikoff in the US and Dr Newhouse in the UK. Both worked independently of the industry, using case data from unions and hospital records respectively.

Selikoff had observed that 15 out of 17 patients from the same asbestos manufacturing plant had asbestos diseases, but as he was refused access to company records he used trade union records to show that the users of asbestos, such as insulation workers, were at even greater risk than manufacturing workers: of the 392 workers examined with 20 years or more asbestos exposure, 339 had asbestosis. The lung cancer rate was seven times normal, and a number had mesothelioma (Selikoff et al, 1964). The excess of lung cancer only became statistically clear after 25 years of follow-up of workers, illustrating one of the serious limitations of so called 'negative' cancer studies, which is that the power of such studies to detect long-latent-period cancers can be very low unless some 20–30 years of follow-up has been possible.

Selikoff was to be described as a 'disturbing sore thumb' by an industry representative from the Asbestos Textile Institute (Tweedale, 2000, p183, footnote 17). This was a similar sentiment to that expressed by the ex-Chief Medical Inspector of Factories, Dr Legge, writing in his then capacity as Medical Adviser to the TUC in 1932 about Ronald Tage, whom he said the TUC could be 'quit of' by paying him a small fee (Greenberg, 1993).

The practice of attacking the purveyors of news about hazards had been well illustrated by Ibsen in his play *An Enemy of the People* (1882), in which the local doctor notices a health hazard which, if fully recognised, would threaten the economy of the local town. He descends from public hero to public enemy as the economic implications of his observations come to be realised by the mayor, the media and most of the citizens.

Newhouse used the long-term pathology records collected by the London Hospital between 1917 and 1964 to show that, of 76 mesothelioma cases, over 50% had occupational or domestic exposure (lived in the house of an asbestos worker), whilst of the others, one third lived within half a mile of the Cape asbestos factory (Newhouse and Thompson, 1965). It was to be 30 years later that children exposed to asbestos in the neighbourhood of factories and who later developed mesothelioma became the first successful environmental exposure cases against Turner Brothers in the UK (Tweedale, 2000, p272).

Both Newhouse and Selikoff presented their findings at a conference in New York in October 1964, organised by the New York Academy of Sciences. A study of Doll's group of workers from the regulated areas of the Rochdale factory was presented as supporting the view that 'it is possible that the specific occupational hazards to life have been completely eliminated', perhaps another example of the 'latency lacuna' (Knox et al, 1965) But neither Selikoff nor the UK Factory Department found such evidence of falling disease rates, mainly because they were including severe cases of dust exposure amongst the users, not just the manufacturers of asbestos, for whom dust conditions were relatively better, at least in the regulated factory production areas.

This failure to appreciate the 'worst case' asbestos exposure scenarios was part of the reason for the delayed and inadequate responses to asbestos. Julian Peto, asbestos cancer researcher, has described the focus of asbestos cancer studies on factories, rather than users, as a 'stupid mistake' (Peto, 1998).

This view was shared by a former director of the world's biggest asbestos company, Johns Manville, when reviewing why, although still profitable, it filed for bankruptcy in 1982 as a means of dealing with asbestos pollution claims. He argued that medical research, assiduous communication, insistent warnings and a rigorous dust reduction programme 'could have saved lives and would probably have saved the stockholders, the industry and, for that matter, the product' (Sells, 1994).

Actions and inactions by regulatory authorities and others

The asbestos regulations of 1931 were only partially enforced, there being only two prosecutions between 1931 and 1968 (Dalton, 1979). Their focus on just parts of the manufacturing process meant that the riskier user activities were neglected. However, the issue of dangerous asbestos was not neglected.

From 1964 to 1975 the media in both the US and the UK kept asbestos high on the political agenda (*Sunday Times*, 1965). The ITV programme 'World in Action' in 1971, and the BBC's 'Horizon' in 1975, about conditions at Cape's Acre Mill asbestos plant in Yorkshire, UK, helped to initiate action by authorities, such as a Parliamentary Ombudsman Report into asbestos regulation enforcement at the factory. This report was initiated by local MP Max Madden, who lodged an official complaint against non-enforcement of the asbestos regulation of 1931. The report was very critical of the Factory Inspectors, and the government responded by appointing a government inquiry, the Simpson

Committee, in 1976. Meanwhile, the 1931 asbestos regulations had been updated in 1969, and a limit for factory asbestos dust exposure of 2 million fibres per cubic metre (m^3) of air was to be gradually introduced.

Unfortunately this 'hygiene standard' did not include consideration of the lung or mesothelioma cancer hazards. It was later to be strongly criticised and associated with high asbestosis levels (one worker in ten would get the disease) by Julian Peto in evidence to the Simpson inquiry (Peto, 1978).

The Simpson Report came out in 1979 with the following recommendations: a ban on 'blue' asbestos, which had already been withdrawn by the industry; a ban on insulation spraying, which was also largely defunct by then; contractors were to be licensed for the removal of asbestos; and the asbestos limit was to be reduced to 1 million fibres/m^3 (or 1 fibre per millilitre) by 1980 for 'white' asbestos, with a target of 0.5 million fibres/m^3 (0.5 f/ml) for 'brown' asbestos, which was considered to be more hazardous than white. An asbestos fibre that is visible is about the diameter of a human hair, 40 microns, but it is composed of a bundle of about 2 million fibrils that can be released by abrasion or physiological processes in the body (Selikoff and Lee, 1978). Electron microscopy is needed to accurately monitor the presence of such fibrils in air or tissues.

There was, and still is, scientific controversy about the relative cancer and asbestosis potencies of the three types of asbestos, with white often being regarded as less hazardous than blue or brown. By 1986 the International Agency for Research on Cancer (IARC) of the World Health Organization (WHO) had concluded that all three types were carcinogenic and, as with other carcinogens, there was no known safe level of exposure to any of them.

There was no similar hygiene standard for the public's protection from airborne asbestos dust until the late 1980s, when the lowest limit detectable by the prevailing dust monitoring method, optical microscopy, was recommended by the UK Health and Safety Executive (100,000 fibres/m^3 or 0.1 f/ml).

In 1982, Yorkshire TV screened a two-hour documentary at prime viewing time, featuring Alice Jefferson, a 47-year-old who had contracted mesothelioma when working for a few months at Cape's Acre Mill asbestos plant. *Alice, a Fight for Life* had an immediate impact, even though some, like Sir Richard Doll, criticised the programme for being unscientific and emotional. The government responded to the programme by implementing the Simpson inquiry recommendations and, in 1984, by introducing the asbestos licensing regulations and a further lowering of the exposure limits to 0.5 million fibres/m^3 (0.5 f/ml) for white and 0.2 million fibres/m^3 (0.2 f/ml) for brown asbestos. A voluntary labelling scheme was introduced for some uses.

Pressure for further improvements continued to come from local MPs, some trade unions and people representing victims, such as asbestos widow, Nancy Tait. She helped reveal that the Turner Brothers' asbestos compensation arrangements, such as £1 a week for the widows of workers with asbestosis, had been largely unchanged since the 1930s.

Her work helped to force Turner Brothers to improve their compensation awards.

New regulations were introduced in 1987 and tightened further in 1989. In 1998 the government adopted a ban on all forms of asbestos, which was imple-

Box 5.1 WTO upholds French and EU ban on asbestos

In 1997 France banned all forms of asbestos fibres and products in order to protect the health of workers and consumers. Existing 'white' asbestos products could be exempt on an exceptional, temporary and annually reviewed basis, if no effective substitute materials were available that posed a lower health risk to workers handling them. Canada objected to this ban at the WTO but the WTO found in favour of France in September 2000 (WTO, 2000). Canada appealed to the Appellate Body the WTO and the EU cross-appealed to uphold the main findings of the panel and to seek correction of some 'errors' of the panel's interpretations and conclusions. The US cross-appealed against the panel's judgement that glass fibres were as carcinogenic as asbestos. The Apellate Body issued a report in early 2001 (WTO, 2001), out of which a number of main points arose, which also have implications for other hazardous agents:

- all forms of asbestos ('white', 'brown' and 'blue') are carcinogenic;
- there is no known threshold of safety for this carcinogen;
- the risk from 'white' asbestos in products is based on evidence which 'tends to show' a risk rather than not;
- workers handling asbestos products, such as building and brake lining workers, are at risk from asbestos exposure;
- there is no WTO requirement for countries to provide quantitative risk assessment data: qualitative evidence is sufficient;
- countries can base their health/environment/animal welfare measures on qualified and respected scientific opinions held by only a minority of scientists: 'a Member is not obliged, in setting health policy, automatically to follow what, at a given time, may constitute a majority scientific opinion' (p64). This means that a WTO Panel need not necessarily reach its decision, on the scientific evidence, based on a 'preponderant weight of the evidence', but on a lower level of proof;
- the efficiency of the 'controlled use' of asbestos products was not demonstrated and the residual risk to the workers would still be significant; this risk management option could not be relied on to protect workers' health, and therefore was not a reasonable 'alternative' measure to the asbestos ban;
- in determining whether asbestos substitutes such as glass fibre were 'like' products, four criteria have been developed by WTO, including the properties and end uses of a substance, and the tastes and habits of consumers. Based on these criteria, the Appellate Body found that the panel had erred in finding that glass fibre products were 'like' products: they were not, principally because they were not as carcinogenic.

mented the following year, along with an EU ban, which is to be implemented by Member States by 2005. Canada filed a trade barriers complaint against the French and EU ban at WTO, but this was rejected by the WTO Disputes Panel. Canada appealed against this ruling to the WTO Appellate Body, which found in favour of France and the EU (see Box 5.1)

The WTO procedures for dealing with the kind of scientific and technological complexity involved in asbestos and other health and environmental hazards has been criticised by one of the scientific advisers involved in the WTO asbestos case (Castleman, 2001).

Meanwhile the annual UK cancer death rate from mesothelioma and lung cancer from asbestos is estimated by the Health and Safety Commission (Health and Safety Commission, 1994–95) to be around 3000 deaths per year and rising (see Figure 5.1). Despite huge amounts of research, many issues of biological mechanisms and dose-response relationships remain unclear, illustrating the limited relevance of more research to disease.

The costs and benefits of actions and inactions

It is beyond the scope of this case study to provide a detailed evaluation of the full costs and benefits of the asbestos story (see Castleman, 1996, pp8–9). However, a few illustrative figures will indicate the dimensions of such an evaluation. At a company level, Turner Brothers made arrangements in 1994 to pay up to £1 billion in asbestos claims. The insurance underwriters Lloyd's of London faced near collapse in the early 1990s from US pollution claims, many of which were for asbestos health compensation and clean-up costs.

If lives are valued at EUR 1 million each, which is common in transport studies, then the costs of the estimated 400,000 European asbestos cancer deaths expected over the next few decades is EUR 400 billion. The human costs in terms of suffering are not calculable. Removing asbestos from buildings safely at the end of their life will cost further billions. Earlier actions to reduce asbestos exposure could have saved many of these costs.

A Dutch illustration of some of the potential savings from earlier risk reduction actions has estimated that a ban in 1965, after the mesothelioma evidence had been widely accepted, instead of in 1993, would have saved the country some 34,000 victims and 41 billion NLG (Netherlands guilders) in building and compensation costs. This is compared to the 52,600 victims and NLG 67 billion guilders in costs expected over the period 1969–2030, estimated by the Dutch Ministry of Health and Social Security (Heerings, 1999). In the US, asbestos compensation settlements reached US$2 billion, with Lloyds syndicates paying around half of that.

On the other hand, asbestos has brought some benefits, including employment. In 1919 it was estimated that fires in the world's theatres in the 1870s and 1880s caused 2216 deaths, 95% of which could have been saved by asbestos fire insulation, it was claimed (Summers, 1919). Asbestos boiler insulation saved energy, and asbestos brake linings saved lives, though the extra vehicle speeds it allowed complicates the picture. *The Lancet*, a UK medical journal, argued in 1967 that 'it would be ludicrous to outlaw this valuable and often irreplaceable material in all circumstances (as) asbestos can save more lives than it can possibly endanger' (*The Lancet*, 1967). Apart from their gross underestimate of the health impacts of asbestos, for which their expertise was at least relevant, the replaceability of asbestos is a technological and economic question which doctors are not well qualified to judge. Little evidence was presented to substantiate their argument that asbestos was 'irreplaceable'.

Substitutes for most uses of asbestos were available by the 1970s and, in some cases, much earlier – many US oil refineries were insulated with mineral wool in the 1940s and 1950s (Castleman, 1996, pp456–7). The slow spread of asbestos substitutes was partly because asbestos industry cartels worked to inhibit their spread (Castleman, 1996, pp34–8), and partly because the market price of asbestos was very low compared to its full production, health and environmental costs. This failure of market prices to reflect full environmental and health costs is the common cause of delay in replacing hazardous materials.

Many jobs, much profit and high dividends were generated by asbestos. Turner Brothers' profits rose strongly after 1947 and peaked at almost £9 million a year in 1965 (Tweedale, 2000, p9). These profits suffered little from the ill health and contamination costs of asbestos, which were 'externalised' onto workers with disease, their families, the health service, insurance carriers and building owners.

An often ignored but significant non-financial benefit of asbestos compensation trials is that they frequently uncover many of the contradictions between company words on asbestos and their actions to reduce hazards (Castleman, 1996).

What are the lessons of the asbestos story?

Asbestos offers many lessons that are relevant to numerous other agents or activities that have long-term hazardous impacts.

- The experiences of victims, lay people and 'competent observers', such as factory inspectors and family doctors, should be taken seriously by governmental and other authorities, and followed up by appropriate investigations. They can anticipate the views of scientific experts, sometimes by many years.
- The early warnings of 1898–1906 in the UK and France were not followed up by the kind of long-term medical and dust exposure surveys of workers that would have been possible at the time, and which would have helped strengthen the case for tighter controls on dust levels. Even now, leading asbestos epidemiologists can conclude: 'It is unfortunate that the evolution of the epidemic of asbestos-induced mesothelioma, which far exceeds the combined effects of all other known occupational industrial carcinogens, cannot be adequately monitored.' (Peto, 1999)
- Long-term environmental and health monitoring rarely meets the short-term needs of anyone, thus requiring particular institutional arrangements if it is to meet society's long-term needs.
- The laws on prevention and compensation introduced in the UK in 1931–32 were not well implemented, and the sanctions were trivial, a pattern that was repeated down the long history of asbestos.
- If early warnings had been heeded, and better control measures adopted, either before 1930 as Dr Legge, Chief Medical Inspector of Factories, and others (Greenberg, 1994; Bartrip, 1931) have noted, or in the 1950s and

1960s, when new cancer hazards emerged and economic circumstances were good, then much tragic loss would have been avoided. Action to curb asbestosis prior to the discovery of the cancers would at least have minimised the impact of these later 'surprises'.More strategically, tighter regulation of asbestos would have raised its market price to capture more of its costs of production and use, thereby stimulating the innovation that belatedly led to better and often cheaper substitutes, as well as to improved engine and building designs that generate, at source, less waste heat.

- Economic factors played a key role as in other cases of worker, public and environmental hazards. These include the employers' need for profits and the workers' need for jobs, which can together produce an alliance which may not be in the long-term interests of workers or society. The greater the size of the 'external' cost of harm (damage costs not borne by the companies), the greater the chance that these diverging private and social costs will inhibit preventative action. Only when full damage costs, including health, building maintenance and site contamination costs, are borne by the polluters via the 'polluter pays' principle, and through liability provisions, regulations, taxes, etc, can the private and social costs of economic activity be brought closer together, thus allowing the market place to operate more efficiently. Penalties on wrongdoing by employers also need to be commensurate with the costs they inflict on others, if private and social costs and benefits are to be more closely aligned. But this is not easy. It is very difficult for governments to overcome powerful economic interests that usually operate on the same short timescales as most politicians, and to implement decisions that are in the best, longer-term interests of society, if they are perceived as imposing short-term costs on powerful groups. Again, appropriate institutional arrangements are needed to help meet society's long-term interests: a 'governance' issue that is taken up in the final chapters of this book.

- One of the main reasons for the failure to implement control measures was the view that 'current exposures to asbestos dust are so much lower than past exposures and should therefore be safe', a view offered to the UK committee of inquiry into compensation for industrial diseases by Dr Murray in 1906, and repeated by many others ever since. As there is a 10–40-year latent period between asbestos exposure and the diseases it causes, by the time that evidence of 'today's' exposure risks becomes available, many years of generally reducing dust levels have ensued, making it once again possible to say that risks in the new 'today' are much less than in the past, or non-existent. The point cannot be proved decisively one way or the other until another 20–40 years have passed. This 'latency lacuna', which is common to all long-latent-period hazards, is an illustration of the common error of assuming that 'absence of evidence of harm' means 'evidence of absence of harm'. It does not.

In the absence of good evidence that today's exposures to carcinogens are safe, it is wiser to apply the precautionary principle, and assume they are unsafe, especially if the disease (or ecological impacts) from higher exposures have no known threshold of exposure below which there are no effects.

This is a key lesson that is relevant to all long-latent-period hazards. The particular preventative measures that would then be required would depend on the proportionality principle – the expected benefits from prevention, including any 'secondary benefits', would need to be significant in relation to the costs of achieving such prevention.

This more precautionary approach to uncertainty and ignorance would also involve switching the current bias within normal scientific methods away from avoiding 'false positives' (with its associated bias of producing 'false negatives' such as asbestos) towards producing a better balance between false positives and false negatives. This would increase the chances of generating the costs of restricting a substance or activity that might later turn out to be safe. However, the asbestos case strongly suggests that society would gain overall from a more ethically acceptable and economically efficient balance between generating false positives and false negatives.

- Implementation of preventative measures was also inhibited by the healthy survivors fallacy. This needs to be widely communicated and avoided as it gives rise to a general but false reassurance of safety, as it does with the general hazard of smoking. It was first described in relation to asbestos by Lucy Deane in 1898:

'Even when the evil reaches such grave proportions as to be capable of easy and tragic proof... there is always a certain proportion of "old workers" – the survivors of their mates – who are found in every unhealthy industry and who... appear to thrive on their unhealthy calling. In less obvious unhealthy conditions the only convincing proof of actual injury, viz, reliable comparative statistics of mortality, or of health standards, is practically unattainable in the case of any given factory, or at any rate with the time and opportunity at present at our disposal.' (Deane, 1898).

This argument has been used throughout the history of asbestos. For example, Dr Knox, the Turner Brothers' UK company doctor, on visiting the Canadian asbestos mines in 1952, said: 'I am assured that many workers over 70 years of age are still employed and are active and vigorous.' (Greenberg, 2000) This view was also presented to one of the authors of this case study (DG) when he visited UK asbestos plants in the 1980s as the union health and safety adviser. Workers pointed to the retired workers who had worked more than 20–30 years or so in the factory without much harm, and who were able to turn up to the annual pensioners' party. Such pensioners were cited as proof of the low or absent risks of asbestos. This could be called the 'pensioners' party fallacy', as it was the workers who did not make it to the party who provided the proof of harm, and their deaths, or illnesses, made them relatively invisible to current workers. As Deane observed, healthy survivors needed to be related to non-survivors via appropriately analysed mortality statistics.

- It seems necessary to establish speedy, affordable and transparent compensation arrangements, based on agreed liabilities, as soon as any harmful effects become known, so as to both increase the incentives to prevent further harm and to improve the chances of recording accurate exposure

Table 5.1 *Asbestos: early warnings and actions*

1898	UK Factory Inspector Lucy Deane warns of harmful and 'evil' effects of asbestos dust
1906	French factory report of 50 deaths in female asbestos textile workers and recommendation of controls
1911	'Reasonable grounds' for suspicion, from experiments with rats, that asbestos dust is harmful
1911 and 1917	UK Factory Department finds insufficient evidence to justify further actions
1918	US insurers refuse cover to asbestos workers due to assumptions about injurious conditions in the industry
1930	UK Merewether Report finds 66% of long-term workers in Rochdale factory with asbestosis
1931	UK Asbestos Regulations specify dust control in manufacturing only and compensation for asbestosis, but this is poorly implemented
1935–49	Lung cancer cases reported in asbestos manufacturing workers
1955	Doll establishes high lung cancer risk in Rochdale asbestos workers
1959–60	Mesothelioma cancer in workers and public identified in South Africa
1962/64	Mesothelioma cancer identified in asbestos workers, in neighbour-hood 'bystanders' and in relatives, in the UK and the US, amongst others
1969	UK Asbestos Regulations improve controls, but ignore users and cancers
1982–9	UK media, trade union and other pressure provokes tightening of asbestos controls on users and producers, and stimulates substitutes.
1998–99	EU and France ban all forms of asbestos
2000–01	WTO upholds EU/French bans against Canadian appeal

Source: EEA

histories. Elements of such anticipatory compensation arrangements were established in the early days of the nuclear industry, when the state in many countries took on future liabilities for nuclear accidents, at least up to certain limits (for example the UK Nuclear Installations Act, 1965). A unique example seems to be the radiation-induced cancer compensation scheme for workers at British Nuclear Fuels (see Chapter 3 on 'Radiation').

• Views should be taken from a wide range of all relevant disciplines and the 'ignorant expert' should be curbed. Specialists in one discipline, for example medicine, provided 'expert' opinions about other disciplines such as dust monitoring and control (occupational hygiene and ventilation engineering) or asbestos substitutes availability. These opinions were often mistaken but went largely unchallenged, and this contributed to misplaced complacency (Greenberg, 2000).

• It is necessary to anticipate 'surprises' and take care with substitutes. If asbestos substitutes reproduce the same physical form as asbestos – long, respirable (< 3 microns in diameter) and durable fibres – it is likely that they too will be carcinogenic (Roller and Pott, 1998), as was predicted by the UK

Health and Safety Executive in 1979, and later confirmed by the IARC for some forms of synthetic mineral fibres. However, mineral wool and glass fibre appear to be much less hazardous than asbestos, and they can be manufactured to be good enough for insulation but not as thin, or durable enough in human tissue, to be carcinogenic. 'Clean' production and user techniques that minimise exposures to atmosphere, whether occupational or environmental, via 'closed loop' and eco-efficient systems, are therefore essential with whatever materials are being used. This then minimises the size of any future 'surprise' impacts from substitutes, which is an important benefit of applying the precautionary principle.

PCBs and the precautionary principle

Janna G Koppe and Jane Keys

Introduction

Polychlorinated biphenyls (PCBs) are chlorinated organic compounds that were first synthesised in the laboratory in 1881. By 1899 a pathological condition named chloracne had been identified, a painful disfiguring skin disease that affected people employed in the chlorinated organic industry. Mass production of PCBs for commercial use started in 1929. Thirty-seven years elapsed before PCBs became a major public issue, recognised as environmental pollutants, and a danger to animals and humans. Large-scale production worldwide, and in particular in some eastern European countries, continued until the mid-1980s. PCBs are the first obvious example of a substance that was not intentionally spread into the environment, but nevertheless became widespread and bioaccumulated to high concentrations.

PCBs are mixtures of synthetic organic chemicals with the same basic chemical structure, and similar physical properties, that range in nature from oily liquids to waxy solids. PCBs were well received in the marketplace as they replaced products that were more flammable, less stable and bulkier. This new group of chemicals facilitated the production of smaller, lighter and what were thought to be safer electrical equipment. In the US the use of PCBs was very important in the Second World War. PCBs were primarily used in electrical equipment, such as capacitors and transformers, because of their insulating properties and resistance to high temperatures. Over the years the number of uses of PCBs increased to include use as heat-transfer fluids in heat exchangers, as hydraulic fluids, as ingredients in PVC plastics, paints, adhesives, lubricants, carbonless copy paper and as immersion oil for microscopes. Sealants containing PCBs were widely used for constructing and renovating buildings. Between 1929 and 1988 the total world production of PCBs (excluding the former USSR and China) was 1.5 million tonnes.

By the late 1930s Monsanto, the US producer of PCBs, was certainly aware of adverse health effects in workers exposed to PCBs. For example, in 1936 several workers at the Halowax Corporation in New York City exposed to PCBs (then called chlorinated diphenyls), and related chemicals called chlorinated naphthalenes, were affected by chloracne. Three workers died and autopsies of two revealed severe liver damage. Halowax asked Harvard University researcher Cecil K. Drinker to investigate. Drinker presented his results at a 1937 meeting attended by Monsanto, General Electric, Halowax, the US Public Health Service and state health officials from Massachusetts and Connecticut. Like the Halowax workers, Drinker's test rats had suffered severe liver damage. Sanford Brown, the president of Halowax, concluded the meeting by stressing the 'necessity of not creating mob hysteria on the part of workmen in the plants' (Francis, 1998). The results were published but did not gain the wider attention of policy-makers (Drinker et al, 1937). Drinker's article did however put the occupational medicine community, labour regulators and manufacturers on notice as to the concerns surrounding PCBs.

The first warning that PCBs were becoming ubiquitous in the environment came from Søren Jensen. In 1966 Jensen, while working on DDT (dichlorodiphenyltrichloroethane), fortuitously detected unknown molecules in the muscle of white-tailed sea eagles in Sweden. The levels were appreciably higher in the fish-eating sea eagles than in fish collected from the same areas. So he concluded that the molecules must be persistent in living tissues and not easily broken down. The mystery chemicals were extremely resistant to degradation, being unaffected even when boiled in concentrated sulphuric acid. It took two further years of study for Jensen to be able to demonstrate that they were PCBs. In 1969 Søren Jensen published his findings (Jensen et al, 1969) which showed remarkably high PCB concentrations in a large proportion of the Baltic Sea fauna (See Figure 6.1). PCBs had entered the environment in large quantities for more than 37 years and were bioaccumulating along the food chain.

In the 1960s it became apparent that the fertility of all three seal species occurring in the Baltic Sea was in decline. By the 1970s nearly 80% of the females were infertile. Some studies drew a link with the presence of persistent pollutants – high levels of DDT and PCBs had been recorded in all three species. A clear correlation was found between the pathological uterine changes and elevated concentrations of contaminants, particularly PCBs. Further studies appeared to link high PCB levels not only with reproductive disorders in seals but with other symptoms such as damage to skin and claws, intestines, kidneys, adrenal glands and skeleton (Swedish Environmental Protection Agency, 1998).

The first well-publicised warning that PCBs could be harmful to humans came from an accident in 1968 in Japan with a mass poisoning among 1800 people who ingested contaminated rice oil. The rice oil was found to contain a large amount of Kanechlor 400, a brand of PCB, that was believed to have leaked from a heating pipe in the factory (Kimburgh et al, 1987). This resulted in serious health problems for those who had consumed the contaminated oil (see Box 6.1). The impact of this incident was such as to give rise to a new word in the Japanese language: *Yusho*, or Japanese rice oil disease. Many debates ensued as to whether it was the PCBs or their breakdown products that had caused these effects. However, it was agreed that PCBs that had been subjected

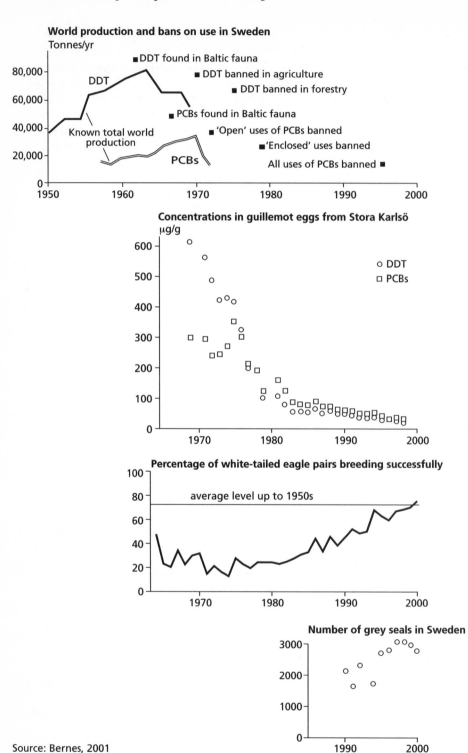

Figure 6.1 *DDT, PCBs and effects on Baltic Sea fauna*

Box 6.1 The Yusho accident

The first clinical sign was a strange skin disease with conjunctivitis, swelling of eyelids and chloracne. The victims' whole bodies, including the extremities, were covered with acne-like pustules. The most common symptoms were pigmentation of nails, skin and mucous membranes; increased sweating of the palms; severe headache; swollen joints and feelings of weakness. About half of the victims coughed persistently with expectoration resulting in a chronic bronchitis. These respiratory symptoms correlated with PCB levels in the blood. It took more than ten years for these symptoms to decline.

Some of the victims were pregnant when they consumed the PCB-contaminated oil. Of 11 babies born to these mothers, two were stillborn. All were 'Coca-Cola' coloured, growth-retarded, had increased eye discharges and nail pigmentation. Follow-up studies of the children showed their growth to be hampered, their IQs to be low, and their demeanour generally apathetic and dull. There was an increased mortality of the whole group of Yusho patients due to malignancies of the liver and respiratory system. Their body burden of dioxins was about 450 micrograms dioxin toxic equivalent (TEQ) level per kilogram, not including the amounts of phenobarbital-like PCBs (Masuda, 1994).

to heating did have harmful effects on humans and that if PCBs were present in places where food was processed accidents like this one could happen.

In the late 1960s press reports about the presence of PCBs in the environment began to appear and in response Monsanto launched its public defence, denying that the chemicals were PCBs. 'The Swedish and American scientists... imply that polychlorinated biphenyls are 'highly toxic' chemicals,' Monsanto said in a widely distributed statement. It continued: 'This is simply not true. The source of marine-life residue identified as PCB is not yet known. It will take extensive research, on a worldwide basis, to confirm or deny the initial scientific conclusions.' (Francis, 1998)

Nevertheless in 1969 Monsanto privately took a different view in its internal 'Pollution abatement plan', which admitted that 'the problem involves the entire US, Canada and sections of Europe, especially the United Kingdom and Sweden.... other areas of Europe, Asia and Latin America will surely become involved. Evidence of contamination (has) been shown in some of the very remote parts of the world.' The plan also stated that stopping the production of PCBs was not an option as it would cause 'profits to cease and liability to soar because we would be admitting guilt by our actions' (Francis, 1998).

Growing evidence of persistence, presence and toxicity

During the 1970s the evidence that PCBs were ubiquitous environmental pollutants continued to build. PCBs were found in remote areas such as the Arctic. In The Netherlands, large amounts of PCBs were found to be entering the environment from the River Rhine. At Lobith, on the German border, inputs measured between 1976 and 1981 ranged from 14,300 kg to 24,000 kg. Most of the PCBs were attached to fine silt in suspension; consequently the levels in the sediments were highest where the flow rates of the rivers were low. The sediments in Rotterdam harbour had the highest concentrations – 12–24 mg/kg. As these sediments were used for reclaimed land, this resulted in The Netherlands being contaminated at the rate of 5000 kg of PCBs a year. Fatty fish caught off the Dutch coast were highly polluted. Eels from the rivers and lakes, tested in 1977 and 1988, contained 3.0–131 mg/kg of PCBs (CBS, 1980; Greve and Wegman, 1983). PCBs were found in fish, mink, seabirds and in humans; these studies provided further evidence that PCBs bioaccumulate. Evidence of actual or suspected harm caused by their bioaccumulation was also being documented (see the case study on the Great Lakes).

What also became clearer throughout the 1970s was an understanding of the major reason for the disagreement between those who said PCBs were harmful in low quantities and those who said they were not. It was found that different forms – 'congeners' – of PCBs have different numbers and positions of chlorine atoms that determine the molecule's physical and chemical properties. Studies in the late 1970s recognised the significance of these different congeners, although at first the differences were wrongly attributed solely to the level of chlorination. This proved too simplistic, and after confusing the debate for a while it became evident that both the position and numbers of the chlorine atoms had an effect on toxicity – and that different congeners have different effects (see Box 6.2).

Action from industry and governments in the 1970s

In 1971 Monsanto realised that its public position was untenable and voluntarily limited the types of PCB mixtures that had the overall group trade name Aroclor to those containing less than 60% chlorine substitution (by weight). They also reformulated one Aroclor to reduce the percentage of higher-chlorinated PCBs. This move was based on the then current scientific opinion that molecules with fewer chlorine atoms were less toxic. Unfortunately, as described above, this opinion was soon found to be an oversimplification.

In 1972, as a result of the reports concerning the presence and effects of PCBs in the environment, Sweden banned these substances for 'open' uses, such as in sealants, paints and plastics, which resulted in uncontrolled losses to the environment. The first international governmental action was in February 1973, when the Organisation for Economic Co-operation and Development (OECD) made Council Decision C(73) 1 (Final) on protection of the environment by control of polychlorinated biphenyls. The OECD's decision was taken as a result of 'concerns about environmental contamination by PCBs, and their health and environmental effects' (OECD, 1973). The decision required use in new open products to be banned in OECD member states. However, large amounts continued to be used in supposedly 'closed systems' such as transformers, probably as the technical problems and costs of measures needed to replace them were considered prohibitive.

Box 6.2 Explanation of the toxicity of PCBs

by Søren Jensen

The basic biphenyl chemical form is shown in Figure 6.2. Theoretically 209 chlorinated biphenyls are possible, but the greater the number of chlorine atoms already present in the molecule, the more difficult it becomes for further substitution of hydrogen with chlorine. Only 135 congeners have been found in technical products or in biota.

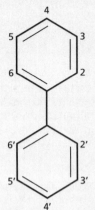

In most PCB congeners chlorine atoms are quite evenly distributed between the two phenyl rings. From a toxicological viewpoint positions 2 and 6 are the most important (see Figure 6.2) – these are called the ortho positions. The chlorine atom is rather bulky, so many chlorine substitutions in positions 2 and 6 will force the biphenyl to twist around the axis. Most molecules have two or more chlorine molecules in the ortho position. Less frequent are molecules with only one chlorine atom in an ortho position, and in this case the molecule is more planar (flat). Finally the non-ortho congeners, called the co-planar PCBs, are only present in trace amounts in technical products.

Source: Søren Jensen

Figure 6.2 *Biphenyl skeleton structure*

Polychlorinated dibenzofurans (see Figure 6.3) are created as accidental by-products during the iron-catalysed synthesis of PCB. They are also formed during fires in oxygen-poor environments such as fires in PCB-containing transformers; in products used as heat-transfer agents; and in other types of PCB wastes exposed to heat or fire.

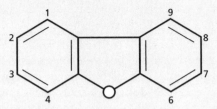

Source: Søren Jensen

Figure 6.3 *Dibenzofuran skeleton structure*

Polychlorinated dibenzo-p-dioxins (see Figure 6.4) are closely related to the dibenzofurans. The 2,3,7,8-tetra chloro congener was first found as a by-product in the 2,4,5-trichloro-phenoxy-acid herbicides. TCDD (tetra-chlorodibenzoparadioxin) is also formed in fires where chlorine is present. TCDD is the most toxic substance of which we know, this being the result of its interaction with a vital cell cytoplasm protein known as the Ah-receptor, which in turn affects enzyme production. This effect, via the Ah-receptor, is often simply referred to as a 'dioxin-like effect'. TCDD is a liver, nerve and bone-marrow toxin and carcinogenic in human beings.

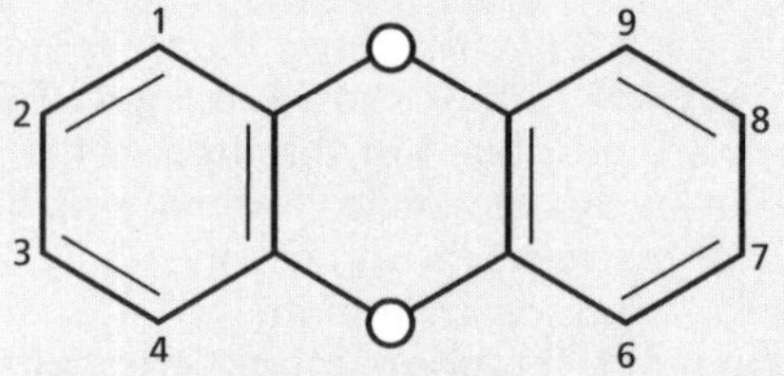

Source: Søren Jensen

Figure 6.4 *Dibenzo-p-dioxin skeleton structure*

Different chlorinated dioxins have been given a TEF-value (toxic equivalent factor), where the ability of TCDD to induce aryl-hydrocarbon-hydroxylase activity via the Ah- receptor was given the value 1. The different chlorinated dibenzofurans could be given a TEF-value as they have been proven to possess a dioxin-like effect. Generally the effect is somewhat lower than the dioxin with the same substitution pattern.

The ability to possess a dioxin-like effect is linked both to the planarity of the molecule and the specific chlorine substitution pattern. Some PCB congeners are planar enough to have a small dioxin-like effect, especially the non-ortho congeners. The same is true, at a still lower TEF-value, for those PCB molecules with only one ortho chlorine. The total dioxin-like effect is, however, the TEF-value multiplied by the total amount present. As a result the net dioxin-like effect of the one ortho congeners can be substantial, as they are present in organisms at a relatively high level.

The majority of the PCB-congeners in biological samples as well as in technical products have two or more ortho substituents; they are too twisted to bind to the Ah-receptor and their TEF-value is zero. They possess however a phenobarbital-like effect, affecting various enzymes in a different manner from dioxins.

In the US, Congress also responded to the dangers associated with the use of PCBs and other toxic chemicals. In 1976 the Toxic Substances Control Act was passed. Although the act covered the regulation of all chemical substances, the severity of the threat posed by PCBs resulted in a section (6(e)) devoted solely to PCBs. No other chemicals received such singular attention. During the debate over the Senate version of the act, Senator Nelson, the author of Section 6(e), noted that PCBs were widespread in the environment and that they posed significant potential dangers to human health and to wildlife (United States Court of Appeal, 1980). The section required that, one year after the act came into effect, PCBs could only be manufactured, processed, distributed and used in a 'totally enclosed manner'. Eighteen months later, all manufacture, processing and distribution of PCBs was prohibited. Production in the UK ended in 1978 and in the US in 1979. However, elsewhere, and in particular in some eastern European countries, large-scale production continued until the mid-1980s (Boersma et al, 1994).

Scientific understanding becomes more sophisticated

In 1979 came another costly reminder of how PCBs can cause serious harm to human health. In Taiwan 2000 people were poisoned by polluted rice oil. The accident, named Yucheng, received more publicity and follow-up than the Yusho accident of the 1960s, demonstrating how awareness of PCBs as an environmental pollutant was changing. Cases with the typical clinical features as seen in the Yusho illness were reported. The children born to poisoned mothers became the subjects of a long-term health study. A quarter of the children died before the age of four years as a result of respiratory infections. At the age of eight years the children still had nail deformities and chronic otitis media (middle ear inflammation) together with bronchitis. Follow up studies of the adult victims of Yucheng showed an increase in skin allergies, chloracne, headache, spine and joint diseases and goitre (Guo, 1999).

A further development in the understanding of the phenomena occurred in the 1980s, when it was realised that PCBs change during bioaccumulation and biodegradation in the environment. This allowed many of the earlier inconclusive studies to be reinterpreted and the apparently conflicting evidence to be resolved. Bioaccumulation through the food chain tends to concentrate congeners of higher chlorine content, producing residues that are considerably different from the original Aroclor mixtures (Schwartz et al, 1987; Oliver and Niimi, 1988). Bioaccumulated PCBs appear to be more toxic than commercial PCBs because some toxic congeners can be preferentially retained (Aulerich et al, 1986; Hornshaw et al, 1983). Mink that were fed Great Lakes fish contaminated with PCBs showed liver and reproductive toxicity comparable to mink fed three times the quantity of Aroclor 1254 (Hornshaw et al, 1983).

Evidence of PCB contamination of human breast milk also became apparent in the 1980s. Due to the high level of PCBs in the Dutch environment, the levels of these chemicals in the Dutch population remain among the highest in the world, with average PCB content in adipose tissue ranging from 1.6–2.5 mg/kg fat (Greve and Wegman, 1983).

In the 1980s came the first published studies on possible developmental effects in children. Examples of endocrine disruption became apparent. The penises of boys affected by the Yucheng accident were underdeveloped and – another sign of endocrine disruption in the prenatal period – their understanding of spatial relationships was diminished, an abnormality also seen in boys of mothers using phenobarbital in pregnancy (Dessens et al, 1998). Children are more vulnerable to the toxic effects of PCBs than adults because they have developmental periods, so called 'windows of time', when metabolic systems develop (see also the case study on DES). During the intrauterine development of a child and in the postnatal period, many processes take place that fix homeostatic systems to states that then persist throughout life. Examples include a steady body temperature of 37 degrees Celsius; the setpoints for circulating hormone levels; and the functioning of the immune system. This 'fetotoxicity' represented a new paradigm for toxicology, one where both dose and timing is important. A natural example is the exposure to viral rubella infection in the first three months of gestation when the different organs are formed. Depending on the day of development of the organs the heart or a leg or an eye or the brain is malformed.

Prenatal exposure to PCBs and furans (polychlorinated dibenzofurans, or PCDFs, see Box 6.2) was associated with negative behavioural effects amongst the Yusho offspring. The children were apathetic and uninterested in their surroundings (Harada, 1976). Monkeys prenatally exposed to PCBs exhibited hyperactive behaviour during infancy, followed by inactivity at four years of age (Bowman and Heironimus, 1981). The four-year-old children of mothers whose diets had included significant amounts of fish from Lake Michigan also displayed reduced activity in relation to their body burdens of PCBs (Jacobson et al, 1990). Furthermore, at the age of 11 years, children more highly exposed in the prenatal period had lower IQ-test scores, and showed difficulties in verbal comprehension and reduced ability to concentrate. They were also more than twice as likely to be two years behind in reading skills and word comprehension (Jacobson and Jacobson, 1996). Further research has demonstrated negative effects as a result of prenatal exposure to background levels of PCBs in the US, Canada and western Europe (see Box 6.3).

Government action in the 1980s and 1990s

The North Sea ministerial conferences, in conjunction with the Oslo and Paris conventions on the protection of the Northeast Atlantic, have been important international fora that have stimulated action on hazardous substances. At the first North Sea conference in 1984, it was agreed that the phasing out of the use and discharge of PCBs should be intensified. At the second North Sea conference in 1987 targets were agreed to reduce discharges of 'substances that are toxic, persistent and liable to bioaccumulate' by the order of 50% by 1995 (DoE, 1987).

In 1987, the OECD made a further decision on PCBs, on the basis that 'current controls of polychlorinated biphenyl have not led to a clear and consistent downward trend of environmental levels of PCBs. Previous concerns about environmental contamination by PCBs, and their health and environmental effects remain unabated. New concerns have arisen over the use of PCBs particularly in situations where highly toxic products such as chlorinated dioxins or chlorinated dibenzofurans might be produced by their decomposition in fires.'(OECD, 1987). The decision recommended that member countries should cease the manufacture, import, export and sale of PCBs by 1 January 1989. The decision also called for the acceleration of the withdrawal of PCBs from use.

During the 1980s some national governments issued health advice suggesting the reduction of consumption of PCB-contaminated fish and time limits on breast-feeding. The advice was controversial and heavily debated because of the positive benefits to health from both breast-feeding and the consumption of fish (Fuerst et al, 1992).

In 1990 the third North Sea conference agreed a specific plan to phase out the use of PCBs by 1999 and safely dispose of them by the same date (DoE,

Box 6.3 Further research on fetotoxicity

In Rotterdam and Gröningen in The Netherlands, starting in 1990 and 1991, a study was performed to investigate the effects of prenatal exposure to background levels of PCBs and dioxins on growth and development of the child (Huisman, 1996; Koopman-Esseboom, 1995; Patandin, 1999; Lanting, 1999). The total study group consisted of 400 healthy mother–infant pairs, of which half the infants were breast-fed and half bottle-fed. Prenatal PCB exposure was estimated by the PCB-sum (PCB congeners 118, 138, 153 and 180) in maternal blood and cord blood and the total dioxin toxic equivalent (TEQ) level in the mother's breast milk (17 dioxin and a total of 8 dioxin-like PCB congeners – 3 planar, 3 mono-ortho and 2 di-ortho PCBs). Postnatal dioxin exposure was calculated as a product of the total dioxin TEQ level in breast milk multiplied by the weeks of breast-feeding.

Of the measured PCB congeners 118, 138, 153 and 180, the first is dioxin-like, but the last three are phenobarbital-like. In general 63% of the total amount of PCBs in human breast milk is ortho-substituted non-planar (PCB-22, -52, -138, -153 and -180) – that is phenobarbital-like PCBs. Current body exposure to the PCB congeners 118, 138, 153 and 180 was measured in plasma at 42 months of age (Patandin, 1999).

The study detected hyperactivity and slower mean reaction times in relation to the current PCB levels in the children at 42 months of age. Irritability and hyperactivity are well-known side-effects of the use of pheno-barbital in childhood. At the age of 42 months attention during free play behaviour was reduced relative to umbilical cord PCB concentrations and maternal PCB exposure. This persistent effect on behaviour from damage that happened prenatally is similar to that found by Jacobson (Jacobson et al, 1990; Patandin, 1999). Effects of prenatal PCB exposure were also adversely associated with neurological outcome at 18 months of age (Huisman et al, 1995), but this was no longer seen at 42 months of age (Lanting, 1998b). In contrast, prenatal and lactational exposure to dioxin-like PCBs and dioxins was not shown to affect attention and activity at 42 months of age (Patandin, 1999).

Thus, negative effects on cognitive and behavioural development, as demonstrated by Jacobson and the Dutch study, are related to the prenatal or current accumulated exposure to phenobarbital-like PCBs and not to dioxin-like PCBs.

A study by Seegal and Schantz (Seegal and Schantz, 1994) also demonstrated the different effects of phenobarbital-like PCB congeners and dioxin-like PCB congeners. Monkeys exposed to di-ortho PCBs were impaired on simple spatial discrimination and reversal problems. However, those monkeys exposed to TCDD (tetrachlorodibenzoparadioxin) performed better than the control group. The di-ortho-substituted PCB-congeners tested in adult monkeys are dopamine neurotoxicants. They reduce the amount of dopamine by inhibiting tyrosine hydroxylase – the enzyme which controls the rate at which dopamine is synthesised. It is probable that this is a long-term or even permanent effect (Seegal and Schantz, 1994). A particular concern is this may have implications relating to an increased incidence of Parkinson's disease.

Dessens found impaired spatial ability in human adults who had been prenatally exposed to anticonvulsants (mostly phenobarbital) (Dessens et al,

1998). The new disease entity 'late haemorrhagic disease of the new-born', first detected in the late 1970s in Japan and western Europe and originally attributed to vitamin K deficiency, might also be related to the effects of phenobarbital-like PCBs (Koppe et al, 1989; Bouwman, 1994). Prenatal exposure to background levels of dioxin-like PCB congeners has also been shown to affect thyroid hormone metabolism (Pluim et al, 1992; Koopman-Esseboom et al, 1994).

1990). In 1995 the Barcelona Convention for the Protection of the Mediterranean Sea against Pollution agreed to 'reduce, by the year 2005, discharges and emissions which could reach the marine environment, of substances which are toxic, persistent and liable to bioaccumulate, in particular organohalogens, to levels that are not harmful to man or nature with a view to their gradual elimination'. In the same year Sweden prohibited the use of old equipment which contained PCBs.

At the May 1995 meeting of the United Nations Environment Programme (UNEP) Governing Council, Decision 18/32 was adopted on persistent organic pollutants (POPs). This decision resulted in a number of studies and meetings culminating in November 1995 with the Washington Declaration, an agreement to a global programme of action to phase out POPs, including PCBs. The declaration was signed by 100 national governments.

In 1996 Directive EC96/59 of the EU called for the elimination of PCBs and PCTs (polychlorinated triphenyls) and their phase-out by 2010. However, transformers filled with PCB oil are still in use. As they become older and rust, the chances of leakage into the environment increase.

Some 100 years after the first serious adverse effects had been documented, closure had finally been reached on the seriousness of the threat. However, the toxic legacy will remain for many decades.

Routes of environmental exposure

When products containing PCBs decompose, or are destroyed by fire, significant amounts of the PCBs survive, because of their stability. During fires in oxygen-poor environments, and where PCBs are otherwise broken down, highly toxic polychlorinated dibenzofurans can be formed and released (see Box 6.2). There have also been accidental releases of PCBs and associated contaminants into the environment via leakage from 'sealed' PCB fluid compartments during commercial use of transformers and capacitors, and from the improper disposal of equipment or products.

By the late 1990s, even organisations generally critical of 'over-regulation' of industry had accepted that: 'In the past, discharges of PCB-laden wastes into rivers, streams, and open landfills were considered acceptable, legal, and hazard-free practices. PCBs were also sometimes intentionally released into the environment – for example, to reduce dust emissions from dirt roads, or as extenders in some agricultural pesticide formulations. In retrospect, these practices were inappropriate and potentially harmful.' (ASCH, 1997)

Once released, PCBs can volatise or disperse as aerosols, providing an effective means of transport in the environment. Strong south to north air flows, especially over west Eurasia, selectively favour the accumulation of PCBs and certain pesticides in the Arctic, once regarded as a pristine environment (AMAP, 1997). PCBs, together with the pesticides DDT, HCH and HCB, are detectable at low concentrations (0.01–40 nanograms (one thousand-millionth of a gram) per gram dry weight) in all samples of freshwater surface sediments from Alaska, northern Canada, Greenland, Norway, Finland and Russia (1995 and 1996). Freshwater and marine ecosystems tend to contain higher levels of PCBs than terrestrial ecosystems. Biomagnification of PCBs is especially significant in food webs dominated by organisms with a high fat content. Additionally, species overwintering at lower attitudes deliver POPs and metal burdens to the Arctic during the summer (Holden, 1970; AMAP, 1998).

Humans absorb PCBs from ingestion, inhalation and through the skin, although over 90% of exposure is via food (Theelen and Lie, 1997). Animal fat is the major source of PCBs. Once absorbed, PCBs equilibrate among lipid compartments in the whole body due to their high affinity for, notably, triglycerides and cholesterol esters and their lower affinity for phospholipids and cholesterol (Lanting et al, 1998a). In the liver PCBs interfere with enzyme systems important for detoxification (Matthews and Anderson, 1975).

The most recent PCB accident

Despite the various international and national regulations and legislation, releases, whether accidental or deliberate, are inevitable. In Belgium, in January 1999, chickens were found to have been fed a mixture of animal fats mixed with 8–50 litres of PCBs and furans. Although the source of PCBs has not been proven it was strongly suspected that they derived from the illegal disposal of old transformers. Levels in chickens and eggs were high, varying for 2,3,4,7,8 PCDF from 1299 picograms (one million-millionth of a gram) per gram in chicken fat to 1103 pg/g in egg yolk. Total dioxin (toxic equivalent (TEQ) level) was respectively 958 and 685 pg/g fat (Hens, 1999). According to WHO guidelines the tolerable daily intake or TDI for people is 1–4 picograms dioxin per kg bodyweight per day (WHO, 1999). The discovery was only made because the levels were so high as to cause chick edema (swelling of tissue due to increased fluid content). It is likely that other food contamination incidents have occurred at lower levels before and will continue to occur in future. This was underlined in 2000, a year later, when in another part of Belgium more animal food was found to be contaminated with PCBs and dioxins.

In 1999 Belgian toxicologists published an analysis of the incident and suggested that it was very unlikely that the isolated episode of contamination in Belgium would have caused health effects in the general population. Without providing data on the background levels of PCBs in the Belgian population, they speculated that a two- to three-fold increase would be comparable with levels in the 1980s of those regularly eating contaminated seafood (Bernard et al, 1999). This fails to take into account Dutch studies showing the effects of background levels of PCBs and dioxins on unborn babies. Since the PCB levels in the Belgian population are comparable to those of the Dutch, their statement is somewhat surprising and appears reminiscent of Sanford Brown of the Halowax Corporation in 1937 when endeavouring 'not to alarm the workforce'. One can legitimately wonder just how much we have learned since then.

Conclusions

By the 1930s there was already evidence, some at a low level of proof, that PCBs could poison people. This information was largely retained within the industry, and does not appear to have been widely circulated amongst policy-makers or other stakeholders. The application of the precautionary principle at that time would have prevented the toxic legacy that now exists.

Thirty years later, by the end of the 1960s, there was a high level of proof, mainly due to the Yusho accident, that in certain circumstances PCBs, or their breakdown products, such as dibenzofurans, could cause serious harm to human health. The findings of Søren Jensen also offered a high degree of proof that PCBs did bioaccumulate and were present in the Baltic food chain. A lower, but still substantial level of proof of the adverse reproductive effects on marine mammals was also available from the Baltic seal studies. Had precautionary action at a level of proof less than 'beyond reasonable doubt' been acceptable to, and applied by, policy-makers of that era, their action would still have resulted in a more manageable, less costly problem than we are faced with today. Many years of use of PCBs would have been avoided.

The 1960s evidence, with attendant worries of future liabilities, is likely to have been a factor that influenced Monsanto to reformulate some of its PCB products in 1971. Unfortunately this action was based on interpretation of the then current, but incomplete, scientific knowledge of how PCBs could cause harm.

During the 1970s evidence increased both of the environmental transport of PCBs to the remotest parts of the world and of the potential of PCBs to cause harm. PCBs were becoming widespread in the environment even though generally not being intentionally spread. It took until the early 1970s for any government to act and even then these actions only affected new 'open' uses of PCBs. By the late 1970s some governments had accepted that there was a greater risk of harm and enacted legislation to stop new 'closed' uses of PCBs. At this point there was no action by any government to address the problem of existing uses or the cleaning up of contaminated sites. It is probable that the technical difficulties and costs of such actions were the reasons behind this half measure. By the late 1970s, a few countries had called for all production to end. By this time alternatives to PCBs in closed uses were available.

In the 1980s a deeper understanding developed as to how PCBs caused harm. This did much to increase the level of certainty because some discrepancies between studies could now be explained as due to different PCB congeners. During this time the first evidence that PCBs could affect the unborn child was published. The North Sea states agreed that there was a danger and in 1987 adopted the political aspiration to reduce inputs to the marine environment by 'the order of' 50%, by 1995.

Also in 1987 the OECD accepted that the level of concern had increased and current legislation had not been effective. At this point all OECD countries agreed to end all new uses of PCBs by 1989. This time the risk posed by existing uses of PCBs was fully acknowledged and the introduction of 'controls' was recommended, as well as the removal of PCB equipment in certain circumstances. Nevertheless, production of PCBs still continued in several countries.

Although nine states within the North Sea catchment agreed in 1990 to phase out the use of all PCBs, it took until the mid-1990s, and the UNEP Washington Declaration, for a significant global response to emerge, acknowledging the problem and agreeing the need to act on PCBs in use.

Even today some of the science is still being debated. Much of this is to do with the different effects of commercial PCB mixes and those found in the environment, especially those that have been bioaccumulated. It could be argued that further scientific study at an earlier time would have allowed an earlier resolution. However, it could also be argued that the call for more science can also be used as a reason to delay justifiable action.

The resistance of PCBs to degradation means they are expensive to destroy. As a result of the many delays, a large percentage of historic PCB production has escaped beyond our control into the environment. Wide dispersal, and bioaccumulative properties, means that in many cases PCBs are in places where their recovery and destruction is not possible. Also, in many countries where they are still in use, the facilities for safe destruction do not exist.

In 1999, during the negotiations for a global convention to phase out all POPs, attention was focused on PCBs still in use, particularly those posing a risk due to accident or leakage. While this focus on prevention of further releases is essential, it is also necessary to pay greater attention to our response to the high levels of PCBs that are already in the environment. Behavioural problems and respiratory diseases affecting children, two of today's most important problems in paediatrics, could be due, in substantial part, to intoxication with PCBs. There is an urgent need to find ways of reducing current body burdens of these chemicals in people. Of course, no equivalent action is possible for other species.

PCBs also highlight issues such as who judges what risks are acceptable, and whether all stakeholders are fairly represented in this debate. Both PCBs and dioxins are fetotoxic. Is it acceptable to tolerate risks for involuntary exposure to unborn babies, when this may affect their future capabilities and those of their offspring?

At almost every stage government action was taken only when there was a high level of scientific proof. The non-application of the precautionary principle has left us with a legacy, the total effects and costs of which can only be guessed at.

Table 6.1 *PCBs: early warnings and actions*

1899	Chloracne identified in workers in chlorinated organic industry
1929	Mass production of PCBs for commercial use begins
1936	More workers affected by chloracne and liver damage
1937	Chloracne and liver damage observed in experiments with rats. Results did not gain attention from policy-makers but both labour regulators and manufacturers were made aware of the concerns surrounding PCBs
1966	Jensen discovers unknown molecules in sea eagles in Sweden – only in 1969 was he able to demonstrate that they were PCBs
1968	Poisoning of 1800 people who had ingested PCB-contaminated rice oil in Japan gives rise to a new Japanese word: *Yusho* – rice oil disease, and to the first well-publicised warning that PCBs are harmful to humans
1970s	High levels of PCBs found in infertile seals of three different species
1972	Sweden bans 'open' uses of PCBs
1976	Toxic Substances Control Act (US) – PCBs to be used only in a 'totally enclosed manner'
1979	2000 people again poisoned, in Taiwan, by polluted rice oil. Follow-up research showed that 25% of children born of poisoned mothers died before the age of four years
1980s	Evidence of PCB contamination of breast milk
1990s	PCBs associated with IQ and brain effects in children exposed in utero to mothers' PCB-contaminated diets. Fetotoxicity represents a new paradigm for toxicology
1996	EU directive to eliminate PCBs, with phase-out by 2010
1999	Chicken food contaminated with PCBs is found in Belgium

Source: EEA

Halocarbons, the ozone layer and the precautionary principle

Joe Farman

Overview

In the second half of the last century some 23 million metric tonnes of CFCs, about 11 million tonnes of methyl chloroform, 2.5 million tonnes of carbon tetra-chloride and 4 million tonnes of a hydrofluorocarbon (HCFC-22) were released into the atmosphere. All of these halocarbons have atmospheric lifetimes[2] long enough for them to be transported to the stratosphere. The amount of chlorine in the stratosphere today is between six and seven times what it was in 1950. There is an ozone hole over Antarctica from September to December each year, less systematic but nevertheless large ozone losses in the Arctic, and moderate ozone losses in the middle latitudes of both hemispheres. The evidence which allows us to conclude, beyond reasonable doubt, that halocarbons are responsible for the damage to the ozone layer, is set out in a series of five reports prepared by the World Meteorological Organization (WMO) for the Parties to the United Nations Vienna Convention and Montreal Protocol (WMO, 1985, 1989, 1991, 1994 and 1999). As a result of this damage, there will be serious impacts including an increase in skin cancer (see Figure 7.1).

The end of what might be called the CFC episode of industrial history is almost in sight. The consumption (consumption = production + imports - exports) and most production of CFCs, halons and methyl chloroform have already ceased in developed countries. Exceptions include feedstock use, a few so-called essential uses[3] and an allowance to supply the needs of developing

---

2 Lifetimes are given as e-folding times. The rate of removal of a constituent is propor-tional to its concentration, so that, in the absence of emissions, the residual concentration after N lifetimes is e-N times the initial concentration.

3 These include medical use of CFCs in metered dose inhalers (now largely replaced by HFCs or PFCs – perfluorocarbons) and the use of halons in fire protection systems in military equipment.

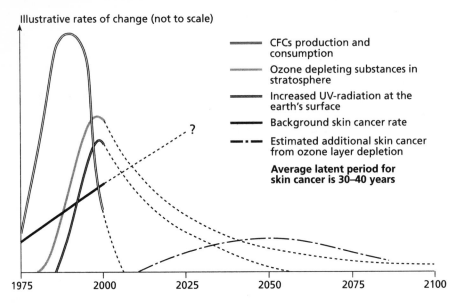

Illustrative rates of change (not to scale)

—— CFCs production and consumption

—— Ozone depleting substances in stratosphere

—— Increased UV-radiation at the earth's surface

—— Background skin cancer rate

—·— Estimated additional skin cancer from ozone layer depletion

Average latent period for skin cancer is 30–40 years

1975   2000   2025   2050   2075   2100

Note: This graph illustrates the approximate time lags between CFC production, the resulting depletion of the stratospheric ozone layer and subsequent extra penetration of UV radiation and the impact this will eventually have on increasing the background rate of skin cancer, given the 30–40 year average latent period for such cancers. Reality is far more complex than this schematic illustration. For example, there are other ozone-depleting chemicals (HCFCs, HFCs and methyl bromide); the ozone hole varies with latitude, time of the year and meteorological conditions; the increased UV radiation varies between different wavelengths and with latitude and cloud cover; and the skin cancer excess comes on top of a rising background rate of skin cancer, with differential effects on the different types of skin cancer, such as malignant melanoma and non-malignant skin cancers. Human behaviour is also a determining effect in skin cancer. Health effects also include cataracts and immune response suppression. However, the figure illustrates the main relationships and time lags between CFC production and skin cancer, and the 'success' in stopping CFC production and averting much more skin cancer from ozone depletion than what is now expected. (Slaper et al, 1996).

Source: EEA

Figure 7.1 *Historical and projected rates of CFC production, ozone depletion, UV radiation and skin cancer*

countries whose own phase-out schedule began with a freeze in 1999 and culminates in cessation of supply in 2010. The reductions in releases are the basis on which the Montreal Protocol (signed in September 1987 and coming into force on 1 January 1989) and its later amendments and adjustments have been hailed as a major success.

However the cessation of releases is not the end of the story for the atmosphere and for the ozone layer. Methyl chloroform has the shortest atmospheric lifetime, about five years, of the major ozone depleting substances (ODS), and only about 2% of the current atmospheric concentration will remain after four lifetimes, or 20 years. CFC-12, on the other hand, has a lifetime of about 100

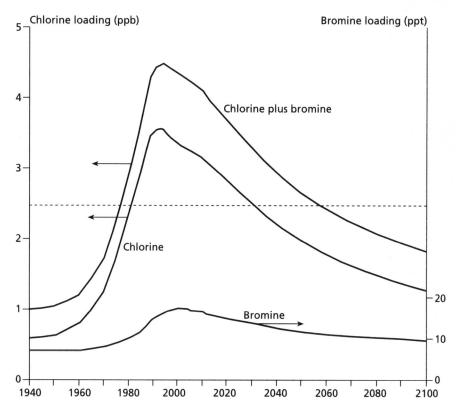

Note: Reactive bromine is scaled in parts per trillion by volume (pptv) on the right, and in parts per billion by volume (ppbv) of equivalent chlorine on the left. The combined loading is expressed as equivalent chlorine. The line at 2.5 ppbv of equivalent chlorine indicates the loading in the late 1970s.

Source: DETR, 1999

Figure 7.2 *Historical and projected total chlorine and bromine loadings of the troposphere*

years and the concentration in the atmosphere in 2100 will be at least 37% of what it is today. The last statement is qualified because even in developed countries where production has ceased releases continue from the bank of past production held in equipment and plastic foams; this was estimated to be 791 kilotonnes in 1995. The production peaked in 1988 and ceased in developed countries at the end of 1993. Whilst there is some production in China, India and Korea, due to cease in 2002, the current releases come predominantly from the bank in developed countries, estimated at 70 kilotonnes in 1995 and being run down at about 4% per year. This halon has an atmospheric lifetime of about 65 years, and its atmospheric concentration will continue to increase until about 2020, unless the protocol is amended to require the destruction of banked halons.

As a guide to past and projected damage to the ozone layer the simplest indicator is the combined loading of chlorine and bromine in the troposphere, expressed as equivalent chlorine. Molecule for molecule, bromine is some 58 times more effective than chlorine in destroying ozone: equivalent chlorine = chlorine + 58 x bromine. Estimates of the historical and projected loadings are shown in Figure 7.2. Opinion is divided over just how far back in time damage to the ozone layer can be traced, but it has become conventional to regard a level of 2.5 ppbv (parts per billion by volume) of equivalent chlorine, first reached in the late 1970s, as significant. Under the latest amendments (1997) to the protocol a return to this level is expected between 2050 and 2060. For comparison it can be noted that under the original protocol, the London amendments of 1990 and the Copenhagen amendments of 1992, there was no guarantee that the equivalent chlorine loading would ever return to 2.5 ppbv. The adjustments in Vienna in 1995 did finally achieve a projected return, and the amendments in Montreal in 1997 brought the return a few years nearer. The failure to act more decisively in the early negotiations can be seen perhaps as the parties to the protocol setting consensus before effectiveness; in retrospect it seems that the negotiators consistently took the view that it would be easier to get agreement at the next meeting.[4]

Should the CFC episode have been avoided? Could it have been avoided? Three sketches of industrial and environmental history may help to put these questions in perspective.

Early history

The first episode is set at the end of the 19th century. The chlorinated derivatives of the simpler hydrocarbons had been studied, finding incidentally many compounds for which there are no significant sources outside the laboratory. Most ODSs are compounds of that sort. Carbon tetrachloride was being produced industrially; it was used as a solvent, for dry cleaning and in fire extinguishers. Methyl chloroform was known but, surprisingly in view of developments after 1950, found no application. A Belgian chemist, Swarts, had laid the foundation of the study of fluorinated hydrocarbons, making CFC-11 and CFC-12 by the catalysed reaction of hydrofluoric acid with carbon tetrachloride. At the turn of the century ozone was an important industrial chemical. In an episode, now largely ignored in textbooks, it was widely used in applications ranging from the chemical laboratory to municipal services. It was the most powerful oxidant known, left no objectionable residue, and was easy, if

---

4 Paragraph 9(c) of Article 2 of the Montreal Protocol states 'In taking such decisions, the Parties shall make every effort to reach agreement by consensus. If all efforts at consensus have been exhausted and no agreement reached, such decisions shall, as a last resort, be adopted by a two-thirds majority vote of the Parties present and voting representing at least 50% of the total consumption of the controlled substances of the Parties.' No issue has yet been put to a vote. Paragraph 11 of the same article states 'Notwithstanding the provisions contained in this Article, Parties may take more stringent measures than those required by this Article.' It has been invoked only once, by the EU in March 1991, suggesting that, on the whole, the negotiators have been quite content to proceed at a pace compatible with consensus.

somewhat expensive, to make. It was used to sterilise public water supplies and to purify the air in the central London underground railway system. As a bleaching agent and a deodorant of oils, waxes and fats, it was widely used in the manufacture of linen, cotton, paint, varnish, linoleum and perfumes. It was used as a preservative for food, and refrigerated warehouses and ships were often equipped with portable ozonisers. Little was known about ozone as a natural constituent of the atmosphere. Measurements at Rouen in 1857 had shown that the mixing ratio near the ground was about 10–8 (10 ppbv) (Houzeau, 1857), and quite dense networks of stations undertaking such measurements had been set up, most notably in Belgium and France. It had been inferred from the cut-off at short wavelengths of the solar spectrum that much larger mixing ratios must occur in the upper atmosphere. At the turn of the century there was a comfortable feeling among meteorologists that the thermal structure of the atmosphere was simple: temperature decreased with height at a rate that was well understood, and the decrease should continue to the limit of the atmosphere. This complacency was shaken in 1901 when Teisserenc de Bort (see, for example, Goody, 1954) reported that the decrease stopped, often quite abruptly, at a height of about 11 km, and that from there to about 14 km, the greatest height attained by his instruments, the temperature remained almost constant. At first he called his discovery the isothermal layer, but later suggested the words troposphere, to denote the well-mixed lower region, and stratosphere for the region above, in recognition of its high static stability. Routine soundings of the stratosphere had to await cheap portable radio, lightweight instruments and improved balloons. A start was made in 1933, but the successive effects of economic recession and world war made progress slow until the 1950s.

The 1930s: the CFC industry is born

The second sketch is for the decade centred on 1930. By then chlorine had largely replaced ozone as an industrial bleaching and sterilising agent. It was cheap, as large amounts were produced as a by-product of the electrolysis of rock salt, a process introduced to satisfy the growing demand for caustic soda for preparing sheet metal for painting. A Norwegian, Eric Rotheim, applied for a patent for the aerosol container (spray can) principle in 1926. (There is no record of use on a large scale until the Second World War, when insecticide sprays were needed in the Pacific sector. Mass production started in the US in 1947 and in Germany in 1953.) In 1929 Thomas Midgely, at General Motors in the US, conducted a survey of chemicals suitable for use as refrigerants, and recommended CFC-12 and CFC-11 as efficient, non-toxic and non-flammable. Du Pont started industrial production of CFC-12 in 1930 and of CFC-11 in 1934.

By this time, the ozone layer had been discovered and, considering the resources available, quite comprehensively investigated. The annual variation in ozone amount had been measured at stations ranging from the Arctic Circle to New Zealand, largely through the efforts of Dobson and his collaborators at Oxford, following up the pioneer measurement of Fabry and Buisson in France.

The broad features of the vertical distribution of ozone had been established, by ground-based measurements of light scattered from the zenith sky at twilight (Götz, Meetham and Dobson), and by the Regeners at Stuttgart, who sent a small solar spectroscope up on a balloon to 31 km, at which point it had passed through about 70% of the ozone layer. These two very different techniques gave results that agreed remarkably well. To complete this sketch it should be mentioned that in 1930 Chapman published the first theoretical treatment of the formation of atmospheric ozone (for more on all this see, for example, Goody, 1954). Within its limitations, equilibrium photochemistry in a static atmosphere, it gave a fair account of the upper part of the ozone layer (above 30 km), but failed completely to explain the observed variations of ozone with latitude and season. More than 50 years were to pass before realistic air motions could be incorporated into models of the ozone layer, and even today there remains a fascinating interplay between uncertainty in the chemistry and uncertainty in the dynamics of the atmosphere.

The 1970s: the seeds of doubt

Concern about the effect of human activities on the ozone layer became an international issue in 1970. Initially fears were expressed about the emissions of nitrogen oxides, carbon monoxide and water from the projected commercial fleets of supersonic stratospheric transport (SST) aircraft. These were heeded – the US abandoned development of SSTs, and the combined total of Anglo-French Concordes and Russian Tupolev-144s never exceeded 40 aircraft. Attention then shifted to the CFC industry, which had expanded enormously throughout the 1960s. A survey, using a recently developed device capable of measuring small traces of CFCs, had shown that these gases, released largely in the northern hemisphere, had spread worldwide (Lovelock et al, 1973). Moreover their concentrations were such as to indicate that processes removing CFCs from the troposphere must be extremely slow – virtually all of the amounts released were still in the atmosphere. In 1974 seminal papers by American scientists pointed out that CFCs were so stable that they would eventually reach the stratosphere, that chlorine would be released there by photolysis, and that an ozone-destroying chain reaction would ensue (Molina and Rowland, 1974; Cicerone et al, 1974). A vigorous debate followed, which was to continue for over a decade.

The first significant move was the agreement in 1977 for a research-oriented 'world plan of action on the ozone layer', and the establishment by the United Nations Environment Programme (UNEP) of a Coordinating Committee on the Ozone Layer, to oversee the plan. It is noteworthy that representatives of non-governmental organisations (NGOs) were given the right to attend meetings of the committee. In the US an effective public campaign, stimulated by the earlier debate on the impact of supersonic aircraft, resulted in regulations in 1977 prohibiting the use of CFCs as aerosol propellants. Canada, Norway and Sweden took similar action. European environmental groups were at the time concentrating on the issue of acid rain, and there was little public pressure on governments over CFCs. However in 1980 European Council Decision 80/372 was passed, aiming to freeze the production capacity for CFC-11 and CFC-12, and to reduce their use in aerosols by at least 30% from 1976 levels by the end of 1981. The effect of these measures on releases is not easily seen. Releases had fallen sharply a few years before the measures came into force, largely as a result of a downturn in world trade following a crisis in the oil market. The reduction in use in the aerosol sector was quickly offset by increased use in the foam-blowing sector. The European freeze was little more than a token gesture, since most plant was running well below its full capacity.

For all that, these measures appear to be the first, and last, unequivocal application of the precautionary principle in the ozone story. It was the only action taken before the evidence against CFCs had become compelling. The 1977 US Clean Air Act explicitly states that 'no conclusive proof... but a reasonable expectation' of harmful effects is sufficient to justify action (US EPA, 1987). This was in stark contrast to the 'wait and see' attitude adopted by industry. Du Pont, the world's first and largest producer of CFCs, had set this out in a full page in the *New York Times* (30 June 1975). It declared that: 'Should reputable evidence show that some fluorocarbons cause a health hazard through depletion of the ozone layer, we are prepared to stop production of the offending compounds.' It was to deny the existence of reputable evidence until 1986. Nevertheless, it should be acknowledged that the industry, through the Chemical Manufacturers Association (an international funding agency), throughout this time gave substantial financial support to institutes and individuals engaged in research into the ozone problem.

In the early 1980s, the problem of the ozone layer seemed to have settled down. Computational models predicted only small long-term reductions of ozone, and this was in reasonable accord with observations, which showed no significant trend. Negotiations for an international convention on the ozone layer, started by UNEP in 1981, proceeded slowly. While the US favoured a range of controls on the use of CFCs in various applications, Europe argued for a cap on production capacity. The differences could not be bridged, and the Vienna Convention for the Protection of the Ozone Layer, agreed in March 1985, contained only pledges to cooperate in research and monitoring, to exchange information on CFC production, and to pass control protocols only if and when justified. By this time the US was not prepared to act unilaterally, claiming that as a result of its earlier action, its production of CFC-11 and CFC-12 had fallen from 46% of the world total in 1974 to 28% in 1985. There was some consolation for those advocating controls; the Parties to the Convention gave UNEP immediate authority to convene working group negotiations for a protocol, to be signed if possible in 1987.

The Montreal Protocol and the ozone hole

The Montreal Protocol was, indeed, signed on 16 September 1987, after a hectic last week of controversy. Richard Benedick, the chief US negotiator, later claimed that this too was an application of the precautionary principle. A simpler interpretation would be that the working group had been overtaken by events. Ozone depletion over Antarctica had been reported in *Nature* (Farman et al, 1985) in May 1985, much more severe than any prediction, and confirmed by NASA in October 1985. In reporting the NASA results, the *Washington Post* gave the world the expressive term 'ozone hole'. Du Pont, reminded of its statement in 1975, wrote to its CFC customers in September 1986, declaring that it now accepted the need for some controls (Cagin and Dray, 1993, p308). Also in 1986, the US National Ozone Expedition (NOZE) to McMurdo Station in Antarctica had produced much evidence to support the view that the depletion was chemically driven. In September 1987 attention was again focused on Antarctica, with press releases expected from NOZE II, and from the US Airborne Antarctic Ozone Experiment (AAOE) whose planes had flown from Punta Arenas in Chile into and under the ozone hole. The timing of the announcement of the protocol makes sense only as a pre-emptive move astutely designed to preserve some credibility for the negotiators, and to give industry time for orderly reorganisation.

Success, compromise, muddle, failure – all these terms have been used to describe the 1987 protocol. There can be no doubt that it was a psychological breakthrough. However the terms were tempered by what was thought practicable, the ultimate objective was not clearly defined, and releases increased rapidly in the period before the next full meeting of the Parties. The protocol was ratified and came into force on 1 January 1989, in line with the timetable. The review procedure was set in motion at once. By then a consensus on the main scientific issues had been reached, NGOs had fought vigorous campaigns for public awareness, and industry was responding much faster to the problem than had initially seemed possible. The London amendments in 1990, although substantially stronger than the original protocol, nevertheless were disappointing by comparison with statements made by most of the Parties in preparatory meetings. However, in addition to the changes in the controls, two important decisions were taken. It was agreed that there should be full reviews every two years instead of every four, and it was agreed (in a new Article 10) to establish a Multilateral Fund for the Implementation of the Montreal Protocol (MFMP) to help developing countries reduce their dependence on ODS.

The main concern in these negotiations was to replace CFCs quickly with new chemicals, hydrochlorofluorocarbons (HCFCs) and hydrofluorocarbons (HFCs) being the options preferred by industry.[5] Some 75% of the global production of CFCs was in the hands of 13 groups of companies, who were quite content to close down old CFC plant if the protocol would allow reasonable time for the industry to profit from investment in HCFC and HFC production. The negotiators readily accepted this; these transitional substances were made subject to guidelines rather than controls and their future was left open-ended, as consensus could not be reached on a phase-out date.[6] In my

---

5 HCFCs are ozone depleting substances, but much less harmful than CFCs. HFCs have zero ozone depletion potential, but they are powerful greenhouse gases.

6 There were sharp differences of opinion on the date by which phase-out could be achieved. Targets ranged from 2010 to 2040.

view, this approach was deeply flawed. Technical surveys had already shown that large quantities of CFCs and halons were released unnecessarily by poor working practices; the quantities of replacements needed were much less than current consumption. More emphasis should have been placed on prudent long-term goals, with active encouragement of the development of halocarbon-free and energy-efficient technologies, to protect the ozone layer, to slow down the forcing of climate change and to reduce the cost of raising living standards in developing countries. The MFMP has been spent largely on the replacement of CFCs by HCFCs, and more money is now needed to phase-out HCFCs. It would surely have been better to stimulate more radical changes in technology from the outset.

The most recent full meeting of the Parties was in Beijing, China, in early December 1999, when 129 governments were represented. Two noteworthy events had taken place during the preparations for the meeting. In March 1999 the MFMP approved US$150 million to fund the complete closure over the next ten years of CFC production in China, now the world's largest producer and consumer of CFCs and halons. A week before the meeting the MFMP approved US$82 million to lead to the complete phase-out of CFC production in India, the world's second largest producer of CFCs. At the meeting the Parties agreed to raise an additional US$440 million for the MFMP; the fund has disbursed more than US$1 billion since 1991. New controls were adopted for HCFCs, including a ban on trade in these chemicals with countries that have not yet ratified the 1992 amendment (for phase-out of HCFCs). A complete phase-out by 2002 of the production of the recently marketed chemical, bromochloromethane, was agreed. A Beijing Declaration was adopted, calling for continued efforts to halt illegal trade in ODS. There was one brief glimpse of the precautionary principle: the Scientific and Economic Assessment Panels were asked to propose means to prevent the development and marketing of new ozone-depleting chemicals.[7] Important issues that were not resolved include the possible destruction of halon banks, an earlier phase-out for methyl bromide and reducing the current scale of CFC and halon consumption in Russia and other countries with economies in transition.

Late lessons

The report in 1985 of rapid and severe seasonal destruction of ozone over Antarctica was an outcome of systematic long-term measurements, begun solely for scientific exploration. It took everyone by surprise, including the authors. The accepted view was that the effects of CFCs should be seen first at high altitudes (30–50 km) in the tropics, and that any changes in the lower stratosphere in polar regions would be very slow. As it happened, two other groups were close to challenging the accepted view – Japanese scientists had presented anomalous ozone profiles from Antarctica, but without identifying a systematic

---

7 For more information on the Beijing meeting visit the web site: www.iisd.ca/ozone/mop11/.

trend, and NASA scientists were re-examining very low ozone amounts flagged as 'suspect' by their software in initial retrievals of satellite data. This was before the Internet, and the absence of effective collaboration, whilst regrettable, was not uncommon in institutions with stretched resources. It should also be noted that the ozone community was just completing the first of the WMO reports – an onerous task for authors and reviewers. The funding of long-term monitoring remains a serious problem. It is simply not practicable to provide open-ended funding at the level needed to cope with uncovering a major environmental issue.

Recession and war restricted the growth of the CFC industry. From 1930 to 1948 the cumulative releases of CFC-12 and CFC-11 were only 25 and 5 kilotonnes respectively. The next two decades brought spectacular growth – in 1970 the annual releases were 300 and 207 kilotonnes. People had been persuaded to buy CFCs and throw them away (aerosols). Industry's dream of 'wonder chemicals' was apparently coming true. This was the time when it might reasonably have been asked whether such development was sustainable.

There can be little doubt that a conventional risk assessment, in say 1965, would have concluded that there were no known grounds for concern. It would have noted that CFCs were safe to handle, being chemically very inert, non-flammable, and having very low levels of toxicity. They were good heat insulators, and some were excellent solvents, mixing readily with a wide range of other organic substances. The assessment might have pointed out that it was not known what happens to CFCs when they are released to the atmosphere, but would no doubt have added that they had been released for more than 30 years with no apparent harm being done. There would probably have been a long list of recommendations for further research. In retrospect, it is easy to see that these should have included investigating the ultraviolet and infrared spectra of CFCs, measuring their atmospheric concentrations, and identifying their decomposition products. As it happens, there were hints of the risk to the ozone layer available (Weigert, 1907; Norrish and Neville, 1934[8]) if it had been recognised that atomic chlorine and fluorine might be released from CFCs in the upper atmosphere. But they would surely have been dismissed on the grounds that there would be at least 10,000 times more ozone than CFCs at the relevant altitudes.

It is just possible that such an assessment might have accelerated the research needed to make out a plausible case against CFCs. But, as history shows, a plausible case brought only limited action. Serious negotiations did not begin until severe depletion had occurred, and strong evidence found to link it with CFCs. The protracted, and frequently amended, schedule for phase-out of ODS suggests that, even at this stage, precautionary management of the environment was not uppermost in the minds of policy-makers.

The recent decision (2001) of the US administration not to ratify the Kyoto Protocol on Climate Change will have disappointed many who were hoping that

---

8 These two papers report laboratory experiments on the decomposition of ozone photosensitised by chlorine. They are cited in a systematic review of stratospheric chemistry, dated 1977, but there is nothing to suggest that they had any influence on workers in the 1960s and early 1970s.

the experience gained with the Montreal Protocol would facilitate getting agreements for further protection of the global environment. One of the lessons should have been that neither governments nor multinational companies have a mandate for global experiments, even when such experiments consist solely of 'business as usual'. The CFC issue provides a stark warning. Practices that appear to be reasonable when introduced (in this case when there were huge gaps in the understanding of atmospheric processes) may later (as understanding improves) be seen to be leading to a major global problem that can neither be avoided, nor rapidly alleviated. There is a deep-seated paradox here. Short-term safety appears to demand that synthetic chemicals in everyday use should be non-reactive. It has taken a long while for it to be realised that this means that they will be extremely persistent.

It should not be assumed that environmental science has reached the stage where all hazards can be foreseen. All too often technology outstrips the science needed to assess the risks involved. If there is to be a solution, policy-makers must learn to recognise, much more rapidly than they have in the past, when ignorance has been replaced by understanding, however rudimentary.

Table 7.1 *Halocarbons: early warnings and actions*

1907	Laboratory experiments by Weigert on the decomposition of ozone photosensitised by chlorine
1934	Ditto by Norrish and Neville
1973	Global survey of CFCs by Lovelock et al showing their distribution in the atmosphere worldwide
1974	Molina and Rowland publish their theoretical arguments that CFCs would be destroying the ozone layer
1977	US bans CFCs in aerosols based on 'reasonable expectation' of damage, followed by Canada, Norway and Sweden.
1977	Research-oriented 'world plan of action on the ozone layer' agreed, overseen by UNEP
1980	European decision restricting use of CFCs in aerosols, but rising use in refrigerators, etc, marginalises this restriction
1985	UNEP Vienna Convention for the protection of the ozone layer agrees research, monitoring, information exchange and restrictions if and when justified
1985	Farman, Gardiner and Shanklin publish results showing hole in ozone layer over Antartica
1987	Montreal Protocol on protection of the ozone layer is signed, with phasing out of ozone depleting substances for both developed and developing countries within different timescales
1990s	Increasing finance to developing countries to help them reduce their dependence on ozone depleting substances
1997	Amendments to the Montreal Protocol in order to restore levels of chlorine by 2050–60
1999	Beijing Declaration calling for efforts to stop illegal trade in ozone depleting substances

Source: EEA

The DES story: long-term consequences of prenatal exposure

Dolores Ibarreta and Shanna H Swan

Introduction

In 1970, Herbst and colleagues reported an unprecedented finding; they had diagnosed a rare vaginal cancer (vaginal clear-cell adenocarcinoma) in seven young women, a cancer that had never before been seen in this age group in this hospital (Herbst and Scully, 1970). The following year, these authors published the startling finding that seven of the eight cases (one more had been identified), but none of 32 matched controls, had been prenatally exposed to the synthetic oestrogen diethylstilboestrol (DES) (Herbst et al, 1971). Seven months after this publication, the US Food and Drug Administration (FDA) withdrew approval for use of DES by pregnant women, for whom this potent synthetic oestrogen had been prescribed since 1947 in the mistaken, but widespread, belief that it prevented spontaneous abortion (miscarriage). In fact, this apparently innocent treatment proved to be a time bomb for the infants exposed during the first third of pregnancy. The discovery that DES was a transplacental carcinogen (and was shown after 1971 to also be a teratogen – causing birth defects) occurred only ten years after the awful discovery (James, 1965) that the use of thalidomide by women in early pregnancy caused severe limb reductions. These tragic lessons forced scientists to abandon their commonly held view of the foetal environment as a safe place, protected by the placental 'barrier', and replace it with an understanding of the extreme vulnerability of the developing foetus, for whom any maternal exposure that occurred during critical periods had the potential to alter development, even long after birth.

Optimistic beginnings

Oestrogens are steroid hormones, made primarily in the female ovaries and the male testes, that act by binding to oestrogen receptors. Oestrogens, together with the other so-called sex hormones (progestins and androgens), are required for the regulation of reproduction and the development of secondary characteristics in both males and females. In 1938, Charles Dodds and colleagues formulated DES, the first orally active synthetic oestrogen (Dodds et al, 1938). This synthetic (non-steroidal) oestrogen has been estimated to be five times as potent as oestradiol, the most potent naturally occurring oestrogen in mammals (Noller and Fish, 1974). DES is inexpensive and simple to synthesise and the developing pharmaceutical industry quickly began worldwide production; DES was marketed under more than 200 brand names. Like other pharmaceuticals produced at that time, DES underwent very limited toxicological investigations. It rapidly became popular in a wide variety of treatments, including those for menopausal symptoms and prostate cancer. Other therapeutic uses were suppression of lactation, post-coital contraception (morning-after pill) and post-menopause syndrome (Noller and Fish, 1974). It was later used as a growth promoter in chicken, sheep and cattle (Aschbacher, 1976).

Among the multiple uses of DES was that for the prevention of spontaneous abortion (miscarriage). It was believed in the 1940s that spontaneous abortion was the result of a decrease in oestrogen levels, now recognised as a consequence, not a cause (Smith, 1948). As early as 1941, Karnaky and others began experimenting with the use of very high doses (100 mg administered intramuscularly into the cervix daily) in women 'threatening to abort', and deemed the drug effective for this purpose, stating that there were no adverse consequences to mother or foetus (Karnaky, 1942). The use of DES for prevention of miscarriage was further promoted by the work of Olive and George Smith, who conducted multiple (uncontrolled) trials of DES for use in pregnancy throughout the 1940s and published extensively regarding its effectiveness (Smith, 1948; Smith et al, 1946).

Paradoxically, Charles Dodds, the scientist who first synthesised DES, a discovery for which he was later knighted, speculated years later about the minimal testing of new drugs at that time. Reviewing the history of stilboestrol (another common term for DES), suggested by Dodds himself (Dodds et al, 1938), he noted that no long-term toxicity tests of this synthetic oestrogen had been conducted. He stated: 'I suppose we have to be very thankful that it (DES) did prove to be such a non-toxic substance.' (Dodds, 1965) Unfortunately, when Dodds wrote this the long-term consequences of DES had not been discovered.

Tragic consequences

Reports that DES increased cancer incidence in laboratory animals appeared as early as 1938 (Lacassagne, 1938; Geschickter, 1939; Shimkin and Grady, 1941; Greene and Brewer, 1941). Since those early reports, extensive research has demonstrated an increased incidence of cancer of the mammary glands, cervix and vagina in multiple rodent species in response to DES. However, until 1971 there was little evidence suggesting that maternal use of DES could result in cancer and reproductive abnormalities in humans, 20 years after exposure.

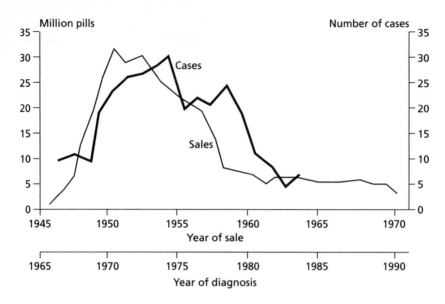

Source: D Ibarreta and S H Swan

Figure 8.1 *Market sales of 25 mg DES versus cases of clear-cell cancer by year of diagnosis*

The 1971 case-control study of Herbst and colleagues identifying prenatal exposure to DES as the likely cause of a rare and often fatal vaginal cancer in young women was startling and unprecedented. This case-control study was followed within a few months by a second, corroborative, case-control study (Greenwald et al, 1971). The relationship between DES use by pregnant women and the occurrence of vaginal clear-cell adenocarcinoma is clearly apparent in Figure 8.1. As can be seen, there is a remarkable correspondence between sale of DES (represented here by market sales figures produced by a large and representative US manufacturer during litigation) and diagnosis of this cancer 20 years later (Melnick et al, 1987).

This shocking finding finally raised a red flag concerning the dangers of DES use by pregnant women, as well as providing convincing evidence of the potential hazards that exposure of the pregnant woman to pharmaceuticals (and other chemicals) pose to the foetus. As a result of this study, the FDA released a bulletin in November 1971 stating that DES use was contraindicated (must not be used) during pregnancy (US Department of Health, Education and Welfare, 1971). Tragically, the use of DES by pregnant women continued even after 1971 outside the US and in some countries was reported many years later (Direcks and t'Hoen, 1986). The number of women who took DES is known imprecisely, but the National Institutes of Health has estimated that it was used by 4.8 million pregnant women in the US alone. Total exposure (to mothers, sons and daughters) worldwide has been estimated to be 10 million (see Table 8.1).

Table 8.1 *Use of DES to prevent miscarriage in Europe and the US*

Country	Period prescribed	Approximate number of pregnancies	Source
Belgium	1950–65		Direcks et al, 1991
Czechoslovakia	1958–76	63,000	Direcks et al, 1991
France	1950–77	200,000	Pons et al, 1988
		60,000–240,000	Direcks et al, 1991
Germany	–1977	200,000	Direcks et al, 1991
Ireland	1550–76		Wingfield, 1992
Italy	–1960(?)		Direcks et al, 1991
The Netherlands	1947–75	189,000–378,000	Hanselaar et al, 1991
Norway	1948–72		Palmlund et al, 1993
Portugal	1960–70		Direcks et al, 1991
Spain	1953–77 (1983?)	25,000	Garcia-Alonso et al, 1988
United Kingdom	1940–71 (1973?)	7000–8000	Kinlen et al, 1974
United States	1943–71	2–6 million	Goldberg and Falcone, 1999

Later studies, including follow-up of a large cohort of DES-exposed women (DESAD cohort, for DES-adenosis) showed that these 'DES daughters' exhibited a wide range of reproductive tract abnormalities. These included epithelial changes (such as vaginal adenosis) as well as structural changes such as cervical stenosis (narrowing of the cervical opening) and uterine malformations. Unlike vaginal clear-cell adenocarcinoma, which was extremely rare among DES-exposed women, these abnormalities were common, particularly in women whose mothers had been prescribed DES in early pregnancy. These changes, at least some of which were found to be prevalent even before birth (Johnson et al, 1979), resulted in serious reproductive consequences for those affected. The risk of all adverse pregnancy outcomes, including ectopic pregnancy (embryo attachment outside the uterus), spontaneous abortion and premature delivery, were significantly increased (Swan, 1992). While studies on 'DES sons' have been much more limited, several have demonstrated increased rates of genital abnormalities in these men (Goldberg and Falcone, 1999).

DES ineffective for prevention of miscarriage

After the first claims of the effectiveness of DES for the prevention of miscarriage, several studies were carried out to assess its efficacy, with mixed results. As these studies became more rigorous, the support for the use of DES declined. Finally, in the early 1950s, two randomised, placebo-controlled trials were conducted. The larger of these trials, conducted by Dieckmann et al (1953), reported no statistically significant differences in adverse pregnancy outcomes when DES was compared to a placebo. The authors concluded (as did the authors of the second, smaller trial) that DES was ineffective in the prevention of miscarriage and complications in late pregnancy. In spite of this, the drug continued to be prescribed even to women without previous pregnancy problems. An advertisement for one of the DES congeners (DesPlex) read, 'Recommended for routine prophylaxis in all pregnancies' (see Figure 8.2).A reanalysis of Dieckmann's data was published in 1978, after the long-term carcinogenic and teratogenic effects of DES were known (Brackbill and Berendes, 1978). The authors reanalysed Dieckmann's published data and found that DES actually increased the risk of the endpoints it was sold to prevent. The methods used in the reanalysis were not new, and had been available in 1953. As the authors noted, had the data been properly analysed in 1953, nearly 20 years of unnecessary exposure to DES might have been avoided. The fact that this drug was prescribed for two decades after its lack of efficacy was clearly demonstrated illustrates a massive failure of the system.

In fact, it was not the lack of efficacy that triggered the end of DES marketing for use in pregnancy, but a fortuitous accident. If the seven cases originally detected by Herbst and colleagues had been diagnosed in several different medical centres, rather than at Massachusetts General Hospital (where DES use had been high because the Smiths had conducted their early experiments on DES there), the dangers of DES might well have gone unrecognised. The cancer that DES caused in young women (vaginal clear-cell adenocarcinoma) is extremely rare. It is estimated to have occurred in less than one in every 1000 exposed daughters (Melnick et al, 1987). In fact, the registry established by Herbst in 1972 to actively register all cases of adenocarcinoma of the genital tract in young women has identified fewer than 800 cases worldwide. Thus, this cancer and its link to DES could well have gone undetected. Had this occurred, it is unlikely that DES-associated genital tract changes, which can only be identified by a physician conducting a special DES examination, and the multiple reproductive consequences of DES exposure, would ever have been identified.

Assessing the extent of the damage

The young age of the women affected made the need for early detection of vaginal clear-cell adenocarcinoma critical. It was of crucial importance to identify the exposed population so that screening and early detection could help prevent fatal consequences. To assemble data on this rare cancer, Herbst and co-workers established the Registry of Clear-Cell Adenocarcinoma of the Genital Tract in Young Females in 1972 (Herbst et al, 1972). Because it became evident, from several studies in which DES cohorts had been screened, that DES also had caused extensive non-cancerous DES changes of the female genital tract, in 1976 the National Cancer Institute established a cohort of over 3000 DES-exposed women and close to 1000 unexposed controls for long-term follow-up. This DESAD has proved invaluable for identifying the range of adverse consequences of DES exposure. Unfortunately, no comparable cohort of 'DES sons' has ever been established.

The exact number of individuals exposed to DES *in utero* is unknown, but estimates range from 2–10 million (see Table 8.1). A study funded by the European Commission and published in 1991 (Direcks et al, 1991) attempted to estimate the prevalence of DES-affected women in Europe. Eighteen countries were surveyed by means of questionnaires. This study found that use was greatest in the UK, France and The Netherlands, followed by Belgium, Ireland, Portugal and Spain. The survey concluded that DES had been prescribed during pregnancy, to a greater or lesser extent, in all countries surveyed except Sweden and Hungary.

The story of DES is far from over. Many of the youngest women exposed *in utero* are not yet 30. The known consequences of its use will continue to appear as this cohort ages. In addition, the cohort must be followed to identify unknown consequences, including a possibly increased cancer risk with age. The use of experimental animal models may help address some of these concerns about the future since the mouse appears to be a good model in which to study the effects of developmental exposure to DES (McLachlan, 1993). Such studies on ageing mice may be useful in predicting DES-effects as the exposed human population ages, as will continued follow-up of exposed cohorts.

What will happen to subsequent generations of the DES-exposed women? There is considerable interest in monitoring the grandchildren of DES-treated women. Studies in mice have shown an increased susceptibility to tumour formation in the third generation (Newbold et al, 1998), suggesting the DES grandchildren may also be at increased cancer risk (Miller, 1999). This is a question that will take many years to resolve.

Lessons from the DES story

It is worthwhile asking how this tragic event might have been prevented and what lessons can be learned from it. First, the DES story demonstrates that long-term and hidden effects of hormonal exposure (as was learned from the thalidomide story and other chemical exposures) are possible, and that such consequences may be devastating. Therefore, extreme caution should be taken before exposing pregnant women to substances that may alter the endocrine system, especially during foetal development. The DES episode also demonstrated that the absence of visible and immediate teratogenic effects cannot be taken as proof of the absence of reproductive toxicity. DES represents not only the first transplacental human carcinogen, but also the clearest example of human endocrine disruption. Although the doses of DES administered to pregnant women were far higher than usual environmental levels of synthetic chemicals, DES remains a clear warning of the consequences of perturbing the endocrine system through synthetic chemicals.

What precautionary action might have prevented the use of DES by pregnant women? First, no long-term toxicity tests were ever carried out. DES is a synthetic oestrogen and the carcinogenicity potential of oestrogens was already known even during the initial experimental use of DES (Cook and Dodds, 1933). Adverse effects of DES on animals had been published (Shimkin and Grady, 1941; Gardner, 1959; Dunn and Green, 1963), but they were largely disregarded. It was also known at the time that chemicals could cross the placental 'barrier'. There were early indications of adverse effects of exposure to oestrogens during development (Greene et al, 1939) and Karnaky in his early experimentation with DES noted darkened areolae (the area around the nipple) and linea alba (the line running from the pubis to the navel) in exposed newborns, indicating the oestrogenic action of DES on the female offspring (Karnaky, 1945). This evidence remained largely ignored, although some modest attempts to pinpoint the risks can be found in the literature. For example, in 1948, Bernard Laplan, a physician who believed in the efficacy of DES, expressed reservations about possible long-term effects: 'The possibility of some latent effects on the reproductive and endocrine system of the infant resulting from the high dosage oestrogen therapy must be borne in mind as indicated by the work of Greene, Burrill, and Ivy in experimental animals. Furthermore, we would avoid this therapy in any patient with a family history of malignant disease.' (Laplan, 1948)

Second, it might have been recognised in premarket testing that DES was never effective for the prevention of miscarriage. The methods used in the clinical trials conducted in 1951–52 that demonstrated this had been available before 1947 when DES was put on the market for use in pregnancy without adequate proof of efficacy. A properly conducted and analysed clinical trial might have avoided the entire episode.

The fact that DES was not patented, and very inexpensive to produce, made it extremely profitable. This, plus the absence of obvious acute toxic effects, undoubtedly contributed to the rapidity with which its use spread worldwide. The widespread use of DES was undoubtedly furthered by the faith in the advances of science and the belief in man-made solutions to nature's problems that were prevalent during the post-Second World War era. Undoubtedly those prescribing DES believed it was safe and effective, and both 'modern and scientific'. In The Netherlands, for example, the use of DES was particularly prominent, aided in part by its endorsement by the Queen's gynaecologist (Brahams, 1988). Consequently, there was strong pressure on physicians to prescribe DES. In 1952, Robinson and Shettles found DES ineffective when compared to untreated cases and therefore discouraged its use. They discussed in their article the 'peer pressure' that doctors were subjected to: 'The synthetic oestrogen, diethylstilbestrol, has more recently become a popular form of therapy in threatened abortion. The public has been so frequently told of the virtue of this drug through articles appearing in lay journals that it now requires a courageous physician to refuse this medication. The mass of pharmaceutical literature, extolling the wonders of this drug, has also rendered most practitioners amenable to his patient's demands. This situation, together with the understandable desire to do something positive toward rescuing a teetering pregnancy, has resulted in the widespread use of DES in threatened abortion.' (Robinson and Shettles, 1952)

The role of another important stakeholder in the wide use of DES, the pharmaceutical industry, should be examined. Pharmaceutical retailers and advertising promoted the effectiveness and safety of DES to doctors and consumers. The pharmaceutical industry ignored the lack of efficacy of their

Source: Des Plex, anonymous

Figure 8.2 *Advertisement for DES*

product and failed to assess its adverse health effects. In fact, some manufacturers promoted it as a panacea for use in all pregnancies (see Figure 8.2).

The eagerness of the pharmaceutical companies to sell this profitable product was compounded by the failure of medical and regulatory agencies to react rapidly to the emerging evidence. While the FDA announced that DES was contraindicated for use in pregnancy only months after Herbst's publication in 1971 (US Department of Health, Education and Welfare, 1971), in Europe the delay to withdrawal was as long as 12 years. It was not until 1974 that the Dutch Ministry of Health advised that DES should not be given to pregnant women (Palmlund et al, 1993); in France, it was not until 1977 that national authorities included the contraindication for pregnancy in the labelling of the drug (Epelboin and Bulwa, 1993). In some countries, such as Spain, there are reports of use as late as 1983 (Direcks et al, 1991). In addition, underdeveloped countries remained an open market for DES for many years. As recently as 1985, DES products were used in maternity care in Brazil, Costa Rica, Kenya, Mexico, Peru, Rwanda and Zaire. In the early 1990s, it was still prescribed during pregnancy in Mexico, Uganda and Poland (Palmlund, 1996).

DES continued to be used for a variety of therapeutic uses for years after the evidence of its adverse effects had been widely publicised. This included use as a post-coital contraceptive. Since DES is less than 100% effective in terminating pregnancy, the use of a chemical potentially carcinogenic to the foetus was not permissible. In 1973, the FDA discouraged the use of DES as a contraceptive, restricting it to emergency situations such as rape or incest (Mills, 1974).

The use of DES as a growth promoter (see Chapter 14 on 'Hormones as growth promoters') began in the 1950s and ended after a heated battle in 1979. Gradually use for other therapeutic purposes decreased and in the spring of 1997 Eli Lilly, the last, and predominant, manufacturer of DES in the US ceased production (Pat Cody, pers comm.).

There has been significant progress in most key areas of drug assessment since 1970, in part spurred by the consequences of DES and thalidomide. In fact, the entire field of teratology was established in response to these episodes. Toxicity testing is much more comprehensive and thorough and sound evidence of efficacy is now required before a drug is marketed. Regulatory authorities are also much more alert to reporting of adverse drug reactions and more inclined to take action than they were in the 1960s and 1970s. Nonetheless several areas of concern remain:

- drugs that were marketed prior to current more stringent regulations may not have been adequately evaluated with respect to efficacy or toxicity;
- monitoring and surveillance in patients taking drugs is neither consistent nor comprehensive. Moreover, it is difficult to demonstrate an association between a drug and a health outcome that is delayed and/or prevalent;
- formalised risk/benefit analyses of new drugs (as well as other chemicals) are not widely utilised; and
- drug surveillance (and evaluation of human health risks from other chemicals) should not be limited to detection of gross malformations and cancers; such limited surveillance would likely have missed most of the adverse effects of DES.

It is clear, in hindsight, that the concerns expressed by scientists regarding the marketing of a drug with known carcinogenic potential should have been heeded. Failure to do so reflects the prevalent attitudes towards health risks, and an absence of precautionary thinking. The lack of a timely response by manufacturers and regulators after DES was demonstrated to be a transplacental human carcinogen in 1971 cannot be excused so easily. Even after the tragic consequences of DES use in pregnancy were confirmed, economic interests predominated, resulting in a 'wait and see' approach.

Those considering the wisdom of precautionary action today would do well to consider the history of DES. This drug was a known animal carcinogen, a suspect human carcinogen and a drug that had been shown to produce observable changes in the offspring of women exposed in pregnancy. Even if marketing in 1947 could have been justified on the basis of insufficient evidence of harm, after DES was proven to be ineffective for use in pregnancy in 1953 a review of its risks and benefits should have resulted in immediate contraindication of this use. At that point there was no longer any justification for subjecting consumers to any carcinogenic risk in the absence of any benefit. Had DES been withdrawn for use in pregnancy at that time, the unnecessary and tragic exposure of millions of mothers, sons and daughters could have been avoided.

Table 8.2 *DES: early warnings and actions*

1938	DES synthesised
1938	First report of increased cancer incidence in animals after DES administration
1939	First report of DES administered to patients
1942	Approval of DES by the American Council of Pharmacy and Chemistry
1942	First report of DES used for prevention of abortion
1947	US Food and Drug Administration (FDA) approves DES for the treatment of threatened or habitual abortion
1948	Use of DES increases following publication of large-scale study in the US
1953	First large placebo-controlled randomised trial shows DES ineffective in the prevention of miscarriage
1970	Published report of seven cases of vaginal clear-cell adenocarcinoma in young women
April 1971	Prenatal DES exposure is linked to vaginal clear-cell adenocarcinoma
November 1971	FDA withdraws approval of DES for use by pregnant women
1972	Registry of Clear-Cell Adenocarcinoma of the Genital Tract in Young Females is established
1978	Reanalysis of 1953 Dieckmann data shows that DES actually increased the risk of miscarriage and other adverse pregnancy outcomes
1985	Last reported use of DES by pregnant women world-wide

Source: EEA

Antimicrobials as growth promoters: resistance to common sense

Lars-Erik Edqvist and Knud Børge Pedersen

Introduction

An antibiotic is defined as a substance produced by microorganisms that inhibits or kills other microorganisms. Synthetic antimicrobial substances are referred to as chemotherapeuticals. The word 'antimicrobial' (as a noun) is often used to encompass any substance of natural, semi-synthetic or synthetic origin that kills or inhibits the growth of a microorganism.

The antimicrobial era began in 1910 with the introduction of Salvarsan into the therapy of syphilis and expanded in the 1930s when the first chemotherapeuticals (sulphonamides) made their way into clinical use in human medicine. The antibiotic, penicillin, was discovered by Alexander Fleming (Fleming, 1929) but was not introduced for therapy until 1941. Shortly after its introduction for use in humans, penicillin was used in animals for the treatment of various bacterial diseases.

Antimicrobials are probably the single most important discovery in the history of medicine. They were considered miracle drugs. Over the years they have saved millions of lives by killing bacteria that cause some of the worst infectious diseases in man and animals.

Antimicrobials for growth promotion

The growth promoting properties of antimicrobial agents in farm animals were discovered in the late 1940s. Trials where fermentation waste from tetracycline production was fed to chickens as a source of vitamin B12 revealed that the chickens fed the waste grew more rapidly than did the controls. It was soon found that this effect was not due to the vitamin content of the feed but to residual tetracycline (Stokstad and Jukes, 1949). The practice of feeding subtherapeutic doses of antimicrobials over long periods of time was readily adopted and soon became an integrated part of the production systems developed in industrialised animal husbandry. Apart from increased growth rate and/or increased feed conversion, examples of other observed effects of antimicrobials at low doses are improved egg production in laying hens, increased litter size in sows and increased milk yield in dairy cows.

Antimicrobial growth promoters are freely accessible and sold over the counter, while antimicrobial drugs for therapy in most cases are available on prescription only. The use of antimicrobial growth promoters over four decades has undoubtedly contributed to the development of current animal production systems. Use of antimicrobial growth promoters apparently provides some protection against certain diseases promoted by intensification and allows, for example, unphysiological early weaning and high stocking rates, raising questions on animal ethics and animal welfare.

Development of resistance

Most antimicrobials are produced by microorganisms and existed long before they were used as medicinal drugs. Microorganisms produce antimicrobial substances to kill other microorganisms in order to create a foundation for their own survival and propagation. The bacteria exposed to antimicrobials develop strategies for survival; development of resistance is one such strategy. This follows the classical concept of survival of the fittest and it is thus not surprising that antimicrobial resistance has probably existed for as long as have bacteria.

Concern about penicillin resistance more or less accompanied its introduction as a medical drug in the early 1940s. The discoverer of penicillin, Alexander Fleming, in a newspaper interview by the *New York Times* (1945), warned that misuse of penicillin could have the result that 'microbes are educated to resist penicillin'. Increasing resistance was noted in several important bacteria known to cause infectious disease. By the early 1950s the problem of antimicrobial resistance was well acknowledged in the medical, veterinary and pharmaceutical press.

Originally it was thought that acquired resistance in a bacterium only occurred through mutation in existing genes, which would mean that the resistance trait would be confined to the mutant clone and spread of resistance confined to that clone (vertical transmission). In the 1960s it was shown that resistance, in addition to mutation, could also be developed through the uptake of existing genes. In this case, the resistance trait through mobile genetic elements can also spread to other bacterial clones, to other bacterial species and even to other genera (horizontal transmission) (for a review see, for example, Amabile-Cuevas and Chicurel, 1992).

The first early warning

The Swann Committee

In the mid-1960s growing concern over food-borne infections with multi-drug-resistant salmonella in the UK led the government to establish an independent advisory committee in 1968. The task of the committee, chaired by Professor Michael Swann, was to examine the issue of transferable antimicrobial resistance and the consequences for human and animal health arising from the use of antimicrobials for growth promotion and in veterinary medicine. The Swann Committee (Swann, 1969) judged the data available 'a sufficiently sound basis for action' and the principal recommendations on antimicrobial growth promoters were that: 'permission to supply and use an antibiotic without prescription for adding to animal feed should be restricted to the antibiotics which:

- are of economic value in livestock production under United Kingdom farming conditions;
- have little or no application as therapeutic agents in man or animals;
- will not impair the efficacy of a prescribed therapeutic antibiotic or antibiotics through the development of resistant strains of organisms.'

Recommendations on specific drugs were also included, for example: 'tylosin should not be available without prescription for use as a 'feed' antibiotic.'

Another recommendation was the establishment of a single permanent committee which 'should have overall responsibility for the whole field of use of antibiotics and related substances whether in man, animals, food preservation, or for other purposes'.

Subsequent action or inaction

Implementation and dilution of the Swann Report

The recommendations in the Swann Report were based on less than full scientific certainty and created much debate and cries for more research, and faced strong opposition from the pharmaceutical industry and farming community in the UK. But most of the main recommendations were adopted in the UK and later on in the EU.

However, subsequent governments in the UK gradually diluted the recommendations of the Swann Report. The recommendation to establish an overarching, strong and permanent committee responsible for the whole field of antimicrobial usage was not fully implemented. For example, no epidemiological studies to monitor antimicrobial resistance development were set up.

Against the Swann recommendations, the EU accepted the macrolides tylosin and spiramycin as growth promoters in 1975. This has probably been one of the major reasons for the widespread macrolide resistance in, for example, enterococci and campylobacter from pigs. Use of the antimicrobial growth promoter avoparcin was extended to other species, such as adult cattle, against the Swann recommendations and its use increased from the mid-1970s at about the same time that its medical equivalent, vancomycin, started to come into hospital use.

One of the scientific arguments put forward to support this use of antimicrobials for growth promotion was that the low dose presents a special case in selecting for resistance. For example, Walton (1988) stated: 'In practical terms the use of a sub-lethal or a sub-inhibitory antibiotic concentration is therefore unable to select resistant strains from a bacterial population, and in this respect the Swann Report's conclusion and recommendations were in error.' However, the recent bans on avoparcin, virginiamycin and tylosin followed the publication of studies demonstrating that this view (Walton's amongst others) was wrong.

Worldwide, there are great differences in the regulatory control of antimicrobials for therapy, prophylaxis and growth promoting purposes. In some countries, such as the US, low doses of tetracycline and penicillin are still used as feed additives for prophylaxis and growth promotion without veterinary prescription, while therapeutic antimicrobials are often prescription-only medicines.

The Swedish ban

Similar to the situation in other countries, some Swedish scientists viewed the practice of routine addition of antimicrobials to animal feeds with scepticism. Following the recommendations of the Swann Committee in the UK, a broader debate was initiated, which eventually led to a reassessment of the use of antimicrobials as feed additives (LBS, 1977).

A working group of the Board of Agriculture concluded, among other things, that: 'the use of antibiotic feed additives entails a risk of increased resistance in bacteria but as the substances in use are mainly active against gram-positive bacteria from which resistance is not transferred, the impact of such development is negligible.' On the other hand, a negative attitude to all kinds of additives among consumers was noted by the group. The benefits, in terms of increased production and prevention of certain diseases, were also acknowledged (LBS, 1977). Legislative changes, especially in the requirements for approval, were proposed in order to mitigate possible risks.

At the same time, farmers were growing increasingly sceptical towards feed antimicrobials. They were concerned that the continued use of antimicrobials might harm consumer confidence. The Federation of Swedish Farmers (LRF) made a policy statement, declaring that Swedish agriculture aimed towards a more restricted and controlled use of antibiotics. In a letter to the Ministry of Agriculture in 1984, the LRF requested a ban on the use of antibacterials as feed additives.

In response to the above, the Ministry of Agriculture drafted a new Feedingstuffs Act (Government Bill 1984/85). Among other things, the draft proposed that the use of antimicrobials in feed should be restricted to treatment, prevention or cure of diseases, meaning that their use for growth promotion should not be allowed. The basis cited for this amendment was the risk of increased resistance, especially the risk of cross-resistance to other substances and the risk of increased susceptibility of animals to salmonella and other enteric pathogens. The government also stressed that 'there is uncertainty on the long-term effects of the continuous use of feed containing chemotherapeutics' (Government Bill 1984/85).

The Feedingstuffs Act was passed by parliament in November 1985 and came into force in January 1986. Since then antimicrobials, whether in feed or administered otherwise, have only been allowed for therapy and on veterinary prescription, and as a result the total consumption of antimicrobials was greatly reduced from around 50 tonnes in 1985 to around 20 tonnes in 1996 (SOU, 1997).

During the accession negotiations with the EU, Sweden was granted a temporary derogation from European legislation concerning the use of antibiotics as growth promoting feed additives. In support of the Swedish view the Ministry of Agriculture appointed a commission to collect and review scientific data on antibiotic growth promoters. In 1997 the commission presented its report and among other points noted that 'antimicrobial feed additives can at levels permitted in feeding stuffs, be used for treatment or prevention of animal disease, which is in violation of Council Directive 70/524/EEC' (SOU, 1997). According to this directive, as amended in 96/55/EEC, Article 3a, authorisation of an additive shall be given only if at the level permitted, treatment or prevention of animal disease being excluded.

The commission concluded that 'the risk for increased resistance associated with the general use of antibiotic growth promoters is far from negligible and the potential consequences are serious for both animal and human health' (SOU, 1997).

The magnitude of the risk is difficult to fully establish because of the complexity of the problem and the lack of pertinent data. The report outlined the research required to be undertaken in a 17-step causal chain, assessed the minimum time required to undertake the research to be five to ten years, and also that the research had to be undertaken for each resistance gene and for each antimicrobial substance, with subsequent updates of the risk assessment.

The report went on to ask who would bear the costs of waiting to do further research, or of taking action then to restrict antimicrobials – the risk-maker or the risk-taker? The commission finally urged: 'As the risks involved are of uncertain magnitude, the decisions on risk management are particularly difficult. The risk can obviously not be excluded with certainty, nor can it be determined as acceptable. Scientists may declare that the information is inadequate for decision making, but for the policymakers, failure to take action is not a neutral position but represents a positive decision to do nothing. In a climate of uncertainty it is preferable to show caution.' (SOU, 1997)

The banning of avoparcin

In March 1995 , when the first information on the occurrence of avoparcin- and vancomycin-resistant enterococci in pigs and poultry had become available (Klare et al, 1995; Bates et al, 1994; Aarestrup, 1995), the Danish farmers' organisations agreed with the feeding industry that there would be a voluntary cessation in the use of avoparcin in animal feed to reduce the spread of antimicrobial resistance. This was followed by a governmental ban implemented on 20 May 1995 and reported to the European Commission as requested by the safeguard clause of Council Directive 70/524/EEC. According to this a Member State can, as a result of new information, temporarily suspend the use of an approved feed additive if its use constitutes a danger to animal or human health.

The scientific background for the Danish ban was the demonstration:

- of cross-resistance between avoparcin and vancomycin;
- that the resistance is transferable;
- that the use of avoparcin as a growth promoter selects for vancomycin-resistant enterococci and that vancomycin-resistant enterococci can be transferred to humans via the food chain (DVL, 1995).

In Norway the use of avoparcin was suspended in June 1995, and in Germany the government issued a ban on avoparcin in January 1996.

In May 1996 the EU Scientific Committee on Animal Nutrition (SCAN) concluded that further evidence was required to establish a risk to human health, animal health or the environment caused by avoparcin. However, the committee accepted that serious questions concerning the safety of avoparcin had been raised and stated that the feed-additive use of avoparcin should be reconsidered at once if it were shown that transfer of resistance was possible from animal to human. The European Commission, however, proposed that in the climate of uncertainty and to avoid taking any risk, a temporary ban should be placed on the use of avoparcin as a feed additive in all EU Member States. This was agreed by a qualified majority vote of the Standing Committee on Feedingstuffs in December and the ban came into force on 1 April 1997.

Danish ban of virginiamycin

On 16 January 1998, the Danish government banned all use of virginiamycin as a growth promoter in Denmark, due to a risk of selection of streptogramin-resistant enterococci in pigs and poultry (Aarestrup et al, 1998). The step was taken to protect human health and to preserve the lifespan of Synercid, which was then undergoing hospital trials but which has now been licensed for the treatment of certain multi-drug-resistant infections in humans.

EU bans four antimicrobial growth promoters

On 14 December 1998, the agriculture ministers of the EU Member States voted in favour of a proposal to ban the use of four antimicrobial growth promoters from July 1999: virginiamycin, bacitracin zinc, tylosin phosphate and spiramycin. The ban was submitted by the European Commission as 'a precautionary measure to minimise the risk of development of resistant bacteria and to preserve the efficacy of certain antibiotics used in human medicine'. The pharmaceutical industry protested against the decision and called for further scientific facts about the risks involved in the use of antimicrobial growth promoters. Afterwards, the decision was challenged before the European Court of Justice by the manufacturer of virginiamycin, who called for an annulment of the entire decision. Final ruling in the case is not expected before the end of the year 2001.

Avilamycin

The latest example of an antimicrobial growth promoter from the EU list of approved products showing cross-resistance with a potential human drug (everninomycin) is avilamycin (Aarestrup, 1998). However, the manufacturers of everninomycin have recently withdrawn it from hospital trials worldwide.

Scientific reports and recommendations

In 1997 the World Health Organization (WHO) organised a scientific meeting which addressed the medical impact of the use of antimicrobials in food animals. The meeting concluded that 'the magnitude of the medical and public health impact of antimicrobial use in food animal production is not known' (WHO, 1997). The recommendations from the meeting stated: 'Increased concerns regarding risks to public health resulting from the use of antimicrobial growth promoters indicate that it is essential to have a systematic approach towards replacing growth promoting antimicrobials with safer non-antimicrobial alternatives.'

The Invitational EU Conference on the Microbial Threat held in Copenhagen, Denmark, in 1998, reached a similar conclusion and stated: 'Most of those at the conference considered the use of antimicrobials for growth promotion was not justified and that it was essential to have a systematic approach towards replacing growth promoting antimicrobials with safer non-antimicrobial alternatives including better farming practice.' (The Copenhagen Recommendations, 1998)

The conference was organised by the chief medical officers of the EU Member States and included both medical and veterinary authorities and researchers, representatives of farmers' organisations, the pharmaceutical industry and the animal feed industry.

Because of concern over the implications for human and animal health of the rapidly increasing rate of development of antimicrobial resistance, the European Commission (DG XXIV, now renamed the Health and Consumer Protection Directorate-General) asked the Scientific Steering Committee (SSC) to evaluate the current position regarding the prevalence and development of antimicrobial resistance, and to examine its implications for human and animal health, particularly with regard to the development and management of infections. In 1999 the SSC concluded in its report that 'action needs to be taken promptly to reduce the overall use of antimicrobials in a balanced way in all areas: human medicine, veterinary medicine, animal production and plant protection' (SSC, 1999). In relation to antibiotics for animal growth the SSC recommends that 'the use of agents from classes which are or may be used in human or veterinary medicine should be phased out as soon as possible and ultimately abolished'.

In the newly issued 'Global Principles for the Containment of Antimicrobial Resistance due to Antimicrobial Use in Animals Intended for Food', WHO recommends that the use of antimicrobial growth promoters that belong to classes of antimicrobial agents used (or submitted for approval) in humans should be terminated or rapidly phased out in the absence of risk-based evaluations (WHO, 2000).

Advantages and disadvantages of the use of growth promoters

Over the entire period during which antimicrobial agents have been used as growth promoters there has been great emphasis on the advantages of these feed additives as a means to improve farm animal production and productivity. Much less attention has been directed towards possible side-effects, and the number of independent scientific studies is relatively small compared to studies and congress contributions supported by the pharmaceutical industry.

Not until recently, when the occurrence of vancomycin-resistant enterococci in animals was found to be associated with the use of avoparcin as an additive to animal feed and the possible consequences for human health were made clear, did the number of independent research studies dealing with these aspects increase significantly.

In the last few years substantial scientific evidence has shown that the use of antimicrobial growth promoters in food animals contributes to the problems of antimicrobial resistance in humans. This has most convincingly been shown for vancomycin-resistant enterococci.

Although the widespread use of antimicrobials in human medicine undoubtedly is of more importance for the emerging antimicrobial resistance problems in humans, this cannot justify ignorance of potential human health risks related to the use of antimicrobials in food animals. The continuous use of antimicrobials in feed is one of the major sources of overuse and misuse of antimicrobials in animal farming.

This ongoing debate has made it clear that the usage of antimicrobial agents as feed additives is a complex issue, with implications not only for human and animal health but also for animal welfare, food safety, environmental aspects and for the development of production systems, feeding practices and management. Some of the positive and negative effects of antimicrobial growth promoters are listed in Table 9.1.

Conclusions and lessons for the future

The original early warning in the Swann Report on the risk of antimicrobial resistance spreading amongst animals, and from animals to humans, was based on a low level of scientific proof, but on a competent microbiological assessment that foresaw possible adverse consequences of the continuous use of therapeutic antimicrobial agents in animal feed. The recommendations were clearly precautionary, although the word 'precaution' was not actually used in the Swann Report.

Subsequent scientific research, developed primarily during the 1990s, has shown that transferable resistance is not restricted to certain bacteria (gram-

Table 9.1 *Positive and negative effects of antimicrobial growth promoters on some broad issues of animal production*

Broad issue	Positive effect	Negative effect
Animal health	Certain diseases – primarily enteric – may be controlled to some extent	Limits treatment possibilities due to development of antimicrobial resistance; masks sub-clinical disease and infection; limits incentives for hygienic improvements
Human health	None	Transfer of resistance to humans with increased societal costs for health care; shortens economic life of medical antimicrobials; occupational hazards through exposure to aerosol and dust contaminated with antimicrobials
Animal welfare	Alleviates and dampens signs of disease	Camouflages stress associated with sub-clinical disease; allows higher stocking rates
Environment	Better utilisation of animal feed; less manure	Increases the environmental pool of antibiotic resistance genes; antibiotic residues
Animal husbandry	Increased production and improved productivity	Stimulates increased intensification of animal production
Production system	Lower labour demand due to possibility of more intense production methods	Hampers the development of animal-friendly production systems
Animal feed	None	Camouflages bad feed quality; hampers improvements in feed formulation and development of alternatives

Source: L-E Edqvist and K B Pedersen

negative), but is much more widespread within the microbiological universe, and that genes can easily move not only between closely related bacterial species, but also even between genera. These results confirm that the Swann Report was both accurate in its evaluation of data at the time and far-sighted in its assessment of future trends.

The justification for the later dilution of its conclusions and compromises on its recommendations was based mainly on narrow considerations of what was precisely known rather than on taking account of what was not known, of the ignorance within the field and the possible consequences for widespread antimicrobial resistance. In other words science that embraces complexities, uncertainties and unknowns with more humility and less hubris is needed.

Table 9.2 *Antimicrobials: early warnings and actions*

1945	Alexander Fleming warns against misuse of penicillin as 'microbes are educated to resist'
1950s	Antibiotic resistance widely recognised – vertical transmission
1960s	Horizontal transmission recognised
1969	Swann Committee recommends severe restrictions on antimicrobials in animal feed
1970s	Most Swann recommendations initially implemented in the UK and EU
1975	Swann recommendations are relaxed: tolysin and spiramycin still permitted as growth promoters as human equivalents; vancomycin comes into use
1977	Swedish Agriculture Board considers potential risk of antibiotic resistance, but concludes it is negligible
1984	Swedish farmers ask for government ban on antimicrobials in animal feed because of health and consumer concerns
1985	Swedish ban on grounds of antibiotic resistance in animals and 'uncertain' long-term effects
1997	Swedish report concludes that risk of antibiotic resistance in humans is 'far from negligible'
1997	WHO scientific meeting concludes that it is 'essential to replace growth promoting antimicrobials'
1998	EU bans four antimicrobials in animal feed as 'precautionary' measure.
1999	EU Scientific Steering Committee recommends phase-out of antimicrobials that may be used in human/animal therapy
1999	Pharmaceutical industry opposes EU bans and takes EU to the European Court; judgement expected end 2001
2000	WHO recommends ban on antimicrobials as growth promoters if used in human therapy and in absence of risk-based evaluation.

Source: EEA

Furthermore, scientific committees which are responsible for the evaluation of confidential information from industry, should consist of a broad panel of independent and up-to-date experts, with relevant expertise and experience from all of the disciplines that are implicated in a broad assessment of the risks, benefits and technological options involved. In this case, expertise from human medicine would have been particularly valuable for every risk assessment.

The experience from this case suggests that assessments of risk need to be much wider, taking into account both positive and negative impacts, the long-term microbiological and ecological effects on human and animal health and the environment, and alternative options, such as better animal husbandry (see Table 9.1).

As the risks involved are of uncertain magnitude, the decisions on risk management are particularly difficult. The risk can obviously not be excluded with certainty, nor can it be determined as acceptable. In a climate of uncertainty it is preferable to show caution. In this situation decision-making needs to involve precaution, particularly when it is unacceptable, inhuman and unethical to wait for ultimate proof, when human fatalities could be involved.

Another clear lesson from this case study is that stakeholders other than regulatory bodies, such as the farmers and their organisations, can take voluntary steps in advance of legislation to stop the use of products which cause concern and loss of confidence amongst consumers. In this case they, as well as the Swann Committee, have been vindicated by history. Common sense and far-sighted use of good scientific evidence which can predict serious impacts should not be ignored whilst waiting for ultimate proof.

Sulphur dioxide: from protection of human lungs to remote lake restoration

Arne Semb

In December 1952 a dense smog – a mixture of fog and coal smoke – descended on London. Records from London's hospitals showed that more than 2000 people died from the exposure to air pollutants during one week, and there was strong pressure that this should never happen again. Yet the 1952 London smog incident was not unique (Brimblecombe, 1987; Ashby, 1981). Worse smog incidents had occurred previously in London, and the air quality there, as well as in other cities in the UK was actually improving, not deteriorating. What was new was the political and social set-up after the war, which meant that the public was no longer willing to accept the situation. The incident was also well documented, both with respect to health effects and air quality. The measurements made by the scientists at St Bartholomew's Hospital showed that the concentrations of smoke particles and sulphur dioxide reached several milligrams per cubic metre. A parliamentary commission prepared a special report named after its Chairman, Sir Hugh Beaver.

The remedies that the Beaver Report could propose were modest. London was entirely dependent on coal for heating and energy purposes, and coal contains sulphur which can only partly be removed prior to use. So, the subsequent Clean Air Act instead considered the smoke component of the air pollution, allowing the local councils to establish 'smoke-free areas', in which the infamous coal fireplaces were to be replaced with more efficient combustion units, electricity and 'smokeless fuel'. Emission sources other than domestic fireplaces were to be 'as far as possible' smokeless. A revision of the Alkali Act in 1958 provided the Alkali Inspectorate with more authority in relation to industrial pollution sources, but did not specify emission limits or standards. 'Best practicable means' was the governing principle. In practice this meant that the main method of reducing sulphur dioxide (SO_2) concentrations at ground levels was the use of tall chimneys, in proportion to the emitted amounts. These were obvious steps in the right direction, but slow, and a second smog incident that occurred in 1962 with about 800 additional deaths further demonstrated the need for action.

Oil from the Middle East became available in large quantities after 1950, and was to become the main source of energy in western Europe during the following two decades (Mylona, 1996). As refining was relatively primitive, a substantial fraction of the production was heavy or residual fuel oil, with a sulphur content of 2.5–3%. Gas oils with less than 1% sulphur were also marketed as fuel oil for use in small boilers and in the domestic market. Heavy fuel oil was used in the new electrical power generating plants in many countries in Europe, particularly in countries with no indigenous coal deposits, but also in the UK. It was also used in boilers for central heating in large building complexes, hospitals and other service buildings, and in industry. However, growing environmental awareness in the 1960s led to concern in cities across Europe about air quality, and restrictions with respect to the use of different qualities of fuel oil and their sulphur contents began to appear. In fact, some cities had experienced black smoke and SO_2 concentration levels comparable to those in London, but caused by the use of sulphur-containing fuel oil with improper combustion.

The OECD had set up an Environmental Section in Europe in the late 1960s and after 1971 representatives of the member countries would meet in an Air Management Sector Group to discuss common problems and experience. In turn, this group took up the problems of urban air pollution, acid rain and photochemical oxidant formation, and made useful contributions to their solution.

The question of air quality standards, or guidelines, was particularly useful in connection with the planning of new industries and licensing of combustion sources. There was a good deal of reluctance to accept fixed limits, which were mainly introduced to Europe under the influence of the example of the US Clean Air Act (United States of America, 1970). However, Professor Lawther of St Bartholomew's had already determined (WHO, 1972), on the basis of the deaths during the London smog, that health damage occurred whenever concentrations of SO2 and black smoke, respectively, rose above 500 and 250 micrograms per cubic metre (Mylona, 1996). Since concentrations of pollutants are extremely dependent on weather conditions, air quality standards have to be fixed at considerably lower average levels, in order to safeguard the public against harmful exposures. Countries have had different attitudes to the establishment of air quality standards, and particularly to their enforcement in relation to emission controls. Nevertheless, by collecting the available documentation about health effects, WHO has since 1979 recommended air quality guidelines that set a standard for the pollution abatement work in Europe (WHO, 1979 and 1987).

Dead fish, dying forests

Increasing energy consumption in Europe during the 1960s resulted in a large increase in emissions of SO_2. Much of the increased energy consumption was in the form of electricity, produced in large thermoelectric power plants, and the SO_2 was released from chimneys more than 100 metres tall. As a consequence of this, as well as from the increased chimney heights in industry and in cities, surface air quality was gradually improved in spite of the increased emissions. Optimistic representatives of the electricity generating industry were confident that the emissions could be diluted and dispersed to levels that were not harmful.

This was not so. While British and other European countries were striving to improve the urban air quality, energy consumption and total emissions of sulphur dioxide in Europe increased dramatically, as shown in Figure 10.1. In Sweden the soil scientist Hans Egnér had initiated measurements of air and precipitation chemistry across Europe (Egnér et al, 1955), supported by the meteorologist C G Rossby. Their primary interest was the supply of plant nutrients by precipitation, and the link with meteorology. However, in 1968 one of their colleagues examined the results and concluded that the precipitation was becoming more acidic as a result of increasing SO_2 emissions, and coupled this to observations of acidification of Swedish rivers. Svante Odén chose to present his results with sweeping statements of their implications, not only in a bulky report but also in a newspaper article (Odén, 1968 and 1967). Sweden chose also to give this as a case study at the 1972 UN environment conference in Stockholm, with evidence of the dispersion, deposition and effects of SO_2 and 'acid rain' (Sweden, 1971). As intended, the creative presentation of this information caught the interest of the international community. Was it really possible that releases of SO_2 in the UK could change the water quality in Scandinavia, causing fish deaths and reducing forest production? Clearly, more documentation was needed.

Plans for a more comprehensive study of the transport of air pollutants across national boundaries in Europe had been discussed in the OECD Air Management Sector Group since 1969. In 1972 a cooperative study was launched, with the participation of 11 member countries. Of the European OECD countries only Spain, Portugal and Italy decided not to participate, because they felt that the issue was not relevant to their situations. By arrangement within the Nordic countries, the Norwegian Institute for Air Research (NILU) was given the task of coordinating this long-range transport of air pollutants programme. The report was completed in 1977, establishing exports and imports within the countries of Europe and determining the relationship between emissions and deposition of sulphur compounds (OECD, 1977). It was now quite clear that acidification in Scandinavia could be quantitatively related to emissions in several European countries, and that these countries were responsible for the damage which occurred from acid rain. A very ambitious Norwegian research programme on Acid Precipitation: Effects on Forests and Fish (SNSF) had been started in 1972, and by 1976 an interim report

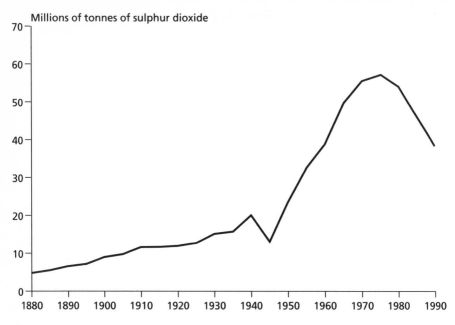

Source: Arne Semb, adapted from Mylona, 1996

Figure 10.1 *Annual emissions of sulphur dioxide in Europe, 1880–1990*

was prepared which showed widespread acidification of rivers and lakes, and strong documentation of the declining stocks of both trout and salmon in such areas (Braekke, 1976). The report was not released, however, as the project was presented to an international audience in June 1976 (Knabe, 1976; *Ambio*, 1976). The suspected effects on forests were, however, much more difficult to demonstrate. The SNSF project was finalized in 1980 (Overrein et al, 1980; Drabløs, 1980).

Although strong scientific evidence was now available, resistance to change was strong. An editorial in the UK-based scientific journal *Nature* (1977) claimed that acid rain was a million-dollar problem with a billion-dollar solution, referring to the value of the fish and the costs of installing and operating flue gas cleaning on electric power plants. The reply from Erik Lykke (Lykke, 1977) at the Norwegian Ministry of the Environment stated that this was obvious, but that the cost–benefit analysis was incomplete. Emitter countries such as the UK should also consider the damages caused by releases of SO_2 in their own countries, to health, materials, agriculture and to natural ecosystems. If all these damages were considered, the economic benefits of reducing the emissions would also be obvious. It was not a case of Europe versus Scandinavia, it was Europe versus itself.

A cost–benefit study carried out, again by the OECD (OECD, 1981), confirmed that the value of the lost fish populations was small in economic terms. The perceived costs in terms of timber production were also not particularly significant, but the damage caused to buildings and construction materials was shown to entail comparable costs to that of reducing emissions by flue gas cleaning and fuel desulphurisation.

In the event, the oil companies would also benefit from fuel desulphurisation, because of the higher profits from light and low-sulphur distillation products, compared to heavy fuel oil. The oil companies were well aware of this, and had already started restructuring the refinery industry to produce less heavy fuel oil, and more light and medium distillates, removing as much as 70% of the crude oil's sulphur content in the process. This move was also a result of the high oil prices following the 1973 oil crisis, which made western European countries aware of their reliance on the oil supply for electricity production. This resulted in the conversion of oil-fired power plants to coal and building of new coal-burning power plants, while France switched to the use of nuclear energy for electricity production.

The situation in central and eastern Europe was different. In the German Democratic Republic (GDR), Czechoslovakia and Poland, energy and industrial production had been increased mainly by the use of large amounts of low quality coals with high sulphur contents, as the old, high-quality coal seams were depleted. The results were dramatic as the SO_2 emissions in these countries increased by a factor of ten from 1960 to 1985, when these three countries alone emitted more SO_2 than all other countries in northwest Europe together.

To combat acid rain and SO_2 emissions without the participation of the Eastern bloc countries was clearly not possible. East–West political relationships were tense during the Cold War period, and the discussions in the Conference of Security and Cooperation in Europe in Helsinki in 1975 were difficult. In fact, the two factions could reach agreement on one issue only: cooperation on the issue of airborne pollutants. Countries from both sides agreed to establish cooperation under the Economic Commission for Europe (ECE), in Geneva, with participation from the World Meteorological Organization and the United Nations Environment Programme. A cooperative programme for monitoring and evaluation of long-range transmission of airborne pollutants in Europe (EMEP), was initiated in 1976, and was followed by the Convention on Long-range Transboundary Air Pollution (CLRTAP), in 1979. This convention expressed the signatories' intentions to investigate the problem, to exchange information about emissions as well as effects, and to reduce, as much as possible, emissions causing harmful effects. The convention also set up a number of task forces and cooperative programmes in addition to EMEP, which were to prepare assessments information for future protocol negotiations.

By this time, forest decline had become a hot issue in Europe. Following releases by German forest scientists at the University of Göttingen (Ulrich et al, 1980), a series of articles in the German popular journal *Der Spiegel* exposed the issue of 'neuartiger Waldschäden', or new forest damage. It appeared that forest damage was widespread across Germany, but mainly along the border with the GDR and Czechoslovakia. It was also most pronounced in freely exposed trees, in hilly areas and on ridges. The symptoms were quite general, and might be interpreted as general stress, although needle yellowing implied magnesium deficiency at some sites. Different schools of thought offered at least three different explanations, but none satisfied a stringent cause-effect relationship. Both soil acidification and direct action of air pollutants were held to be responsible, continuing the division of opinion dating back to when concerns first emerged in Germany in the 19th century. Meanwhile, reports of even more serious forest diebacks came from Bohemia and Poland. In the border areas between the GDR and Czechoslovakia, several square kilometres of dead spruce forest were present in the areas now identified as those with the highest concentrations and deposition of airborne sulphur compounds and acidity (Moldan et al, 1992).

By this stage, public opinion and the press had been alerted. Acid rain and fish-kills in remote lakes and rivers were identified in North America as well as in Europe. When forests and terrestrial ecosystems were so apparently endangered, the situation seemed obvious to the public, even if the scientists did not agree on the mechanisms.

In March 1983 the official Council of Environmental Advisers in Germany issued a report to the German Bundestag relating to forest damage (Council of Environmental Advisers, 1983). In their opinion, flue gas desulphurisation should already have been installed at coal-fired power plants where emissions exceeded 400 milligrams per cubic metre of SO_2. But the council was not convinced by the scientific explanation of the new forest damage, and cautioned that SO_2 emission reductions might not improve this particular situation. Action justified on this basis alone might jeopardise the credibility of the environmental policy if subsequently found to be incorrect. In its own words:

> *'As long as the preventive measures aim at reducing the emissions of the pollutants in question within the scope of a long-term strategy and in appropriate relation, there is hardly any danger of their being classified as unreasonable. This is also valid if the immission situation in clean air areas can only be improved slowly as a result and if positive influences on the vegetation can initially only be surmised. A balanced reduction of the emissions means that one must proceed from the objective criteria which speak for greater or lesser hazard potential of the individual pollutants, and that one must reduce the total spectrum proportional to the apprehension, not in an unsystematic manner or only under the influence of certain popular fears.'*

Since much of the damaged forest was located near the borders with Germany's neighbouring countries, international cooperation in research and policy development was also necessary.

The 1985 CLRTAP Protocol and beyond

The 1985 CLRTAP Protocol, committing countries to 30% reduction in sulphur emissions, was carried through by the so-called 30% club, consisting of the Nordic countries, The Netherlands, Switzerland and Austria, and joined by the Federal Republic of Germany. Two countries did not sign the protocol, Poland and the UK. A somewhat superfluous research programme carried out by the

UK Royal Society and the research academies in Norway and Sweden concluded that acid rain did indeed kill fish (Mason, 1992), and the Chairman of the Central Electricity Generating Board in the UK was impelled to explain to the UK Prime Minister that the accusations made by the Norwegian government regarding the long-range impact of the UK's coal-burning power stations were scientifically well founded.

Several severe winters with prolonged anticyclonic conditions and easterly flow over northern Europe provided strong reminders of the deterioration of the environment in the Eastern bloc countries during the 1980s. Over large areas of Germany, including western Germany, levels of SO_2 and black smoke were observed that far exceeded the air quality guidelines recommended by WHO (Bruckmann et al, 1986). This experience again demonstrated that tall stacks did not necessarily solve the problem of air pollution with the increased emissions of SO_2 that had occurred. Health warnings were issued to the inhabitants of West Berlin, which were gleefully commented on by the official news services in the GDR. But the source was East Germany, together with the adjoining parts of Poland and Czechoslovakia, in the so-called 'black triangle'. The collapse of the communist regimes which followed was in many ways related to the uneconomic development of energy-consuming heavy industries in these countries, and to the collapse of the Soviet empire which had paid for the products with expensive fuel oil and petroleum products.

Negotiations for a follow-up protocol on sulphur emissions took advantage of this new situation (ECE, 1994). In addition, Germany and some other countries had started on an ambitious programme of emission reductions, installing flue gas desulphurisation and denitrification in both new and old coal-burning electric power plants. In addition to desulphurised oil products, natural gas from Russia and from the North Sea was available to replace coal and sulphur-containing fuel oil. By now, also, the scientific knowledge accumulated in the various bodies and task forces under the CLRTAP could be used to ensure a cost-efficient use of the emission reductions in relation to environmental damage.

One of the main reasons for the wish to reduce the emissions continued to be forest damage, which had been demonstrated in many countries through series of national inventories of tree vitality, involving assessments of crown thinning and leaf and needle yellowing. However, there was still no consensus with respect to the cause, nor was there any indication of quantitative cause-effect relationships. The problem, therefore, had to be attacked from another angle, more precautionary than the prevailing approach, which came to be known as the 'critical load' concept (Nilsson et al, 1988). By definition, the critical load is the highest deposition of a pollutant that does not change the ecosystem in an unacceptable way. For soil acidification this implies a deposition of sulphur (and nitrogen) which is balanced in relation to the release of base cations (such as calcium) from the weathering of soil minerals. In the case of lakes and rivers the acid input must be less than the leaching of base cations in the watersheds. The critical loads may be derived from soil surveys, or surveys of lake chemistry, and have been extensively mapped all over Europe (Hettelingh et al, 1991), providing a rational basis for the negotiations of the

1994 sulphur protocol. Because the sulphur deposition exceedances were mainly located in northern Europe, and because of the state of technical developments, emission reductions were largely called for in this area. It also proved to be too difficult to satisfy the most stringent requirements with respect to critical loads: only a 60% gap closure was found to be achievable for the grids where the relative exceedances of the critical loads were the highest.

These international negotiations also have implications for urban air quality. It has long been realised that reducing air pollutant concentrations in the cities will have added benefits for human health as well as in terms of reducing material damage. New and stringent limit values for SO_2 and other air pollutants are now included in EU legislation, taking into account both the benefits of improved air quality and the desirability of reducing emissions (European Commission, 1999). It is interesting, however, to see that the short-term limit for protection of human health, which is set at 350 micrograms per cubic metre for one hour, is still not very much lower than the values proposed on the basis of the experience from the London smog. Limits are also set for 24-hour exposure, at 125 micrograms per cubic metre. It would seem that progress has been slow, as this limit was exceeded for 34% of Europe's population in 1990 (Stanner et al, 1995).

Damage due to air pollutants has been substantial to materials and historical monuments, particularly to masonry and iron constructions. As concentrations rise above 10–20 micrograms per cubic metre the damage to building materials and historical monuments significantly exceeds the natural degradation occurring in clean environments (Coote et al, 1991). Disfigurement of medieval ornaments and other building details in carved sandstone, sculptures and other works of art, and stained-glass windows, are among the costs not easily quantified. However, a number of retrospective studies have shown that the costs of reducing the emissions have more than been recovered in terms of generally reduced maintenance costs for buildings and steel constructions in the urban environment.

Sulphur dioxide emissions over northern Europe have now been reduced by more than 50% since the maximum in 1980. Through the use of clean fuels, particularly natural gas, concentration levels in the urban environments have been even more reduced. In the UK, average urban concentration levels have been reduced by more than 70%. A new and more stringent protocol to the CLRTAP has been negotiated (ECE, 1994), which will lead to further SO_2 emission reductions. The main emphasis is shifting towards interactions between pollutants such as nitrogen oxides, ammonia and volatile organic hydrocarbons, the combined acidifying effects of sulphur and nitrogen deposition, the formation of photochemical oxidants, and the eutrophication effect of transboundary transport of nitrogen compounds.

The acid lakes and streams show a slow, but steady, recovery (Skjelkvåle et al, 1998). Even forest vitality is improving, according to the latest surveys (ECE and EC, 1997), although the evidence is not unambiguous. It seems that the trout and salmon populations, however insignificant in economic terms, have played an important educational part in making Europe understand the full implications of the emissions of air pollutants.

Late lessons

So what role has precaution played in this story? Generally action has only been taken on the basis of proof beyond reasonable doubt, and protagonists have felt compelled to justify action on such a basis. Only when the issue was taken to the international level could significant change occur. It was relatively easy for the Scandinavian countries to argue for action, as the initial perception was that they were bearing most of the costs, but few of the benefits, of fossil fuel combustion in other countries. The UK regarded itself as bearing high costs but gaining little benefit from action to reduce long-distance transportation of sulphur emissions; arguably it was only when it was appreciated that acid rain had costs closer to home that the political climate changed. In the case of eastern Europe, the countries could not afford the short-term costs involved, no matter what the merits of action. Throughout the early history of SO2 pollution and acid rain, the precautionary approach was altogether absent, mainly because decision-makers had limited understanding of the problems. The tall stack approach was a clear example of the reluctance to accept effects beyond the immediately obvious.

All this was to change perceptibly when the issue came to be the subject of an ECE convention, which was also seen as an important instrument in the improvement of political relations between eastern and western European countries in the 1980s. Another major element was the political pressure of the Green Party in Germany. It is noteworthy that the German Council of Environmental Advisers was concerned that statements about forest damage, couched unjustifiably as a scientific fact, established in terms of proof beyond doubt, could undermine the wider basis for action if these should subsequently be demonstrated as unfounded. If there was general acceptance of the need for action based on a lower standard of proof – a precautionary approach – such potential problems could be side-stepped. In reality, the council's argument was for the record. Politically, the decision had already been taken.

At the international level, the machinery of the CLRTAP had to find a rational approach to negotiations about the limitation and reduction of SO2 emissions. In principle, the task was to find an approach which minimised the adverse effects, while distributing the costs of emission reductions evenly among the different countries. The many task forces and committees within the convention provided substantial scientific advice and knowledge for this task, and served also to guarantee that the signatories' national interests were taken into account. What the task force on effects came up with was the critical load concept. This can be regarded as related to the precautionary approach because it aims at a situation where no damage or adverse effects are expected to occur. This has the effect of shifting the burden of proof, from demonstrating and calculating in economic terms the damage which could occur in the future from decreased growth of forests, or loss of species, to the relatively simple task of determining which level of deposition can be accepted without perceptible chemical changes in soil composition. With respect to water acidification, the critical loads calculated also represent some simplifications, which are accepted only because of reasonably wide safety margins regarding the survival of sensitive species.

Thus, while not exactly representing an application of the precautionary principle, the application of critical loads represents a rational way of dealing with uncertainties regarding the environmental effects of acid rain.

Table 10.1 *Sulphur dioxide: early warnings and actions*

1952	A dense smog kills more than 2000 people in London
1952	The Beaver Report prepared by a parliamentary commission proposes modest remedies
1962	Second smog incident kills 800 people in London
1968	Acidification of precipitation and rivers in Sweden is linked to sulphur dioxide emissions in other countries
Late 1960s	An OECD Air Management Sector Group is set up, contributing to solving air problems
1972	Further evidence of acidification of Swedish lakes presented to the UN environment conference, Stockholm
1972	OECD acid rain study is launched
1972	OECD programme on long-range transport of air pollutants is launched
1977	OECD report is published, determining the relationship between emissions and depositions of sulphur compounds
1979	Convention on Long-range Transboundary Air Pollution (CLRTAP) is agreed
1979	WHO recommends air quality guidelines, setting a standard for the pollution abatement work in Europe
1980s	Forest death from 'acid rain' in Germany, Poland, Czechoslovakia and North America
1985	CLRTAP Protocol agrees 30% reduction in sulphur emissions
1988	The EU directive on large combustion plants is published, and amended in 1988. These were very efficiently used by Germany against the British opposition to emission controls
1994	Second sulphur protocol, based on the critical load concept that had already been mapped all over Europe

Source: EEA

MTBE in petrol as a substitute for lead

Martin Krayer von Krauss and Poul Harremoës

Introduction

A core notion of sustainability is that of futurity, whereby development in the present should not compromise the ability of future generations to meet their needs. Although it may not be possible for us to predict exactly what the needs of the future will be, we can respond by developing procedures for making robust and flexible decisions.

The goal of this case study is to examine how foresight, embodied in the precautionary principle, can lead to robust and flexible decisions that meet the needs of the present, but that can be adapted to meet the changing needs of the future. Recently there has been much debate over the use of methyl tert-butyl ether (MTBE) in petrol. Concerns in particular over the potential for contamination of groundwater supplies have prompted regulative authorities in western nations to reassess the risks associated with the use of MTBE.

After presenting the background, this case study will examine whether, at the time of MTBE's introduction, it would have been possible for the petrochemical industry and regulatory agencies to foresee that MTBE's physical, chemical and microbiological properties might eventually be deemed to be undesirable characteristics. The analysis will then be pursued to illustrate how foresight, in the form of some essential precautionary questions, can be applied to arrive at robust and flexible decisions.

This chapter was completed in May 2001. Undoubtedly, the debate on MTBE will continue and some aspects of the chapter may become quickly outdated, but it is hoped that it will be a valuable contribution to the debate on the precautionary principle.

Lead in petrol

The toxicity of lead has been known to man since ancient times. The Ancient Romans were aware of the fact that the lead they used to make their utensils was poisoning people. The field of occupational health formally established the toxicity of lead in the 1800s. Already in the early 1920s, at the very beginning of the car industry, the wisdom of using lead in petrol was questioned. The debate was reignited in the 1960s. There developed a widespread consensus that a long-term trend of rising airborne lead concentrations was undesirable and it was eventually decided by most western nations to phase out lead in petrol. The gradual phase-out of lead in petrol began in the late 1970s and by the mid-1990s, most western countries had phased out lead in petrol. As a substitute for lead, the petrochemicals industry chose MTBE.

The MTBE case

The choice of MTBE as an engine anti-knocking agent to replace lead was made on the basis of a variety of advantageous properties: it is a low-cost and easily produced chemical with favourable transfer and blending characteristics; it can be produced at the refinery; it blends easily without separation in petrol; and the blend can be transferred through existing pipelines (Squillace et al, 1996).

Commercial production of MTBE started in Europe in 1973 and in the US in 1979 (DeWitt & Company Inc, 2000). Italy introduced MTBE into petrol in the late 1970s, followed by other European countries, mainly in the mid-1980s. Total worldwide annual production was about 21.4 million tonnes in 1999. Roughly 3.3 million tonnes of MTBE were produced in the EU in 1999. Some 2.3 million tonnes were used domestically, 1.1 million tonnes were exported and 0.2 million tonnes were imported (DeWitt & Company Inc, 2000). In 1995 MTBE was the third most produced organic chemical in the US, at approximately 8 million tonnes per year (Johnson et al, 2000). MTBE is therefore a very high production-volume chemical.

In the US, the use of MTBE greatly increased following the 1990 amendments to the Clean Air Act requiring petrol 'oxygenates', such as MTBE or ethanol, to be added to petrol to reduce atmospheric concentrations of carbon monoxide (CO) or ozone. In January 1995 a special blend of petrol (dubbed 'reformulated gasoline', RFG) containing more MTBE was introduced for use in metropolitan areas in the US that had severe ozone pollution problems. The present average MTBE content in RFG in the US is around 11% (NSTC, 1997; ENDS Environment Daily, 2000). There is also a large volume of conventional petrol sold in the US, with a 2–3% MTBE content.

In the EU, the application of MTBE was regulated by a 1985 directive (85/536/EEC) on additives to petrol, by which no Member State can prevent the use of organic oxygenates at concentrations lower than regulated by the directives. For MTBE this is a maximum of 15% by volume. In 1999 in the EU, the average was 2.1%, calculated from the total consumption figures on motor petrol and MTBE consumption. Actual concentrations of MTBE in petrol are highly variable, from 0 to 15%, depending on petrol grade, oil company and country (Finnish EPA, 2001).

In the following sections we will attempt to summarise the relevant background information. As the aim is to examine the potential use of the precautionary principle, particular attention will be focused on areas of uncertainty within current scientific knowledge.

The benefits of MTBE

The original purpose of adding MTBE to petrol was to prevent 'knocking'. In addition MTBE or other oxygenates allow more complete combustion, which in turn leads to a reduction of CO emissions and a reduced emission of precursors for ozone formation (Koshland et al, 1998). MTBE also achieves some elevation in the octane rating that alternative components of fuel such as benzene (a class 1 carcinogen) and other aromatics provide.

The role of MTBE in reducing air emissions has however been questioned. In this respect, it is important to distinguish between the general effects of using RFG and those associated specifically with the presence of MTBE in RFG. During the 1990s the US saw a significant decrease in CO, low-level ozone and nitrogen oxide (NO_x) pollution in major cities using RFG. But, although the use of RFG results in significant reductions in automotive pollutant emissions relative to conventional petrol, studies have shown that CO, NO_x and volatile organic compound (VOC) emissions are not significantly affected by including MTBE in petrol (NRC, 1996). In a more recent report investigators concluded that the use of oxygenates in RFG had a negligible impact on ambient ozone concentrations (NRC, 1999). It has also been reported that the benefits of MTBE are decreasing, because these mostly apply to older vehicles, which are progressively being replaced by vehicles with more effective emission controls (Keller et al, 1998b).

The impacts of MTBE

Persistency in groundwater

Concerns regarding the use of MTBE began to arise following studies indicating that MTBE moves at about the same speed as groundwater, making it a very mobile chemical (Barker et al, 1990). These concerns became widespread following a report published by the US Geological Survey in 1996. Of VOCs analysed in samples of shallow ambient groundwater collected from eight urban areas during 1993–94, MTBE was the second most frequently detected chemical (Squillace et al, 1996). Its solubility is in the order of 50,000 mg/l (milligrams per litre). A level of 10% MTBE in petrol gives an equilibrium concentration in water of the order of 5000 mg/l.

Persistency can be discussed in terms of physical, chemical or microbiological persistency. Uncertainties concerning the persistency of MTBE in soil and groundwater still remain. MTBE is rapidly photodegraded in the atmosphere.

The available data in the sub-surface is limited, there being few well-documented reports concerning attenuation of MTBE in the field. Two studies have shown that biodegradation could not be detected in the groundwater under field conditions (Borden et al, 1997; Schirmer and Barker, 1998). However, in subsequent laboratory studies, a very slow but measurable biodegradation was observed (Landmeyer et al, 1998). Each of these three investigations occurred under aerobic conditions. The results of field investigations have shown that MTBE can be degraded anaerobically (Sufflita and Mormile, 1993; Mormile et al, 1994; Yeh and Novak, 1994; Hurt et al, 1999). But significant rates of MTBE degradation, either biologically (Eweis et al, 1998a and b) or chemically have only been observed under laboratory conditions. Thus, because of its high solubility, mobility and persistency, MTBE poses a potential risk to groundwater.

Aesthetics

The aesthetic impact of MTBE contamination of groundwater is considerable. The potent terpene-like odour in water is detectable by people at very low concentrations. The odour threshold was determined to be 180 ug/l (micrograms per litre) in Denmark (Larsen, 1997), but as low as 5 ug/l in California (CAL-EPA, 1999). Based on current monitoring data, MTBE has been shown in some cases to be present in drinking water at concentrations exceeding taste and odour thresholds.

Relatively small amounts of MTBE may thus render large reserves of groundwater useless. When the taste and odour threshold in water is exceeded, contaminated drinking water is normally not used, requiring the utilisation of alternative supplies. When a large and important groundwater reservoir is contaminated the consequences can be remarkable, both in terms of cost and disruption.

Leaking underground storage tanks and spillage from overfilling the tanks are the main cause of groundwater contamination (Finnish EPA, 2001). The severity of the consequences may vary greatly between countries depending on, for example, the level of groundwater utilisation for drinking water and the condition of petrol station underground storage tanks. The number of pollution cases varies significantly from country to country in the EU. The EU risk reduction report (Finnish EPA, 2001) states that 'MTBE concentrations are currently not routinely monitored in groundwater. There is only limited data on MTBE concentration trends'. In a recent report to the European Commission (Arthur D Little Limited, 2001) it is stated that 'little public information is available across Member States regarding monitoring of groundwater contamination by MTBE'. The report refers to unpublished data as a significant source of information, combined with data available from six Member States (Denmark, Finland, France, Germany, Sweden and the UK). It concludes that 'none of the findings indicated widespread or serious groundwater contamination by MTBE on the same scale as the USA'. However, according to the EU risk assessment study, the 'documented cases provide sufficient justification for concern that MTBE poses a risk for the aesthetic quality of drinking water from groundwater supplies'. The EU risk reduction report states: 'It is justified to conclude that

MTBE is causing a risk for the aesthetic quality of drinking water.' (Finnish EPA, 2001)

Cancer

The classification of the carcinogenicity of MTBE is the focus of a continuing controversy (see Box 11.1). The recent EU risk assessment concluded that MTBE was a borderline case for classification as a carcinogen (Finnish EPA, 2001). Nonetheless, the European Chemicals Bureau has decided that MTBE should not be classified as a carcinogen (Dixson-Decleve, 2001). For the purpose of this case study, it is noteworthy that the issue of carcinogenicity was not addressed until long after the marketing of MTBE as a high production-volume chemical: no comprehensive pre-marketing carcinogenicity testing was carried out. Even today, after in-depth investigations, uncertainties about the carcinogenicity of MTBE remain. The ongoing debate in the US and the EU over the classification of MTBE illustrates the difficulty of dealing with uncertainty and borderline results.

Asthma

A similar debate is taking place regarding whether the use of MTBE in petrol has contributed to an increase in urban asthma. In an editorial published in the *Archives of Environmental Health* in February 2000 (Joseph, 2000), concerns were raised over epidemiological studies indicating an increase in the occurrences of asthma and other conditions of respiratory and/or inflammatory natures in the years following the introduction of MTBE to the cities of Philadelphia (Joseph, 1997) and New York (Crain et al, 1994; Leighton et al, 1999). The past five years have seen reports of alarmingly high rates (above 20%) of asthma among children in several large cities on the east coast of the US where MTBE was in use (Mangione et al, 1997; McBride, 1996; Hathaway, 1999; Leighton et al, 1999). It has been suggested that the increase in asthma is due to an unknown exhaust product of MTBE combustion entering the ambient air (Joseph, 1999; Leikauf et al, 1995).

The University of California, Davis report states that it is plausible that combustion products of MTBE could exacerbate or even cause asthma, but that there have been no studies to date designed to address this issue. They conclude that 'there is little evidence at present either to implicate or exonerate MTBE as a cause or exacerbating factor in asthma' (Keller et al, 1998b).

Other impacts

There are a few investigations indicating that MTBE may function as an endocrine disrupter (Williams et al, 2000; Moser et al, 1998; Day et al, 1998). However, the mechanisms by which MTBE may disrupt endocrine systems remain unclear and further research is required. In this respect, the EU risk assessment concluded: 'Because the data is not considered to be sufficient, no NOAEL (no observed adverse effect level) is assigned.' (Finnish EPA, 2001)

Box 11.1 Carcinogenicity: complex science, borderline results and conflicting interests

Comprehensive investigations of carcinogenicity were initiated in the 1990s. Evidence from three animal bioassay studies demonstrated that chronic exposure to MTBE – either by inhalation or orally – causes cancers in animals. MTBE inhalation exposure caused an increased incidence of kidney and testicular tumours in male rats (Bird et al, 1997; Chun et al, 1992), and liver tumours were identified in mice (Burleigh-Flayer et al, 1992). Oral administration of MTBE produced a statistically significant increased incidence of lymphomas and leukaemias in female rats and testicular tumours in male rats (Belpoggi et al, 1995 and 1998).

Based on these results, it would seem that MTBE induces benign and malignant tumours at multiple sites, in multiple species, and via multiple routes of exposure. However, the results have been criticised on the grounds that the 'conduct and reporting in the carcinogenicity studies is inadequate, interpretation of the obtained results is difficult and a relation of the observed increases in tumour incidences to MTBE-administration is questionable. Moreover, rodent-specific mechanisms of action have been established for several of the tumours induced by MTBE, thus making the results inapplicable to man.' (Dekant, 2000)

According to WHO's International Agency for Research on Cancer (IARC), no analytical epidemiological studies have addressed a possible association of MTBE with human cancer. IARC concluded that because there is 'inadequate evidence in humans' for carcinogenicity, and only 'limited evidence' for experimental animals, 'MTBE is not classifiable as to its carcinogenicity to humans' (IARC, 1999). The US National Toxicology Program's (NTP's) Board of Scientific Counselors voted six to five not to list MTBE as being 'reasonably anticipated to be a human carcinogen' (BSC, 1998). The International Programme on Chemical Safety (IPCS), a joint programme of the International Labour Organisation, the United Nations Environment Programme and WHO, echoed the IARC's conclusion, recommending that in order to provide quantitative guidance on relevant limits of exposure and to estimate risk, the acquisition of additional data in several areas remains necessary (IPCS, 1999).

Other institutions and individual scientists have decided that the evidence provided by the animal bioassay studies is sufficient to conclude that MTBE is likely to cause cancer in humans and should therefore be labelled a probable human carcinogen (Mehlman, 2000). A review of the existing studies by the University of California (Keller et al, 1998b), indicated that MTBE is a potential human carcinogen, although further studies would be needed to make a conclusive determination. The White House National Science and Technology Council concluded that 'there is sufficient evidence that MTBE is an animal carcinogen' and that 'the weight of evidence supports MTBE as having carcinogenic hazard potential for humans' (NSTC, 1997). The US Environmental Protection Agency (EPA) concluded that 'the weight of evidence indicates that MTBE is an animal carcinogen, and MTBE poses a carcinogenic potential to humans' (US EPA, 1997).

The most recent in-depth review of the available carcinogenicity data was performed by the Finnish EPA in the context of the EU Risk Assessment on MTBE (Finnish EPA, 2001). In the draft risk assessment report, the conclusion on carcinogenicity states: 'There are indications of carcinogenicity in two species. However the treatment relation of the occurred tumours is equivocal in some studies (mouse adenoma) and the relevance of the mode of action is questionable in others (Leydig cell). Moreover, the tumours appear mostly at very high and systemically toxic doses, and MTBE is not genotoxic *in vitro* or *in vivo*. On the other hand, the human relevance of the testicular interstitial adenomas observed in rats on two separate rat strains cannot be neglected. In addition, some uncertainty remains as to the significance of the lymphatic tumours found, especially in the light of the limitations of the study and somewhat inadequate study quality reporting. The rapporteur considers MTBE as a borderline case between non-classification and Carcinogenicity Category 3.' (Finnish EPA, 2001)

The classification and labelling of MTBE for hazard was discussed by the Working Group on the Classification of Dangerous Substances at the European Chemicals Bureau in November 2000. A proposal to classify MTBE as a carcinogen in Category 3, with an R40 risk phrase was rejected (R40 states that a substance poses 'possible risk of irreversible effects') (Dixson-Decleve, 2001).

The probable basis for this decision is that it is generally accepted that there is a threshold concentration below which no effects can be observed for carcinogenic substances that are not mutagenic. For MTBE, several *in vitro* mutagenicity assays with metabolic activation are positive, while *in vivo* studies are negative. It is believed that the positive responses occur when cells *in vitro* are exposed extracellularly to the MTBE metabolite formaldehyde, and that formaldehyde will not exert this effect when it is generated intracellularly, in the intact organism. For this reason, MTBE is regarded as non-mutagenic (Finnish EPA, 2001).

Thus the level of concern for MTBE is not as high as it would be for a mutagenic carcinogen where, in theory, effects can be expected at all doses, right down to infinitely small concentrations. For non-mutagenic carcinogens, the effect is often connected to some other damage to the target organ, for instance the kidney or liver. The high regeneration and growth of cells that then takes place in connection with tissue regeneration in the damaged organ can be accompanied by an increased tumour production. For the primary damage on the target organ, there will be a threshold value. This threshold value is the no observed adverse effect level (NOAEL). By remaining below the threshold value, damage to the organs is prevented, as is the formation of tumours (Østergaard, 2001). Thus, the risk of carcinogenicity posed by such substances is considered manageable.

MTBE in drinking water

In late 1995, the authorities in the city of Santa Monica in California detected MTBE in a well that supplied the city with drinking water. By June the following year the problem had escalated and the city authorities were forced to shut down some of the potable water supply groundwater wells. A review of known and suspected petroleum spill sites identified about ten potential sources of contamination within 1 kilometre of the well field (Johnson et al, 2000). As a result of the MTBE contamination the city lost 71% of its local water supply. About half its total water consumption must now be bought from outside sources at a cost of US$3.5 million a year (Rodriguez, 1997). Some MTBE plumes have originated from very small spills. For example, a spill resulting from a single car accident in Standish, ME, led to MTBE transport through more than 0.7 kilometres of fractured rock and the contamination of more than 20 domestic wells (Johnson et al, 2000; Hunter et al, 1999). By now there are many documented cases of MTBE pollution of groundwater in the US, the number is increasing and where pollution occurs the consequences can be serious. Assuming treatment by granular activated carbon, the cost of purifying MTBE contaminated drinking water sources could be enormous, due to the extremely low concentration limits for MTBE in drinking water (in the order of 5 to 30 μg/l). The cost of dealing with underground storage tank and pipeline leaks and spills could be of the order of tens to hundreds of millions of dollars per year in California alone (Keller et al, 1998a). This however could change in light of yet unpublished results from work indicating that MTBE could potentially be biologically degraded in ordinary waterworks using sand filtration (Arvin, 2001).

Responses

In Denmark, a report on MTBE was published in 1998 (Miljø og Energiministeriet, 1998). The introduction acknowledges: 'In 1990 The Danish EPA received information from Professor Erik Arvin, Institute for Environmental Science and Engineering, Technical University of Denmark, that there might be a problem in relation to groundwater, because of the mobility and apparent persistency in groundwater.' The Danish EPA did not consider that to be a problem at the time, because leakage from tanks was considered a minor problem, and 'because problems with petrol components were rarely found in groundwater at the time'. In 1998, the Danish EPA introduced a tentative limit for drinking water at 30 ug/l.

In California, the first US state to suffer the consequences of MTBE, the California Legislature created a task force within the University of California. The task force evaluated the available evidence, produced an assessment of health and environmental impacts and made several recommendations to the governor and the legislature, including the phase-out of MTBE (Keller et al, 1998b). As a result, a Governor's Executive Order in March 1999 recommended developing 'a timetable by July 1, 1999 for removal of MTBE from petrol at the earliest possible date, but no later than December 31, 2002' (Davis, 1999). The University of California study also concluded that: 'A lesson to be learned from the MTBE story is that addition of any chemical compound to the environment in quantities that constitute a significant fraction of the total content of petrol may have unexpected environmental consequences. Therefore, we recommend a full environmental assessment of any alternative to MTBE.' The intention here is to emphasise that any alternative to MTBE should undergo a full assessment prior to its introduction. This measure is in particular due to the 'potential adverse health effects associated with incomplete combustion products of ethanol'. The report also observed that: 'The current structure of state agencies which focus on specific media (land, air, water), leads to fragmented and incomplete environmental impact assessments.'

A 'Blue Ribbon Panel' was established by the US EPA in 1998 'in response to the growing concerns from State and local officials and the public' (Blue Ribbon Panel, 1999). The report of September 1999 concluded *inter alia*: 'The Panel agreed broadly that, in order to minimise current and future threats to drinking water, the use of MTBE should be reduced substantially. Several members believed that the use of MTBE should be phased out completely.' One lesson, the panel concluded, is that: 'In order to prevent future such incidents… EPA should conduct a full, multi-media assessment (of effects on air, soil, and water) of any major new additive to petrol prior to introduction.' In March 2000, the US EPA announced that steps would be taken to 'significantly reduce or eliminate' MTBE as a petrol additive, as a 'possible carcinogen' and in order 'to protect America's drinking water supplies' (ENDS Environment Daily, 2000).

Present trends

The future in the US is likely to see a shift towards other oxygenates such as ethanol, as well as equivalent non-oxygenated petrols, which meet the strict emission requirements (Keller et al, 1998b; CEC, 1998). In Europe, the comparatively low use of MTBE has meant that concerns and possible problems associated with MTBE have developed later than in the US (Morgenroth and Arvin, 1999). The EU regulations introduced on fuel quality covering both petrol and diesel in 1998 (98/70/EEC) call for compounds such as benzene (class 1 carcinogen) and overall aromatics to be reduced in steps by the years 2000 and 2005. This could result in an increase in the use of MTBE in Europe. In August 2000 the Danish EPA placed MTBE on its list of undesirable substances and announced that it planned to introduce economic instruments to discourage the use of MTBE. The recent EU risk assessment of MTBE concluded that because of the risk that MTBE poses to groundwater reservoirs, risk reduction measures are justified (Finnish EPA, 2001). A report to the European Commission on risk reduction for underground storage tanks was released on 19 April 2001 (Arthur D Little Limited, 2001) as a supplement to the risk reduction report written in connection with the risk assessment (Finnish EPA, 2001). The reports stress the difference between the US and EU situations. The anticipation is that 'MTBE octane requirements will settle out in the 1–4% volume range, depending on the available octane, and will still be well below the 10–15% currently used in reformulated petrol in the USA'. Many EU countries have recently adopted regulatory measures against leakage from underground storage tanks to ensure that the risk of groundwater contamination 'remains low in the future'. The report points at the risks posed by existing underground storage tanks not complying with the new regulations in the interim period until full enforcement. The regulations are anticipated to have taken full effect by 2005. The report emphasises the need for 'strong enforcement of the underground storage tank specifications' and suggest 'penalties to prove an effective deterrent'.

Accordingly, it seems that the position in the EU tends to be that oxygenates such as MTBE should have their place to improve combustion and help reduce emissions of CO and organic compounds. The increased risk associated with leaking underground storage tanks is seen as a technical problem that can be managed by risk reduction. However, studies in the US have shown that even sophisticated, double-walled underground storage tanks with detectors may leak undetected due to improper installation (Couch and Young, 1998). This explains the push for 'strong enforcement' and follow-up monitoring of groundwater in the report to the European Commission (Arthur D Little Limited, 2001).

Discussion in relation to the precautionary principle

Our analysis will first take a historical perspective in order to highlight the questions that could have been asked at the time of the introduction of MTBE in the early 1980s. The objective here is to illustrate the potential of applying foresight as part of the precautionary principle.

As early as 1954, studies were published indicating the very low biodegradability of the ether family (Mills and Stack, 1954). By 1960, the resistance of ethers to biological degradation had become textbook knowledge (Sawyer, 1960). On this basis we consider it reasonable to believe that at the time of the introduction of MTBE, competent chemists and microbiologists could have anticipated that MTBE might be persistent in groundwater. Documentation for this argument has however not been found. It appears that the first warnings against persistency of MTBE in groundwater, based on the first experimental facts (although only at the laboratory scale), were published in 1990 (Barker et al, 1990; Jensen and Arvin, 1990). However, the regulatory agencies did not react to these first warnings. It was not until the full-scale results emerged in 1996 that the regulatory system was alerted to the seriousness of the problem. That delay is documented in the US and Denmark.

On the other hand, it is reasonable to believe that there were no indications of any obvious harmful effects associated with MTBE at the time it was chosen to replace lead in petrol. Accordingly, the fundamental issue is not whether a persistent *and* harmful chemical poses an unacceptable risk. The fundamental issue is whether or not the prevailing knowledge was adequate at the time to foresee that persistency in itself might eventually be considered problematic.

The historical perspective

Widespread concern over the persistency of chemicals first arose following the publication of the landmark book *Silent Spring* (Carson, 1962). In her book, Rachel Carson described the disastrous effects of large-scale applications of pesticides on insects, birds and ecosystems. At the time, the debate was closely connected to what was known as the 'dirty dozen' of pesticides, now referred to as persistent organic pollutants, or POPs. In connection to this debate, research on biodegradability and mobility, as well as other characteristics of pesticides, has been ongoing since the early 1960s.

A similar debate emerged in Europe in the early 1960s, following incidences of foaming in rivers caused by the use of non-biodegradable detergents. The soap and detergent industry became actively involved in efforts to develop criteria and methodology for testing the persistency/degradability of detergents (ASDA, 1965; Swisher, 1987) as did the OECD (1970).

It would therefore appear that industry and regulators would have had reason to suspect that persistency could entail complications when present in combination with detrimental properties. The experience with pesticides and detergents provided scientific evidence that in combination with certain other chemical properties, persistency could cause lasting undesirable effects, such as persistent toxicity or foaming rivers.

Based on this, we may further ask if at the time of the introduction of MTBE there were any indications that society was formulating and implementing responses to address the issue of chemical persistency combined with other negative characteristics.

In 1978/79, an OECD working group on test methods for degradation and accumulation was formed to pioneer the development of the specific detergent methods into more general methods for measuring persistency (OECD, 1981). At these workshops, representatives from governments, industry and academia discussed the technical details of the already accepted concept of persistency. As well as the OECD, a number of governmental, industrial and non-governmental organisations were active in developing standard test methods for biodegradability during the 1970s and the early 1980s (US EPA, 1979; ECETOC, 1982; ISO, 1984).

Persistency appeared early in the development of EU environmental legislation as an undesirable property of a chemical (European Commission, 1967 and 1984). According to the sixth amendment (European Commission, 1979) to the EC classification and labelling directive for new substances (European Commission, 1967) adopted in September 1979, all new substances intended to be manufactured or marketed in the EU must be notified to the competent authority in one of the Member States. This pre-marketing notification must be accompanied by a set of data on the identity, use and properties of the substance. The size of the data set is dependent on the foreseen production-volume of the substance involved. Together with toxicity, bioaccumulative potential and suspected carcinogenicity, persistency could trigger a classification as 'particularly dangerous to the environment'.

However, MTBE was not legally bound to these 'new substance' regulations, which only applied to chemical substances that were not marketed within the EU in the ten years prior to 18 September 1981. Because MTBE had been marketed prior to this date, it was classified as an 'existing substance' in the EU. Regulations for the evaluation and control of existing substances were adopted in 1993 (European Commission, 1993). The Finnish Environmental Institute is currently conducting the risk assessment of MTBE required under this regulation. Draft versions of the risk assessment, already referred to, became available by the end of 2000. The final version is expected during 2001.

The large amount of effort dedicated to developing test methods for persistency indicates that at the time society did in fact deem it important to identify persistency in a chemical. The subsequent incorporation into law of persistency as being an undesirable characteristic of a chemical further indicates that society was indeed prepared to implement responses to address the impact of chemical persistency in combination with other negative characteristics.

At the time it could have been expected that the projected high production-volume of MTBE would have given rise to concern. These concerns could have prompted further investigations, although there was no requirement at the time. Such investigations would have revealed the persistency of MTBE to decision-makers.

Had industry and regulators taken account of the persistency of MTBE, it is reasonable to assume that they could have considered the following question: does MTBE exhibit any other characteristic which, when combined with persistency, requires a response by society due to the risks involved?

As has been mentioned previously, the taste and odour problems associated with MTBE have been known for a long time. These were, however, overlooked during the screening of MTBE. It seems that the possibility that MTBE could pose a threat to groundwater reservoirs was never considered. Furthermore, the carcinogenicity of MTBE did not start to be investigated in detail until the 1990s and the classification of MTBE with regard to carcinogenicity remained uncertain long after the introduction of the chemical as a high production-volume chemical. There is no doubt that the introduction of a high production chemical displaying a combination of persistency, taste and odour characteristics, potential carcinogenicity and other adverse effects could have sparked concern in the early 1980s. Studies should therefore have been done at that time.

The choice of MTBE as a long-term replacement to lead in petrol was not grounded in precaution, as the possible threats associated with the choice were not adequately characterised. By applying foresight, it could have been possible for the petrochemicals industry and regulative authorities to identify that the persistency of MTBE could eventually become problematic.

The modern-day perspective

Of all the negative features of MTBE, persistency is unique in that it implies irreversibility. A persistent chemical remains present in the environment long after its use has been discontinued, thus dramatically increasing the risk associated with a false diagnosis of known detrimental effects, and with other detrimental effects of which science is still unaware. Indeed, the release of persistent chemicals into the environment begs the following questions: should a response be implemented on the sole basis of persistency, and should persistency motivate systematic, comprehensive and thorough investigations of perceivable negative effects?

These questions are still pending today, but the high production volume and the high solubility of MTBE should definitely give rise to concern. The list of known negative features of chemicals, other than persistency, is still expanding. Only now, for example, are we beginning to investigate the mechanisms that induce endocrine disruption. Should new information become available associating any new negative effect to a persistent chemical, the financial and technological resources required for remediation are likely to be out of reach once this chemical is spread throughout the environment.

In this case the interpretation of the precautionary principle is that the risk of being wrong and the potential consequences should always be considered. In the case of persistent chemicals, that risk is significantly greater than with other chemicals due to *irreversibility*. Lack of full scientific understanding of cause-effect relationships cannot be used as an excuse to postpone action. Moreover, scientific uncertainty and ignorance warrant precautionary measures.

Alternatives

The precautionary approach invokes the principle of substitution, seeking out safer alternatives to potentially harmful activities. There is no doubt that MTBE is a reasonably better option than lead. However, because we have reason to believe that there could be irreversible detrimental effects associated with the use of MTBE, we also have to investigate substitution as an alternative to risk reduction. There are alternatives to MTBE and it is likely that more could be discovered if sufficient research were conducted in this direction. Thus, the important follow-up question in the implementation of the precautionary approach is: what is the status of the alternatives to MTBE? The most recent account is presented in the EU report on risk reduction drafted in connection with the risk assessment (Finnish EPA, 2001)

The most commonly considered alternatives to MTBE include other oxygenates, improved engine technology and altered petrol composition (Morgenroth and Arvin, 1999; CEC, 1998).

Other oxygen-containing compounds include ethanol, ETBE (ethyl tert-butyl ether), TAME (tert-amyl methyl ether), and DIPE (di-isopropyl ether). However, other oxygenates could also have adverse impacts on the environment. For example, the area of agricultural land required to grow the plant matter for the production of biological ethanol would be significant and the ecological impact of the fertilisers and pesticides required to produce this crop need to be considered. Moreover, ethanol production requires considerable amounts of energy and this option may not lower greenhouse gas emissions significantly when the entire production cycle is considered. Other ethers could have health effects similar to those of MTBE which, as we have noted, are not fully understood.

Another alternative is the introduction of vehicles with improved engine technology, such as gasoline direct injection (GDI). At part load, GDI does not require as high an octane rating as conventional engines. At full load however the differences are not as important. With the reduction of the aromatics in petrol being called for in Europe, the addition of oxygenates would remain necessary even with improved engine technology.

Another widely considered alternative could be to improve the composition of the petrol. An increase in the octane rating of the petrol could be achieved by changing the structure of the 'branch alkanes' in petrol. This option may however be opposed by the petrochemicals industry, as it would imply process changes at the refinery, entailing major investment costs.

The use of MTBE as a petrol additive to reduce emissions of pollutants from motor vehicles is indicative of a deeper issue of which MTBE is only the symptom. As countries like India and China pursue the process of industrialisation, it is clear that future generations cannot afford to operate a mass transit system resulting in the emission of VOCs, CO, carbon dioxide, NO_x and other pollutants. Although the above mentioned alternatives could improve the current situation, it is not likely that the benefits they provide will be significant enough to meet the needs of future generations. Thus, the precautionary principle would now beckon us to invest seriously in the development of alternatives entirely different from the ones considered above.

In this respect, some European governments have been advocating a response directed at the very driving forces that lead to environmental degradation. In essence, they are questioning the basic need for a mass transit system. For example, the position of the current government in Denmark is that with advances in communication technologies, personal vehicles are increasingly becoming a 'want' versus a 'need'. They have therefore enacted various economic policies that aim to discourage citizens from driving personal vehicles.

Another point of view is that society will always have a need for a means of rapid transportation, but that a radical shift in engine technology can eliminate the pressures exerted on the environment by personal transport. One example of such a technological intervention is the hydrogen fuel cell. The emission by-products of this system are limited to oxygen and water. Pilot projects using hydrogen-based fuel cell buses have been set up, for example, in Chicago and Vancouver.

A feature of all these options is that none of them has been investigated to the point where they could be implemented on a wide scale in the short term. As we are currently realising the problems associated with the use of MTBE, foresight would beckon us to actively research and develop alternatives to this option.

Cost–benefit analysis

A cost–benefit analysis should ideally incorporate all costs and all benefits – or a reasonable approximation thereof. In the face of ignorance, a cost–benefit analysis is of only limited value to decision-makers and cannot, of itself, form the sole basis for a policy decision. Nevertheless, a systematic and comprehensive assessment of all the options can serve as an important tool for their relative assessment, even under situations of partial ignorance.

A cost–benefit analysis on the use of MTBE in California was conducted in 1998 (Keller et al, 1998a). The analysis examined the human health benefits derived from controlling air pollution, and then analysed the costs associated with the use of MTBE across the following categories:

- human health costs due to an increase in cancer cases caused by air pollution from MTBE and its combustion by-products (aldehydes);
- costs of averting human health damages through water treatment or by using alternative water supplies;

- direct costs paid by the consumers in the form of increased petrol prices as well as decreased petrol efficiency due to the oxygenates;
- monitoring costs;
- recreational costs; and
- ecosystem damage.

The analysis compared the costs and benefits of using MTBE, of using ethanol, and of the use of non-oxygenated petrol with either toluene or iso-octane. Conventional petrol sold prior to the introduction of RFG was used as a baseline comparison.

The air quality benefits associated with the three options were essentially the same, as all formulations achieve approximately the same reduction in CO and ozone precursors emissions. The air quality benefits of the three options were estimated to be relatively minor, between US$14 million and US$78 million per year.

The water treatment costs associated with MTBE made it the most expensive option, when all costs were considered. Based on an estimate of the number of groundwater supplies and surface water reservoirs currently contaminated with MTBE, the estimated aggregate cost of water treatment in California was found to be between US$340 million and US$1480 million per year. These costs were based on the premise that contaminated water would be treated to a concentration below 5 ug/l using granular activated carbon. As described earlier, there may be cheaper methods. For non-oxygenated petrol and ethanol blends, the differential cost of remediation and/or water treatment relative to conventional petrol would be small. Other important costs associated with the use of MTBE included the direct price paid by consumers for oxygenated petrol (US$435 million to US$1055 million per year), and the potential loss of recreational boating activities in order to prevent this source of MTBE contamination of surface water reservoirs (US$160 million to US$200 million per year). The report concluded that non-oxygenated petrol achieves air quality objectives at the least cost, followed by ethanol-based petrol formulations.

Given the ignorance surrounding our understanding of the health effects of MTBE, a cost–benefit analysis will always be provisional. It is possible that many potential costs still remain unknown to us. For example, if new information became available establishing a clear link between the use of MTBE and an increase in asthma occurrences, the health costs associated with the option of MTBE would increase significantly. On the other hand, if new information showed that MTBE could be degraded in municipal waterworks, the costs associated with MTBE could decrease significantly.

But on the basis of what is currently known with reasonable certainty, water treatment costs make MTBE a very expensive option. Furthermore, if we assume a worst-case scenario for the health effects of using MTBE, the cost of correction of damage would increase even further, far outweighing the cost of prevention. It is widely agreed that in the pursuit of the precautionary principle, the cost of any precautionary measures taken should be proportionate to the benefits that can be achieved by them. The potentially very high costs associated with MTBE would therefore justify a proportionately costly response.

It remains unclear who should be held responsible for the costs incurred as a result of the use of MTBE. Our analysis suggests that both industry and society (represented by regulators) were short-sighted in their decision to replace lead in petrol with MTBE. Because of this, it is difficult to single out who will bear the cost for the response. Who is the polluter, who should pay? Until now, the majority of the costs associated with the use of MTBE have been borne by society in the form of risk reduction, water treatment or alternative water supply costs, costs to industry carried over to consumers and human health costs. The consequences of any decision relating to our mass transit system will be far reaching. Because of this, foresight would now beckon society to select those alternatives to MTBE that are based on best environmental practices, even if these alternatives are more costly in the short term. The alternatives selected must be the best for the needs of the present day and for the needs of the future.

Conclusions

By applying foresight at the time of the introduction of MTBE, it could have been possible to predict that the persistency of MTBE would eventually be deemed problematic by society. The persistency, mobility and high production volume of MTBE should have prompted systematic, comprehensive investigations into perceivable adverse characteristics of the substance. This could have identified taste and odour problems and suspicions of carcinogenicity of MTBE at an earlier stage, and could have acquitted the chemical or confirmed suspicions.

The risk to groundwater due to persistency and the strong odour and taste of MTBE was ignored for a long time but has now been recognised. The classification of MTBE with regards to its carcinogenicity remains uncertain, long after its introduction as a high production-volume chemical. A state of near ignorance characterises our knowledge of the possible endocrine disrupting and asthma inducing effects of MTBE. Additional research is still recommended in these areas.

Because of its persistency in groundwater, the use of MTBE poses an ongoing, everlasting risk of having irreversible adverse effects. These adverse effects could come in the form of known effects such as taste and odour in contaminated drinking water, as well as in the form of presently unknown adverse effects.

The key question of principle is: does persistency alone, without indication of other adverse effects, give reason to apply the precautionary principle? It seems reasonable to conclude that systematic, comprehensive and thorough investigations into all known possible adverse effects should be exercised before any release of large volumes of a persistent chemical into the environment. These investigations should be reopened and pursued as new categories of adverse effects are discovered. It also seems reasonable to answer that, because persistent chemicals expose us and future generations to a variety of possible negative effects of which we are still ignorant, alternatives to the use of persistent chemicals should be sought out whenever possible. There are now a considerable number of examples of persistent chemicals (including CFCs, PCBs and tributyltin) that caused unwelcome 'surprises' with serious consequences.

Foresight beckons us to investigate alternative decisions thoroughly and to reconsider these alternatives when we realise the limitations of the current decisions. Best environmental practices, like risk reduction, should be pursued. Due to the possibility of risk reduction being insufficient, research and development into alternatives should be actively encouraged in order to render them feasible as soon as possible. Such thorough investigations ensure that decisions are robust and flexible so that they may be adapted to unforeseen circumstances in the future. Thus, foresight, embodied in the precautionary principle, is the guarantor of futurity within the concept of sustainability.

Table 11.1 *MTBE: early warnings and actions*

1954	First scientific paper demonstrates low biodegradability of the ether family in water
1960	Information about taste and odour in water and low biodegradability available in textbook
1990	First indications of the potential for groundwater pollution with MTBE at laboratory scale
1990	Significant increase in use of MTBE in the US due to amendments to the Clean Air Act
1990	Comprehensive investigations of carcinogenicity initiated in the 1990s
1995	MTBE detected in wells that supplied drinking water in Santa Monica, California. These had to be closed and the city lost 71% of its local water supply
1996	Concerns become widespread following a US Geological Survey report
1997	Field studies demonstrate that MTBE is highly soluble, mobile and persistent and therefore a potential risk to groundwater
1998	A Danish EPA report acknowledges that the government was informed in 1990 that MTBE might give rise to groundwater problems and presents an action plan for MTBE remediation and risk reduction
1999	California recommends removal of MTBE from petrol as soon as possible, but not later than end 2002
2000	Indications that MTBE might be linked to asthma in some US cities
2000	Indications that MTBE might be an endocrine disrupter
2000	US EPA announces that steps will be taken to significantly reduce or eliminate MTBE as a petrol additive
2000	Danish EPA places MTBE on its list of undesirable substances
2001	EU reports on analysis of risks and risk reduction related to MTBE. European Chemicals Bureau decides that MTBE should not be classified as a carcinogen
2001	The debate goes on

Source: EEA

12

Early warnings of chemical contamination of the Great Lakes

Michael Gilbertson

The first significant early warnings

The growth of chemical manufacturing and use of organochlorine compounds in the 20th century has resulted in global contamination with a wide variety of toxic and persistent organochlorine residues. Probably the most significant 'early warning' was the publication of *Silent Spring* by Rachel Carson (1962). This book compiled the existing evidence of previous early warnings of the effects of organochlorine pesticides on fish and wildlife and warned particularly of the threat posed by these chemicals in relation to cancer in humans.

One area of North America where the scientific and policy implications of organochlorine contamination have been intensively studied, particularly since the publication of *Silent Spring*, is the Great Lakes basin. The US and Canada share a boundary in four of the five Great Lakes. Early warnings of the contamination of this large ecosystem came from a variety of sources, not only as chemical analytical observations of the presence of residues of these organochlorine compounds, but also as observations of effects on populations of wild organisms, and particularly predatory birds.

The first analytical results of the presence of organochlorine compounds in organisms in the Great Lakes were published by Dr Joseph Hickey and co-workers and concerned the bioaccumulation of DDT (dichlorodiphenyl-trichloroethane) and metabolites, and dieldrin in a Lake Michigan food chain (Hickey et al, 1966). Additional organochlorine pesticides including lindane, heptachlor, aldrin and endrin were identified in samples of Lake Erie water (Pfister et al, 1969). After the discovery of PCBs in a white-tailed sea eagle in Sweden (Jensen, 1966), analytical methods were developed to detect the presence of PCBs (Reynolds, 1969) in Great Lakes samples. Subsequent application of these methods led to the finding of hexachlorobenzene in samples of eggs of common terns from Hamilton Harbour, Ontario (Gilbertson and

Reynolds, 1972). The flame retardant and pesticide mirex was subsequently identified in fish sampled from Lake Ontario (Kaiser, 1974).

The first reports of the effects of organochlorine compounds on Great Lakes populations of birds were those of Dr Joseph Hickey's students and co-workers (Keith, 1966; Ludwig and Tomoff, 1966) who documented the effects of DDT and metabolites, and dieldrin on reproduction and mortality in Lake Michigan herring gulls. Previous observations of the decline in the population and reproductive failure of Florida bald eagles had been published (Broley, 1952; Broley, 1958) but research on Great Lakes bald eagles did not start until the mid-1960s, by which time most of the population had been destroyed (Sprunt et al, 1973). The first observation of changes in eggshell quality was reported by naturalists visiting Pigeon Island in Lake Ontario in 1963 (Edwards et al, 1963) when two soft-shelled eggs were found in the nest of a pair of double-crested cormorants. The first published observation of a deformed chick of a Great Lakes fish-eating bird was of a juvenile bald eagle (Grier, 1968). Systematic studies of the incidence of deformities in the chicks of various species of colonial fish-eating bird were undertaken in the early 1970s (Gilbertson et al, 1976). In the mid-1960s, there was an outbreak of adult and kit mortality in ranch mink that fed on fish from the Great Lakes that had serious effects on this economic activity (Hartsough, 1965).

Concerns about the possible effects of organochlorine compounds on human health were first addressed in 1974 in a cohort of Great Lakes fisher-men (Humphrey, 1983). Consumption of contaminated fish resulted in elevated levels of PCBs in humans but was not associated with any recognised acute effects in fish eaters. These concerns were heightened in the spring of 1978, when Lois Gibbs, a resident living in a housing development built next to the Love Canal, Niagara Falls, New York started to investigate the incidence of diseases in her community and the possible relationship to the 20,000 tonnes of toxic wastes that had been disposed of in the canal by the Hooker Chemical Company during the previous 20 years. These inquiries set off a series of psycho-social dynamics within families, among workers, and between communi-ties and institutions such as the local university, hospitals, churches and the medical profession (Levine, 1982). Out of desperation, Lois Gibbs organised her neighbours into the Love Canal Homeowners Association and struggled for more than two years for relocation. Opposing the group's efforts, though, were the chemical manufacturer, Occidental Petroleum which had bought the Hooker Chemical Company, and local, state and federal government officials who insisted that the leaking toxic chemicals, including dioxin, the most toxic chemi-cal known, were not the cause of high rates of birth defects, miscarriages, cancers and other health problems. Finally, in October 1980, President Jimmy Carter delivered an Emergency Declaration which moved 900 families from this hazardous area and signified the victory of this grassroots movement. In 1981, Lois Gibbs responded to the growing public perception of the pervasive nature of the contamination and created the Center for Health, Environment and Justice (formerly Citizens Clearinghouse for Hazardous Wastes), an organisa-tion that has assisted more than 8000 grassroots groups with organisational, technical and general information nationwide.

In 1980, based on the concerns raised in the preliminary studies of elevated levels of PCBs in fish eaters as well as the concerns at the Love Canal, a cohort of infants was established to investigate the developmental effects of maternal consumption of Lake Michigan fish contaminated with persistent toxic substances. At birth, infants exposed to the highest levels of PCBs weighed less and had smaller head circumferences (Fein et al, 1984) and exhibited one or more behavioural deficits (Jacobson et al, 1984). Subsequent assessment and testing indicated that the growth retardation was irreversible, and that there were effects on short-term memory at seven months and at four years, and effects on attention (Jacobson et al, 1990; Jacobson and Jacobson, 1993). Testing at 11 years of age indicated that the children most highly exposed *in utero* had IQ scores that were more than six points below the reference group (Jacobson and Jacobson, 1996). The strongest effect was on memory and attention, and the most highly exposed children were three times more likely to have low average IQ scores and twice as likely to be at least two years behind in reading comprehension.

Date and nature of subsequent action or inaction

The information about the presence and effects of organochlorine chemicals in the Great Lakes in the 1960s had been foreshadowed not only by the publication of *Silent Spring* in 1962, but also by surveys in the UK of the risks to workers applying pesticides (1951), residues in food (1953) and risks to wildlife (1955) (cited in Cook, 1964). In 1961 the authorities decided on a voluntary ban on the use of aldrin, dieldrin and heptachlor for seed dressing for spring-sown cereals. Further restrictions were decided in 1964 based on the observations of high mortality of seed-eating birds and the widespread decline of the peregrine falcon (Ratcliffe, 1972). These moves were opposed by the Shell Chemical Company which stated (Robinson, 1967): 'the correlations between the time of usage of aldrin/dieldrin and the declines in populations are difficult to assess as there is insufficient quantitative data which can be used to establish precise relationships for any of the raptor species. It is impossible from these surveys to establish, in a rigorous manner, the nature of the relationship between the usage of aldrin/dieldrin and the breeding status of the peregrine falcon.'

This scepticism was mirrored on the other side of the Atlantic. Linda Lear (1997), in her biography of Rachel Carson, has detailed the intense controversy surrounding the use of organochlorine pesticides in the 1950s and 1960s and the partisan review of the US National Academy of Sciences National Research Council in its highly controversial report entitled 'Pest control and wildlife relationships'. The serialised publication of parts of *Silent Spring* in the *New Yorker* in 1962 resulted in a letter from general counsel of the Velsicol Chemical Company to Houghton Mifflin, publisher of *Silent Spring*, threatening legal action unless the last instalment in the *New Yorker* was cancelled (Lear, 1997). After publication of *Silent Spring*, the National Agricultural Chemicals Association (NACA) produced and distributed a critical information booklet entitled 'Fact and fancy' and sent it with letters to editors of magazines and newspapers indicating that future advertising revenues might be affected if *Silent Spring* were to receive favourable reviews (Lear, 1997).

In November 1963 there was a massive fish kill in the lower Mississippi River that was eventually traced to the organochlorine pesticide endrin and its chemical manufacturing by Velsicol Chemical Company at Memphis. The political response was to stimulate the production of a draft Clean Water Bill and a precautionary ruling by Stewart Udall as Secretary of the Department of the Interior prohibiting the use of pesticides where there was a reasonable doubt about safety (Lear, 1997). But even four years later, the Shell Chemical Company (1967) published a report that stated: 'The implication of endrin in the 1963 Mississippi River fish kill has not been verified by recent studies'.

The authorities in the US were reluctant to take action and the US Department of Agriculture responsible for registration of pesticides tended to align itself with the pesticide manufacturers and the farmers. A suit brought by Victor Yannacone in 1966 on behalf of the Brookhaven Town Natural Resources Committee to stop the use of DDT by the Suffolk County (Long Island, New York) Mosquito Control Commission, led to the formation of the Environmental Defense Fund in 1967. This group of lawyers, scientists and economists eventually brought a suit against the US Department of Agriculture, first in Wisconsin and subsequently in Washington, DC, to cancel the registration of DDT. Responsibility for pesticide registration was transferred to the newly formed US Environmental Protection Agency, and the Environmental Defense Fund suit eventually led to judicial administrative decisions to suspend the registrations of DDT, in 1972, and dieldrin, in 1973. In Canada, Professor Donald Chant (1969), on behalf of the newly formed Pollution Probe at the University of Toronto, successfully petitioned the Minister of Health and Welfare and the Minister of Agriculture to ban DDT and related pesticides. These national decisions had an immediate effect on the concentrations of organochlorine pesticides in the Great Lakes environment that was reflected in gradual improvements in the status and reproduction of bald eagles (Grier, 1982).

Other national and international decisions were being made that affected the concentrations of organochlorine compounds in the Great Lakes. The 1972 Federal Water Pollution Control Act laid the groundwork for regulating pollutant discharges into US waters. In Canada, the 1970 revisions to the Fisheries Act were being used to implement federal controls on water pollution. In 1970, Monsanto, as the sole manufacturer of PCBs in North America, announced that it was restricting the sale of PCBs for open uses, such as adhesives, sealants, chlorinated rubber, special paints and fire-resistant hydraulic fluids (Monsanto, 1970).

At the regional level, the governments of the US and of Canada had referred the matter of the pollution of the lower Great Lakes to the International Joint Commission (IJC). While the primary concern in the 1960s was eutrophication of the Great Lakes, particularly Lake Erie, the report of the IJC (1969) drew attention to the presence of organochlorine compounds in fish and wildlife. The report led to the negotiation of the 1972 Great Lakes Water Quality Agreement signed by President Nixon and Prime Minister Trudeau. In the 1970s, new information about the presence and effects of persistent toxic substances in the Great Lakes was affecting the political and regulatory processes in both countries. For example, the finding of mirex in Lake Ontario fish (Kaiser, 1974) led to a New York State prohibition of the possession of fish caught in Lake Ontario. This precautionary approach was, however, met with such flagrant violation of the regulation that it was rescinded after only a few months.

Similarly, when the Great Lakes Water Quality Agreement was renegotiated in 1978, it included a precautionary policy which stated that 'the discharge of any or all persistent toxic substances be virtually eliminated'. However the politics of the 1980s were very different, in both countries, from those of the 1970s when the Great Lakes Water Quality Agreement was renegotiated. The statements about the effects of persistent toxic substances on Great Lakes wildlife and humans were met with scepticism by government officials and demands for proof of a causal relationship before 'massive' appropriations and expenditures of public or private funds on remedial works.

Consequences of institutional responses

The past 30 years have been a period in which these institutional responses have led to significant improvements in water quality in the Great Lakes and particularly in relation to decreases in the sources, loadings and concentrations of persistent toxic substances. Early in the process, indicator organisms, such as lake trout and the eggs of herring gulls (Pekarik and Weseloh, 1998) were selected and analysed to follow the trends in concentrations. The evidence from these analyses demonstrate that the concentrations decreased markedly between about 1975 and the early 1980s (Stow et al, 1999). The trends in concentrations have generally followed a first order decline, and while technically the decreases continue at the same logarithmic rates, in practice the curves have become non-zero asymptotes at concentrations that are still of toxicological significance.

For example, the present concentrations of PCBs in water are about two orders of magnitude higher than the established water quality criterion for the protection of human health based on a cancer risk assessment. The changes in the politics in both countries in the 1980s do not seem to have led to the level of control of releases of organochlorine compounds or to the clean-up of non-point sources, such as contaminated landfill sites, sediments and atmospheric emissions, that are required to protect human health. The question remains whether present levels are affecting human development and whether the effects are serious enough to warrant implementing the stringent requirements of the Great Lakes Water Quality Agreement, particularly concerning restoration of water quality.

In 1990, the late Dr Helen Daly set up a team to replicate the Lake Michigan epidemiological studies by establishing a cohort centred on Oswego, New York and comprised of infants whose mothers had eaten Lake Ontario fish. While the researchers did not find the same relationship between maternal fish consumption prior to pregnancy and effects on body weight and head circumference, the same behavioural effects were observed (Lonky et al, 1996). In addition, based on rat studies (Daly, 1993), it was shown that the infants of the mothers with the highest fish consumption could not adapt to frustrating events. Subsequent chemical analytical determinations have shown the specific relationship between these behavioural anomalies and prenatal exposures to the highly chlorinated biphenyls (Stewart et al, 2000).

To address the pervasive scepticism of the 1980s and 1990s, a small group of scientists started applying new methods (Fox, 1991) for integrating evidence to infer causal relationships between the observed injury to wildlife and human health and exposures to persistent toxic substances. This process has resulted in a series of case studies linking the effects in a variety of organisms, including humans, with specific chemical causes (reviewed in Gilbertson, 1996). There has, however, been a variety of objections to this approach. For example, O'Brien (1994) has objected that the approach is not precautionary. The precautionary principle is, by definition, applicable to circumstances in which there is a high degree of uncertainty. The application of this a posteriori process is designed to reduce uncertainty using all the existing evidence to infer a causal relationship, thereby precluding the special need for applying the precautionary principle.

Similarly, the application of post-normal science (Funtowicz and Ravetz, 1993) to the implementation of the Great Lakes Water Quality Agreement, based on the premises of system complexity and uncertainty, has recently resulted in a singular legitimacy for multi-causal ecological statements (Shear, 1996; Hartig et al, 1998; Donahue, 1999). This supposed complexity and uncertainty has not been inconvenient to those interests reluctant to implement the costly remedial policies contained in the Great Lakes Water Quality Agreement. In contrast, the causal statements of the toxicologists are based on the integration of a diversity of evidence drawn from traditional science based on simple linear systems. These yield, first, a high degree of certainty, and thus dispense with the need to apply the precautionary principle. Second, the causal relationships could be used as a reliable and scientifically defensible basis for remedial action to restore water quality. This is particularly valuable in situations, such as the Great Lakes, where water quality has been chronically impaired by releases of persistent toxic substances and where organisms, including humans, have already been injured over a long period of time. Remedial actions, based on these statements, to address the extensively contaminated sediments and to secure the leaking chemical landfill sites, could be precautions against the production of another generation of infants prenatally exposed to chemicals that profoundly alter structural and functional development (Colborn and Clement, 1992; Colborn et al, 1998). In this sense, there is a powerful cognitive dissonance between the scientific information produced during the past 20 years on the injury to health (Johnson et al, 1998 and 1999) and the response of governments to implementing the policies contained in the Great Lakes Water Quality Agreement.

Costs and benefits

What have been the costs and benefits of these actions and their distribution across time? There have been significant improvements in the past 20 years in the development and application of methods for estimating costs and benefits in relation to chemical pollution (see, for example, Swanson and Vighi, 1998). A few cost and benefit analyses have been undertaken of the effects of persistent toxic substances in the Great Lakes and of their removal from discharges, contaminated landfill sites and sediments. For example, Burtraw and Krupnick (1999) have described methods to measure health benefits in monetary and non-monetary terms in the context of reductions in pollutants as part of a programme to improve Great Lakes water quality.

In the development of the Great Lakes Water Quality Guidance (US EPA, 1993) under the Clean Water Act, there was an analysis of the costs and benefits. Incremental costs were calculated for additional construction of treatment facilities and process changes including pollution prevention and waste minimisation programmes; for additional monitoring programmes; and for pre-treatment programmes. These were evaluated for 316 major municipal dischargers, 272 major industrial dischargers and 3207 minor dischargers using four different scenarios. Non-point sources were not covered. The total annual costs of compliance in the US were estimated in 1992 to be between US$80 and US$200 million (ca 80–200 million) depending on the scenario.

The Detroit Wastewater Treatment Plant is one of the largest point sources to the Great Lakes and discharges more than 100 kilograms of PCBs per year. Since 1971, nearly US$1 billion has been spent in upgrading the sewer infrastructure and US$120 million was recently spent in improving the operation through construction of a pumping station. There are plans for additional improvements costing US$1 billion, including an increase in the primary treatment capacity. Whether these costs will result in improvements in the PCB discharge from the plant is uncertain.

There are also a few studies of the costs and benefits of remedial actions for chemical landfill sites. One study was undertaken (Sudar and Muir, 1989) concerning the leaching of organochlorine pollutants from four of the largest dump sites located next to the Niagara River, upstream from Lake Ontario. The following three options were examined: no action; containment; and removal and thermal destruction, with consideration of short and long time horizons, and from the viewpoint of who pays and who benefits, with different discount rates. The cheapest option is containment, through capping the waste site and collecting and treating the contaminated groundwater, involving costs of US$100 million with a ten-year horizon, and nearly US$300 million with a 35-year horizon. This option essentially leaves the problem to another generation. The most expensive option is also containment with leaks that, over a 100-year horizon, would cost more than US$19 billion. The removal and thermal destruction option for the four sites would entail capital expenditures of about US$50 million and annual operating costs of about US$75 million for 15 years. The no action option, over 35 years and 100 years, respectively, would cost society more than US$1 billion and 16 billion. These same costs to society would be involved if industry spent about US$300 million over 35 years or US$3 billion over 100 years and was unsuccessful in stopping the plumes from reaching the face of the Niagara Gorge. These estimates were for four dump sites, but there are several hundred around the Great Lakes basin that are leaking persistent toxic substances.

The Great Lakes Science Advisory Board of the International Joint Commission recently toured nine of the hazardous waste sites in the Niagara Falls area. Extensive engineering work has been successfully undertaken to intercept and treat contaminated groundwater leachate from the hazardous waste sites and prevent movement to the Niagara River and to Lake Ontario. However, these are costly systems to construct and maintain. For example, at the Occidental Chemical Corporation's Hyde Park hazardous waste site between 1998 and 2000, some 100 million gallons of water (ca 375 million litres) were intercepted and treated, and between 1989 and 2000, nearly 300,000 gallons of non-aqueous phase liquids (ca 1.135 million litres) were collected and destroyed. The annual operation and maintenance costs at this site alone are US$2 million. Many of the remedial costs borne by the industries are unavailable, but available remedial costs to industry and governments, incurred to date for the New York landfill sites, are at least US$370 million. Remediation costs at New York hazardous waste sites are expected to total over US$630 million (US EPA and NYSDEC, 2000). There is a need for estimates of the benefits that will accrue from remedial actions at these and at other sites around the Great Lakes, or public and political support for these costly schemes is likely to wane.

The costs of remediation of contaminated sediment in the US part of the Great Lakes have been detailed (US EPA, 1998) with about US$580 million spent on 38 sediment remediation projects since 1985. However this only represents a small fraction of work necessary. Costs of remedial work for the Outboard Marine Corporation site at Waukegan, in Illinois, were US$21 million to remove 136,000 kilograms of PCBs from OMC property. A further 900 kilograms of PCBs is in the navigational channel and will be removed starting in 2002, at an estimated cost of US$12–14 million which will include construction of a confined disposal facility. Similarly, estimates for treatment costs for remedial work on the sediments of Hamilton Harbour range from CA$ 60 million to 1 billion. There seem to be few benefits analyses to supplement these cost estimates.

Conclusions and lessons for the future

The Great Lakes have provided a valuable if unwitting laboratory for studying the effects of organochlorine compounds, not only on the health of wildlife and humans, but also on the political responses to pollution of large ecosystems with persistent toxic substances. The record indicates the extraordinary lengths of time between the introduction of a new technology, the detection of an effect, the demonstration of a causal relationship, and the appropriate and sufficient response from the authorities (Lawless, 1977). It is only after more than half a century of exposures to organochlorine compounds from the Great Lakes that scientists are beginning to comprehend the scale of damage that occurred to human health and to wildlife.

Over this long period of time, scientists have been faced with a dilemma of whether, on the one hand, to investigate injury to populations of fish, wildlife and humans suspected to have been caused by persistent toxic substances, or to

Table 12.1 *Great Lakes: early warnings and actions*

1962	*Silent Spring* by Rachel Carson is the significant early warning of the effects of organochlorine pesticides on fish and wildlife as well as the threat of cancer in humans
1963	First observation of changes in eggshell quality on Pigeon Island in Lake Ontario
1966	Hickey et al publish the first analytical results of the presence of organochlorine compounds in organisms in the Great Lakes
1969	DDT and related pesticides are banned in Canada
1972	DDT is banned in the US (dieldrin is banned in 1973) and gradual improvements in wildlife begin in the Great Lakes
1974	Concerns of possible effects of organochlorine compounds on human health
1978	Association of incidence of diseases (high rates of birth defects, miscarriages, cancers, etc) in Love Canal, Niagara Falls with the disposal of toxic wastes (including dioxin) denied by Hooker Chemical Company
1978	Renegotiation of the Great Lakes Water Quality Agreement, including a precautionary policy, but it is not properly implemented
1980	President's Emergency Declaration moves 900 families from the hazardous Love Canal area
1984	Studies show that, at birth, infants exposed to high levels of PCBs (maternal consumption of Lake Michigan contaminated fish) weighed less and had smaller heads
1996	Studies of Lake Ontario affected children published that observed same behavioural effects as in affected children from Lake Michigan
2000	The specific relationship between behavioural anomalies and prenatal exposures to the highly chlorinated biphenyls is determined
2000	Reluctance to undertake costly remedial actions even after causal relationship is proven

Source: EEA

make a special plea to stop the sources and exposures even though they origi-nally had little more than a suspicion. Ironically, even though a causal relationship has now been proven between the injury to health and exposures to persistent toxic substances, Great Lakes scientists have found it difficult to communicate their scientific evidence within the social, economic and political contexts in which their work is undertaken to effect remedial actions. These various case studies demonstrate that the length of time between the introduc-tion of a new technology, product or undertaking, the discovery of its deleterious effects, and the regulatory, judicial or administrative action to reduce exposures, is seldom less than 25 years.

The existing evidence concerning the persistence of the organochlorine compounds released into the Great Lakes during the past 60 years indicates that it will probably be several more decades before the necessary remedial actions will have reduced concentrations sufficiently to protect human reproduction and development from chemically induced injury, particularly from consumption of contaminated Great Lakes fish. The scientific aspects are characterised by a high degree of certainty. In essence, we are engaged in the trans-generational transmission not only of the legacy of contamination and the associated dilemmas, but also of chemically induced injury to the structural and functional development of exposed infants. But for the health, fisheries and environmental researchers and administrators there is a complex array of social, economic and political dilemmas. For example, should health administrators draw attention to the contamination and recommend that children and women of child-bearing age should not eat Great Lakes fish, or would this advice jeopardise commercial, sport and tribal fisheries interests? Similarly, should health and environmental researchers report on the injury to fisheries and wildlife populations, and on the injury to human health from the continuing exposures to elevated concentrations of persistent toxic substances? Or would the requisite response to this information by the environmental administrators represent an apparently impossible financial burden for the US and Canadian taxpayers?

TBT antifoulants: a tale of ships, snails and imposex

David Santillo, Paul Johnston and William J Langston

Introduction

There is little doubt that, without some form of control, the accumulation of marine fouling communities on vessels and man-made structures at sea increases drag and, in the case of vessels, fuel consumption, with substantial consequences in terms of economics and emissions. There is no doubt, also, that tributyltin (TBT) compounds (and the less widely used triphenyltins) are extremely effective and relatively economical as antifouling biocides, contributing to the rapid take-up of organotin-based paints by the shipping industry and small boat owners in the 1970s. These two arguments have formed the basis of the defence of TBT antifouling formulations since the first undesirable consequences of their use became apparent in the late 1970s, and indeed are still cited today by proponents of their continued suitability (for example, see Evans, 2000; Abel, 2000). What is missing from such evaluations, of course, is proper consideration not only of the quantifiable financial losses suffered by the aquaculture industry and imposed upon harbour authorities as a result of the widespread application of TBT paints, but also of the broader environmental 'costs' which led initially to restrictions on use and which now underlie the decision for a global phase-out.

The TBT story presents, in some ways, a rather unusual case study. Firstly, the widespread use of TBT paints is a relatively recent development, with its origins in the late 1960s. Secondly, initial concerns about adverse effects were raised during the period in which its use became most popular, concerns that led rapidly to some national and regional restrictions. Thirdly, the adverse effect most commonly associated with TBT, that of imposex in marine gastropod molluscs resulting from interference with steroid hormone metabolism, represented a highly sensitive, chemical-specific phenomenon. This factor contributed greatly to the early acceptance of a direct causal relationship and, in turn, of the need for controls. The paint manufacturers, in concert with other interested parties, mounted challenges to restrictions imposed in the 1980s, but the strength of the evidence for severe effects on biota, including regional extermination of some species, could hardly be denied.

The prohibition of the use of TBT paints on vessels under 25 metres in length, effective in France from 1982, in the UK from 1987 and more widely from the end of the 1980s and early 1990s, did much to improve the situation within marinas and sheltered harbours where use on leisure craft had predominated. Some regional recovery of affected mollusc populations has since been recorded. Through the late 1980s and 1990s, however, a picture of more widespread TBT contamination and population-level effects emerged, coincident with improved monitoring and understanding of the properties and environmental distribution of organotins. Vos et al (2000) estimate that imposex has now been documented in the wild for as many as 150 species of marine prosobranch snails worldwide. Evidence relating the prevalence of imposex to density of shipping traffic, along with poor recovery of affected populations in some areas and widespread accumulation of butyltin residues in marine mammals, led to renewed calls for prohibitions to be extended to use on all vessels, irrespective of size. As we stand on the brink of just such a prohibition, developed under the auspices of the International Maritime Organization's Marine Environmental Protection Committee (MEPC), what can we learn from the process of its evolution?

The emergence of the TBT problem

Organotin compounds were first developed as moth-proofing agents in the 1920s, and only later used more widely as bactericides and fungicides (Moore et al, 1991). Dibutyltin and tributyltin compounds have been produced since the late 1940s (Laughlin and Linden, 1985), although use of TBT in marine antifouling paints dates only from the 1960s (Balls, 1987; ten Hallers-Tjabbes, 1997) and then initially as a booster biocide in copper-based formulations. As a result of its superior effectiveness over copper (Wade et al, 1988a), the use of TBT paints by private and commercial users accelerated greatly in the 1970s, during which these formulations captured a major proportion of the antifouling market (Evans, 2000). 'Free association' paints, which released the biocide rapidly at first but demanded frequent reapplication, were gradually replaced by 'self-polishing copolymer' formulations which ensured a more constant release of biocide and reduced repainting frequency.

At the same time as its explosive increase in use, the first observations were made of TBT effects on non-target organisms. While toxicity to fouling organisms was intentional, its propensity for wider impacts on the marine environment had been grossly underestimated. An early focus on acute effects, especially mortality (Laughlin and Linden, 1987), failed to identify sub-lethal consequences of prolonged exposure in some taxa. For example, imposex (the development of male sexual structures in females) can be initiated in some gastropod molluscs by TBT in the low ng/l (nanograms per litre or parts per trillion) range (Bryan et al, 1986; Alzieu, 1998), concentrations also known to cause shell deformity and larval mortality (Alzieu et al, 1986).

The phenomenon of imposex was first described by Smith (1971), from studies of the American mud-snail (*Nassarius obsoletus*) in the vicinity of harbours on the US east coast. Around the same time, Blaber (1970) recorded the appearance of a penis in female dogwhelks (*Nucella lapillus*) in Plymouth Sound, UK, at much greater prevalence close to the harbour than further away. Despite the severity of the phenomenon, however, the causal agent remained unknown. Only as analytical capabilities improved in the late 1970s and early 1980s was the connection with shipping made and the extent of damage already done recognised.

Two regional case histories were instrumental in identifying low-dose effects of TBT and initiating development of the first regional controls; the collapse of the shellfish industry in Arcachon Bay (Atlantic coast of France) and the reporting of widespread imposex in dogwhelks from southern UK coastal waters.

Arcachon Bay

Until the mid-1970s, Arcachon Bay had been an important area for oyster (*Crassostrea gigas*) culture, with production of 10,000–15,000 tonnes per year (Evans, 2000) covering substantial areas of the tidal mud flats. The bay was also popular with leisure craft, with vessel numbers increasing from 7500 in the mid-1970s to 15,000 at the start of the 1980s. Estimated inputs of TBT to the bay peaked at around 8 kg per day (Ruiz et al, 1996).

Imposex was first observed in the bay in 1970, affecting the predatory gastropod *Ocenebra erinacea* (oyster drill), leading rapidly to its near extirpation from the bay (Gibbs, 1993). TBT was identified as the responsible agent only in the early 1980s.

Had the adverse effects been limited to the loss of this species, considered a pest within the shellfish industry for its damage to oyster stocks, little if any action may have followed. However, this early warning was quickly followed by failure of the oyster stocks themselves. Despite a normal spawning event in summer 1976, few of the larvae survived. Larval settlement largely failed through the late 1970s and into the 1980s, resulting in massive financial losses by the shellfish industry. By 1981, annual oyster production had fallen to only 3000 tonnes (Ruiz et al, 1996). In addition to reproductive failure, adult oysters were rendered unsaleable by shell deformation leading, in severe cases, to 'ball-shaped' specimens (Alzieu et al, 1989).

Such observations pre-dated analytical techniques sensitive enough to describe in detail environmental distributions of TBT. Alzieu et al (1986) provided the first reliable survey of organotins in the waters of Arcachon Bay, while sediment data were not available until the 1990s (Sarradin et al, 1994). Nevertheless, the severity of impacts on the ecology of Arcachon Bay, manifest in heavy financial losses, was sufficient to stimulate relatively swift action by the French government. Acting on the best information available linking the oyster collapse to the presence of TBT, France was the first country to introduce legislation prohibiting the application of TBT paints to small (< 25 metre) vessels, in 1982 (Michel and Averty, 1999a). These controls undoubtedly markedly reduced TBT inputs from marinas throughout France. In the case of Arcachon, implementation was probably aided by the local provenance of many boat-owners and their interest in preserving a local industry. Their effectiveness in addressing more widespread TBT contamination remains questionable, however (Michel and Averty, 1999a).

UK harbours and coastal waters

Following Blaber's (1970) observations in Plymouth Sound, other research began to identify imposex as a more widespread problem. Frequency of imposex in *N. lapillus* was greatest close to ports and harbours, although evidence was also growing for the spread of the phenomenon through coastal waters of the southern UK (Bryan et al, 1986 and 1987). In addition, Waldock and Thain (1983) linked the failure of attempts to introduce Pacific oyster culture into the UK in the early 1980s to TBT exposure rather than to fine sediment particles as previously thought. Reproductive failures and shell deformities in the UK showed many parallels with those recorded in Arcachon Bay.

Based on emergent concerns, the UK government introduced controls on the sale of TBT paints for use on small vessels in 1985. These included controls on retail sales, guidelines for handling paints and the setting of an environmental quality target (EQT) of 20 ng/l TBT (8 ng/l as tin), a level considered at the time to be sufficiently protective of marine biota (Waldock et al, 1987). TBT concentrations in many coastal waters consistently exceeded the EQT. Moreover, as understanding developed through the 1980s, it became clear that concentrations well below the EQT could cause severe effects.

Sterilisation of female dogwhelks occurs at TBT concentrations as low as 3–5 ng/l TBT (Gibbs et al, 1988), with almost all females affected once concentrations reach 10 ng/l and more fundamental changes at higher concentrations (including testes development and suppression of egg production).

During the 1980s, butyltin concentrations exhibited strong seasonal trends relating to boating activity and maintenance. Summer-time concentrations in marinas regularly exceeded 100 ng/l and occasionally 1000 ng/l (Waldock et al, 1987). Langston et al (1987) reported similar concentrations in marina waters within Poole Harbour (southern UK). These marinas regularly served 5000 leisure craft, engaged in hull maintenance and berthing. Even beyond the marinas, TBT concentrations above 100 ng/l were sometimes encountered. The overlap between field concentrations and those known to have severe developmental effects highlights the extent of the problem faced, and illustrates the inadequacy of the EQT as a protective instrument.

Evidence continued to accumulate during the 1980s. Bryan et al's (1986) study of dogwhelks in southwest England was particularly influential, concluding: 'that the incidence of "imposex"… is widespread, that all populations are affected to some degree… Populations close to centres of boating and shipping activity show the highest degrees of imposex'.

The study also noted that the rapid increase in imposex in Plymouth Sound strongly coincided with contemporary increases in TBT applications, and revealed a strong correlation with tissue concentrations of organotin residues. The significance of this study was profiled in September the same year in the journal *Marine Pollution Bulletin* ('TBT linked to dogwhelk decline', 1986), in many ways marking wider acceptance of the central role of TBT in observed declines.

The geographical extent of the TBT problem in Europe had been recognised by the late 1980s (Bailey and Davies, 1988a and 1989; Gibbs et al, 1991). Balls (1987) reported that use of TBT paints on salmon-farming cages had resulted in contamination of a Scottish sea loch, and noted the generally higher prevalence of imposex within sea lochs used for aquaculture. Cleary and Stebbing (1987) highlighted the additional concern of accumulation of organotins in the lipid-rich sea-surface microlayer, a threat considered particularly relevant to buoyant fish larvae (because of resulting exposure during sensitive developmental periods) and intertidal organisms (exposed to the microlayer during tidal ebb and flow) (Cleary et al, 1993). Concerns over persistence and impacts in sediments were also emerging at this time (Langston et al, 1987; Langston and Burt, 1991).

Faced with the accumulation of research, the UK government considered options for further retail restrictions and, in January 1987, reduced the maximum permissible content of organotins in applied paint, helped by technological developments (Side, 1987). These limits were rapidly superseded, however, by the introduction in May 1987 of a total ban on the retail sale of TBT paint (Waldock et al, 1987 and 1988) for use on vessels under 25 metres and on fish cages (earlier voluntary measures having failed adequately to address this latter application). At this time, work by the UK Water Research Centre was under way to recommend environmental quality standards (EQS) for organotin compounds in water (Zabel et al, 1988), involving consideration of toxicity and environmental behaviour of a range of organotins. It became apparent that for TBT, in particular, no-effect levels could not be achieved in the environment without use restrictions. Two years later, and in recognition of the low-dose effects, the 1985 EQT was replaced by an EQS of only 2 ng/l (Cleary, 1991).

In June 1987, the Paris Commission (PARCOM), responsible for administering the Paris Convention (1978), recognised that the use of TBT paints was causing 'serious pollution in the inshore areas of the Convention waters (NE Atlantic)' (PARCOM, 1987). PARCOM Recommendation 87/1 called for a harmonised ban on retail sales for application to pleasure boats and fish cages and, furthermore, for consideration of restrictions for seagoing vessels and underwater structures.

Though strong in intent, it quickly became apparent that PARCOM could not achieve restrictions within the commercial shipping sector. As this issue had already been referred to the International Maritime Organization (IMO), PARCOM instead turned its attention to inputs from docking activities, especially hull maintenance operations, in PARCOM Recommendation 88/1 (PARCOM, 1988). The effectiveness of such measures remains difficult to evaluate, though it is indisputable that shipyards and docks remain important point sources of organotins.

A global pollutant

Concerns over the impacts of TBT soon extended worldwide, leading to a series of national and regional measures towards the end of the 1980s. The annual Oceans symposia, organised by the US Marine Technology Society, did much to disseminate the growing body of research (Wade et al, 1988b; Krone et al, 1989). The NOAA (US National Oceanic and Atmospheric Administration) Mussel Watch programme highlighted the ubiquitous distribution of butyltins in bivalves from US coasts (Wade et al, 1988a and b; Uhler et al, 1989), while work in New Zealand confirmed accumulation in sediments (King et al, 1989). Prohibitions addressing small vessels were adopted in the US in 1988, followed in 1989 by similar measures in Canada, New Zealand and Australia, and by European legislation in 1991 harmonising controls throughout the EU (Evans, 2000).

Effectiveness of controls on small vessels

Retail restrictions undoubtedly resulted in a major shift away from the use of TBT paint on leisure craft (although the extent of illegal application remains unknown) and substantial reductions in inputs. In some regions at least, this was manifest in partial recovery of mollusc populations. In Arcachon Bay, monitoring of the effectiveness of regulations in reducing water column concentrations of butyltins was limited by the high detection limits of early analytical methods. While Alzieu et al (1986) were able to demonstrate that concentrations fell from 900 ng/l tin in 1983 to below 100 ng/l by 1985, it took until the late 1980s to confirm that concentrations had fallen below 10 ng/l in most parts of the bay. Hydrodynamic disturbance has largely prevented reconstruction of sediment concentration trends (Ruiz et al, 1996).

Recovery of the oyster beds, and resumption of commercial operations, in the mid-1980s provided the first indirect evidence of the effectiveness of the ban. Indeed, the recovery of the bay is frequently cited as an illustration of how the limited controls of the 1980s 'solved' the TBT problem (Nicholson and Evans, 1997; Evans, 2000), a view which has met substantial disagreement.

Evidence for partial recovery of severely affected mollusc populations certainly exists from several parts of Europe. For example, Minchin (1995) reported recovery of the flame shell (*Lima hians*) and associated flora in Mulroy Bay (Ireland), previously decimated through use of TBT on salmon cages between 1981 and 1985. In the sheltered inlet of Sullom Voe, Shetland Islands, and adjacent Yell Sound, imposex in dogwhelks was significantly less prevalent in 1995 than in 1991 (Harding et al, 1997) although overall prevalence remained high. Evans et al (2000a) suggest that there has been a more general recovery in UK dogwhelk populations over the last decade.

Other studies provide less cause for optimism. Minchin et al (1997) stressed that recovery of dogwhelk populations in Ballybegs (Ireland) had been slower than expected, and recoveries in Sullom Voe and Yell Sound occurred against a continuing high background of imposex, and continued absence of dogwhelks from worst affected areas. In Canada, St-Jean et al (1999) noted that butyltin concentrations in blue mussels (*Mytilus edulis*) and sediments from the southern Gulf of St Lawrence remained remarkably high eight years after retail restrictions. Despite initial declines in French coastal waters, dissolved TBT concentrations have since stabilised and remain at levels often well in excess of those known to cause adverse effects in some species (Michel and Averty, 1999a). In some areas of Arcachon Bay, concentrations remained high enough to cause imposex in sensitive species ten years after the 1982 regulations (Ruiz et al, 1996). Similar concerns have been voiced for UK estuarine and coastal locations (Cleary, 1991; Langston et al, 1994).

The underlying causes of continued contamination and failure of ecosystems fully to recover undoubtedly differ from location to location. In some cases (eg Huet et al, 1996), isolated but significant illegal use of TBT paints on small vessels has been implicated, while other researchers have stressed the importance of release from historically contaminated sediments (Waldock et al, 1990; Langston et al, 1994). High larval sensitivities (Gibbs, 1993) and long life histories (Rees et al, 1999) undoubtedly also contribute to the slow rate of recovery of some species.

Potentially the most significant single contributor to continued widespread presence of TBT in the marine environment, however, and currently the most fiercely debated, is use on seagoing vessels.

The significance of seagoing vessels

At the time of the first national and regional prohibitions, the use of TBT paints on commercial and military ships was viewed as a lesser concern because, it was argued, those vessels spent most of their operational lives on the open seas. Nevertheless, these ships use inshore waters and port facilities on a regular basis. The scale of TBT inputs from hull maintenance of large vessels has been recognised for some time. Waldock et al (1988) recorded TBT in wash water from a naval frigate at approximately 1 million times the lowest biologically effective concentrations, and estimated total input from cleaning a single vessel at 100 g of freely available TBT. Including TBT bound to paint-chips, which might act as a long-term reservoir of butyltins to the environment, led to estimates of almost 1 kg TBT per vessel per cleaning operation. Guidelines to control inputs from such operations have been in use in many countries for some time, although their effectiveness is difficult to evaluate.

Studies surrounding the Sullom Voe oil terminal (Bailey and Davies, 1988b) provide evidence for significant inputs of organotins from normal transport operations of TBT-coated ships. Although uses on small service vessels and marker buoys contributed to early inputs, more recent inputs arise predominantly from movements of oil tankers themselves. Significant contributions from heavy commercial traffic have also been highlighted in the Gulf of St Lawrence (St-Jean et al, 1999).

While ongoing inputs from commercial shipping to coastal waters are now generally accepted, the significance of such sources to remote coastal and offshore areas remains the subject of intense debate (ten Hallers-Tjabbes, 1997;

Evans, 2000). This is despite the increasing body of evidence supporting a link between density of shipping traffic and occurrence of biological effects (predominantly imposex) in offshore waters. Among the first to highlight imposex in the common whelk (*Buccinum undatum*) from the open North Sea and describe a positive correlation with shipping intensity were ten Hallers-Tjabbes et al (1994). Similar correlations have since been reported in the Strait of Malacca, connecting the Bay of Bengal with the South China Sea (Swennen et al, 1997; Hashimoto et al, 1998), and in remote parts of the Galician coast (Ruiz et al, 1998). Cadee et al (1995) speculated that organotins might be responsible for local destruction of whelks in the Dutch Wadden Sea. More recently, Davies et al (1998) estimated total annual inputs of 68 tonnes TBT to the North Sea from shipping, with continuous leaching from painted hulls when in port or under way the major contributor.

Nicholson and Evans (1997) provided further evidence supporting the pioneering work of ten Hallers-Tjabbes et al (1994) but questioned the significance of what they termed 'mild' imposex against a background of overexploitation by shell fisheries. There is little doubt, however, that detection of population-level effects in offshore regions was an important factor underlying calls for the extension of restrictions in the mid-1990s.

During the same period, the truly global nature of the TBT problem was acknowledged (Ellis and Pattisina, 1990; Kannan et al, 1995a, b and c). Though data remain limited for areas outside Europe and North America, recent studies in Japan and the Philippines (Harino et al, 1998a, b, c and 1999; Prudente et al, 1999) have gone some way towards redressing the balance, confirming (as suspected) the occurrence of similar relationships.

Recent research has also highlighted the widespread accumulation of organotins in organisms higher in the food chain, including cetaceans. Iwata et al (1995) were among the first to determine concentrations in marine mammals, suggesting that the high levels recorded (up to 10 parts per million (ppm) in porpoise liver) reflected a low potential for metabolism of these compounds. Tanabe et al (1998) later extended the data set, including species from North Pacific and Asian coastal waters. Kannan et al (1996) described butyltin accumulation in dolphin, tuna and sharks from the Mediterranean, noting markedly different ratios of TBT breakdown products within the different taxa. First reports of butyltin residues in European cetaceans and seals, including in pelagic cetaceans that feed in remote offshore waters, were published by Ariese et al (1998) and Law et al (1998 and 1999).

Although uncertainty remains, evidence suggests that accumulation of butyltins in top predators might adversely effect the immune system. Kannan et al (1997) reported high levels of TBT and its breakdown products (primarily dibutyltin) in bottlenose dolphins associated with mortality events on the US Atlantic and Gulf coasts. Similar correlations have been reported for Californian southern sea otters (*Enhydra lutris nereis*) exhibiting various infectious diseases (Kannan et al, 1998).

Human intake of organotins from seafood, especially from fish farmed in TBT-treated cages, has long been recognised (Davies and McKie, 1987; Ishizaka et al, 1989). Only more recently, however, has such intake been evaluated.

Cardwell et al (1999) reported that residues were widely detectable in US seafood but that estimated intakes were significantly below levels judged to be of concern for human health. In contrast, Belfroid et al (2000) concluded that average intakes of TBT from seafood could lead to exceedance of tolerable daily intakes based on more sensitive immunotoxicological end-points for some products retailed in North America, Europe and Asia, while stressing that, for the majority of countries, data were simply unavailable.

Progress towards a global phase-out

Despite uncertainties regarding 'far-field' effects, contamination of the marine environment with organotins is clearly a persistent and pervasive problem. In 1995, and in spite of a decision by MEPC in 1994 that no further controls were necessary, ministers at the fourth Conference on the Protection of the North Sea in Esbjerg agreed: 'to undertake concerted action within IMO aiming at a worldwide phase-out of the use of TBT on all ships' (MINDEC, 1995).

Their preference for global action within IMO, in common with the position taken by the OSPAR (Convention for the Protection of the Marine Environment of the North-East Atlantic) Commission, recognised the limits of regional measures in addressing a transboundary problem. On the basis of emerging research, MEPC agreed in 1996 to look again at the need for a global TBT ban (ten Hallers-Tjabbes, 1997). The possibility of such a ban was explicitly recognised at MEPC's 40th session (MEPC, 1997), marking a sea change in the thinking of that committee. Draft mandatory regulations were duly adopted the following year (MEPC, 1998).

The deadlines now incorporated in the draft International Convention on the Control of Harmful Anti-fouling Systems (2003 for phase-out of application of organotin paints, 2008 for their presence on ship hulls) were adopted under IMO Assembly Resolution A.895(21) in November 1999, and formal adoption of the convention is expected in 2001.

The question of alternatives

With the advent of such a progressive measure, attention is focusing increasingly on the availability of effective and economically viable alternatives to TBT (Evans et al, 2000b). It is clear that some of the preparations in use prior to the widespread introduction of TBT (including those containing mercury or arsenic compounds) are not acceptable alternatives. Copper-based systems generally require booster biocides in order to be effective, biocides which themselves may present additional problems. Those containing the triazine herbicide Irgarol 1051, used extensively in some areas as a replacement for TBT on leisure craft, are commonly cited examples. Widespread occurrence of this herbicide in certain estuaries (Scarlett et al, 1997), coupled with direct effects on plant growth in the field (Dahl and Blanck, 1996; Scarlett et al, 1999), in some ways mirror early findings with respect to TBT.

Some commentators use such examples as justification against substitution of TBT in commercial shipping applications (Abel, 2000; Abbott et al, 2000). This is a somewhat negative argument. The more appropriate question is, can fouling control be achieved without recourse to such highly toxic, persistent and bioaccumulative substances?

Research into use of natural antifouling chemicals is developing rapidly (Clare, 1998), though commercial application may remain some time away. Perhaps the most promising contemporary solution is biocide-free, 'non-stick' coatings which simply present a physical barrier to settlement. Such coatings have been commercially available for many years, and retain a significant market share for leisure craft. Their viability and performance on larger vessels remain under evaluation, although applicability for fast-moving craft has been demonstrated. Although significant technical issues remain to be resolved, advances towards antifouling mechanisms which do not release hazardous substances to the sea would seem desirable.

Late lessons from the TBT story

The above discussions indicate the degree to which the hazards of TBT were initially underestimated. It was initially assumed, for example, based on acute toxicity tests that concentrations in the ug/l (micrograms per litre) range were necessary to initiate biological effects and that, as a consequence, an EQT of 20 ng/l would be sufficiently protective. It quickly became apparent that, even if the EQT could be met (and it was greatly exceeded in some areas), severe biological effects could be expected. Had the endocrine-mediated mechanisms underlying imposex (Matthiessen and Gibbs, 1998) been identified earlier, the potential for low-dose effects would have been clear. Of course, much of our knowledge of organotin toxicity has been obtained through hindsight and is likely to continue to develop (Langston, 1996; Bouchard et al, 1999; Morcillo and Porte, 2000). In the meantime, it may be hoped that the lessons gained will allow earlier identification and, wherever possible, avoidance of future problems in advance.

The persistence of organotins, permitting their accumulation and wider dissemination, was also underestimated. Early predictions that TBT would degrade rapidly in surface waters (see reviews by Simmonds, 1986 and Lee et al, 1989) failed to account for the high lipophilicity and sediment-binding properties of organotins in seawater. Half-life estimates in the order of days for eutrophic surface waters must be contrasted with up to several years for residues in nutrient-poor waters (Michel and Averty, 1999b) and marine sediments (de Mora et al, 1989), especially anaerobic sediments. The persistence of TBT, and toxicity to sediment communities, raises the prospect of delayed recovery of damaged ecosystems (Langston et al, 1994; Dahllof et al, 1999) and represents a substantial legacy to be borne by authorities responsible for dredging operations. This problem is only now receiving formal recognition within international conventions (London Convention 1972, OSPAR Convention 1992) regulating the dumping of dredge materials at sea.

Organotin bioaccumulation was also underestimated, and the specific role of biofilms in enhancing bioaccumulation and toxicity has only recently been recognised (Labare et al, 1997). Accumulation in top predators was simply not envisaged.

Hindsight is a wonderful thing, of course. Nevertheless, increasing awareness of pathways and interactions within the marine environment, coupled with an appreciation of their complexity and indeterminate nature (Santillo et al, 1998), should equip us to reduce or even avoid the potential for future TBT-style scenarios involving other persistent organic pollutants.

Two key factors contributed to early ignorance of the geographical extent of the TBT problem: low sensitivity of analytical methods and absence, in most regions, of adequate baseline data on the distribution and ecology of non-commercial species. The first of these was subject to an unavoidable process of methods development, partly overcome by the high specificity of imposex as a biomarker for TBT exposure. The second limitation illustrates a more general concern which could have been avoided through greater focus on the collection of 'baseline' data. Where such data were available (eg southwest England), they were invaluable in the early detection of effects on non-commercial species. Though frequently underrated, baseline studies play a vital role in the early detection of adverse trends and may consequently serve the application of precaution. Equally important is the need for continuing long-term monitoring of TBT-affected areas, as this will provide us with unique insights into recovery of pollutant-damaged environments.

The continuation of the TBT problem in coastal waters of Japan (Iwata et al, 1995; Harino et al, 1998a and b), despite a national ban on all applications of TBT for marine antifouling, clearly illustrates the transboundary nature of the problem. It would seem that universal, global restrictions are the only way to address the totality of the TBT problem and to achieve environmental quality standards in all coastal systems.

Finally, though the selection of alternatives to hazardous chemicals is never a simple task, this does not justify inaction. Several of the existing TBT 'alternatives' carry their own problems, though thankfully, on a global scale, none has yet proved as damaging as TBT. In selecting appropriate alternatives, those which do not rely on the release of hazardous substances to the marine environment should, perhaps, be viewed most favourably. Broader consideration of problems may give rise to more beneficial solutions than simple 'chemical for chemical' substitution.

Conclusions: precaution or retrospective action?

The use of organotin antifoulants has and continues to result in widespread and sometimes severe environmental effects. Unusually in the field of ecotoxicology, the evidence linking cause and effect (with respect to TBT-induced imposex) is irrefutable. Vos et al (2000) refer to the phenomenon as 'the best example of endocrine disruption in invertebrates that is causally linked to an environmental pollutant'.

Table 13.1 *TBT: early warnings and actions*

Early 1970s	Rapid increase in the use of TBT antifouling paints on vessels of all sizes and first reports of imposex in marine snails (Blaber, 1970; Smith, 1971)
1976–81	Repeated failure of larval settlement leads to near collapse of oyster fishery, Arcachon Bay, France
1982	France introduces legislation prohibiting the use of TBT paints on small vessels
1985	First controls introduced in UK limiting concentrations of TBT in paints
1986	Bryan et al (1986) report widespread imposex in dogwhelks on southern coast of UK, linked to TBT
January 1987	UK announces further restrictions on TBT content of applied antifouling paint
May 1987	UK introduces ban on retail sale of TBT paint for use on vessels < 25 m and on fish cages
June 1987	PARCOM Recommendation 87/1 calls for similar ban over entire convention area (Northeast Atlantic)
1988	US introduces restrictions. Waldock et al (1988) highlight significance of inputs from shipyards
1989	Restrictions introduced in Canada, Australia and New Zealand
1991	Harmonised ban on retail sale of TBT paint introduced at EU level
1994	Early reports of imposex in whelks from offshore areas of North Sea linked to shipping activity
1995	Ministerial declaration of fourth North Sea conference (Esbjerg) commits to working for global phase-out of TBT paint within IMO
1997	Concept of global phase out of organotin containing paints agreed at MEPC's 40th session
1998	Draft mandatory regulations aimed at such a phase-out adopted. OSPAR (Convention for the Protection of the Marine Environment of the North-East Atlantic) prioritises organotins for action to cease all releases. Cessation of all releases of organotins to marine environment, under OSPAR's hazardous substances strategy in 2020
November 1999	Deadlines for phase-out adopted under IMO Assembly Resolution A.895(21)
2001	Text of International Convention on the Control of Harmful Antifouling Systems to be finalised. In 2003 worldwide prohibition on new application of organotin antifoulants to all vessels and in 2008 the existing organotin antifouling coatings will be replaced on all vessels worldwide

Source: EEA

It would be difficult to argue, therefore, that any of the actions to address TBT to date have been precautionary, resulting as they have from extensive documentation of ecological impacts. Actions have undoubtedly contributed towards remediating the most severe problems, but this is not precaution. The 1987 UK restrictions, for example, stemmed from a realisation that environmental concentrations were already well above those known to cause chronic effects and had already resulted in widespread declines in gastropod populations. It could be argued, similarly, that agreement of the IMO convention which will bring about elimination of organotin antifoulants has come only after the consequences of continued use have been well documented. Although the significance of this global, legally binding treaty should not be underestimated, it too is fundamentally retrospective in action.

Complete phase-out of organotin paints from the global shipping fleet by 2008 will mark the closure of an important chapter in the TBT story. Persistence in sediments and long-lived biota will remain to be addressed, but widespread inputs from shipping should, at least, be a thing of the past. Organotin inputs will continue, of course, through their use as additives in a wide range of consumer products. Whether efforts to address these emerging challenges will draw on the lessons of the past remains to be seen.

Hormones as growth promoters: the precautionary principle or a political risk assessment?

Jim W Bridges and Olga Bridges

Introduction

Oestrogenic steroid hormones ('oestrogens') have a crucial role in cellular regulation in all vertebrate species. The levels required to bring about such changes are very low, around 0.1–1 pg/ml (picograms per millilitre) of serum. It has been known for over five decades that oestrogens affect the development of the male reproductive system of mammals (Zuckerman, 1940). Nonetheless, oestrogenic steroid hormones are often called 'female hormones'. The female reproductive system initially develops independently of the hormone regulatory system. This means that by default an animal is female if hormone stimulation is absent (Wilson and Lasnitzki, 1971). Nonetheless, in both sexes oestrogens are needed for fertility.

At a level above the physiological one, natural oestrogens produced by mammals, such as oestradiol-17β, have a lasting effect on males. Experimental studies have shown, for example, that the administration of oestradiol-17β to mice, rats, guinea pigs and rabbits, during both foetal and perinatal life, can result in significant defects in the pituitary-hypothalamic function in males. This, in turn, may disrupt testicular function during adulthood (Takasugi, 1979; Orgebin-Crist et al, 1983; Davies and Danzo, 1981; Brown-Grant et al, 1975).

For maximum growth a combination of both oestrogens and androgens (male hormones) is required. The growth promoting effects are attributed principally to the ability of combinations of oestrogens and androgens to increase the retention of dietary nitrogen through protein synthesis through several mechanisms (European Commission, 1996). After the Second World War, the recognition of the growth promoting properties of oestrogens, either alone or in combination with androgens, led to their introduction as a tool to increase meat production. Diethylstilboestrol (DES), as a cheap, better absorbed analogue of the natural hormone oestradiol-17β, became the favoured growth promoter for cattle, sheep and poultry in many countries (Schmidely, 1993).

As with many steroid growth promoters, DES was administered as an implant under the skin of young animals or as a feed additive. In the early 1970s concerns about its safety were raised when DES was confirmed to be a human carcinogen. In the scientific community, however, consensus was reached that the health risk was insignificant. The DES residues in meat were very low (below the limit of analytical detection) compared to those which individuals were exposed to when DES was used as a drug. Use of DES as a growth promoter continued in some Member States of the EU longer than in the US. It was finally banned for this use throughout the EU in 1987 because of uncertainty as to whether there was a definable 'no effect' dose for its potential tumour inducing effects in humans (European Commission, 1996), although some Member States had introduced an earlier ban. In the US a totally different pattern of events took place. DES was banned initially as a growth promoter in 1972 on the grounds that it was a carcinogen, violating the so-called 1958 Delaney Clause. This clause prohibits food for human consumption that contains carcinogenic substances, but was very difficult to apply in practice because the majority of foods contain trace amounts of carcinogenic substances. However, public opinion ensured that the clause remained on the statute books. The regulators had been forced to refer to 'minimum detectable levels' in justifying their inaction regarding the Delaney Clause in the case of DES. The US Food and Drug Administration (FDA) estimated that the economic burden to the consumers from a DES ban would be approximately US$500 million per annum. The calculation of this estimate involved a number of questionable assumptions. The estimated health risk was one cancer in 133 years (Jakes, 1976).

In 1974 the use of DES as a growth promoter was temporarily reinstated because of procedural deficiencies in the original bill banning DES in the US. The farming lobby made strong claims regarding the serious economic consequences of a further ban. These claims were made despite the fact that there were alternative growth promoters already on the US market (see Table 14.1). The 'breathing space' enabled the pharmaceutical industry to develop additional hormonal growth promoters. At the same time a scientific debate was taking place on what residue level of DES could be regarded as without significant risk to human health. In 1976 the FDA set the minimum detectable level of DES (the regulatory level) at 2 ppb (parts per billion). The FDA estimated that levels of DES in meat were of the order of 0.5 ppb (McMartin, 1978), but was not able to verify this estimate by measurements. The safety of oestrogens in the oral contraceptive pill and the high levels of natural oestrogens in pregnant women were cited as crucial evidence of low residues of DES in food being without risk to the consumer. This argument did not take into account that young children with low natural levels of oestrogens were the likely 'at risk' group (McMartin, 1978). The FDA also omitted the fact that DES has many structural differences from both oestradiol and the oestrogenic components of the oral contraceptive pill.

In 1979 DES was finally banned because there were no toxicological grounds for identifying a residue level below which a carcinogenic effect would not occur (Jakes, 1976).

The concerns of the high cost to the consumer from a DES ban were probably groundless. When the ban was eventually implemented there was little evidence of a sustained increase in the costs of meat production. In the case of the US the lack of increase in costs could be explained by the availability of alternative growth promoters and, in part, by the wrong assumptions made in the preliminary calculation of costs. It is worth noting that the FDA has continued to support the use of other oestrogenic compounds as growth promoters in cattle, (including oestradiol, trenbelone and zeranol) because of the perceived importance for the economic efficiency of meat production.

In 1982, an EU expert working group (the Lamming Committee) comprising members of the Scientific Committee for Food and the Scientific Committee for Animal Nutrition (the lead committee for issues concerning growth promoters), reached an interim conclusion that oestradiol and several other growth promoters with a hormonal action were safe as a growth promoting agent in cattle. This decision was clearly unpopular with the EU officials. Further work was carried out by the Lamming Committee over the next few years, but this did not change its opinion. The committee was disbanded in 1987 and the EU did not publish its interim conclusions. However, members of the committee published their opinions independently of the EU in the scientific literature (Lamming et al, 1987).

In 1988, a risk assessment by the Joint FAO/WHO Expert Committee on Food Additives (JECFA) reached a similar conclusion to that of the Lamming Committee. JECFA used the standard approach for risk assessments still employed by scientific advisory committees today. JECFA only considered the following (JECFA/WHO, 1988):

- risk when the growth promoters are used according to authorised use (though at the time and since there have been indications of significant accidental or deliberate misuse, which might be expected to lead to higher meat residues);
- individual growth promoters (rather than their combinations); and
- data provided by the manufacturers.

Shortly after the publication of JECFA's conclusions the EU issued a ban not only on the use of oestradiol but also on the use of other natural and synthetic steroid hormones as growth promoters. This ban was first adopted in 1985 but was disputed before the European Court by the UK. It was annulled because of procedural deficiencies. The ban was finally agreed in 1988. It encompassed a ban on the use of oestradiol 17-β, testosterone, progesterone, zeranol, trenbelone acetate and melengestrol acetate within Member States. In 1989 it was extended to imports from third world countries except where such growth promoters were already banned or countries were operating hormone-free cattle export programmes. This action could be regarded as an application of the precautionary principle, although the principle was not formalised at the time.

It is important to analyse the reasons why the European Commission decided to overrule the views of both committees. Three factors appear to have had a particular influence on the Commission's decision regarding DES's use as a growth promoter:

1   the scientific evidence that DES, which had been extensively used as a growth promoter, caused vaginal clear-cell adenoma in young women (Herbst and Bern, 1988);
2   increasing public concern about the health risks from hormones generally. The first generation oral contraceptive pill was blamed for increased incidence of breast cancer and thrombosis;
3   several epidemiological studies published at the time claimed that oestrogenic environmental contamination could result in anomalies in growth, sexual development and puberty. In Puerto Rico over 10,000 cases of anomalous sexual development, including premature development of breasts and body hair and pseudo precocious puberty, were reported (Perez-Comas, 1988).

These changes were associated by the authors with high serum total oestrogens. However, the source of the oestrogen contamination was not clearly identified. Similar adverse effects were observed in Italy, believed to result from accidental contamination of food by DES (Fara et al, 1979). In addition, in 1980, analysis of Italian baby food made with homogenised veal showed the presence of DES at significant levels. This was claimed to result from implants that were not removed after slaughtering of animals.

It is evident that the human risk associated with the use of oestradiol and oestradiol-related compounds is governed by many interrelated factors:

•   the nature of the growth promoter(s) used, the site and dose administered to cattle and the time period which has elapsed between its administration and the slaughter of the animal;
•   the amount of meat and meat products derived from slaughtered animals treated with the growth promoters which is consumed by individual over an extended period of time;
•   indirect contact with substances with oestrogenic properties through environmental contamination or other forms of exposure;
•   the susceptibility of the individual consumer.

In addition, there exists a potential for accidental or deliberate misuse of oestradiol and other hormonally related substances in the cattle industry. This misuse may take several forms:

•   use of a dose higher than considered acceptable;
•   a complex mixture of oestrogenic steroids;
•   an inappropriate injection site;
•   failure to remove an injection site or an implant (likely to have much higher hormone levels than elsewhere) from a slaughtered animal;

- a shortened withdrawal period;
- use of illegal substances.

Illegal use of growth promoting substances in Member States was the subject of the 1989 Pimenta Report. The report found no evidence in the use of oestradiol-17β, but nonetheless endorsed the ban because it facilitated controls and consumer confidence in meat. There have been claims that the EU ban on steroid hormones has led to illegal use, not only of the 'safer' steroids but also the more toxic ones, such as DES (Loizzo et al, 1984). In other words, the ban may have led to an increased risk to the consumer, rather than a reduction in risk. In the absence of a substantial regular monitoring programme, the extent of such misuse and the consequent increased risk, if any, to the consumer is hard to gauge. It is noted, however, that DES was detected last year in US meat imported into Switzerland.

In most reported cases of accidental contamination of food by oestrogenic substances, the anomalous effects have been considered to be transient and reversible. However, the long-term effects of exposure of prepubescent children to oestrogenic substances are as yet unknown. The absence of a demonstrable threshold concentration, below which there is no effect, adds to this uncertainty (European Commission, 1996).

Impacts of oestrogenic compounds on wildlife

This issue was not considered by either the Lamming Committee or JECFA. Two sources of information have emerged on possible impacts of oestrogenic compounds on the environment, namely:

1   effects of natural and synthetic oestrogens themselves on endocrine function in wildlife;
2   effects of non-steroid chemicals which impact wildlife through endocrine disruption.

No comprehensive studies were conducted until the late 1980s. However, there was sufficient information generated in the 1970s to raise concern about the environmental impacts of compounds with oestrogenic properties. For example, it was reported in 1970 that dichlorodiphenyltrichloroethane (DDT) decreased oestradiol blood levels and deposition of medullar bone (Scientific Committee on Veterinary Measures Relating to Public Health, 1999). It was suggested that the oestrogenic property of DDT was responsible for the observed effect.

Growth reduction was observed in catfish exposed to DES as long ago as 1972, indicating that DES was likely to affect a wide range of species in the environment (Peakall, 1970). Johnstone et al (1978) subsequently described a significant suppression of both length and weight of rainbow trout following dietary administration of oestradiol-17β (Bulkey, 1972).

A number of chemicals widely present in the environment (DDT, PCBs and alkylphenols) disrupt oestrogen receptor function in wildlife (Johnstone et al, 1978; Mueller and Kim, 1978; Reijnders, 1986; Bergman and Olsson, 1985; Aulerich et al, 1985). Feminisation of male birds (having both ovarian and testicular tissue) was induced by ethinyloestradiol-17β (Delong et al, 1973).

The studies cited above were ignored until the late 1980s, when concerns regarding the possible impact on the environment of veterinary drugs and growth promoters were raised. This was discussed in the 1989 Collins Report, but no in-depth evaluation resulted. This may be ascribed to the lack of interest of drug agencies in the environment and to the widely held assumption that any excreted drugs or growth promoters would be in a very diluted form and quickly degrade in the environment. The extent of the environmental impact of the use of oestrogenic growth promoters remains to be established. The recent international workshop on hormones and endocrine disrupters in food and water (in Copenhagen in 2000) confirmed concerns about this issue.

What were the uncertainties regarding the use of oestrogenic growth promoters for human health?

First, oestrogenic growth promoters were introduced to improve efficiency in cattle production. Human health issues, possible environmental impacts and farm animal welfare were not given significant attention. Histological changes in the prostate and bortholinic gland have been detected in cattle following oestradiol-17β administration. However, the physiological significance of these changes remains unclear.

Second, residues of the compounds in meat were subsequently measured and shown to be low (in the case of oestradiol-17β within the 'physiological range'), although what constitutes the physiological range continues to be controversial. The other limitation in these studies was the suitability of the analytical measurements. One aspect of this is the failure to assay metabolites with potential oestrogenic activity, for example oestradiol esters.

The EU has continued to encourage scientific evaluation of the safety of these growth promoters. In 1995 in Brussels the European Commission organised an international conference on growth promoters and meat production, involving the major stakeholder groups. No definitive conclusions were drawn. The expert opinions of the Scientific Committee on Veterinary Measures Relating to Public Health have been published since. The conclusion of both opinions is that further attention needs to be given to the exposure of sensitive populations to these substances because of the possible effects on the immune system, the endocrine system and cancer. The EU is also sponsoring a number of ongoing research projects in this area. JECFA continues to hold to its original view that each of the growth hormones with steroid-like action is safe for the consumer.

Prepubertal boys are identified as being at risk. The reliability of measurements of their endogenous levels and production of oestrogens is very questionable since these levels were close to the limits of detection. It means that any additional exogenous oestrogen represents a relatively high percentage of the total body oestrogen. This is particularly relevant in the context of the safety criterion applied by the FDA, that intake of any hormone from food should constitute less than 1% of the individual's daily endogenous production.

Neither possible human exposure via release of oestrogenically active excreta from cattle into the environment, nor possible effects on wildlife, were properly taken into account.

Public concern in Europe was initiated by the association of DES with vaginal clear-cell adenoma and increasing worries about the carcinogenic effects of some hormones. It is pertinent in this regard that recent research has demonstrated that oestradiol-17β (although a natural hormone), is a genotoxic carcinogen. This finding has further fuelled the debate on what is a safe level.

Has the approach adopted by the European Commission proved to be sound?

There is a growing consensus that cancer of the breast in women and prostate cancer in men may be promoted by high oestrogen exposure. North America has one of the highest breast cancer rates in the world, while Asia and Africa have much lower rates. The pattern is similar for prostate cancer. It has been noted that women with high levels of oestrogen, particularly free oestrogen, have a higher risk of breast cancer development (Adkins, 1975). Studies on migrant populations indicate this risk is principally due to environmental rather than genetic factors.

There is, so far, no good evidence that the EU ban on the use of growth promoters has protected the health of the public. However, it can also be argued that in those countries where these growth promoters have continued to be used, reliable evidence has not been accumulated on their safety to the consumer. Although potential risks to the environment have been identified, no conclusive evidence that growth promoters constitute a significant environmental risk has been produced.

The case for DES use as a growth promoter was a purely economic one. There was no benefit either for the cattle (or other species to which DES was administered) or for the environment. Agricultural specialists continue to debate the extent of the benefits of anabolic steroids as growth promoters. The economic consequences of this parting of the ways between the US and the EU with regard to anabolic steroids as growth promoters are very considerable and have yet to be fully evaluated. The divergence of opinions has led to a trade dispute between the EU and the US (Henderson et al, 1988). From 1989, the US took unilaterally retaliatory measures in the form of a 100% *ad valorem* duty on a variety of EU exports at a value of US$93 million (ca 93 million) per annum. In 1996 these measures were withdrawn as not compatible with World Trade Organization (WTO) law. In 1997 the legal basis for the EU ban was challenged by the US and Canada in front of a WTO panel. The panel found largely against the EU. On appeal, several of the grounds were reversed. The only aspect where the panel's view was upheld was that the EU had in its ban not focused specifically enough on residue in meat of each growth hormone. The dispute raises the issue of where the benefit of doubt should lie. An issue of concern is that attempts to resolve the problem are being made in the absence of any formal mechanisms for trading risks and benefits for the public. Potential environmental impacts or animal welfare issues have not been considered in this dispute.

The EU is currently experiencing sanctions against its exports of the order of £100 million (ca 160 million) per annum. The success of the US in the WTO hearings on anabolic steroid growth promoters has encouraged further actions on other products where the EU has adopted a precautionary approach on health grounds. The question is whether, if the EU applies the precautionary principle on health grounds to any product(s), it would prove acceptable to the WTO. Some issues have, however, been clarified by the WTO appeal, namely a sanitary protection measure (including a ban) can be permitted if supported by a risk assessment, even if this:

- is not necessarily quantitative in nature;
- takes into account real world issues such as difficulties in control measures;
- is based on 'qualified and respected sources'(WT/DS, 1997), even if these are in the minority.

Table 14.1 *US FDA approval dates for anabolic agents*

Trade name	Anabolic agent	Approved date
Synovex-S	200 mg progesterone/ 20 mg oestradiol benzoate	20 February 1956
Synovex-H	200 mg testosterone propionate/ 20 mg oestradiol benzoate	16 July 1958
Ralgo	36 mg zeranol or 12 mg zeranol	5 November 1969
MGA	0.25–0.50 mg/day MGA	3 June 1977

Source: Henderson et al, 1988

Conclusions

The EU took action in 1985 and again in 1988 to ban growth promoters with a steroid-like action, principally in response to public concern about involuntary and unnatural hormone exposure. This action was not at the time supported by the EU's own scientific committee (the Lamming Committee) nor that of WHO (JECFA). It is appropriate to apply the precautionary principle in those situations where the science base is inadequate to confirm the safety of a product. Neither committee was required to properly characterise the degree of uncertainty in their assessment. As this question was never asked, the original EU ban was, in reality, a political risk assessment. More recent scientific research, however, probably justifies the application by the EU of the precautionary principle to continue the ban.

The handling of the issue of steroid hormones as growth promoters has wider implications in determining acceptability of the use of chemical substances, namely that:

- it is very important, in arriving at their conclusions, that scientific committees are requested to identify the uncertainties in their assessments;
- rigorous and transparent mechanisms must be developed for evaluating risks against benefits.

Table 14.2 *Hormones as growth promoters: early warnings and actions*

1970s	Concerns about growth promoters' safety, as DES confirmed a human carcinogen
1972	Peakal publishes that DES likely to affect a wide range of species in the environment (wildlife) but this was ignored until the late 1980s
1972	DES banned as a hormone growth promoter in the US
1974	Use of DES reinstated in the US
1976	US Food and Drug Administration (FDA) sets the minimum detectable level of DES
1979	DES banned again on the grounds of the impossibility of identifying levels below which it would not be carcinogenic
1982	EU expert working group (Lamming Committee) concludes that some growth promoters are safe
1985	First EU ban is adopted, ignoring results from the Lamming Committee because the scope of their assessments had not been broad enough
1987	Lamming Committee disbanded by EU and their results were not published
1988	Ban of several growth promoters throughout the EU based on uncertainty of their effects on humans
1988	WHO/FAO Joint Expert Committee on Food, using standard risk assessments, reaches same conclusions as Lamming Committee
1989	EU ban extended to other growth promoters and to imports from third world countries
1989	Pimenta Report finds illegal use of growth promoters in some Member States
1989–96	US takes unilateral retaliatory measures on EC exports
1995	European Commission organises an international conference on growth promoters and meat production where uncertainties remain regarding effects on the immune system, endocrine system and cancer
1999	The EU Scientific Committee on Veterinary Measures Relating to Public Health publishes a report concluding that no threshold levels can be defined for six growth promoters
2000	International workshop on hormones and endocrine disrupters in food and water confirms impacts on the environment (wildlife) of veterinary drugs
2001	EU still suffers from sanction to its exports of around 160 million per year

Source: EEA

'Mad cow disease' 1980s–2000: how reassurances undermined precaution

Patrick van Zwanenberg and Erik Millstone

Introduction

Many of the UK policy-makers who were directly responsible for taking policy decisions on bovine spongiform encephalopathy (BSE) prior to March 1996 claim that, at the time, their approach exemplified the application of an ultra precautionary approach and of rigorous science-based policy-making.[9] We argue that these claims are not convincing because government policies were not genuinely precautionary and did not properly take into account the implications of the available scientific evidence.

The BSE saga is enormously complex and this account is necessarily selective. It is, however, essential to appreciate that UK public policy-making was handicapped by a fundamental tension. The department responsible for dealing with BSE has been the Ministry of Agriculture, Fisheries and Food (MAFF) (since 2001, the Department for Environment, Food and Rural Affairs (DEFRA)), and it was expected simultaneously to promote the economic interests of farmers and the food industry whilst also protecting public health from food-borne hazards. The evidence cited here suggests that because MAFF was expected simultaneously to meet two contradictory objectives it failed to meet either.

A new cattle disease

The first cases of BSE were officially acknowledged in November 1986. The pathological characteristics of the new cattle disease closely resembled scrapie, a transmissible spongiform encephalopathy (TSE) that is endemic in the UK

---

9 Gillian Sheppard (BSE Inquiry transcript, 1998, 15 December, pp10–11); John Gummer (BSE Inquiry transcript, 1998, 8 December, p50).

sheep population. TSEs are a group of very poorly understood, untreatable and invariably fatal brain diseases that afflict both animals and humans. Creutzfeldt-Jakob disease (CJD) is the best known human TSE.

MAFF scientists suspected that BSE had been caught from sheep infected with scrapie and was being transmitted through contaminated feed. The rendered remains of sheep, cattle and other animals were routinely incorporated into animal feedstuffs. Contaminated feed was quickly confirmed as the principal vector of the disease but whether BSE had in fact derived from scrapie, or from a spontaneous TSE in cattle, or from another source, remains unclear.

There was no evidence that eating sheep meat from scrapie-infected animals could cause CJD, but unfortunately policy-makers could not be sure that the agent which caused BSE had in fact derived from scrapie. Moreover, even if the scrapie pathogen had jumped species into cattle, policy-makers could not be sure that BSE would subsequently have the same transmission characteristics as scrapie. Experimental evidence indicated that it was then not possible to predict what the host range of a given strain of scrapie would be once it had jumped to another species (Kimberlin et al, 1987). Even if policy-makers assumed that BSE was pathogenic to humans they could not quantify the risk. No one knew, for example, which cattle tissues, if any, would be free of the infectious agent, or what the levels of infectivity in the various tissues would be, or how this could vary over the period of incubation, and no one knew if there might be a threshold of human exposure below which the risk would be negligible. In the late 1980s there was no test that could reliably detect the pathogen in live animals before clinical symptoms appeared. Asymptomatic cattle could not be identified nor differentiated from cattle which were uninfected.

As soon as the first cases of BSE had been diagnosed senior officials realised that BSE posed a possible risk to human health (BSE Inquiry, 1999b, para. 22). As the Under Secretary in MAFF's Animal Health Group told his colleagues in early 1988: '... we do not know whether (BSE) can be passed to humans... There is no evidence that people can be infected, *but we cannot say there is no risk... we have to face up to the possibility that the disease could cross another species gap*' (emphasis added) (BSE Inquiry, 1999c, para. 59). Policy-makers had no choice but to take urgent decisions about a novel disease the implications of which were unknown.

Initial decisions

In the early stages of the BSE epidemic a wide spectrum of possible policy responses was available to policy-makers. The spectrum ranged from the most to the least precautionary. They could also be ranked in terms of their likely costs, but the order was then reversed. The total eradication of the disease and its pathogen from agriculture and foods would have required, *inter alia*, the slaughter and exclusion from the food chain of all the animals which had received feed known, or suspected, to have been contaminated with the pathogen. As there were no ways of knowing which batches of feed were contaminated, and because almost all dairy herds had received feed containing

Box 15.1 Early warnings

Rendered animal slaughterhouse wastes have been recycled into animal feed since at least the beginning of the 20th century (Cooke, 1998). The known risks of that practice included the transmission, recycling and amplification of pathogens. Those concerns prompted the 1979 Royal Commission on Environmental Pollution to recommend minimum processing standards in the rendering industries (RCEP, 1979). Before the Labour government could follow that advice, it lost the 1979 election. It is not yet clear what effect such regulations might have had in diminishing the BSE epidemic because the incoming Conservative government decided to withdraw the proposed regulations, deeming them to be unnecessary and excessively restrictive. The Thatcher government indicated that the industry should be left to decide for itself how its equipment should be operated (Barclay, 1996, Section II B, p13). After 1996, minimum process standards were introduced in the rendering industry and deactivation experiments have been conducted and are in progress. We might eventually learn what the effect on the spread of TSE agents would have been if those standards had been introduced in 1979.

In the mid-1970s the US Department of Agriculture decided that carcasses of sheep and goats afflicted with, or exposed to, scrapie should not be used in human or animal foods, partly to prevent transmission of scrapie to other flocks but also because of their concern about a possible link between scrapie and CJD (Martin, 1998). No similar action was taken in the UK. If BSE was indeed caused initially by scrapie jumping from sheep to cattle then similar, relatively inexpensive, restrictions might have prevented the BSE epidemic.

The possibility that BSE might transmit to humans was recognised by veterinary officials in MAFF as soon as the disease was first diagnosed in 1986; however they thought that the probability that BSE might be pathogenic to humans was acceptably slight. The earliest documented official acknowledgement, of which we are aware, that the probability of transmission might be more than remote was made at a meeting at the National Institute for Biological Standards and Control in May 1988. The minutes of a meeting reported the conclusion that 'by analogy (with scrapie and CJD) BSE may be transmissible to humans' (BSE Inquiry, 1999c, para. 186). Senior government advisers participated in that meeting.

Between 1990 and 1995, evidence gradually emerged indicating that BSE exhibited distinct transmission characteristics from scrapie in sheep, thus indicating that BSE had an unknown and unpredictable host range. The most significant evidence was the discovery, from 1990 onwards, that BSE was transmissible, via food, to domestic cats, a species that is not susceptible to scrapie.

Evidence that BSE could cause CJD did not emerge until 1995 when cases of an unusual form of CJD (later called variant CJD) in exceptionally young people began to be discovered. The temporal and geographical association between the two diseases was circumstantial evidence of causation.

In 1996 and 1997 direct evidence indicative of a causal relationship between BSE and variant CJD was produced. This included studies indicating that the pathological and clinical features of BSE and variant CJD were identical whilst both differed from the distinctive features of scrapie and sporadic CJD.

meat and bone meal, and because the majority of the beef herd were bred from dairy herds, that would have entailed slaughtering almost the entire British herd which might have cost in the order of £12–15 billion.[10] On the other hand, there were numerous other options which could have been selected, which would have substantially reduced the risks without spending a great deal of public money. These might have included, for example, a ban on the use of animals from affected herds as human food, or a ban on the use in the food chain of all bovine tissues that were suspected of harbouring the pathogenic agent, or even just a ban on the use of clinically affected animals as human food. In 1987, and the first half of 1988, approximately 1200 clinical cases of BSE were recorded (though at that time the disease was not notifiable and the actual incidence must almost certainly have been higher) and most of those were sold as human food. The costs of compensation for removing those clinically diseased animals would have been no more than £1000 per animal, totalling approximately £1.5 million. It is not yet possible to estimate the harm which eating those animals may have caused.

Even if the science had been massively less uncertain, scientific considerations would never by themselves have indicated where on the policy spectrum an appropriate response would have been. Policy-makers had to make political judgements about which actions to take, and how the costs should be distributed between public and private sources.

One problem with taking any regulatory measures, as then seen from the perspective of the UK government, was that any regulatory response – indeed any admission that consuming meat, milk or dairy products from British cattle might be harmful – would have undermined domestic and international confidence in the safety of British beef with adverse consequences for the meat industry. Even the virtually cost-free option of sharing information about the disease with those outside MAFF might have alerted domestic consumers and potential importers of UK cattle and meat to the presence of a new potentially fatal zoonotic disease. Fear of those consequences, and a reluctance to increase public expenditure, dominated policy-making in MAFF for the first 20 months of the epidemic. For example, when MAFF's Chief Veterinary Officer first told his minister about BSE he warned that '… the disorder could have potentially serious implications, not only domestically but for UK exports'. He advised that it was not appropriate to impose regulatory restrictions, noting that 'irresponsible or ill-informed publicity is likely to be unhelpful since it might lead to hysterical demands for immediate, draconian Government measures and might also lead other countries to reject UK exports of live cattle and bovine embryos and semen' (BSE Inquiry, 1999b, pp27–8). Even the option of making the disease notifiable, an essential tool for disease surveillance, was rejected in part, because, as one official put it, such action '… might imply to the general public

---

10 Assuming a compensation rate of £865 per slaughtered cow (the real rate of compensation paid to farmers in 1996), a herd of approximately 12 million cattle, the costs of slaughtering and incinerating cattle, and the knock-on effects on employment produces a maximum estimated figure of £15 billion ('Cash for cows', 1996).

we know something they don't, like the meat or milk is a source of danger for humans' (Phillips et al, 2000, Vol 3, para 2.130).

As the epidemic rapidly began to escalate, UK policy-makers not only chose to avoid taking any regulatory action at all, but they also decided to try to keep information about BSE within the confines of the ministry. One of MAFF's scientists later recalled: '... in December 1986 when recognition of the disease began to crystallise, we were at the Central Veterinary Laboratory placed under strict confidentiality as to discussing it with outside people...' (BSE Inquiry, 1999b, p13). As the Phillips Inquiry into BSE concluded, during the first half of 1987 '... there was a policy of restricting, even within the State Veterinary Service, the dissemination of any information about the new disease' (Phillips et al, 2000, Vol 3, para 2.137). Most of the scientific research community, the medical profession, and senior officials and ministers in other government departments did not learn about BSE until early 1988.

In February 1988, with the media beginning to devote attention to the new cattle disease and increasing numbers of affected cattle, senior MAFF officials changed their views and recommended that their ministers introduce a slaughter and compensation policy for clinically diseased cattle which, at the time, were being sold for human food. Officials argued, privately, that without a slaughter policy the government would be held responsible if it later transpired that BSE was transmissible to humans. The Agriculture Minister, John MacGregor, rejected that advice. The minister's private secretary explained why: 'He (the minister) does not see how we could *proceed without being clear where the offsetting savings are coming from*... More importantly... the argument that slaughter compensation policy would help to stem the spread of the disease (advocated in these papers) is precisely the one sugar beet growers have been making, and which we have strongly and publicly been rejecting. He also thinks that *action along the lines recommended now would make the export position much worse*, not better' (emphases added) (Minute, 1988).

The government's policy was not precautionary. Its primary objective was rather one of trying to diminish, as far as possible, the short-term adverse impact of BSE on the profitability of the food industry and the level of public expenditure.

Expert advice and regulatory controls

In mid-1988, and for the first time, a small expert advisory committee was set up to provide advice on BSE. This only occurred at the insistence of the Chief Medical Officer (CMO) at the Department of Health, who was first informed about the new disease only in March 1988 – 17 months after MAFF was first alerted (BSE Inquiry, 1999c, para 115). That only occurred because agriculture ministers were advised by their officials that they needed the support of the CMO for the ministers' decision not to remove clinically affected cattle from the human food chain (BSE Inquiry, 1999c, para 76).

The advisory committee, under the chairmanship of Sir Richard Southwood, insisted on the day of their first meeting (20 June 1988) that clinically affected cattle should cease to go into the human and animal food chains and that farmers should be compensated. Another major change occurred when MAFF announced, on the very same day, that they would be introducing a ban on the use of potentially contaminated ruminant protein in ruminant feed. The feed ban only applied to ruminants. Animals such as pigs and poultry could still be fed with the contaminated protein even though no one knew whether or not they might also be susceptible to BSE. MAFF officials had in fact considered, and then rejected, a ban on feeding ruminant protein meal to all animals because that would have deprived the rendering industry of its principal market (the bulk of animal protein was fed to pigs and poultry) (BSE Inquiry transcript, 1998, 29 June, p35). Senior veterinary officials were nevertheless aware that their decision was a gamble. In June 1988, the Chief Veterinary Officer, Keith Meldrum, admitted privately to a colleague that 'the most we could say is that any ruminant protein fed to (pigs) might contain the agent of BSE or scrapie. Whether or not infection would be established in the pig and whether it might replicate is unknown' (BSE Inquiry transcript, 1998, 16 June, p99). One unfortunate consequence of that decision was that for the next six or so years cross-contamination occurred between feed destined for cattle and feed destined for other animals, greatly prolonging the BSE epidemic.

Although Southwood's advisory committee had been quick to insist that clinically affected animals be removed from the human food chain it did not recommend controls on the use in food of sub-clinically infected animals, the tissues of which would also harbour the infectious agent. (In the absence of an ante-mortem diagnostic test any controls would have had to have been imposed on the entire British herd.) Southwood acknowledged in March 1996, after the acute BSE crisis erupted, that a ban on the use of all cattle brains might not have been a politically feasible option in 1988. He explained: 'We felt it was a no-goer. They (MAFF) already thought our proposals were pretty revolutionary' (*New Scientist*, 1996).

A ban on the use of cattle brains and other offal from all cattle in the human food supply was introduced by MAFF in November 1989, nine months after the Southwood Committee reported. That regulation was only introduced after it emerged that one of the government's own expert advisers had told officials, in confidence, that he had undertaken private consultancy work for the pet food industry and had subsequently recommended a bovine offal ban in pet food, and after ministers decided that they did not wish to be upstaged by the meat products industry and the pet food industry, both of which had told MAFF that they would be unilaterally removing bovine offals from their products (BSE Inquiry, 1999e, paras 87–9 and 135).

The ruminant feed ban, the slaughter and destruction of affected cattle, and what became known as the specified bovine offal (SBO) ban were all in place by the end of 1989. The controls were not designed to eradicate the BSE agent, however, but only to diminish the risk. For example, the tissues selected for the SBO ban were chosen not because they alone harboured the infectious agent but because they could most easily be removed, and because they were of the lowest commercial value. There were no experimental data, at that time, indicating which cattle organs might be contaminated with the pathogen, although analogies with other species and their TSEs indicated that many other tissues would also have carried the agent. For example, lymph nodes and peripheral nerves would almost certainly be highly infectious but could not practicably be removed and organs such as the liver would, by analogy with other TSEs, also contain (lower) levels of the infectious agent but were commercially valuable (BSE Inquiry, 1999e, para 85). Moreover, the SBO ban excluded cattle under six months old. The carcasses of calves were not normally split in abattoirs so the removal of their spinal cords would have raised abattoir costs. The exclusion of calves would only have been sensible if one could have assumed that vertical transmission of BSE from cow to calf could not occur. That assumption was implausible because it was already known that scrapie did transmit from ewes to their lambs and because MAFF did not start funding research into maternal transmission of BSE until 1989 (Barclay, 1996, p16; *Nature*, 1990).

The delay in implementing the principal regulations also meant there had already been repeated human exposures to the pathogen. For example, from mid-1988, after Southwood recommended that all clinically affected cattle be destroyed, to the end of 1989, when the SBO ban was actually introduced, an estimated 30,000 infected cattle that were at least halfway through the average incubation period for BSE had been consumed (Dealler, 1996).

Constructing a house of cards

In 1987, UK policy-makers adopted the hypothesis that BSE was an innocuous version of scrapie and they struggled to remain wedded to it, in the face of accumulating evidence to the contrary, because that narrative enabled the UK government to offer a reassuring and optimistic message by suggesting that the presence of BSE in British dairy and beef herds posed no threat to human health. MAFF repeatedly asserted that their reassuring statements were fully supported by scientific evidence, expertise and advice. That was, however, a misrepresentation.

Policy-makers were repeatedly told, both by the scientific experts on whom they claimed to rely, and by the wider scientific community, that it was impossible to be certain that consuming meat, milk and dairy products from animals with BSE posed no risk. For example, in May 1990, the government's Spongiform Encephalopathy Advisory Committee (SEAC) told policy-makers that: 'in the present state of knowledge, it would not be justified to state categorically that there was no risk to humans, and it was not appropriate to insist on a zero risk' (BSE Inquiry transcript, 1998, 24 March, p71). Ministers and senior policy-makers insisted otherwise in public. On 7 June 1990, for example, the Agriculture Minister told the House of Commons that there was '… clear scientific evidence that British beef is perfectly safe' (*Hansard*, 1990, column 906). Policy-makers repeatedly claimed a certainty which was unavailable and which they knew to be unavailable. Occasionally policy-makers acknowledged that they could not be certain that BSE was an innocuous form of scrapie, but they always claimed that regulatory controls introduced in November 1989 prevented all potentially contaminated material from entering the food chain (*Radio Times*, 1992).

Regulatory controls were never intended, however, to eliminate exposure to the BSE agent, but only to diminish exposures, and MAFF scientists and expert advisers made sure that senior policy-makers knew that (see, for example, BSE Inquiry, 1999e, para 275). For example, in 1990 SEAC produced a draft document about the safety of beef intended for the Chief Medical Officer, in which it made statements such as: 'some of the edible offal... that have on rare occasions demonstrated low titres of infectivity are not included in the offal ban' and 'there are some who insist on nothing less than an absolute guarantee of safety. No scientist is in a position to do that at present for British (or Irish) beef' (Phillips et al, 2000, Vol 11, para. 4.120). That document was circulated within the Department of Health and MAFF for suggested amendments. The MAFF official who subsequently forwarded the document to ministers told those ministers, and other MAFF officials, that: 'the most potentially inflammatory pieces of drafting in earlier versions (including the citations above) have now been edited out' (Phillips et al, 2000, Vol 11, para 4.118). But then as Phillips concluded, in a memorable phrase, ministers and officials followed an approach to information provision 'whose object was sedation' (Phillips et al, 2000, Vol 1, para 1179).

The assertion that beef was entirely safe was not only misleading but it also made it increasingly difficult for MAFF to take a range of other precautionary steps. Any new regulatory measure, no matter how useful or cheap, risked not only raising questions about the government's reassurances, but might also provoke serious doubts about the logic of not introducing further and more expensive controls (zero risk was always going to be unattainable without slaughtering and restocking the entire British herd and cleaning out the feed chain). In other words, partial reductions in risk were difficult from the point of view of presentation; the only credible options, given the rhetoric, were to draw a line, maintain that it provided total protection and stick to it, or alternatively to try to eradicate the agent entirely.

Numerous precautionary measures were not therefore introduced, not because of their immediate costs but because of their liability to undermine the government's reassuring message. For example, mechanically recovered meat (MRM) was widely acknowledged to contain residual pieces of potentially highly infectious nervous tissue (BSE Inquiry transcript, 1998, 6 July, pp104–6 and 127). Banning MRM would have made explicit the risks associated with peripheral nervous tissue, most of which could not practicably be removed from the carcass. As the minutes of a meeting held at MAFF in September 1989 indicate: 'Mechanically recovered meat (MRM) – the possible danger raised by several of those consulted was recognised and during the discussion there was an expression of the illogicality of what was being done and in particular how easy it would be to have to concede the possible dangers of material other than those listed in the proposed ban. It was agreed not to raise it' (BSE Inquiry, 1999e, para 263).

In February 1990 the Institute of Environmental Health Officers (IEHO), whose members were responsible for enforcing controls in slaughterhouses, raised concerns with MAFF about existing practices for removing cattle brains from heads, none of which, the IEHO argued, could be accomplished without contaminating the head meat. The IEHO sensibly recommended that all removal of head meat should take place prior to splitting the skull for the removal of the brain. Although agriculture ministers had 'qualms' about the practice of removing brains before removing head meat, and felt that the practice ought to be banned, civil servants argued, successfully, that no new controls should be introduced. As a senior official in MAFF's Meat Hygiene Division explained to the Minister for Food: 'Amendment regulations would fuel debate on BSE generally and, inevitably, lead to demands for similar action on spinal cords... A ban on splitting (spinal columns) would have grave consequences for the industry and for the export trade. Nor would it end with spinal cords. Concern would then be directed at nerve trunks and lymph nodes, which cannot be removed from carcasses' (BSE Inquiry, 1999f, p7).

Again, a cheap, simple and risk-reducing measure was avoided in order to maintain a reassuring and misrepresentative message about safety and to counteract political pressure for ever more precautionary controls. If MAFF had publicly acknowledged some of the uncertainties and risks, and admitted that some measures of control might be too impractical and/or too expensive, and therefore that a lower but acceptable level of risk might have to be tolerated, policy-makers might have found it easier to introduce precautionary control measures without threatening the ministry's credibility.

As events and evidence eventually prompted additional regulatory controls, it became increasingly hard to reconcile those responses with the government's reassuring narrative, particularly if those additional regulations made explicit further areas where controls ought to be introduced. Policy-makers therefore sometimes misrepresented their reasons for introducing regulations in an attempt to prevent their narrative from unravelling. For example, MAFF insisted that the SBO ban was not necessary on scientific grounds (see, for example, House of Commons Agriculture Committee, 1990, pp9 and 71), and it was therefore difficult to convince industry and other stakeholders that those regulatory measures were crucially important for public health. In 1995, during unannounced visits by enforcement officers to UK abattoirs, some 48% were found to be failing to comply with the SBO regulations (House of Commons Agriculture and Health Select Committees, 1996, p10). As a representative of those responsible for enforcing slaughterhouse regulations put it: 'We were being given the message that really there probably wasn't a problem anyway so this was maybe a bit of window dressing as opposed to serious public health matters...' (*Panorama*, 1996).

It was not only new regulatory measures, however, that threatened the government's claims that risks were zero. Sustaining the government's reassuring message also entailed that unwelcome information and evidence could undermine the official narrative. Expert advisers were therefore carefully selected and those who did not share the ministry's policy framework, or who might refuse to acquiesce to restrictions on the dissemination of information, were excluded. As one MAFF official put it: '... you have to turn to external bodies to try to give some credibility to public pronouncements, you are very dependent therefore on what the Committees then find... Really the key to it is setting up the Committee, who is on it, and the nature of their investigations' (BSE Inquiry transcript, 1998,

29 June, pp79–81). Some experts were also excluded because their institutional location might provide the wrong impression. For example, the UK Public Health Laboratory Service (PHLS) – the established disease surveillance institution in the UK for new and emerging diseases – was always excluded from BSE policy. As the Welsh Chief Medical Officer has recalled: 'the basis of the consistent opposition to the involvement of the PHLS was the anxiety that their involvement would be tantamount to admitting the possibility of a human health risk (Phillips et al, 2000, Vol 11, para 4.28).

Senior policy-makers also attempted to ensure that the commissioning, conduct and reporting of BSE research were tightly controlled. Many key experiments were never started or were seriously delayed, information and evidence were sometimes withheld, and data and materials were not always shared with other researchers. For example, a random post-mortem survey of animals in abattoirs would have helped to provide estimates of the numbers of infected but asymptomatic animals entering the human food chain. The laboratory resources were available and the costs would have been relatively low but only one such survey has been conducted in the UK and that was in 1999 and only in cattle that were not permitted to enter the human food chain. A crucially important experiment to see whether cattle fed on rations deliberately infected with scrapie would get BSE was not started until 1996 (BSE Inquiry transcript, 1998, 11 March, p132). Once BSE became notifiable, all infected cattle brains became the property of MAFF and the ministry showed extraordinary reluctance to provide some of the most senior scientists in the US with pathogenic material (BSE Inquiry, 1999a, paras 493–505). A precautionary approach to policy-making, on the other hand, would have involved producing and disseminating far more information and evidence.

The failures and eventual collapse of the policy edifice

In the years following the Southwood Report, MAFF's reassuring narrative repeatedly and progressively unravelled. It did so partly because the scientific evidence, which was never entirely reassuring, became progressively less reassuring, because the ministry's control of the diffusion of information was imperfect, and because actors and agents outside the ministry's control took independent decisions. This occurred despite MAFF's vigorous attempts to sustain the policy in the face of its inherent weaknesses and accumulating counter-evidence.

By late 1995 a lengthy series of events and evidence had obliged MAFF progressively to tighten regulations, though in a reactive, rather than in an anticipatory, fashion. By then, a growing proportion of the national and global scientific and research community had become increasingly concerned about the risks from BSE. MAFF's policy eventually collapsed in March 1996 after a new variant of CJD (now, with the passage of time, labelled variant or vCJD) had emerged in the UK, and after SEAC had concluded that consuming food contaminated with BSE was the most probable cause.

Box 15.2 The European dimension

Although BSE first emerged in the UK, it spread to other countries, especially in continental Europe, as a consequence of trade in animals and feedstuffs. Individual Member States and the European Commission have therefore had to grapple with many of the same difficulties and dilemmas as the UK. Countries such as Ireland, Portugal and France have had sufficiently high rates of BSE that, during the 1990s, their governments recognised the need to establish controls on their domestic production systems. Other countries, with lower incidences of BSE, such as Belgium, The Netherlands and Italy occasioned some concern and regulatory activities, but primarily in relation to traded animals and feedstuffs. The various jurisdictions have, nevertheless, responded in quite different ways, regardless of their levels of industrial development or the number of BSE cases in each country. A full account of how and why those responses differed is beyond the scope of this case study.* Nevertheless, it is clear that the location of responsibilities for BSE policy-making was fundamental in framing the ways in which the BSE problem was defined, evaluated and responded to. In general, those jurisdictions in which industrial sponsorship and responsibility for consumer protection were located within the same institutions (eg Ireland) adopted less precautionary approaches to protecting public health than those where sponsorship and regulation were split or shared between more than one institution (eg Austria) (BASES, n.d.).

For example, within the European Commission, prior to 2000, responsibility for BSE policy was located primarily within DG III (now renamed the Enterprise Directorate-General, with responsibility for the EU's internal market and enterprise) and DG VI (now the Agriculture Directorate-General and Fisheries Directorate-General). Although the UK introduced domestic legislation banning the use of contaminated ruminant protein for use in ruminant feed in June 1988, at which point it informed the European Commission of its actions, EU-wide legislation to control the spread of BSE was not introduced for another six years. After June 1988, the UK continued to export contaminated feed to other Member States and some of that was subsequently fed to cattle. For example, exports of meat and bone meal to the EU had jumped from 12,553 tonnes in 1988 to 25,005 tonnes in 1989 (European Parliament, 1997, p8). In the summer of 1989, the Commission asked the UK to introduce an export ban on those feedstuffs but the UK refused to do so (BSE Inquiry, 1999d, para 257). The Commission has since claimed that it did not have the legal basis itself, prior to the Single European Act, to ban exports of UK meat and bone meal (although the European Parliament has disputed that assertion); instead the Commission invited all Member States to introduce a national ban on the import from the UK of ruminant-derived meat and bone meal (European Parliament, 1996, p10). Some Member States then did so, or had already introduced such a ban (eg The Netherlands), whilst some did not ban imports of UK meat and bone meal until much later (eg Portugal). The European Commission did not insist on an EU-wide ban on the feeding of ruminants with meat and bone meal until 1994. Not until 1996 did the Commission ban the exports of UK produced meat and bone meal (and all other cattle products). The European Parliament has concluded that the Commission consistently subordinated the protection of animal and public health to maintenance of the internal market (European Parliament, 1997).

As a result of the 1996 BSE crisis, there has been an on-going reorgani-sation of scientific advice and food safety policy-making in both the European Commission and Member States. In the European Commission, the scientific advisory system has been reformed and management of scientific advice has moved to DG XXIV, now renamed DG SANCO or the Health and Consumer Protection Directorate-General. In 2000, the regulatory and sponsorship functions of DG III and DG VI were split and the regulatory functions were also transferred to DG SANCO. The European Commission's 2000 White Paper on food safety has now proposed a further institutional split by proposing the creation of a European Food Authority to provide independent science-based advice to DG SANCO (European Commission, 2000). Analogous reforms and proposals for reform have occurred in many of the Member States.

As of 2000, many individual Member States have discovered that they have rising cases of BSE (eg France and Ireland) and those countries that previously thought they might be free of the disease have discovered cases amongst their domestic cattle population (eg Germany and Spain). Substantial historical differences in the types of controls that have been imposed by different Member States, and the extent to which those controls have been enforced, will mean that some jurisdictions face considerable animal and public health challenges for many years.

* National reports about the policy responses to BSE in 11 European countries, conducted as part of a European Commission sponsored research project, provide more information. These are available at: www.upmf-grenoble.fr/inra/serd/bases/.

Conclusions

BSE was always going to be a difficult issue to apply a precautionary approach to once it had been discovered in the UK cattle herd. In November 1986, many infected cattle had already been consumed and even at that stage it would have been hugely expensive to eradicate.

Nevertheless, there was a great deal which the government could have done to diminish the risks to consumers, and in the long run to the meat industry and to the Exchequer, especially if they had openly acknowledged what the scientific evidence did, and did not, indicate. Instead the UK government claimed to be prudently protecting public health, while in practice it covertly subordinated the protection of public health to the support of agricultural sales, with a view also to minimising state intervention and public expenditure. The regulations which were set were, consequently, too little and too late, and even then they were not properly enforced. Moreover, too little was invested in scientific research and the involvement of independent scientists was actively discouraged.

If the UK government had adopted a genuinely precautionary approach, it would have necessitated, firstly and most fundamentally, reforming policy institutions so as to separate responsibilities for regulation from those of sponsorship. The BSE saga has provoked a reappraisal of the ways in which risks to public and environmental health are assessed and managed in the UK.

Box 15.3 The costs of BSE

BSE has had substantial, and as yet incomplete, ramifications, some of which can be defined in monetary terms but others of which are incalculable.

In 1998, the cumulative expenditure by UK agricultural departments in response to the BSE crisis, from 1996 to 2001, was forecast to be £4.2 billion (House of Commons, 1999). The bulk of that expenditure was, and will be, for compensating commercial enterprises, especially compensation to farmers for the removal of cattle over 30 months of age from the human food chain and support to the slaughtering and rendering industries. The figures also include expenditure on research programmes and administration. Other costs since 1996 that have been borne by public expenditure include the public inquiry into BSE, at an estimated £25 million (Farmers Weekly Interactive Service, 1999).

The costs to the private sector of BSE have also been considerable. The ban on British beef exports in March 1996 led to the complete loss of a trade worth £700 million per year (DTZ Pieda Consulting, 1998). In the first 12 months since March 1996, the total value of the market for UK produced beef fell by an estimated 36% in real terms (a combination of loss of exports and the drop in domestic demand), amounting to an estimated loss of value added to the UK economy of £1.15 billion (DTZ Pieda Consulting, 1998).

It would be premature to try to provide precise estimates of the total costs of BSE, not least because we still cannot estimate how many people will eventually succumb to new variant CJD; there may be no more than another 100 cases, or there may eventually be up to a million (Collinge, 1999).

Since May 1997, the UK government has acknowledged that there was a fundamental contradiction at the core of MAFF's remit, and that recognition informed the decision to create the Food Standards Agency.

A precautionary approach would also have necessitated acknowledging how little 'sound science' was available, and would have involved open and accountable discussions of the possible costs and benefits of taking, or failing to take, a wide range of different possible courses of action. A Freedom of Information Act might have the effect of initiating a cultural change in the way policy-making bodies represent scientific evidence. An institutional separation between those responsible for providing scientific advice, risk assessments and research and those responsible for regulatory policy-making might also have encouraged more open and robust discussion of possible risks. Furthermore, the more support there is for research, conducted by a wide range of disciplines and interdisciplinary groups and in a wide range of institutions with open access to evidence and data, the harder it would be to conceal uncertainties, and therefore the uncertainties might be more readily diminished.

One of the factors which, prior to March 1996, helped MAFF to sustain its optimistic narrative was the willingness of expert scientific advisers to acquiesce to an arrangement under which the scientists provided advice which was based on both scientific and non-scientific considerations but which was represented to the general public as if it was purely scientific. That suited ministers because

Box 15.4 Conclusions from the Phillips Inquiry

In January 1998, an inquiry into BSE was set up by the Labour government to 'establish and review the history of the emergence and identification of BSE and variant CJD and of the action taken in response to it up to 20 March 1996' and 'to reach conclusions on the adequacy of that response, taking into account the state of knowledge at the time'. The inquiry committee, chaired by Lord Justice Phillips, reported in October 2000 after having taken oral and written evidence from over 600 witnesses.

The 16-volume report focused primarily on procedures rather than outcomes; indeed, the inquiry team was reluctant to comment on the extent to which policy was or was not proportionate, preferring instead to highlight issues of communication within and outside government, the use of expert advice and cooperation between government departments. Phillips' main criticism was that public policy was dominated by the political objective of reassuring the public. The inquiry team maintained, nevertheless, that appropriate policy decisions were taken although they were not always timely, properly designed, or adequately implemented or enforced.

Two of the conclusions reached by Phillips and his colleagues were that 'the government was anxious to act in the best interests of human health' and that 'it was not (the Ministry of Agriculture, Fisheries and Food's (MAFF)) policy to lean in favour of the agricultural producers to the detriment of the consumer'. It is, however, difficult to see how the evidence available to the inquiry, some of which is summarised in this case study, is consistent with those conclusions.

The Phillips Report contains 160 individual lessons. Many of these are specific to animal health policy and agricultural production practices but the main generic conclusions concern:

- the appropriate use and role of advisory committees;
- the maintenance of sufficient in-house expertise;
- greater cooperation between animal and human health professionals;
- the proper implementation, operation and enforcement of policy measures;
- coordination of research to diminish policy-relevant uncertainties;
- the principle that uncertainty can justify action;
- the importance of establishing credibility and trust;
- communication of uncertainty;
- openness and transparency.

Many of those conclusions are relevant to debates about precaution but none provided an explicit discussion of what precaution might imply in practice for the conduct of policy-making and research.

it allowed them to argue that they were doing what, and only what, their scientific advisers recommended, and it flattered the scientists by representing them as authoritative and influential. A more precautionary approach could have been expected if the role of the scientific advisers had been more strictly delineated, and open to expert and public scrutiny. Since risk assessments are always framed by socio-economic considerations, the responsibility for articulating and justifying those framing assumptions should be the responsibility of democratically accountable ministers, and expert scientific advisers should be responsible for showing how they have gathered and interpreted all the appropriate evidence. Since March 1996, members of SEAC have become more independent than their predecessors. When advising on the possible risks from eating 'beef on the bone' SEAC set out the possible consequences of various courses of action, and explicitly indicated the decisions which ministers would have to take. Policy-making on BSE has become more precautionary, and in part that has been because it has become more open and accountable, especially following the creation of the UK's new Food Standards Agency.

Table 15.1 *BSE: early warnings and actions*

Mid-1970s	US bans scrapie-infected sheep and goat meats from cattle food chain
1979	UK Royal Commission on Environmental Pollution recognises risks of pathogens in animal feed and recommends minimum processing standards in rendering industries
1986	First cases of bovine spongiform encephalopathy (BSE) are officially acknowledged
1988	First documented official acknowledgement that BSE may be transmissible to humans
1988	Southwood Committee is set up and recommends that clinically affected cattle should not go into human and animal food
1989	Ruminant feed ban, slaughter and destruction of affected cattle and specified bovine offal (SBO) ban
1995	Almost 50% of the abattoirs checked are found to be failing to comply with the SBO ban
1995	Evidence that BSE may cause Creutzfeldt-Jakob disease (CJD)
1996	At last, experiments start to see whether cattle fed on rations deliberately infected with scrapie would get BSE
1996	BSE crisis, after a new variant of CJD emerged in the UK and consuming BSE contaminated food was considered the most probable cause
1998–2000	The Phillips Inquiry takes place and its 16-volume report is published. Its conclusions do not seem sufficiently rigorous on judging government actions over time. These conclusions state that appropriate policy decisions had been taken, although not always timely, or adequately implemented or enforced.

Source: EEA

Twelve late lessons

Introduction

The case studies provide a wealth of 'late lessons' for future policy. To attempt to summarise them all would effectively replicate the studies. Returning to the four broad questions that we posed to the authors and trying to distil a number of specific lessons seemed more useful. These then might be applied to future policy in order to minimise repetition of the mistakes – or at least the oversights – of the past.

The first question posed was: When was the first credible scientific early warning? The second was: When and what were the main actions or inactions on risk reduction taken by regulatory and other responsible bodies? The key point here is the length of the gap between the specific problem being identified and effective action being taken. The answer for many case studies was that the gap was long, certainly many years or decades, and in some cases over a century. This might not be so surprising before the need for the precautionary principle had been explicitly identified in the 1970s and 1980s. But even after that, examples of unequivocal precautionary action were relatively scarce. It is also notable that, while the precautionary principle debate has sometimes been characterised as a battle between the EU and North America, the case histories suggest another story, one of different degrees of acceptance of the need for precaution within different institutions in both North America and Europe.

In many of the case studies, adequate information about potential hazards was available well before decisive regulatory advice was taken, but the information was either not brought to the attention of the appropriate decision-makers early enough, or was discounted for one reason or another. It is also true that in some of the case studies, early warnings – and even 'loud and late' warnings – were effectively ignored by decision-makers because of short-term economic and political interactions (see the case studies on asbestos, PCBs, the Great Lakes, and sulphur dioxide and acidification).

The third question was: What were the resulting costs and benefits of the actions or inactions? This proved to be the most difficult question for the case study authors to answer, at least in a comprehensive manner. In part this is due to the background of many of our authors, who are generally technical experts in the field, rather than experts in assessing the economic costs and benefits, or the wider pros and cons of action. But this is also an intrinsically difficult and controversial area. There is no credible way of reducing the pros and cons of alternative courses of action to a single figure, economic or otherwise, not least because of the problem of comparing incommensurables and because the pros and cons are unlikely to be spread evenly across all interest groups. There are constructive ways of dealing with these complications, but ultimately a general analysis lay beyond the scope of the current publication.

However, dealing with some aspects of costs and benefits is inevitable when addressing the fourth question posed to the authors, namely: What lessons can be drawn that may help future decision-making?. For the purposes of this publication, this is a key issue.

The European Scientific Technology Observatory (ESTO) project on technological risk and the management of uncertainty (see, for example, Stirling, 1999) provided the initial framing of this analysis. This sets out a comprehensive structure for the consideration of issues relating to precaution. Not only did this help in organising the consideration of the lessons, it also gave an opportunity to test or elaborate many of the points arising from the ESTO studies against the large body of historical material contained in the case studies. Most of the key issues that emerged from the case studies could be addressed by 12 late lessons:

1   Acknowledge and respond to ignorance, as well as uncertainty and risk, in technology appraisal and public policy-making.
2   Provide adequate long-term environmental and health monitoring and research into early warnings.
3   Identify and work to reduce 'blind spots' and gaps in scientific knowledge.
4   Identify and reduce interdisciplinary obstacles to learning.
5   Ensure that real world conditions are adequately accounted for in regulatory appraisal.
6   Systematically scrutinise the claimed justifications and benefits alongside the potential risks.
7   Evaluate a range of alternative options for meeting needs alongside the option under appraisal, and promote more robust, diverse and adaptable technologies so as to minimise the costs of surprises and maximise the benefits of innovation.
8   Ensure use of 'lay' and local knowledge, as well as relevant specialist expertise in the appraisal.
9   Take full account of the assumptions and values of different social groups.
10 Maintain regulatory independence from interested parties while retaining an inclusive approach to information and opinion gathering.
11 Identify and reduce institutional obstacles to learning and action.
12 Avoid 'paralysis by analysis' by acting to reduce potential harm when there are reasonable grounds for concern.

The distinctions between these different aspects are intended to be illustrative, rather than definitive. Many are clearly interlinked. Some might be combined together or further distinguished. However, the issues summarised here provide a basis for the practical implementation of the precautionary principle. Many of the lessons relate to the type, quality, processing and utilisation of information set within the context of a more participative and democratic process. Such an integrated and comprehensive process of hazard and options appraisal clearly needs to be related to the likely scale of the potential consequences (environmental, social, economic) of the activity in question.

In elaborating these lessons the rule was of not to introduce material extraneous to the case studies. However, in a final section some more general points are raised, which attempt to set the conclusions within the context of other developments in the field.

Twelve late lessons

Respond to ignorance as well as uncertainty

A central lesson of this book concerns the importance of recognising and fully understanding the nature and limitations of our knowledge. What is often referred to as 'uncertainty' actually hides important technical distinctions (see Box 16.1). All the activities in the case studies were subjected to some form of (formal or informal) assessment of risk. What remained neglected, however, was the virtual certainty that there would be factors that remained outside the scope of the risk assessment. This is the domain of ignorance – the source of inevitable surprises, or unpredicted effects.

No matter how sophisticated knowledge is, it will always be subject to some degree of ignorance. To be alert to – and humble about – the potential gaps in those bodies of knowledge that are included in our decision-making is fundamental. Surprise is inevitable. Just as one basis for scientific research is the anticipation of positive surprises – 'discoveries' – so it will always yield the corresponding prospect of negative surprises. By their nature, complex, cumulative, synergistic or indirect effects in particular have traditionally been inadequately addressed in regulatory appraisal.

Thus a key element in a precautionary approach to regulation involves a greater willingness to acknowledge the possibility of surprise. This does not mean resorting to blanket opposition to innovation. But acknowledging the inevitable limits of knowledge leads to greater humility about the status of the available science, requiring greater care and deliberation in making the ensuing decisions. It also leads to a broadening of appraisals to include more scientific disciplines, more types of information and knowledge, and more constituencies.

The consequences of ignorance can be dramatic, as demonstrated by the case study on halocarbons. Prior to the hypothesis of a mechanism for stratospheric ozone depletion in 1974, the now well-known impact of CFCs was a very strong candidate for ignorance extending over many decades. Not only the likelihood, but the very possibility of an 'ozone hole' was unappreciated. Chemicals that were relatively inert and benign under 'normal' conditions (and less conventionally hazardous than the substances they replaced) turned out to behave very differently under conditions that were not considered in the risk appraisal. The effects of the synthetic oestrogen diethylstilboestrol (DES) on the next generation of the treated patient came as a complete surprise, while the

Box 16.1 Risk, uncertainty and ignorance

The precautionary principle is seen principally as a way to deal with a lack of scientific certainty. A basic foundation for our conclusions concerns the nature of scientific certainty itself. There is an urgent need for a more complete and systematic basis for thinking about the different ways in which scientific uncertainty may pervade regulatory appraisal.

First there is the familiar condition of **risk**, as formally defined in probability theory. This is where all possible outcomes are known in advance and where their relative likelihood can be adequately expressed as probabilities. Where this condition prevails, risk assessment is a valid technique that can save lives, prevent damage to the environment and provide a robust basis for decision-making. Still, the judgements over what is defined as at risk, and over the right balance to strike in decision-making, are necessarily laden with subjective assumptions and values.

Under the condition of **uncertainty**, as formally defined, the adequate empirical or theoretical basis for assigning probabilities to outcomes does not exist. This may be because of the novelty of the activities concerned, or because of complexity or variability in their contexts. Either way, conventional risk assessment is too narrow in scope to be adequate for application under conditions of uncertainty. Although techniques such as safety factors, scenario or sensitivity analysis can be useful, they do not provide a way adequately to assess the impacts of different options. Here, more than ever, judgements about the right balance to strike in decision-making are laden with subjective assumptions and values.

Many case studies in this book involve examples where regulatory appraisal laboured not only under a lack of certainty as to the likelihood of different outcomes, but where some of the possibilities themselves remained unknown. Here, decision-making is faced with the continual prospect of surprise. This is the condition formally known as **ignorance**. Even more than uncertainty, this underscores the need for a healthy humility over the sufficiency of the available scientific knowledge and, crucially, for an institutional capacity for open reflection on the quality and utility of available bodies of knowledge. Regulatory appraisal must explicitly address the implications of alternative assumptions and systematically document how these relate to the perspectives of different social groups and to the environment.

Once it is acknowledged that the likelihood of certain outcomes may not be fully quantifiable, or where certain other possibilities may remain entirely unaddressed, then uncertainty and ignorance, rather than mere risk characterise the situation. The adoption of robust, transparent and accountable approaches towards the various aspects of risk, uncertainty and ignorance can be identified as one crucial means of regaining public confidence in regulatory decision-making.

The decision-making process needs to be more explicit and systematic about the level of proof needed to justify reducing hazards. Examples include 'scientifically based suspicion', 'reasonable grounds for concern', the 'balance of evidence' and 'beyond reasonable doubt' (see Table 16.1, in the last section of this chapter, and its elaboration in the last part of this report) There is therefore a range of choices of levels of proof for determining the basis for action, each with different cost and benefit implications for different groups. These different levels of proof provide a more sophisticated basis for the weighing up of potential benefits and harm than do simple pronouncements of truth or falsity.

accumulation of organotins in top predators, arising from tributyltin (TBT) antifoulants was simply not envisaged. According to the authors of the antimicrobials case study: 'The justification for the later dilution of (the Swann Committee's) conclusions and compromises on its recommendations was based mainly on narrow considerations of what was precisely known rather than on taking account of what was not known, of the ignorance within the field ... In other words science that embraces complexities, uncertainties and unknowns with more humility and less hubris is needed.'

The lesson seems clear. Rather than focusing only on the most straightforward and direct impacts, the process of regulatory appraisal should extend attention to as wide a range of conditions and effects as can reasonably be anticipated. Whilst accepting that even the broadest appraisal processes may still fail to foresee 'surprises', there is much that can be done to guard against some of the consequences of the ubiquitous experience of ignorance and surprise.

This insight lies at the heart of the case studies and is a central element of what it means to be precautionary. At first sight, responding to ignorance may seem to ask the impossible. How can strategies be devised to prevent outcomes, which, by definition are not known? Yet the case studies suggest that it is possible to do rather better than in the past.

For example, although not quite as simple as it seems, account can be taken of the potential irreversibility of actions, even if the consequences might not be known. For halocarbons, PCBs and methyl tert-butyl ether (MTBE), as artificial chemicals, their very novelty might be taken as a warning sign. Enough was known at the outset regarding their persistence in the environment to serve as another warning. They would also readily disperse to become ubiquitous throughout the physical environment – one more warning. It could have been deduced from the outset that if these substances were released into the environment, and if a problem subsequently developed, it would take many years for both them and the problem to 'go away'. The Great Lakes case study illustrates long-term hazards associated with other persistent organic pollutants (POPs). For other cases, while it may not have been known in the first instance how irreversible an action was, when this did become apparent regulators were often slow to react. It was relatively quickly established that TBT was more persistent than first assumed; and the permanence of asbestos dust has been known to be part of the problem for many decades. In neither case did hazard reduction actions take account of the long-tem effect early enough. If persistence and bioaccumulation are used as screening for eliminating potential hazards, then the size and seriousness of future 'surprises' are likely to be smaller.

Of course, irreversibility is not restricted to the possible consequences of chemicals. Resistance to antimicrobials, it is now known, is long term. For fisheries, stocks can take a long time to recover from a crash, if ever. Consideration of the irreversibility, or slow reversibility, of actions is a necessary component of a more broadly based approach to the appraisal process. The scale of the potential hazard, particularly if global, where there is only one 'experimental' model, is also a relevant consideration in the appraisal.

The case studies also provide some confirmation that potential problems can be anticipated. For antimicrobials in animal husbandry, confidence over the low risks of transmission of antibiotic resistance to humans was progressively qualified as new understandings developed. Yet as early as the 1960s the UK expert Swann Committee had anticipated many of the subsequent difficulties. This early example of sensitivity to possible sources of ignorance was subsequently overwhelmed by scientific over-confidence in the safety of antimicrobials. Similarly, for PCBs, early results – such as those obtained in animal testing in 1937 – might have been taken as more of a warning.

If a harmful property of a chemical is identified, then it may be prudent to consider that this may be correlated with other potentially harmful but less obvious effects. Of the case studies, short-term acute effects that were readily identified preceded – sometimes by many decades – less obvious chronic problems for sulphur dioxide emissions, ionising radiation, benzene, asbestos, TBT and PCBs. However this should not necessarily be taken as a general rule. At the very least the relationship is an asymmetrical one. While the presence of acute effects may be correlated with chronic impacts, chronic effects will not necessarily be preceded by acute ones – as illustrated by bovine spongiform encephalopathy (BSE) and halocarbons. Similarly, harmful effects seen in wildlife can be useful 'sentinel events' warning us of potential hazards for humans. This calls for integrated ecological and health hazard appraisals.

It is also necessary to draw a distinction between a condition of ignorance that is located at the point of decision-making itself and a condition of ignorance endemic throughout society as a whole. The former predicament, which might be termed 'institutional ignorance', refers to a situation where information relevant to the decision may be extant in society, but is not available to the decision-makers. Here, the consequent 'surprises', though they can be serious, may be quite localised. This problem is exemplified in most of the case studies in this book. It can be remedied by a series of provisions for more effective communication and social learning. The latter condition of 'societal ignorance' is more intractable. This problem is also exemplified in many of the case studies (including BSE) and requires rather different remedies, involving scientific research and the fostering of greater diversity, adaptability and flexibility in decision-making and technological choices. These issues are returned to in the final section of this chapter.

Research and monitor for 'early warnings'

General research and long-term monitoring can be dismissed as being too expensive and unfocused. Yet well-planned research and monitoring are essential to the systematic identification of areas of uncertainty. It is, however, necessary to consider how to conduct general monitoring to increase the prospect of timely alerts to problems arising out of ignorance. Awareness of uncertainty and ignorance helps the posing of appropriate research questions for scientific evaluation. It follows that the adequate funding of research and monitoring intended to pick up early warnings is central to a robust approach to regulatory appraisal of potential hazards.

The case study on halocarbons and the ozone hole carries a mixed message. It was 'curiosity driven' general research for another purpose that resulted in the discovery of stratospheric ozone depletion in the Antarctic. The discovery was essentially serendipitous (see next section). While emphasising the value of purely academic scientific enquiry, it is hardly a reassuring reflection on the status of deliberate monitoring.

Many case studies indicate the value of thorough, long-term, monitoring. While for asbestos, benzene and PCBs evidence was accumulating of the adverse health effects as early as the 19th century, no role was then played by systematic monitoring. Data were either not collated (benzene), or became available only in a slow and rather ad hoc fashion over a period of many decades. Presumably the assumption was made that if there were harmful effects, evidence would emerge of its own accord and in good time for corrective action. A different attitude could have prevented harmful effects at an earlier stage. As for the current relevance, if the trend is for human actions to become geographically more widespread and less reversible, then the use of the 'world as a laboratory' becomes increasingly problematic. It is probably still true that in many cases the underlying assumption remains that any major problems will emerge in good time for corrective action. However, there ought to be more ecological and biological surveillance of the only biosphere we have.

It is also a feature of the case studies that even 'critical path' issues, identified at an early stage, were not necessarily followed up in a timely or effective fashion. For BSE, research into a number of crucial issues was not undertaken in the UK until late in the story. BSE was first identified as a new disease in cattle in 1986, but research to verify its supposed absence of maternal transmission in cattle – important to the early position of the UK Ministry of Agriculture, Fisheries and Food (MAFF) – was not initiated until 1989. Ultimately it showed that maternal transmission did occur. Similarly, experiments concerning the transmissibility of sheep scrapie to cattle (a favoured hypothesis of the source of the disease) were not begun until 1996. No surveys of the number of infectious but asymptomatic cattle entering the food chain have ever been conducted. Yet, throughout this period, reassurances on the part of the UK government continued prominently to cite the absence of evidence, when no evidence was actually being sought. This was a classic example of 'no evidence of harm' being misinterpreted as 'evidence of no harm'.

Similar delays in the conduct of relevant scientific research are documented in other cases. Regarding the routine use of antimicrobials in livestock management, concerns over the implications of the development of resistance, identified by the 1967 Swann Committee, were not followed up until the 1990s. This was despite longstanding knowledge that widespread antibiotic usage could lead to the rapid development of resistance. Likewise for asbestos, there was no systematic monitoring of health impacts, despite clear warnings and recommendations on mortality studies between 1898 and the 1920s, and despite the fact that techniques for workforce health monitoring were well within the capabilities of the day. The authors of the TBT case study concluded that: 'Though frequently under-rated, baseline studies play a vital role in the early detection of adverse trends and may consequently serve the application of precaution'. The case studies on MTBE and PCBs also comment on the relative lack of research on identified causes of concern. Monitoring alone is not enough. Adequate reporting, dissemination and utilisation of research and monitoring results are also essential.

However, neither long-term monitoring specifically, nor environmental science in general, offers a panacea. They may answer some questions, but they raise others and the science progresses from relatively simple and often linear proposition to more dynamic and complex 'system' science. Research may convert some aspects of our ignorance into uncertainty – and even uncertainties into risks – but this will not necessarily be the case. There are examples where research can compound uncertainty and reveal new sources of ignorance. For fisheries, a Canadian mathematical model of the interactions between various fish species suggested that these became more unpredictable as progressively more biological data were incorporated into the model. For the Great Lakes, intensive research amplified the uncertainties. It progressively raised more questions about the possible causes of the observed bird population crashes. At face value this presents a serious challenge to the notion that further scientific research is necessarily a precautionary measure, or indeed whether broadening out the appraisal process to different disciplines is necessarily precautionary (see 'Identify and reduce interdisciplinary obstacles to learning', below). Of course, where thorough research genuinely reveals that concerns over particular agents are unfounded – perhaps by demonstrating a convincing alternative mechanism for an observed effect – then it is in no way precautionary to persist in restricting the original agent of concern.

Other case studies, such as those on antimicrobials, sulphur dioxide and PCBs, illustrate the opening up of the research domain and of sources of ignorance as increasing complexities are discovered. Finally, as the antimicrobials case study illustrates, hazard appraisals should be as specific as possible about the nature of the scientific question that further research needs to address; the time such research may take and the source of the funding needed; and the independence of the relevant organisation carrying it out. The appraisal should also say, as the Swann Report did, whether actions to reduce hazards should happen before or after the research is completed.

Search out and address 'blind spots' and gaps in scientific knowledge

Several of the case studies illustrate blind spots existing within the dominant discipline involved in the regulatory appraisal process. For halocarbons the chemical mechanism for depletion of stratospheric ozone was identified in the prestigious journal *Nature* in 1974. Nevertheless, this did not prevent regulatory neglect until firm empirical evidence of actual effects became available. Even then, as has already been noted, the manner of the emergence of that empirical evidence presents a salutary lesson. The confirmation of an Antarctic 'ozone hole' in 1985 was essentially by accident – a by-product of an experiment conducted for other purposes. A dedicated satellite observation programme to monitor stratospheric ozone had earlier detected major depletion, but the results were considered suspect and set aside. This provides a pertinent example of where assumptions adopted in analysis can prejudge the results, leading to serious blind spots for policy-making. In this case these were not only at the centre of the main scientific disciplines involved in regulatory appraisal, but they involved both the theoretical mechanism and the empirical evidence.

A blind spot within a scientific discipline was also apparent in the case of agricultural antimicrobials. Evidence available in 1968 to the UK Swann Committee allowed explicit anticipation of a series of potential environmental, animal welfare and human health problems that were to become of pressing concern. Although initially influential, the Swann recommendations became marginalised over the ensuing decades. Had they been implemented and sustained, they might at least have mitigated the difficulties now recognised. Similarly, for MTBE the key problematic property of persistence was apparent at the outset, and this might reasonably have been expected to lead to more questions over the potential environmental problems of widespread use of this chemical than were actually raised in the formal regulatory process. In the case of TBT, rates of degradation were based on assumptions about the nature of the marine environment that were evidently incorrect for many areas. For hormones as growth promoters there was a failure to appreciate that young children with low natural levels of oestrogens were the likely 'at risk' group. Radiation risk estimates of typical doses long overlooked the uncertainties resulting from their derivation largely from the health records of the survivors of the atomic bombings in Japan at an atypical high dose and dose rate.

Another blind spot can occur where the adoption of a new practice is held, of itself, to have solved historic problems. For asbestos successive claims were made that past health impacts were due to conditions that had been superseded. The long lineage of claims that 'the disease is not so likely to occur (in future)' can be traced back to 1906. With each successive minor incremental improvement in conditions, the persistent risks associated with the new conditions would then in turn take further decades to become evident. Remarkably, when the recognised magnitude of the health effects eventually prompted asbestos substitution, this was initially attempted with fibrous minerals that shared some of the properties that had led to the effects of asbestos (such as fibre size). In their turn, these substitutes also came – eventually – to be recognised as sources of essentially similar, if much lower, risks. For sulphur dioxide, the building of taller smokestacks, while helping to ameliorate local effects, did not address the wider problem arising from cumulative emissions and long-range transport.

A more precautionary approach therefore means systematically searching out blind spots at the heart of the disciplines historically involved in the regulatory process. This will be easier if multiple relevant disciplinary and other sources of knowledge are engaged, helping to stimulate the sometimes uncomfortable interactions that will be more likely to expose false assumptions and other questions. This leads directly to the next lesson.

Identify and reduce interdisciplinary obstacles to learning

Where effects that are the domain of a particular specialist field may initially be more pronounced, or discovered at an earlier stage, this can lead to a situation where regulatory appraisal becomes unduly dominated by, even 'captive' to, a particular discipline. This can lead to a form of 'institutional' ignorance, as opposed to the society-wide ignorance discussed above. For both asbestos and ionising radiation the setting of standards was strongly influenced by the preoccupation of medical clinicians with immediate acute effects. In both cases, the toxicology and epidemiology of long-term chronic effects remained relatively neglected. The introduction of MTBE was based on bodies of knowledge concerning engines, combustion and air pollution. The water pollution aspects associated with persistence and significant taste and odour problems were essentially disregarded, though the information was available. For sulphur emissions the regulatory appraisal was initially focused on human health concerns. When ecological effects became apparent, a regulatory process constructed to address health issues experienced problems assimilating and reacting to these. Similarly, for the use of hormonal growth promoters in livestock, the initial emphasis was also on human health effects. Although concerns over the impact on wildlife were raised, they initially appeared to attract little attention from the regulators.

In contrast, for both livestock antimicrobials and BSE, considerations of the human impacts were initially marginalised by the regulatory focus on veterinary science. Indeed, for antimicrobials this concern underlay the early 1968 recommendation, by the Swan Committee, that a single advisory process be established which 'should have overall responsibility for the whole field of use of antibiotics and related substances whether in man, animals, food preservation, or for other purposes'. This recommendation was not taken up, in the UK or elsewhere, for many years. In the case of BSE, UK veterinary officials considered the possibility of transmissibility to humans as acceptably slight. This contrasts with the attitude in the US, where the possible link between sheep scrapie and human Creutzfeldt-Jakob disease (CJD) had been regarded as a possibility since the 1970s, when the entry of infected animals into the food chain was banned.

Ensure that real world conditions are fully accounted for

'Real world' conditions can be very different from theoretical assumptions, and these differences can have serious consequences. In principle this problem is well recognised, and it is possible to considerably reduce exposure to oversights of this type. Yet in practice the case studies reveal a variety of incomplete assessments, resulting in erroneous regulatory appraisals and decisions.

In the human sphere it is often assumed that technologies will perform to the specified standards. Yet real life practices can be far from ideal; and it may be a long time before we realise that this is the case. Sometimes actions are taken that appear to be in defiance of prior experience. The leakage from petrol station storage tanks was underestimated in the US regulatory appraisal of MTBE and so led to an underestimation of the resulting exposures. Although storage tanks can be redesigned to reduce the chance of leakage, this benefit can be lost by incorrect installation. For PCBs it was assumed that these could be constrained within 'closed' operating systems. This proved impossible, resulting in accidents such as Yusho and Yucheng, losses from poorly maintained equipment and even illegal disposal into the human food chain. Similarly optimistic assumptions as to the performance of engineered containment equipment, or the efficiency of decommissioning, also played a role in reducing the effectiveness of halocarbon control measures. While some aspects of public exposure to benzene have received rigorous control, these are not necessarily the routes of greatest exposure. The failure to develop mitigation practices, or even warnings, regarding benzene exposure via petrol is one notable example. For the clinical use of radiation, the importance of establishing, and using, the optimal dose for any examination can be traced back to 1949. Yet the dosage for the same examination in different hospitals can still vary by a factor of 100. And for growth promoters scientific advisory committees such as the WHO/FAO Joint Expert Committee on Food considered only a restricted range of options, including just those circumstances relating to authorised use, and assessments of individual growth promoters, rather than in combination. They also gave little attention to the misuse of growth hormones, such as higher doses than recommended, inappropriate injection sites, failure to withdraw hormone implants from slaughtered animals and shortened withdrawal periods.

A gap can also open between assumptions and the real world when applications change without corresponding adjustments to their regulation, such as the expansion of the use of asbestos in consumer products and housing as well as boiler insulation. Asbestos is also notable for the long delay before it was acknowledged that real world conditions meant that users (or even local residents around a factory), as well as workers, could be at risk from exposure. Significantly, the 2001 World Trade Organization Appellate Body ruling on asbestos concluded that 'controlled use' risk management could not be relied on to protect workers' health in real world conditions.

In some cases there will be deliberate non-compliance. Apart from the illegal disposal of PCBs already noted, this included poor practice in the agricultural use of antimicrobials that increased the spread of resistance, and the circumvention of attempted regulation of fisheries that helped deplete stocks. Similarly, unrealistic assumptions were made about the implementation of changes to UK slaughterhouse practices as a crucial part of the response to the BSE crisis. Acute human effects observed in Puerto Rico and Italy were blamed on the illegal or incompetent use of animal growth promoters. Similarly, the smuggling of halocarbons is threatening the effectiveness of global controls.

False assumptions about the real world also affect our interpretation of events in the natural environment. The PCBs case study describes the surprising potential for these chemicals (along with certain other POPs) to concentrate disproportionately on a global scale in high-latitude regions. Also for PCBs, in the real world bioaccumulated PCBs were found to be disproportionately more toxic, with the result that the effects were greater than those indicated by experiments using the original commercial formulations. For fisheries, stock assessment models tend to concentrate on single stocks, downplaying the interactions between stocks or other marine species. There are enormous, perhaps insoluble, problems in broadening the scope using the stock modelling approach. Nevertheless, the single stock approach does not reflect actual conditions. The unexpected consequences of halocarbon degradation in the stratosphere is another example of the unanticipated complexity of the real world. In these, and many other cases, the behaviour of real natural systems can prove far removed from the standard assumptions made in regulatory appraisals and consequent decisions. The issue of hormone growth promoters illustrates how the real world also contains groups of particularly sensitive individuals (young boys, for example) who may react differently to exposures compared with assumptions based on the 'average' response.

Systematically scrutinise and justify the claimed 'pros' and 'cons'

One feature of debates about environmental risk is how all protagonists typically call for greater and more systematic attention to be paid to the claimed benefits of the technologies in question. Some are concerned that undue attention on, or inaccurate appreciation of, the risks might diminish recognition of the anticipated benefits of their favoured technologies. Others are concerned that the justification for new technologies, and claims as to their efficacy, are insufficiently critically scrutinised. Either way, both positions effectively call for the regulatory appraisal process to more deliberately and systematically examine the claims made about the benefits of a technology or product, including an identification and assessment of the conditions under which the claimed benefits might, or might not, materialise.

Problems can arise from the partial assessment of environmental protection measures. Raising the height of smokestacks and shifting to smokeless fuel were an effective response to the serious episodes of respiratory illness from European sulphur emissions and urban air pollution in the 1950s. Yet this very effectiveness may have inhibited attention to the problems of long-distance transport of acid gases and the consequent acceleration of environmental problems in vulnerable areas. This was a classic case of an end-of-pipe 'solution' only creating other, less visible hazards. A more integrated approach eventually reduced all the problems. Similarly, because MTBE apparently promised a simple solution to the serious environmental problems caused by lead emissions from motor vehicles, the environmental problems associated with taste and odour in combination with persistency in groundwater were perhaps more readily overlooked than might otherwise have been the case. The introduction of hormonal growth promoters can also be considered to be an example of narrow and partial assessments of the pros and cons. Human health issues, possible environmental impacts and farm animal welfare were 'not given significant attention', according to the case study authors.

Another dimension of the sulphur dioxide case study was that the distribution of the pros and cons between the UK and the Scandinavian countries was very different, or at least was perceived to be very different. In relation to the effects on the natural environment, Sweden seemed to be suffering the most. It was only with the realisation of major damage to buildings in the UK – caused by air pollution – that both countries realised that they were suffering from the impact of acid emissions.

In two cases, BSE and fisheries (the Canadian cod collapse), the pros and cons of taking early action were identified prior to the event. But because the uncertainties were significant, and the financial costs of action high, limited action was taken. This resulted in the far greater costs (many of which were anticipated) when the measures proved inadequate. In the case of fisheries, even in the absence of stock collapses, major economic, social and environmental benefits accrue from allowing depleted stocks to recover.

One might think medicines would be validated for efficacy. However, for DES, the data from 1953 trials showed that DES was ineffective as a means of reducing risks of spontaneous abortion in certain groups of mothers and that it was positively harmful. This seems not to have been appreciated at the time. As a result the rate of reduction in use of the drug was more gradual than might have been the case; there was no regulatory action; and marketing continued unabated. It was not for another 20–30 years that use of this drug was actually banned in different countries, in response to the discovery of an increase in a rare cancer of the vagina in daughters of treated women. Had greater critical attention been paid at the outset to the claims of efficacy, then some of these second-generation cancers might have been avoided.

A step beyond passive assessment of the pros and cons is actively directed prior to justification. Ionising radiation is a rare example of such a 'justification principle', developed by the International Commission on Radiological Protection (ICRP) in the 1950s. This was a response to the burgeoning of a variety of dubious or ineffective uses of radioactive materials (for instance in countering ringworm, fitting shoes for children, the cosmetic removal of hair and the treatment of mental disorders). Yet even with this criterion, the degree to which exposure to ionising radiation is justified by the benefits remains open to question. Surveys of radiography practices over the past decade or so conclude that, while doses have reduced drastically, a large proportion of medical X-rays are still of doubtful clinical use. The reduction of the use of antimicrobials, initially in Sweden, can also be considered to be an example of the wider assessment of the pros and cons.

The appropriate allocation of costs and benefits is an essential pre-condition for optimising resources between technological options. A host of risk management measures are available under the broad remit of the 'polluter pays principle' – including taxes, subsidies and liability regimes, which offer a way to ensure more equitable social distributions of the costs and benefits associated with risk governance decisions. The failure, in cases like asbestos, halocarbons and PCBs, to reflect full environmental and health costs in market prices gave these products an unjustifiable advantage in the marketplace. This in turn helped to keep technically superior substitutes off the market for longer than was optimal from society's point of view. Although the mechanisms for the internalisation of external environmental costs and the practical implementation of liability regimes are controversial, such measures are essential if both efficiency and equity objectives are to be addressed effectively.

Evaluate alternatives and promote robust, diverse and adaptable solutions

Even where the pros are scrutinised alongside the cons, if attention is restricted simply to isolated technologies or products then important practical insights may be missed. One concern is that, once a technological commitment is made, a host of institutional and market processes act to reinforce its position, even if markedly inferior to potential alternatives.

So while in principle the function of MTBE might be substituted by alternative oxygenates such as bioethanol, improved engine technology or an increase in the octane rating of the fuels themselves, little formal scrutiny appeared to have been undertaken at the time of adoption of MTBE. In California, the search for a successor to MTBE has recognised that all the proposed alternatives must be fully evaluated. The authors of the TBT case study note that 'Broader consideration of problems may give rise to more beneficial solutions than simple 'chemical for chemical' substitution', and give examples of such alternatives. For ionising radiation, substitutes for the diagnostic use of X-rays remain underutilised. The ozone-depleting properties of second-generation CFC substitutes were perhaps also unduly tolerated, simply because of their relatively low impacts when compared with the original substances, and the existence of more benign substitutes or alternative approaches was not properly looked at. And while effective husbandry practices not involving the routine large-scale administering of antimicrobials are increasingly used in a number of European countries, these more benign alternatives are not actively promoted.

This raises some challenging issues about the relationship between regulatory processes and product development by private companies. The promotion and production of alternatives needs to take place within a culture of 'eco-efficiency', 'clean production' and closed-loop material flows so as to minimise the size of any future 'surprises' in the use and impact of technologies. These issues are returned to in the concluding section of this chapter.

Use 'lay' and local knowledge as well as all relevant specialist expertise

The importance of ensuring that regulatory appraisal includes the full range of relevant disciplines has already been covered. A related but distinct lesson concerns drawing upon knowledge held by lay people. These may include industry workers, users of the technology and people who live in the locality or, because of their lifestyle or consumption habits, stand to be most strongly affected. The point is not that lay people are necessarily more knowledgeable or environmentally committed. Rather the benefit of attending to lay knowledge rests in its complementary character, its sometimes firmer grounding in real world operational conditions – as already discussed – and the associated independence from the narrow professional perspectives that can be a downside of specialist expertise. Often too, lay knowledge of a technology or risk may be based on different assumptions about what is salient, or what degree of control is reasonable to expect or require, whereas technical specialists may simply respond to granted authority without further reflection.

One prominent contribution from lay knowledge relevant to the regulatory process concerns workplace awareness of emerging patterns of ill health. The histories of usage of asbestos and PCBs provide examples where workers were aware of what regulators subsequently recognised to be a serious problem. Similarly, local communities may become aware of unusual concentrations of ill health before the authorities, such as the Love Canal example cited in the Great Lakes case study.

Another form of lay knowledge concerns remedial measures. Fisheries highlight several aspects and, although fishers can be less precautionary about stock depletion than others, there are many examples where fishers wish to act in a precautionary manner but are prevented from doing so because of a systems failure. There is an increasing emphasis in Canada and elsewhere on the need to involve fishers in management, and take full account of their knowledge and perspectives. Similarly for livestock antimicrobials, Swedish farmers' knowledge of alternative animal husbandry techniques allowed them to promote animal health and growth without the large-scale use of antimicrobials. Not only did they bring valuable insights to the regulatory debate, but they were able to undertake voluntary controls in advance of regulatory requirements. Another aspect to emerge from this case study is the need for knowledge to be widely based in order for less harmful alternatives to be effectively implemented – indeed it is fundamental to ensuring that the existence of possible alternatives is actually recognised.

Another aspect of lay knowledge is where workers know that real practices do not match the theoretical assumptions of risk assessors. The UK slaughterhouse rules over BSE separation of specified bovine offal from meat were widely flaunted, yet failures in the inspection regime meant that this was not drawn to the attention of the regulators. In this case, workers in the industry in question were apparently better informed about the operational realities than were high-level regulatory advisers and officials.

Of course lay knowledge should be subject to the same intensity of critical scrutiny as specialist expertise. Lay perspectives are not immune to the pitfalls and difficulties noted in these conclusions – and may be more vulnerable. One example is the 'pensioners' party fallacy' amongst asbestos workers who pointed to the presence of healthy pensioners at the firm's Christmas party as evidence of the apparent harmlessness of asbestos.

Nevertheless, workers, users and neighbours evidently can bring important information to the regulatory appraisal process, requiring greater attention to be devoted to the development of methods to enable those groups with potentially valuable knowledge to provide this, and for this to be fully taken into account. Such broadening of the knowledge base can strengthen the appraisal, improve governance and democracy, and enhance the acceptability and legitimacy of the process.

Take account of wider social interests and values

Gathering available knowledge is not the only reason for opening up the appraisal process. Historically there is little doubt that social and political conflicts can be aggravated by a regulatory preoccupation with expert judgements and a lack of attention to public perspectives and values. In part this relates to a wider assessment of the pros and cons, as already discussed. The meeting of specialists and interest groups with different viewpoints can be productive, helping ensure a reflective approach, and allowing the implicit assumptions of all parties to be tested. The Swedish farmers in the antimicrobials case study show how lay views can help ensure that the regulatory process remains (or becomes) attached to prevailing ethical and socio-cultural values.

It is implicit that the intuitions embodied in public values may sometimes prove quite robust in relation to the framing of the regulatory science itself. An aversion to situations far outside the bounds of normal experience, or at least a desire to proceed with caution, can certainly be defended as a rational response to uncertainty. A key feature of the public reaction to the emerging evidence of BSE in the late 1980s was the surprised revulsion that ruminants were being fed on offal and bodily wastes. It seems likely that avoiding offal in ruminant feed would have at least significantly limited the scale of the subsequent BSE and CJD problems. Similarly, had widespread public misgivings over the use of antimicrobials in animal husbandry been heeded, the development of resistance would have been held in check. The fisheries study illustrates how the objectives of a precautionary approach – to prevent stock collapses, to maintain maximum sustainable yields or to ensure the protection of other species – depend on the value judgements of the interest groups.

Maintain regulatory independence from economic and political special interests

A major element of a broader approach to regulatory appraisal is to ensure that an appropriate distance is maintained between those responsible for regulatory appraisal and various contending interest groups seeking to influence their decisions. It is a necessary part of the regulatory process that claims over the pros and cons should be actively advanced and argued by interested parties. It then becomes a matter for independent, accountable institutions to adjudicate between the contending claims.

There is evidence in the case studies that interested parties are often able to unduly influence regulators. As a result decisions that might reasonably have been made on the basis of the available evidence were not taken. Benzene was demonstrated to be a powerful bone marrow poison in 1897; the potential for acute respiratory effects of asbestos was first identified in 1898; and the first cases of PCB-induced chloracne were documented in 1899, with effects on workers known by the late 1930s. Yet it was not until the 1960s and 1970s that significant progress began to be made in restricting the damage caused by these agents. One factor in the slow UK response to BSE was that the governmental regulatory body was responsible first to the industry and only second to consumers. Similarly, the temporary lifting of the ban on DES as a growth promoter in the US in 1974 followed strong pressure from the farming lobby, and occurred despite the availability of alternatives.

It is also notable how poorly substantiated some of the sustained 'refutations' of critical findings have been. This was true of the identification of PCBs as widespread environmental pollutants in the 1960s and of the UK response to the impact of acid deposition in the 1970s and early 1980s. Asbestos provides a clear example of persistent obstruction and misinformation by vested interests, and of drastic miscalculation in the wider regulatory process. The accumulation of medical and pathological evidence, while having very little impact on regulation, was sufficient to make parts of the US and Canadian insurance industry wary about providing cover by 1918; a precautionary attitude that ironically was not maintained as evidence accumulated – an error that was to cost the insurance industry billions of dollars. Although benzene had been unequivocally identified as a human carcinogen, human health protection measures continued to be impeded by claims over a lack of evidence for animal carcinogenicity. Similarly demonstrably erroneous claims (based, for example, on basic statistical errors) were later repeated regarding evidence of effects arising from very low benzene exposures.

Even where the evidence is essentially not contested, data and reports are sometimes suppressed, or publishers intimidated, as reported in the Great Lakes case study. For antimicrobials, research that might have been expected to reinforce a critical position was delayed. Efforts were made in the case of BSE and asbestos unjustifiably to discredit independent critics. In the Californian sardine fishery in the 1930s, critical agency scientists were dismissed. 'Shooting the messenger' has been a typical response to those bearing disturbing news ever since Galileo, but it rarely, if ever, promotes societal welfare. BSE provides an explicit example of independent expert advisory committees who advise the regulators subjecting themselves to self-censorship, based on a judgement of what was 'realistic' or 'achievable'. The Southwood BSE Committee considered in 1988 that a ban on the use of all cattle brains in the human food chain might be justified on scientific grounds, but it was considered not to be a politically feasible option.

Regulatory appraisal frequently fails due to the dependence of risk assessment on information produced and owned by the very actors whose products are being assessed. Independent sources of risk information are a necessary, if not sufficient, condition of independent, rigorous and trustworthy regulatory appraisal. Independent information about risks and possible risks was often lacking in the cases studied. In some of the examples cited above, for example benzene, PCBs, asbestos, halocarbons and DES, knowledge concerning hazards was available long before any regulatory action was decided. Not all of these cases demonstrate the delaying or distorting effect of non-independent sources of such knowledge. Nevertheless, the emergence of hazard evidence can be accompanied by vigorous though often low public profile interpretative jockeying to try to justify inaction. What is very difficult to dispute is that had such information – from wherever it emerged – been taken to be the rightful subject of control and disseminated by an independent public body whose very *raison d'être* was the provision of salient public policy information, then the corresponding interpretative debate about policy intervention would have been more open, and more pluralistic. Diverse interests would have been more equitably, thoroughly and probably more rationally represented. Independent information institutions, allied to corresponding rights, resources and responsibilities, are thus a key element of authentic regulatory independence and robust governance and appraisal. This is increasingly being recognised, for example by the shifting of advisory committees from 'producer' directorates in the European Commission (for example, agriculture) to the Health and Consumer Directorate. The setting up of independent food agencies in some Member States and at the EU level also reflects this concern for more independent hazard appraisal institutions.

Identify and reduce institutional obstacles to learning and action

The progressive unfolding of the asbestos, benzene and PCB episodes from the late 19th century provide various examples of how short-term horizons, notably government and business cycles, can militate against social welfare in the medium and long term. However, institutional obstacles against timely protection of health and the environment can take other forms as well. The case studies illustrate three other areas which can present difficulties: those resulting from periods of transition (for example between succeeding elected administrations) or from tensions between different departments or levels of government and 'their' agencies, and the issues that can arise from differing national approaches.

One instance where a change in political administration may have contributed to poor implementation of prior knowledge is provided by the case of BSE. An official UK commission in 1979 recommended the setting of minimum processing standards in the rendering industries. A new administration later that year decided to withdraw the resulting proposed regulations, deeming them to be an unnecessary burden on industry. It is not clear to what extent such tighter standards might actually have inhibited the later BSE outbreak, but it is notable that the implementation of standards of this sort featured prominently among that same government's later responses to the BSE crisis in 1996.

Similarly, in the Californian sardine fishery, what was in effect a precautionary programme of stock conservation was reversed with a change in government. The Californian fishery also provides a clear example of tension between different levels of government, albeit dating back to the 1930s, where the state agency's recommended precautionary action was strongly opposed by the US Federal Bureau of Fisheries on the grounds that it would unduly inhibit commercial activity. An example of similarly fraught communication between different governmental departments may be found in the case of BSE in the UK. Here, the Department of Health was not informed by MAFF about the emergence of the new disease until some 17 months after MAFF was first alerted, and only then because its assent was required for a decision not to remove clinically affected cattle from the human food chain. Regulatory agencies can face a difficult relationship with government, who can exercise more or less subtle influence, even where the agency has explicit independence. Difficulties can also arise where the regulatory agency becomes part of the issue through its past decisions. Both situations are illustrated by BSE, where identification and recognition of the problem was influenced and delayed as a consequence of wider policy considerations (the economic impact on farming) and the concern that lack of consistency would undermine the credibility of government and agencies alike.

Scepticism over the scientific results obtained in other countries was a key feature of the attitude of UK regulatory authorities to the sulphur emissions in the mid-1980s. Although research results suggesting both the seriousness of the environmental effects, and the identity of the responsible agent, were accepted in Norway in 1976, it was not until 1985 that the scientific case for a causal link was acknowledged in the UK. As already noted, during this period the distribution of pros and cons was perceived to be unevenly balanced between the contesting parties, and it would not have been surprising if this influenced the level of scepticism on the part of the UK.

Similar tensions have existed between Sweden and the EU in the case of antimicrobials, where different regulatory systems were based on different presumptions. Whatever one may consider to be the pros and cons of the argument, EU membership requirements were an institutional obstacle to the continued implementation of a national policy. At a different level, global problems clearly require a global response. This is brought into focus by the circumstances surrounding the TBT issue. Here, effective action to regulate the use of antifouling biocides on the hulls of wide-ranging commercial vessels is dependent on agreement within global institutions such as the International Maritime Organization.

For BSE it is notable that the same scientific evidence was available to the US and the UK in the mid-1970s concerning the transmission of scrapie and possible links between scrapie and CJD. However, it led the US Department of Agriculture, but not the UK MAFF, to decide that scrapie-affected animals should not be used in human or animal foods. The different timing of national decisions on the use of DES both as a pharmaceutical and as a growth promoter in animals also illustrates how widely decisions can vary even though based on the same information. In these, and other examples, institutional obstacles appear to have played a role.

Avoid paralysis by analysis

The general tenor of the lessons so far is to 'know more', for example by searching out blind spots within disciplines, reaching out to other disciplines, accessing lay and local knowledge, and taking account of wider social perspectives. One response is to ask how much information is enough to justify action to reduce potential hazards. An obvious concern is that of the danger of paralysis by analysis where either information overload or lack of political will leads to a failure of timely hazard reduction measures. One example is the evidently anti-precautionary straitjacket imposed upon US benzene regulation by a Supreme Court decision, which required layer upon layer of additional information before regulatory action to reduce risks was possible.

Experts have often argued at an early stage that 'we know enough' to take protective action. For antimicrobials the UK Swann Committee in 1969 concluded: 'despite the gaps in our knowledge... we believe... on the basis of evidence presented to us, that this assessment is a sufficiently sound basis for action... the cry for more research should not be allowed to hold up our recommendations'. Other case studies, such as asbestos and BSE, suggest that more, or better-targeted, research, at an earlier stage, would have helped minimise future costs. Similarly, for fisheries, the Ecosystems Principles Advisory Panel to the US Congress concluded: 'There will always be unmeasured entities, random effects, and substantial uncertainties, but these are not acceptable excuses to delay implementing an ecosystem-based management strategy.'

On the other hand, the Great Lakes study argued that more uncertainty was generated as the field was opened up to new disciplines, and that this indeed could lead to paralysis by analysis if a precautionary approach was applied. The Great Lakes case raises a very important issue that is best understood by appreciating the significant distinction between this and the other case studies. Most deal with concerns raised in relation to particular identified agents. The issue in such cases is the 'prospective' assessment of risks, starting with an agent and seeking possible effects. The Great Lakes case, however, is an example of a rather different, 'retrospective' process. This starts with the documenting of a series of manifest health or environmental effects and seeks the identification of possible agents. The broadening out of prospective appraisal is precautionary because it has the effect of focusing attention on a greater number of possible effects. The broadening out of retrospective appraisal, however, may have the effect of raising uncertainties over the basis for regulating individual agents.

As has been pointed out in discussing monitoring, it is in no way precautionary to persist in restrictions of the wrong agent. However, the precautionary principle applies as much to uncertainties over agents as to those over effects. If a broad-based retrospective process raises scientific uncertainties or ambiguities about the grounds for targeting a particular agent, the precautionary principle may nonetheless be invoked, entirely legitimately, to defend continued action on this agent, until such uncertainties are resolved.

The fact that the precautionary principle was not invoked in this fashion in the Great Lakes case is more a reflection of the value judgements in the prevailing legal and socio-political context than it is of intrinsic inconsistencies in the concept of precaution itself. The prospects for successful appeal to the precautionary principle will depend on the culture within which the appeal is made. If the culture is not prepared to act even when there is demonstrable evidence of cause and effect, then appeals to precaution are unlikely to succeed. In reality the regulatory and wider culture of a society may vary between these extremes, and even between different regulatory sub-cultures (cf the differing US approach in the case studies on BSE, fisheries, MTBE, benzene and the Great Lakes).

Whether or not the need for more information risks 'paralysis by analysis' or is merely part of a 'prudent and careful evaluation' of the situation, will be influenced by the individual, social or interest group's assessment of the likely pros and cons as they impinge upon them. If the benefits of taking early precautionary action are large, and the adverse consequences deemed relatively small, and if these are evenly spread across interest groups, then early action is likely to be considered. If the advantages are less certain and, like the costs, are very unevenly spread across different interest groups, or time periods, then reaching consensus about the appropriate amount of research, or about actions to reduce hazards, will be more difficult.

Of course, it may be that in some cases it will be necessary to severely curtail or end innovation in a particular field or technological direction where society judges the risks to be unacceptable. But there is an enormous difference between the discouraging of a particular innovatory pathway, and the channelling of innovation into alternative routes. As illustrated by asbestos, halocarbons, PCBs and antimicrobials, the curtailment of a particular option may actually serve to foster and intensify innovation in other areas. It may also provide a competitive edge to the economies of the countries leading such innovations. The intelligent use of foresight and the precautionary principle may therefore not only reduce overall costs to society of some economic developments, but can stimulate innovation, encourage better and more systems-based science, and improve public decision-making.

Some of these wider implications of a more precautionary approach to potential hazards and innovation are further elaborated in the next section.

The wider implications of precaution

The 12 broad lessons for policy-making on risk just described have been developed under a number of criteria. First, they are well grounded in the empirical detail of particular case studies. Second, they are sufficiently general in nature to be found relevant to virtually any risk management problem. Third, taken together, they address a balanced and fairly comprehensive range of considerations, spanning a large part of the current debate on the management of hazards and the implementation of the precautionary principle. Finally, although necessarily general in nature, they are sufficiently concrete to inform practical policy measures and institutional procedures, even though the precise nature of these in a given case will necessarily be defined by variable local circumstances.

That said, it is not possible to anticipate in one short discussion, or one set of 'lessons', the full range and diversity of detailed practical precautionary measures and procedures, still less to explore the specific contextual considerations bearing on their application. Such matters are the subject of a wide and burgeoning literature (see, for example: O'Riordan and Cameron, 1994; Harding and Fisher, 1999; Raffensperger and Tickner 1999; Stirling, 1999; O'Riordan et al, 2001). Although not always labelled as 'precaution', many of these lessons have been strongly developed and elaborated by a variety of influential policy studies in industrialised countries over recent years.

In the US, for instance, the seminal study by the National Research Council (NRC), 'Understanding risk' (NRC, 1996) and the subsequent report by the presidential commission (Omen et al, 1997) documented the limitations of conventional narrow risk assessment and highlighted the importance of interdisciplinary, lay knowledge and divergent stakeholder viewpoints in the characterisation of risk issues and of appropriate assessment approaches. The 1998 report of the UK Royal Commission on Environmental Pollution developed this theme (RCEP, 1998), underscoring the potential significance of uncertainty and different 'framing assumptions' in the shaping and interpretation of formal appraisal. In France (Kourilsky and Viney, 1999) recommendations on implementation of the precautionary principle stressed the need to organise systematically national expertise capacities, including both scientific and technical expertise, alongside economic and social expertise. In Germany, the importance of more broad-based discursive procedures is recognised in the major report of the German Advisory Council on Global Change (WBGU, 2000). The development of the Swedish chemicals policy is based on recognition of many of the lessons noted here concerning the fundamental limitations of risk assessment, particularly the use of persistence and bioaccumulation as 'proxies' for unknown but possible impacts.

Various specialists have also detailed the general points of these lessons in respect of the structural limitations of EU regulatory risk assessment of genetically modified organisms (GMOs) (van Dommeln, 1997). In the light of these cogent critiques of the overly reductionist and narrow character of European scientific risk assessment of GMOs, it is worth remembering that this same EU risk assessment is regarded by US counterparts as irrationally exaggerated when measured against what they define as 'sound science'. At any rate, it is abundantly clear that in most of these issues, a scientific framing of the questions as if they were all resolvable by existing or available knowledge of risks is radically incomplete – and not only in respect of the answers, but more particularly in respect of the questions which are deemed salient to address even if answers are difficult or impossible to achieve.

In the light of recognition of these wider dimensions, some practical yet more broadly based institutional procedures such as consensus conferences and scenario workshops have been developed in Denmark and The Netherlands to try to articulate public questions and values with respect to scientific presumptions about the answers, and these have been exported widely over recent years (Renn et al, 1996). In the UK, the advent of new 'strategic commissions', on food, human genetics, and agricultural genetics and environment, is a recent innovation that opens up the risk policy process in the way suggested by some of these lessons. Detailed policy appraisals in areas such as BSE (Phillips et al, 2000) and mobile phones (IEGMP, 2000) have seen various of these lessons explored in some detail, with specific recommendations on how to handle issues such as institutional conflicts of interest and unrealistic expectations of the role of science as a touchstone, or arbiter, of ultimate truth.

The 12 lessons should be useful aids to policy-making. However, one should avoid caution against over-reliance on any single set of prescriptions for what constitutes a 'precautionary approach' in any given case. The implementation of the precautionary principle involves drawing on an entire spectrum of methods, procedures and instruments, many falling on the same continuum as orthodox risk management approaches. The business of deciding upon one particular set of responses rather than another must necessarily remain, at some level, an essentially political business – subject to all the normal processes of rational policy deliberation, professional review and democratic debate and accountability.

Finally, it is worth remembering that the precautionary principle began life as an environmental policy approach but it has been rightly recognised that constructive and effective environmental policy demands integration of environmental objectives into all areas of decision-making and technological, as well as public policy, commitment. Therefore it is axiomatic that a proper framework for measured and effective precautionary policy-making must encompass these wider domains, even if only indirectly. Beyond the 12 lessons, some general principles and specific practical messages are proposed, covering the relationships between precaution and science, precaution and innovation, and precaution and governance.

Precaution and science

The precautionary principle raises important issues for science. Some are to do with what many might perceive as the mechanics of science, such as issues of statistical proof and the framing of hypotheses. But it also raises some very fundamental interdisciplinary issues regarding the very nature of knowledge-gathering.

'Statistical proof' and the framing of hypotheses

For the environmental sciences, issues of proof and precaution often come up via the interpretation of statistics. Given that it is impossible to prove a hypothesis (such as 'all swans are white'), only to disprove it (the discovery of Australia, and with it the Australian black swan), the statistical workaround is to attempt to falsify a 'null hypothesis'. This is the opposite of the hypothesis of interest, for example that chemical concentrations have increased. If an increase exceeds, by some arbitrary threshold, that which might be expected by chance fluctuation, the null hypothesis is rejected and it is assumed that an increase has occurred. However it is still possible that the result is a freak and that the increase is due to chance. This is known as a 'Type I' statistical error, or a 'false positive'. Traditionally there has been a strong emphasis on avoiding Type I errors. In the example here, a recorded increase in the chemical would be assumed to reflect a real underlying change only if there is a very small probability of the change occurring by chance – typically less that 1 in 20 or 1 in 100 (a result that is significant at the 95% or 99% level). In effect not being wrong is more important than being safe. However this issue is being increasingly recognised in policy. Table 16.1. gives some examples of policy action taken at different levels of proof. This is further elaborated in an EEA response to this book (EEA, forthcoming 2002).

But there is another fundamental statistical problem. Because environmental monitoring is expensive it is usually limited in scope. Yet the smaller the sample size and/or the greater the natural variation, the less likely it is that a real increase could be identified through the statistical noise. The possibility of calling a real effect false is known as a 'Type II' error, or a 'false negative'. Underwood (1999) concluded 'Typically there has been little concern about Type II error. The chances of erring in 'favour' of the environment (a Type I error) is deliberately kept small, whereas the chances of erring 'unfavourably' to environmental issues is not!' A great deal of money can be wasted, for example on expensive ship-borne marine monitoring, if the actual amount of sampling that can be carried out on a few trips has no prospect of separating adverse effects from statistical noise, that is, it has low statistical power (HELCOM,

Table 16.1 *Different levels of proof for different purposes: some illustrations*

Verbal description	Examples
'Beyond all reasonable doubt'	Criminal law; Swedish chemical law, 1973 (for evidence of 'safety' from manufacturers)
'Balance of evidence'	Intergovernmental Panel on Climate Change, 1995 and 2001
'Reasonable grounds for concern'	European Commission *Communication on the Precautionary Principle*
'Scientific suspicion of risk'	Swedish chemical law, 1973, for evidence required for regulators to take precautionary action on potential harm from substances

Source: EEA

1996). On top of this come complications arising from the formulation of the hypothesis to be tested, and of experimental design: for example, asking the wrong question; dismissing a factor from assessment due to an erroneous prior assumption that it is unimportant; deciding when, what and how frequently to monitor; the importance to be accorded to rare events; or deciding how to deal with complex interactions, or non-linear responses such as chaos.

Similarly, even small misclassifications of exposure in epidemiological studies can result in major reductions in relative risks, with associations being more likely to be missed than falsely implicated (Copeland et al, 1977). In general, the power of epidemiological studies to detect relevant risks is critical but often overlooked, leading to a false sense of security from so-called 'negative' studies that fail to find a risk.

The bias in science towards avoiding false positives inevitably involves generating false negatives, which, if they are human and or environmental disasters, as in most of these case studies, is not sound public policy. Clearly, such a bias in favour of generating false negatives does not conform to the precautionary principle, and is an issue that is taken up briefly in the EEA's response to this book (EEA, forthcoming 2002).

While such issues are often seen as simply a matter of scientific judgement, in fact they lead on to some rather deeper points.

Fundamental issues

The commonly used word 'uncertainty' needs to be differentiated at least into risk, uncertainty and ignorance. A wider examination of just how agreement can be reached on what are the 'facts' would have to take account of other distinct dimensions such as complexity, indeterminacy, ambiguity, and the nature of disagreement (Wynne, 2001; Stirling, 1999). The concept of precaution has resulted in new thinking in the fields of sociology of science and in philosophy, and with it the recognition of new kinds of ignorance underlying the very processes of knowledge procurement. Authors such as Krohn and Weyer (1994) have explained how full knowledge of the consequences of innovations can only be gained by treating society and the larger environment as themselves the experimental laboratory. This point has profound though as yet unrealised implications for democratic policy-making about new, and indeed existing, technologies.

Society's growing commitment to the precautionary principle is essentially a response to a growing tension between two aspects of science: its growing innovative powers were increasingly outrunning its capacity to anticipate the consequences. Moreover, too often from within the scientific community there was a denial of the waning ability to predict those consequences. This encouraged the reasonable democratic response of demanding more circumspection. This circumspection was not about innovation and risk themselves, but about our ability to know. In other words, it was about science and its presumed powers. It is not at all anti-scientific to raise such questions. Indeed it could be said that it is anti-scientific to deny them. There is nothing scientific about the 'pretence at knowledge' (von Hayek, 1978). Such pretence has the consequence of undermining the authority and credibility of the institutions of science – society's most powerful intellectual resource.

With this in mind some further observations are relevant. For example, in discussions between peers, it is accepted that the nature of scientific proof is essentially complex, open, and always provisional. Yet externally it has in some quarters become a requirement that science provide the policy process both with simple answers and certainty. This dual identity for 'science' causes considerable tensions, not least because the contradiction between intrinsic provisionality and pretended certainty often goes unacknowledged – but not, it appears, unnoticed.

This brings us to a deep dislocation between policy institutions and the public about understandings and representations of scientific uncertainty and ignorance. Public surveys in relation to GMOs on both sides of the Atlantic (Levy and Derby, 2000; Wynne et al, 2000), indicate that non-experts do make a basically correct distinction between uncertainty and ignorance. Whilst scientific risk assessment focuses on (known) uncertainties, public concerns instead centre on unacknowledged ignorance lying behind even the best science. Especially with the rapid expansion of very novel innovations, a major public concern is the possible consequences of ignorance. The reaction can be summed up as 'if we can never fully know the consequences, then we had better at least ensure that the purposes driving the enterprise, and the interests which control the responses to the resultant surprises, are good ones' (Wynne, 1992 and 2001). In other words the issues of what are the driving purposes and who benefits are foremost in people's minds.

Yet the policy response, in order to reassure the public, has often been to intensify research on identified uncertainties, with the intention of demonstrating intellectual mastery of the issue, and to show that concern about (known) risks is unfounded. These policy responses to what are believed to be misconceived public demands for zero risk and zero uncertainty are futile, because they presume the problems of public mistrust lie with the public's erroneous expectation of certainty, and the public's supposed misunderstandings of science, risk and uncertainty. This institutional approach fundamentally misunderstands typical public attitudes and expectations; and it only feeds public mistrust by inadvertently demonstrating its own denial of ignorance and lack of intellectual mastery – which the public appears intuitively to understand rather better than does institutionalised science itself.

Thus whereas some views critical of precaution see it as pandering to populist anti-science sentiment, in the form of supposed demands for certainty before sanctioning any innovative commitment, there is ample evidence that people are typically quite ready to accept a much more radical kind of uncertainty than institutional science is able to acknowledge – namely ignorance, and corresponding lack of control. As Stirling (1999) and colleagues have elaborated in detail elsewhere, the precautionary principle has nothing to do with anti-science, and everything to do with the rejection of reductionist, closed and arbitrarily narrow science in favour of sounder, more rigorous and more robust science.

Perhaps the most fundamental general insight to emerge is that scientific uncertainty, like scientific knowledge itself when deployed to provide authority to policy, is emphatically not just a private matter for scientific bodies to autonomously resolve, define, or otherwise interpret on behalf of the public policy domain, before it is rendered visible to the latter. As the NRC (1996) in the US and the RCEP (1998) in the UK independently concluded, prior questions need public deliberation. These include: what questions should the science be addressing, what are the salient factors and what general principles should define good science (for example, the balance between comprehensiveness and precision) for environmental policy, as distinct from other more confined domains such as engineering risks.

These questions lead on to the importance of distinguishing between facts and values. It is sometimes assumed that, having agreed to adopt a precautionary approach, this should automatically lead to one 'correct' outcome. This is an oversimplification. What is at issue itself will vary. Preferred outcomes will also vary depending on people's interests, objectives and values. As Popper pointed out long ago, it is rationally impossible to derive a proposal for a policy from facts alone (Popper, 1962). Policies that unduly emphasise the factual basis of decisions, without explicitly acknowledging and engaging with the value judgements that are also part of such decisions, are unlikely to achieve consensus, or at least acceptance, where substantial divisions of opinion exist. (RMNO, 2000)

It is for these reasons that the involvement of stakeholders in regulatory appraisal needs to begin at the beginning rather than being artificially confined to the later 'risk management' stages of the conventional approach. The stages of hazard and risk appraisal, management and communication are not sequential, as in the traditional model, but require stakeholder involvement at the earliest stage. This has been recognised by the NRC, the RCEP and the Nice Council of Ministers conclusions on the precautionary principle in 2000.

Again, it is emphasised that the raising of such issues should not be seen as creating a new form of 'paralysis by analysis'. The case studies, and the lessons that emerge, do provide a positive and robust way forward. But if these complexities are not explicitly addressed, progress will be slower and the mistakes made will be more serious.

Precaution and innovation

In the Introduction it was noted that, the German *Vorsorgeprinzip* ('foresight' or 'precautionary' principle) of the 1970s considered the stimulation of innovation, employment and forward planning to be integral components of the precautionary principle. An overarching principle arising from all the case studies, as well as from much wider analysis and experience, is that the polarised processes of technological innovation and risk regulation need to become less separate and antagonistic. Many of the lessons are as applicable to the innovation process itself as to the regulation of the resulting products and technologies. Indeed, accommodating them within the innovation process could overcome the adversarial relationship between innovation and regulation.

For example, traditional risk assessments of chemicals concentrate on the risks associated with a particular chemical. The use of the chemical is identified, but this identification of use is not then used in a more integrated way to assess the potential of alternatives. It is not the first time that the need for the integration of innovation and risk regulation, and for the integration of technology-appraisal approaches more generally is identified. It is addressed, for instance (at least in part), by the techniques of constructive technology assessment (CTA) developed in The Netherlands (Rip et al, 1996; Wynne et al, 2001). CTA starts from recognition that technologies are more than hardware. Their promotion and adoption depends upon the goals, relationships, understandings and skills of different sectors of society. The greater the scope, power, complexity or interconnectedness of the technological systems concerned, the more important a consideration of these social and institutional aspects becomes. In essence, CTA attempts to foster the recognition of this neglected but fundamental dimension of technology and innovation. By a variety of means it aims to improve integration, from the outset, of the perspectives of innovators, regulators, users and other stakeholders. In this way, innovation benefits from creative inputs at a stage when these may realistically be harnessed, rather than forcing such wider social interaction simply to take the form of an (often adverse) downstream reaction to a technology already developed through a more closed process. The analysis underlying CTA recognises how technological systems otherwise have a tendency to 'lock-in' to particular configurations at a relatively early stage in their development, thus foreclosing other options and raising the costs of shifting to alternatives. The particular technologies that gain ascendancy in this way may do so for arbitrary reasons which have nothing to do with intrinsic qualities, and everything to do with chance and first-leader advantage. CTA attempts to highlight such questions and to provide the intellectual resources for resolving them.

The potentially positive relationship between regulation and innovation is also emphasised in the technological options analysis (TOA) approach, developed in the US (Ashford, 1981 and 1994; Tickner, 2000). Here, a variety of practical procedures are routinely employed in order to include consideration of 'off the shelf' and 'on the horizon' alternatives alongside the technology or process in question. Again, like CTA, TOA can be performed by regulatory agencies or private companies, depending on the context. Together, they form part of a broader culture of 'alternatives assessment' (O'Brien, 2000), which highlights the importance of innovation and understands this as an open-ended process, subject to deliberate choices and commitments. These innovative approaches represent a more reflective and intelligent approach to the design, assessment, choice and implementation of technologies. By addressing innovation at the earliest stages, they offer a means to implement the lessons developed here in a fashion that minimises economic inefficiencies and social tensions, and actively fosters innovation pathways that are more sustainable over the longer term.

The promotion of robust, diverse and adaptable technologies not only helps to stimulate innovation but it can also provide 'insurance' against surprises, such as the case study examples of the asbestos cancer, mesothelioma, and the halocarbon damage to the ozone layer. This is because the size of any future surprises will be smaller if there are several competing technologies that are being used to meet human needs, rather than just one, global, near monopoly, as was the case with asbestos, halocarbons and PCBs. Diverse technologies and other ways of meeting needs can help deal with the seemingly intractable problem of 'societal ignorance' and attendant surprises.

Precaution and governance

'Governance' is about the manner in which something is governed by methods of management and systems of regulations, be they formal or informal. More broadly, it refers to the conduct of life or business in general and the mode of living, or behaviour, in society. The challenges which the precautionary principle heralds involve more than simply new decision rules and technical instruments, and this implies a learning process in public policy, industry, science and civil society at large. Here three aspects of governance relevant to precaution are considered, namely: how current institutions associated with the appraisal of risk might evolve to take account of precaution; the relevance of participatory approaches and subsidiarity; and the importance of greater awareness within civil society, including ethical awareness, so as to better exercise both rights and responsibilities.

Evolution, not revolution

Beyond the disciplines of CTA, there are a variety of perspectives to be found among established approaches to the regulatory appraisal of risk which could be constructively enlarged and developed. Suitably amended and interpreted, many of these offer ways to respond to the lessons discussed here. Multi-criteria mapping (MCM), for instance, combines the flexibility and scope of qualitative approaches with the transparency and specificity of quantitative disciplines. It offers one way to accommodate a diverse array of stakeholder perspectives with different technical and scientific factors, including uncertainties, without placing undue constraints on the divergent framings of the issues in question (Stirling and Mayer, 1999). Likewise, life cycle analysis (LCA) has developed an array of methods to ensure that attention extends to encompass the full technical life cycles and resource chains associated with different options (van den Berg, 1995). Cost-benefit analysis, for all its idiosyncrasies and serious limitations, is unusual in upholding the importance, emphasised in these lessons, of considering the 'pros' (justifications and benefits) alongside the 'cons' (risks and costs) (Hanley and Spash, 1993). Although rather infrequently used, sensitivity and scenario analysis techniques offer ways to explore the implications of different assumptions and perspectives and so be more 'humble' about the status of any particular understanding of a risk issue (Godet, 1992).

One broad approach that has emerged over the past decade or so, integrated environmental assessment (IEA), offers an architecture for constructing a new synthesis of these kinds of positive attributes in existing approaches to the appraisal of the pros and cons of contending alternatives (EFIEA, 2000; Dowlatabadi and Rotmans, 2000). Specifically developed to address large, complex environmental problems, IEA provides a means to integrate such methods into the kind of broad-based, multi-perspective and more humble and open-ended approach highlighted in these lessons. IEA in its present form addresses the interface between science-engineering and policy with emphasis on the need for interdisciplinarity; integration across the environmental media: water, air and soil; mass balance accounting in society and sectors; and analysis of alternatives. In view of the lessons identified in the case studies, equal emphasis on the following issues would improve the perspectives of IEA: more openness and deliberation about framing agendas; distinguishing between risk, uncertainty and ignorance; taking better account of the risk and consequences of being wrong; accounting for all values; expansion of cost-benefit analysis to the appraisal of wider pros and cons (as defined in this book); and much earlier involvement of these broader concerns in the relevant decision-making processes. Here, the use of 'what-if' scenarios and participatory scenario development techniques can assist greatly in the management of surprises and uncertainties.

Participatory approaches and subsidiarity

The historic trend of legal and economic regulation has been to centralise at global, regional or national government level, and to disenfranchise many interest groups. While there are signs of change, attempts to create participatory approaches are as vulnerable as any other initiative to centralising pressures. For example, the consensus conference, without safeguards, can potentially degenerate into little more than a form of consultation driven by the sponsor's agenda. Appeals procedures may also involve participatory approaches, but at far too late a stage in the process of regulation to deal with anything other than marginal issues. It follows from the 'late lessons' that participation of interest groups should be at an early stage, broadly drawn, and carried down to the appropriate local level.

Of course, local involvement is only meaningful in the context of democratically legitimate strategic frameworks of innovation and overall policy. The basic point is that often experts involved in technological developments – and officials in government – need better sensitivity to (often under-articulated) public values, priorities and concerns, at a variety of levels, from local to international. This can be achieved without the need for what would be paralysing indiscriminate full public participation in every single decision. In addition to

European examples already mentioned, there are also developments outside the EU worthy of evaluation. These include the environmental laws of New Zealand, where the principle of subsidiarity has been introduced as an alternative approach to centralised regulation (Ministry for the Environment, 2001), and where the stated aim is for procedures for local participation and consensus-building to take prominence over central regulation. Both the development and implementation of Australia's ocean policy include significant attempts to involve stakeholders (National Oceans Office, 2000). Among many other findings, the research underlying the ocean policy made the relevant point that the views of local interest groups are not necessarily identical to their national or international equivalents, be these, for example, environmental non-governmental organisations or industry.

The tools for participatory approaches are in various stages of development, and the challenges are far from trivial (Brookes, 2001). But this has to be set against traditional approaches, where the costs of failure can also be high, as illustrated by the public rejection of irradiated foods, the abandoned attempt to dump the North Sea Brent Spar oil installation and the response to GMOs.

Awareness and ethics

Participatory approaches cannot work without heightened awareness, interest and engagement on the part of stakeholders and the public at large. Broadening the scope of environmental assessment will have a lower chance of success without a development of society's attitudes, responsibilities and ethics in relation to the environment. Parallel efforts are needed to increase society's awareness, foster discriminating involvement, and increase the educational basis for consensus building, by increased knowledge of all aspects of the environment over the whole range of the disciplinary spectrum. This process starts at home and school and reaches its full potential by engagement in participatory procedures as a matter of interest and commitment. In stating this indoctrination to any one point of view is not implied, but rather the development of skills to critically assess arguments, express a point of view and engage in the democratic process.

A related area is the professional communication of the issues surrounding precaution. It is evident that at least some communication of the complexities involved is necessary to move forward, for the sake all interest groups. It is therefore ironic that the media and other professional communicators have been moving in the opposite direction, emphasising only 'positive knowledge' and the 'clear and simple message' in a sound-bite culture. This tends to exclude the communication of ignorance, of complexity and of responsibility in face of the essential limits of all knowledge.

There is also an ethical and cultural issue raised by the important need for institutional recognition of ignorance as well as uncertainty. This arises because of the way in which the ethical boundaries of acknowledged responsibility for uncertainties about the consequences of human innovative commitments have been drawn by scientific knowledge. Any possible future consequence which lies beyond existing scientific knowledge and predictability is deemed by definition to be beyond responsibility. This is defined as such even though it is known that such surprises will occur as a result of choices and commitments. The precautionary principle implies the need, as a matter of cultural change, for society's institutions to enlarge existing notions of ethical responsibility to encompass these unknowns, which are predictable in principle even though not in specifics. Suggestions have been made as to how this process of intellectual enlargement might begin, starting with the 12 late lessons.

This report expresses the honest conviction that to achieve sustainable environmental policies and a properly balanced practice of the precautionary principle requires the achievement of a cultural shift towards a greater civil sense of responsibility and involvement in policy-making (including science policy and technological innovation). This in turn will demand that the expert-led institutions of science, industry and policy learn to trust, to challenge and to build the opportunities and the frameworks for civil society to take on those responsibilities.

From the case studies, the 12 late lessons and these wider considerations of science, innovation and governance, it is evident that the precautionary principle – the need to exercise foresight – once accepted, leads far beyond the simple definition. Rather it is playing its part in the development of civil society and policy-making during the early 21st century which, it appears, will have its own distinctive character, as great in its differences as those which set apart previous centuries.

17

Conclusions

The case studies reviewed in this book show that there is much that can be learnt from history. Such learning begins with two basic observations:

1 Regulatory appraisal and control of technologies and economic development involves balancing the costs of being too restrictive on innovation with the hazards and costs of being too permissive, in situations of scientific uncertainty and ignorance. The case studies provide many examples where regulatory inaction led to costly consequences that were not – and sometimes could not have been – foreseen.

2 The case studies also provide many examples where 'early warnings', and even 'loud and late' warnings, were clearly ignored; where the scope of hazard appraisal was too narrow; and where regulatory actions were taken without sufficient consideration of alternatives, or of the conditions necessary for their successful implementation in the real world.

If more account, scientifically, politically and economically, is taken of a richer body of information from more diverse sources, then society may do substantially better in the future at achieving a better balance between innovations and their hazards. Discussion of the case studies led to the distillation of 12 late lessons which, if applied to future decision-making, could help achieve this better balance.

The precautionary principle is an overarching framework of thinking that governs the use of foresight in situations characterised by uncertainty and ignorance and where there are potentially large costs to both regulatory action and inaction.

However, the intrinsic difficulties of applying the precautionary principle to issues of complexity, uncertainty and controversy are compounded by a lack of agreement on the definition and meanings of key terms.

The table below is a contribution to clarifying the meaning of six basic concepts that lie at the heart of this debate. What is sometimes loosely referred to as 'uncertainty' mixes up the analytically distinct concepts of 'risk', 'uncertainty' and 'ignorance'. The public action concepts of 'prevention', 'precautionary prevention', and 'precaution' can then be usefully related to these three states of knowledge, as in Table 17.1.

The procedures for dealing with the situations of risk, uncertainty and ignorance need to be fair, transparent and accountable, key elements of the

Table 17.1 *Uncertainty and precaution: towards a clarification of terms*

Situation	State and dates of knowledge	Examples of action
Risk	'Known' impacts; 'known' probabilities eg asbestos causing respiratory disease, lung and mesothelioma cancer, 1965–present	**Prevention**: action taken to reduce known risks eg eliminate exposure to asbestos dust
Uncertainty	'Known' impacts; 'unknown' probabilities eg antibiotics in animal feed and associated human resistance to those antibiotics, 1969–present	**Precautionary prevention**: action taken to reduce potential hazards eg reduce/eliminate human exposure to antibiotics in animal feed
Ignorance	'Unknown' impacts and therefore 'unknown' probabilities eg the 'surprises' of CFCs and ozone layer damage prior to 1974; asbestos mesothelioma cancer prior to 1959	**Precaution**: action taken to anticipate, identify and reduce the impact of 'surprises' eg use of properties of chemicals such as persistence or bioaccumulation as 'predictors' of potential harm; use of the broadest possible sources of information, including long term monitoring; promotion of robust, diverse and adaptable technologies and social arrangements to meet needs, with fewer technological 'monopolies' such as asbestos and CFCs

Source: EEA

'good governance' which is needed to regain public confidence in policy-making on technologies, their benefits and potential hazards.

Most of the cases in this book involved costly impacts on both public health and the environment, two fields of science and policy-making that have become specialised and somewhat polarised during the last 100 years. Individuals experience their health and their environment as one, interconnected reality: science, regulatory appraisal and policy-making need to be similarly integrated. *The Precautionary Principle in the 20th Century* should make some contribution to this integration of health and environment.

The scope of regulatory appraisal needs to be broadened to include adequate consideration of relevant social issues alongside the physical, chemical, biological and medical aspects of technologies.

Involving a wide range of stakeholders, and taking account of their values and interests at the earliest stage of the appraisal and choice of technological and social options for meeting human needs, brings two key benefits. It not only augments the information available to policy-making, but may also improve public trust in society's capacity to control hazards, without necessarily stifling innovation or compromising science.

Recent controversies over emerging technologies such as genetically modified organisms and oil-rig disposal have much to do with public values and scientific uncertainties, in contrast to the previously low emphasis on values and to the demand for unequivocal scientific proof before action to reduce hazards. An open recognition of this changing context for such controversies is a first step towards their improved governance.

However, the inclusion of different socio-political perspectives in regulatory appraisal becomes not just a matter of better policy-making: it can make for better science as well.

For example, reductionist science and linear causality are useful approaches, but they are limited. They do not cope well with the dynamics of complex and sometimes chaotic systems, characterised by feed-back loops, synergisms, thresholds, and equilibria/instability issues, and linked by multi-factoral and interdependent causal chains. Such complex reality demands better science, characterised by more humility and less hubris, with a focus on 'what we don't know' as well as on 'what we do know'.

One important consequence of acknowledging both scientific uncertainties (including ignorance) and the urgency of hazard reduction in situations of high stakes is the need for agreement on the sufficiency of evidence of harmful effects that is required to justify action. Such 'levels of proof' can vary from the 'reasonable grounds for concern' of the European Commission's *Communication on the Precautionary Principle*, to the 'beyond reasonable doubt' of criminal law. Choosing which level to use in particular situations involves a decision that can radically shift the size, nature and distribution of the costs of being wrong. This is a key political decision with profound ethical implications. The level of proof that is appropriate for particular issues depends upon the size and nature of the potential harm, the claimed benefits, the available alternatives, and the potential costs of being wrong in both directions, ie of acting or not acting in the context of uncertainty, ignorance and high stakes. This type of public decision-making is not unknown: military intelligence has long adopted similarly precautionary approaches to uncertainty and high stakes, where the costs of being wrong can be catastrophic.

Late lessons from early warnings

The case studies in this book both support and illustrate the need for the 12 late lessons derived from the century of history reviewed:

1 Acknowledge and respond to ignorance, as well as uncertainty and risk, in technology appraisal and public policy-making.
2 Provide adequate long-term environmental and health monitoring and research into early warnings.
3 Identify and work to reduce 'blind spots' and gaps in scientific knowledge.
4 Identify and reduce interdisciplinary obstacles to learning.
5 Ensure that real world conditions are adequately accounted for in regulatory appraisal.

6   Systematically scrutinise the claimed justifications and benefits alongside the potential risks.

7   Evaluate a range of alternative options for meeting needs alongside the option under appraisal, and promote more robust, diverse and adaptable technologies so as to minimise the costs of surprises and maximise the benefits of innovation.

8   Ensure use of 'lay' and local knowledge, as well as relevant specialist expertise in the appraisal.

9   Take full account of the assumptions and values of different social groups.

10 Maintain regulatory independence from interested parties while retaining an inclusive approach to information and opinion gathering.

11 Identify and reduce institutional obstacles to learning and action.

12 Avoid 'paralysis by analysis' by acting to reduce potential harm when there are reasonable grounds for concern.

Most of these lessons involve improvements in the quality, availability, utilisation and processing of information in public policy-making on environment and health. However, none of the lessons would themselves remove the dilemmas of decision-making under situations of uncertainty and high stakes. They cannot eradicate uncertainties or avoid the consequences of ignorance. However, they would at least increase the chances of anticipating costly impacts, of achieving a better balance between the pros and cons of technological innovations, and of minimising the costs of unpleasant surprises. The use of the precautionary principle can also bring benefits beyond the reduction of health and environmental impacts, stimulating both more innovation, via technological diversity and flexibility, and better science.

The 'late lessons' may also help to achieve a better balance between proportionate and precautionary public policies, recognising that over-precaution can also be expensive, in terms of lost opportunities for innovation and lost lines of scientific inquiry.

It is the central conclusion of this report that the very difficult task of maximising innovation whilst minimising hazards to people and their environments, which is ultimately a matter of political discourse, could be more successful if it embraced the 12 late lessons from the histories of hazards reviewed.

About the authors[11]

Jim Bridges has been Professor of Toxicology and Environmental Health at the University of Surrey since 1979. He is a member of the EU Scientific Steering Committee (since 1997) and Chairman of the UK Veterinary Residues Committee (since 2001). He was previously a member of the EU Scientific Committee on Animal Nutrition (1991–97) and the UK Veterinary Products Committee (1982–97). He acted as a scientific adviser to the EU (World Trade Organization hearing in Geneva) on the legitimacy of the EU ban on the use of hormones as growth promoters. He is author/joint author of more than 300 research papers and reviews.

Professor Jim W Bridges, Dean for International Strategy, Vice Chancellor's Offices, University of Surrey, Guildford GU2 5XH, United Kingdom
Tel: +44 (0)1483 873 802
Email: j.bridges@surrey.ac.uk

Olga Bridges is a lecturer in Environmental and Public Health at the University of Surrey. Her research interests are the impact of chemicals in the environment and the diet, public perception of environmental risks and application of HACCP (hazard analysis critical control point). She has participated in a number of public enquiries, and has recently been involved in the training programmes of environmental health officers abroad.

Dr Olga Bridges, European Institute of Health and Medical Sciences, University of Surrey, Guildford GU2 5XH, United Kingdom
Tel: +44 (0)1483 873 802
Email: o.bridges@surrey.ac.uk

Lars-Erik Edqvist DVM, PhD is Director General of the National Veterinary Institute (SVA), Uppsala, Sweden. The antibiotics department at SVA has been involved in research for many years and has advocated prudent use of antimicrobials in veterinary medicine. In 1995 the Swedish government appointed Professor Edqvist chairman of the Commission on Antimicrobial Feed Additives. The commission gathered and evaluated scientific information on the use of antimicrobials as feed additives in relation to the temporary derogation from Community legislation that Sweden had when it became a member of the EU. The commission completed its task in 1997.

---

11 The views expressed in the chapters are those of the authors and do not necessarily reflect those of the institutions where they work.

Professor Lars-Erik Edqvist, Swedish National Veterinary Institute, Ulls vag 2A-C, Box 7073, 750 07 Uppsala, Sweden
Tel: +46 (0)18 67 40 00
Email: lars-erik.edqvist@sva.se

Joe Farman, CBE and Polar Medal, is currently a consultant to the European Ozone Research Coordinating Unit in Cambridge, and is a member of the Science Panel on Stratospheric Ozone Research of the European Commission. From 1956 to 1990 he worked for the British Antarctic Survey. He is on the UNEP Global 500 Roll of Honour, and has received the UNEP Global Ozone Award, the Environment Medal of the Society of Chemical Industry and the Charles Chree Medal of the Institute of Physics. He is an Honorary Fellow of Corpus Christi College, Cambridge.

Dr J C Farman, European Ozone Research, Coordinating Unit, Cambridge, United Kingdom
Email: general@ozone-sec.ch.cam.ac.uk

David Gee graduated in economics and politics but has been working at the interface of science, economics, production and policy-making, within occupational and environmental health, since 1974, for trade unions and non-governmental organisations (he is a former Director of Friends of the Earth, England, Wales and Northern Ireland). Since 1995 he has worked with the EEA on emerging issues and scientific liaison.

David Gee, Information Needs Analysis and Scientific Liaison, European Environment Agency, Kongens Nytorv 6, 1050 Copenhagen K, Denmark
Tel: +45 33 36 71 42
Email: david.gee@eea.eu.int

Michael Gilbertson has worked with the Canadian federal government since 1969, when he initiated research on the outbreaks of reproductive and developmental disorders in fish-eating birds in the lower Great Lakes. He has been at the interface between forensic environmental science and regulatory action since 1975. His interest is in the social processes involved in moving from use of inappropriate technologies that require causal demonstrations of injury for their control to appropriate technologies based on sound ecological principles.

Dr Michael Gilbertson, International Joint Commission, 100 Ouellette Avenue, 8th Floor, Windsor, Ontario N9A 6T3, Canada
Tel: +1 519 257 6706
Email: gilbertsonm@windsor.ijc.org

Morris Greenberg is a former Medical Inspector of Factories, Health and Safety Executive, UK, and a former member of the Environmental Toxicology Unit, UK Department of Health. He helped in setting up the first asbestos mesothelioma register in the UK and is an expert in the medical aspects of inhaled fibres.

Dr Morris Greenberg, 74 End Road, London NW11 7SY, United Kingdom.
Tel: +44 (0)20 8458 2376
Email: gillmorris.greenberg@talk21.com

Poul Harremoës has been a full Professor at the Technical University of Denmark in Environmental Science and Engineering since 1972. He has carried out research in urban water issues, water pollution and purification, and environmental management. He is a member of the Scientific Committee of the EEA and former president of the International Water Association. He has the following international awards: the Stockholm Water Prize (1992) and the Heineken prize for environmental science (2000). He has published five textbooks and some 350 further publications (see www.er.dtu.dk).

Professor Poul Harremoës, Department of Environment and Resources,
Technical University of Denmark
Email: ph@er.dtu.dk

Dolores Ibarreta is a biologist with a PhD in genetics from the Universidad Complutense, Madrid, Spain. She has worked as a researcher at the Centro de Investigaciones Biologicas (CIB-CSIC) in Madrid and Georgetown University Medical Center in the US. She is currently a scientific officer at IPTS (Joint Research Centre, European Commission), where her main focus has been the risk assessment of endocrine disrupters (DES being one the main references), specifically hormonally active substances in the diet.

Dr Dolores Ibarreta, IPTS Institute for Prospective Technological Studies (Joint Research Centre), European Commission, Edificio Expo-WTC, C/ Inca Garcilaso, s/n, E-41092 Seville, Spain
Tel: +34 (9)5 448 84 45
Email: dolores.ibarreta@jrc.es

Peter Infante DDS, DrPH has, for the past 25 years, evaluated and regulated toxic substances found in US workplaces for the Department of Labor. He is the author of more than 100 scientific publications. He has a doctorate in public health from the Department of Epidemiology, University of Michigan and is a Fellow of the American College of Epidemiology. He has served on numerous panels and advisory committees related to the US National Cancer Institute, the President's Cancer Panel, the Office of Technology Assessment of the US Congress and the National Academy of Sciences, and most recently as an expert consultant to the World Trade Organization in its deliberations on the banning of products containing asbestos in the EU countries.

Dr Peter F Infante, Health Standards Programs, Occupational Safety and Health Administration, US Department of Labor, Washington, DC, United States
Email: peter.infante@osha.gov

Paul Johnston is an aquatic toxicologist who established the Greenpeace Research Laboratories in 1987 and continues as its principal scientist. He has more than 15 years research experience in the field of marine pollution.

Dr Paul Johnston, Greenpeace Research Laboratories Department of Biological Sciences, University of Exeter, Exeter EX4 4PS, United Kingdom
Email: p.johnston@exeter.ac.uk

Jane Keys is a freelance researcher. Since the late 1980s she has researched environmental issues for industry, environmental non-governmental organisations and the EEA. Recent work includes, on behalf of the UK Forestry Commission and others, the identification of feasible and sustainable economic activities to fund and support the UK's semi-natural ancient woodlands and urban street trees.

Jane Keys, 22 Brook End, Potton, Bedfordshire, SG19 2QS, United Kingdom
Tel: +44 (0)1767 261 834
Email: jane.keys@btinternet.com

Janna Koppe studied medicine at the University of Amsterdam and went on to specialise in paediatrics and neonatology at the university. She became an assistant professor in neonatology in 1969 and a full professor in 1986, becoming head of the neonatology department in 1977, and retiring in 1998. Her contribution to this book was written as part of her role as Emeritus Professor of Neonatology, University of Amsterdam and Chair of the Ecobaby society. Studies on the effects of dioxins and PCBs on the unborn and newborn human baby were started in 1985 and are still ongoing.

Professor Janna G Koppe, Emeritus Professor of Neonatology, University of Amsterdam, Hollandstraat 6, 3634 AT Loenersloot, The Netherlands
Tel: +31 294 291 589
Email: janna.koppe@inter.nl.net

Barrie Lambert is an independent radiation biologist. He has researched and taught the subject for more than 30 years, with particular reference to the comparative long-term risk of radiation exposure. He is a consultant to environmental groups, the nuclear industry and government.

Dr Barrie Lambert, St Bartholomew's and the Royal London School of Medicine, Charterhouse Square, London EC1M 6BQ, United Kingdom
Tel: +44 (0)1273 471 973
Email: barrie.lambert@which.net

Bill Langston is a research scientist at the Plymouth Marine Laboratory and has been engaged in studies of tributyltin behaviour and impact in the marine environment since the early 1980s.

Dr William J Langston, Plymouth Marine Laboratory Citadel Hill, Plymouth PL1 2PB, United Kingdom

Malcolm MacGarvin has a PhD in ecology. Since the mid-1980s he has worked as a consultant on environmental issues for industry, environmental non-governmental organisations, the European Commission and the EEA. In addition to the precautionary principle, recent work includes that on marine eutrophication and on marine fisheries.

Dr Malcolm MacGarvin, modus vivendi, Ballantruan, Glenlivet,
Ballindalloch AB37 9AQ, Scotland
Tel: +44 (0)1807 590 396
Email: macgarvin@modus-vivendi.co.uk

Erik Millstone trained initially in physics and philosophy. Since 1974 he has been researching the causes, consequences and regulation of technological change in the food industry. Since 1998 he has been investigating the links between the science and politics of bovine spongiform encephalopathy for projects funded by the European Commission.

Dr Erik Millstone, SPRU – Science and Technology Policy Research, University of Sussex,
Brighton BN1 9RF, United Kingdom
Tel: +44 (0)1273 877 380
Email: e.p.millstone@sussex.ac.uk

Knud Børge Pedersen DVM, PhD, DVSc has been Director of the Danish Veterinary Laboratory (DVL) since 1985, and of the Danish Veterinary Institute for Virus Research since October 2000. His doctoral thesis was on infectious keratoconjunctivitis in cattle, and he is author/joint author of a number of scientific articles on microbiology and infection pathology. During recent years, DVL has established research groups on antimicrobial resistance mechanisms and epidemiology, particularly concerning antimicrobial growth promoters. Dr Pedersen has initiated the formulation of a veterinary antibiotic policy and guidelines for prudent use of antimicrobials in veterinary medicine.

Dr Knud Børge Pedersen, Danish Veterinary Laboratory, 27 Bülowsvej, DK-1790
Copenhagen V, Denmark
Tel: +45 35 30 01 23
Email: kbp@svs.dk

David Santillo is a marine and freshwater biologist and a senior scientist with the Greenpeace Research Laboratories. He represents Greenpeace International at various international conventions addressing marine environmental protection.

Dr David Santillo, Greenpeace Research Laboratories Department of Biological Sciences,
University of Exeter, Exeter EX4 4PS, United Kingdom
Email: d.santillo@exeter.ac.uk

Arne Semb graduated in chemistry from the University of Oslo and has worked on a number of different air pollution problems at NILU since 1971. His major involvements include the OECD long-range transport of air pollutants programme 1972–77, the Norwegian SNSF project on acid precipitation and its effects on forests and fish 1972–80, and the EMEP programme for monitoring and evaluation of long-range transmission of airborne pollutants in Europe from 1977 to the present.

Dr Arne Semb, Norwegian Institute for Air Research (NILU), PO Box 100, N-2027 Kjeller, Norway
Tel: +47 63 89 80 00
Email: arne.semb@nilu.no

Andrew Stirling is a Senior Lecturer at SPRU. He has researched and published widely on issues relating to technology assessment, environmental appraisal and risk analysis. He has worked with a variety of academic, public interest, industry and government organisations and served on a number of Advisory Committees.

Dr Andrew Stirling, SPRU – Science and Technology Policy Research, University of Sussex, Brighton BN1 9RF, United Kingdom
Tel: +44 (0)1273 877 118
Email: a.c.stirling@sussex.ac.uk

Shanna Swan PhD is an epidemiologist and statistician who studies the reproductive risks of DES, other hormones and environmental exposures. She is currently Research Professor at the University of Missouri, Columbia and directed the Reproductive Epidemiology Section of the California Department of Health Services 1981–98. Her approach to public health, particularly in relation to risks to the unborn foetus, has always been precautionary.

Professor Shanna H Swan, Research Professor, University of Missouri, Columbia, Department of Family and Community Medicine, Medical Sciences Building MA306L, Columbia MO 65212, United States
Tel: +1 573 884 4534
Email: swans@health.missouri.edu

Paddy van Zwanenberg trained initially in environmental science before taking postgraduate degrees in science and technology policy. His research focuses on issues of science and governance, with a particular emphasis on the role of scientific expertise in public and environmental health policy-making. He has worked on two European Commission funded projects on the science and politics of bovine spongiform encephalopathy.

Dr Patrick van Zwanenberg, SPRU – Science and Technology Policy Research, University of Sussex, Brighton BN1 9RF, United Kingdom
Tel: +44 (0)1273 877 141
Email: p.f.van-zwanenberg@sussex.ac.uk

Sofia Guedes Vaz is an environmental engineer who has worked at the EEA since 1997, specialising in data, reporting, targets and environmental emerging issues. She has an MSc in Environmental Technology from the Imperial College and before working at EEA did environmental consultancy.

Sofia Guedes Vaz, Integrated Assessment and Reporting, European Environment Agency, Kongens Nytorv 6, 1050 Copenhagen K, Denmark
Tel: +45 33 36 72 02
Email: sofia.vaz@eea.eu.int

Martin Krayer von Krauss has a BEng from the Royal Military College of Canada and has worked as project engineer on petrol-contaminated site investigations. He has an MSc in environmental engineering from the Technical University of Denmark. His PhD study is on 'Incertitude and its implications for environmental engineering'.

Martin Krayer von Krauss, PhD student, Department of Environment and Resources, Technical University of Denmark
Email: mkvk9@yahoo.com

Brian Wynne is Professor of Science Studies at the Institute for Environment, Philosophy and Public Policy. He was a member of the EEA's management board and Scientific Committee from 1995 to 2000. He has completed extensive research and publications on risk, environmental and science studies issues and on public understanding of science and risk.

Professor Brian Wynne, Centre for the Study of Environmental Change, Institute for Environment, Philosophy and Public Policy, Furness College, Lancaster University, Lancaster LA1 4YG, United Kingdom
Tel: +44 (0)1524 592 653
Email: b.wynne@lancaster.ac.uk

References

Preface

EEA (European Environment Agency), forthcoming 2002. 'An EEA response to late lessons from early warnings: Some implications for policymakers and the public', European Environment Agency, Copenhagen

Chapter 1 Introduction

Beck, U, 1992. *Risk Society*, Sage, London

Boehmer-Christiansen, S, 1994. 'The precautionary principle in Germany: Enabling government', in T O'Riordan and J Cameron (eds), *Interpreting the precautionary principle*, p3, Cameron May, London

Brody, H et al, 2000. 'Map-making and myth-making in Broad Street: the London cholera epidemic, 1854', *Lancet* Vol 356, pp64–8

Deane, L, 1898. 'Report on the health of workers in asbestos and other dusty trades', in HM Chief Inspector of Factories and Workshops, 1899, *Annual Report for 1898*, pp171–2, HMSO, London (see also the Annual Reports for 1899 and 1900, p502)

European Commission, 2000. Communication from the Commission on the Precautionary Principle, COM (2000) 1, Brussels

Gee, D, 1997. 'Approaches to scientific uncertainty', in T Fletcher and A J M Michael (eds), *Health at the crossroads: Transport policy and urban health*, Wiley, London

Hill, A B, 1965. 'The environment and disease: Association or causation?' *Proceedings of the Royal Society of Medicine* Vol 58, pp295–300

James, W H, 1965. 'Teratogenetic properties of thalidomide', *Br Med J* October 30; 5469, p1064

Lieberman, A J and Kwon, S C, 1998. *Facts versus fears: A review of the greatest unfounded health scares of recent times*, 3rd ed, revised June, American Council on Science and Health, New York, at www.acsh.org

Marine Pollution Bulletin, 1997. Vol 34, No 9, pp680–1

Millstone, E, 1997. *Lead and public health*, Earthscan, London

Peto, J, 1999. 'The European mesothelioma epidemic', *B J Cancer* Vol 79, February, pp666–72

Raffensperger, C and Tickner, J, 1999. *Protecting public health and the environment: Implementing the precautionary principle*, Island Press, Washington, DC

Small, I, van der Meer, J and Upshur, R E G, 2001. 'Acting on an environmental health disaster: the case of the Aral Sea', *Environmental Health Perspectives* Vol 109, No 6, June 2001

Smith, J (ed), 2000. *The Daily Globe: Environmental change, the public and the media*, Earthscan, London

Snow, J, 1849. *On the mode of communication of cholera*, London

Chapter 2 Fisheries

ACFM ICES, 1999. *Report of the working group on the assessment of dermersal stocks in the North Sea Part 1*, ICES CM 2000/ACFM:7, Advisory Committee on Fishery Management, International Council for the Exploration of the Sea, Copenhagen

ACME ICES, 2000. *Report of the working group on ecosystem effects of fishing activities*, ICES CM 2000/ACME:2 Ref.:ACFM+E, Advisory Committee on the Marine Environment, International Council for the Exploration of the Sea, Copenhagen

ACFM ICES, 2000a. *Cod in sub-area IV (North Sea), division VIId (Eastern Channel) and division IIIa (Skagerrak)*, Advisory Committee on Fishery Management, International Council for the Exploration of the Sea, Copenhagen, at www.ices.dk/committe/acfm/comwork/report/2000/Oct/cod-347d.pdf (accessed 15 April 2001)

ACFM ICES, 2000b. *Report of the CWP intersessional meeting: Working group on precautionary approach terminology and CWP sub-group on the publication of integrated catch statistics for the Atlantic*, Advisory Committee on Fishery Management, International Council for the Exploration of the Sea, Copenhagen, p55, at www.ices.dk (accessed 25 April 2000)

Atlantic Fisheries Policy Review, 2000. *The management of fisheries on Canada's Atlantic coast: A discussion document on policy direction and principles*, Atlantic Fisheries Policy Review, Ottawa, at www.dfo-mpo.gc.ca/afpr-rppa/linksto_discodoc_e.htm (accessed 19 March 2001)

Bertram, J G, 1865. *The harvest of the sea*, John Murray, London

Daan, N, 1998. 'Structure and dynamics of the North Sea ecosystem' in *Workshop on the ecosystem approach to the management and protection of the North Sea, Oslo, Norway, 15–17 June*, TemaNord 1998, 579, pp56–9, Nordic Council of Ministers, Copenhagen

Day, D, 1995. 'Tending the Achilles heel of NAFO: Canada acts to protect the nose and tail of the Grand Banks', *Marine Policy* Vol 19, pp257–70

DFO, 2000. *Northern (2J3KL) cod*, DFO Science Stock Status Report A2–10, Department of Fisheries and Oceans, Ontario, at www.dfo-mpo.gc.ca/csas/csas/status/2001/a3-01e.pdf (accessed 24 March 2001)

Earl, M, 1994. *A precautionary approach to the management of fisheries in the North Atlantic*, Greenpeace International, Amsterdam

Ecosystems Principles Advisory Panel, 1998. *Ecosystems-based fisheries management: A report to Congress by the Ecosystems Principles Advisory Panel*, Ecosystems Principles Advisory Panel, Seattle

European Commission, 1995. 'Second report of the Scientific, Technical and Economic Committee for Fisheries', EC's Staff Working Paper SEC(95)2160, European Commission, Brussels

European Commission, 2000. Communication from the Commission to the Council and European Parliament: Application of the precautionary principle and multiannual arrangements for setting TACs, 01.12.2000, COM(2000) 803 final, European Commission, Brussels

European Commission, 2001a. Green Paper on the future of the Common Fisheries Policy Volume 1, 20.3.2001, COM(2001) 135, European Commission, Brussels

European Commission, 2001b. Green Paper on the future of the Common Fisheries Policy Volume 2: Report on the economic and social situation of coastal communities, COM(2001) 135, European Commission, Brussels

FAO, 1995. *Code of conduct for responsible fisheries*, Food and Agriculture Organization of the United Nations, at www.fao.org/fi/agreem/codecond/ficonde.asp#7 (accessed 25 April 2000)

Finlayson, A C, 1994. *Fishing for truth: A sociological analysis of northern cod stock assessments from 1977 to 1990*, Social and Economic Studies Vol 52, Institute of Social and Economic Research, Memorial University of Newfoundland, St Johns

Fowler, C W, 1999. 'Management of multi-species fisheries: From overfishing to sustainability', ICES Journal of Marine Science Vol 56, pp927–32

Garcia, S M, 2000. 'The precautionary approach to fisheries 1995–2000: Progress review and main issues', *Report of the CWP intersessional meeting: working group on precautionary approach terminology and CWP sub-group on the publication of integrated catch statistics for the Atlantic*, Advisory Committee on Fishery Management, International Council for the Exploration of the Sea, Copenhagen, p22, at O:\ACFM\WGREPS\Cwp\Reports\2000\CWP 2000.Doc

Gomes, M do C, 1993. *Predictions under uncertainty: Fish assemblages and food webs on the Grand Banks of Newfoundland*, ISER, Memorial University, St Johns

Guénette, S, Pitcher, T J and Walters, C J, 2000. 'The potential of marine reserves for the management of northern cod in Newfoundland', *Bulletin of Marine Science* Vol 66, pp831–52

Harris, L, 1990. *Independent review of the state of the northern cod stock*, Communications Directorate, Department of Fisheries and Oceans, Ontario

Hjort, J, 1914. 'Fluctuations in the great fisheries of northern Europe', *Rapports et Procès-verbaux des Réunions, Conseil international pour l'exploration da la Mer* Vol 20, pp1–228

Huxley, T H, 1881. 'The herring', *Nature* Vol 23, pp607–13, cited in Sinclair, M, 1988, *Marine populations: An essay on population regulation and speciation*, Books in Recruitment Fishery Oceanography, Washington Sea Grant Program, University of Washington Press, Seattle

Huxley, T H, 1883. 'Inaugural address', *The Fisheries Exhibition Literature, International Fisheries Exhibition, London* Vol 4, pp1–22, cited in Ecosystems Principles Advisory Panel, 1998, *Ecosystems-based fisheries management: A report to Congress by the Ecosystems Principles Advisory Panel*, Ecosystems Principles Advisory Panel, Seattle

Keats, D, Steele, D H and Green, J M, 1986. *A review of the recent status of the northern cod stock (NAFO divisions 2J, 3K, and 3L) and the declining inshore fishery*, Report to the Newfoundland Inshore Fisheries Association, cited in Finlayson, A C, 1994, *Fishing for truth: A sociological analysis of northern cod stock assessments from 1977 to 1990*, Social and Economic Studies Vol 52, Institute of Social and Economic Research, Memorial University of Newfoundland, St Johns

Kent Smedbol, R and Wroblewski, J S, 2000. *Metapopulation theory and northern cod population structure: Interdependency of subpopulations in recovery of a groundfish population*, Canadian Stock Assessment Secretariat Document 2000/087, at www.dfo-mpo.gc.ca/csas/csas/English/Research_Years/2000/2000_087e.htm (accessed 24 March 2001)

McEvoy, A, 1986. *The fisherman's problem: Ecology and law in the Californian fisheries 1850–1980*, Cambridge University Press, Cambridge

MacGarvin, M, 2001a. *A comparison of the fate of Canadian and UK whitefish fisheries*, modus vivendi/WWF-UK, Glenlivet/Godalming, UK

MacGarvin, M, 2001b. 'Precaution, science, facts and values' in T O'Riordan et al (eds), *Reinterpreting the precautionary principle*, Cameron May, London

MacGarvin, M and Jones, S, 2000. *Choose or lose: A recovery plan for fish stocks and the UK fishing industry*, WWF-UK, Godalming, at www.wwf-uk.org/orca/info.htm (accessed 15 March 2001)

March, E J, 1953. *Sailing trawlers: The story of deep-sea fishing with long-line and trawl*, Percival Marshall & Co, London

Murawski, S A, Brown, R, Lai, H-L, Rago, P J and Hendrickson, L, 2000. 'Large-scale closed areas as a fisheries-management tool in temperate marine systems: The Georges Bank experience', *Bulletin of Marine Science* Vol 66, pp775–98

Murphy, O and O'Boyle, R, 2000. *Proceedings of the ecosystem approaches to fisheries management workshop, 31 August–2 September 1999*, Canadian Stock Assessment Proceedings Series No 99/38, Fisheries and Oceans Canada, Maritimes Region, Dartmouth

Nordic Council of Ministers, 1998. *Workshop on the ecosystem approach to the management and protection of the North Sea, Oslo, Norway 15–17 June*, TemaNord 1998:579, Nordic Council of Ministers, Copenhagen

Norwegian Ministry of the Environment, 1997. *Statement of conclusions from the intermediate ministerial meeting on the integration of fisheries and environmental issues: Intermediate ministerial meeting on the integration of fisheries and environmental issues, Bergen, 13–14 March 1997*, Norwegian Ministry of the Environment, Oslo, at www.odin.dep.no/nsc/meeting1997/conclusions.shtml (accessed 2 May 2000)

O'Reilly Hinds, L, 1995. 'Crisis in Canada's Atlantic sea fisheries', *Marine Policy* Vol 19, pp271–83

Pauly, D, Christensen, V, Dalsgaard, J, Froese, R and Torres Jr, F, 1998. 'Fishing down marine food webs', *Science* Vol 279, pp860–3

Peters, R H, 1991. *A critique for ecology*, Cambridge University Press, Cambridge

Report, 1866. *Report of the commissioners appointed to inquire into the sea fisheries of the United Kingdom*, presented to both Houses of Parliament, London

Report, 1885. *Report of the commissioners appointed to inquire and report upon the complaints that have been made by line and drift net fishermen of injuries sustained by them in their calling owing to the use of the trawl net and beam trawl in the territorial waters of the United Kingdom*, presented to both Houses of Parliament, London

Restrepo, V R et al, 1998. *Technical guidance on the use of the precautionary approaches to implementing National Standard 1 of the Magnuson-Stevens Fisheries Conservation and Management Act*, NOAA Technical Memorandum NMFS-F/SPO, 17 July

Richards, L J and Schnute, J T, 2000. 'Science strategic project on the precautionary approach in Canada' in R Haigh and C Sinclair (eds), *Proceedings of the second workshop*, pp59–60, Canadian Stock Assessment Proceedings No 99/41, Fisheries and Oceans Canada

San Diego Natural History Museum, 2000. *Ocean Oasis Field Guide, Sardinops sagax caerulea, California pilchard, Pacific sardine, Sardina Monterrey*, at www.oceanoasis.org/fieldguide/sard-cae.html (accessed 5 May 2001)

Scottish Office, 1898 to present. *Annual Report of the Fisheries Board for Scotland for 1898*, Scottish Office, Edinburgh, et seq

Sutherland, I, n.d. *From herring to seine net fishing on the east coast of Scotland*, Camps Bookshop, Wick (ISBN 0 9508697 2 4)

Swain, D P, Sinclair, A F, Chouinard, G A and Drinkwater, K F, 2000. *Ecosystem effects on pre-recruit survival of cod in the southern Gulf of St Lawrence*, Canadian Stock Assessment Secretariat Document 2000/147, at www.dfo-mpo.gc.ca/csas/csas/English/Research_Years/2000/2000_147E.htm (accessed 15 March 2001)

Thompson, W F, 1919. 'The scientific investigation of marine fisheries, as related to the work of the Fish and Game Commission in Southern California', *Fisheries Bulletin* (Canada) Vol 2, pp3–27

UN, 1982. UN Convention on the Law of the Sea, United Nations, at gopher://gopher.un.org:70/11/LOS/UNCLOS82 (accessed 25 April 2000)

UN, 1995 Draft Agreement for the Implementation of the Provisions of the United Nations Convention on the Law of the Sea of 10 December 1982 relating to the Conservation and Management of Straddling Fish Stocks and Highly Migratory Fish Stocks United Nations, accessable via www.igc.org/habitat/un-proc (accessed 13 September 2001)

van Beek, F A and Pastoors, M A, 1999. 'Evaluating ICES catch forecasts: the relationship between implied and realised fishing mortality', *Theme session: Fishing capacity, effort and mortality*, ICES CM 1999/R:04, International Council for the Exploration of the Sea, Copenhagen

Whitmarsh, D, James, C, Pickering, H and Neiland, A, 2000. 'The profitability of marine commercial fisheries: A review of economic information needs with particular reference to the UK', *Marine Policy* Vol 24, pp257–63

Chapter 3 Radiation

Albers-Schönberg, H E, 1903. 'Über eine bisher unbekannte Wirkung der Röntgenstrahlen aurden Organismus der Tiere', *München med. Wchnschr.* Vol 50, pp1859–63

Colwell, H A and Russ, S, 1934. *X-ray and radium injuries. Prevention and treatment*, Oxford University Press, London

Dennis, J, 1899. 'The roentgen energy today', *Dental Cosmos* Vol 41, p853

Desjardins, A U, 1923. 'Protection against radiation', *Radiology* Vol 1, p221

Doll, R, 1989. 'The epidemiology of childhood leukaemia', *J Royal Statistic Soc* (Series A) Vol 152, pp341–51

Edison, T A, 1896. 'Effect of X-rays upon the eye', *Nature* Vol 53, p421

'Editorial', 1921. *Archives of the Roentgen Society* Vol XVII, pp50–1

ICRP, 1977. 'Recommendations of the International Commission on Radiological Protection (Publication 26)', *Ann ICRP* Vol 1, No 3

Ionising Radiations Regulations (Sealed Sources), 1961. HMSO, London

Macklis, R M, 1993. 'The great radium scandal', *Scientific American* Vol 269, pp94–9

Martland, H S and Humphries, R E, 1929. 'Osteogenic sarcoma in dial painters using luminous paint', *Arch Pathol* Vol 7, pp406–17

Mutscheller, A, 1925. 'Physical standards of protection against roentgen ray dangers', *Amer J Roentgen* Vol 13, p65

National Bureau of Standards Handbook No 59 (1954)

NRPB, 1990. 'Patient dose reduction in diagnostic radiology', *Docs of National Radiological Protection Board* Vol 1, No 3

POPUMET, 1988. Ionising Radiation (Protection of Persons Undergoing Medical Examination or Treatment) Regulations, HMSO, London

RCR, 1993. *Making the best use of a department of clinical radiology*, Royal College of Radiologists, London

Roentgen, W C, 1895. 'Über eine neue Art von Strahlen', *Sitzungs-Berichte der Physikalisch-medicinischen Gesellschaft zu Wurtzburg* Vol 9, pp132–41

Rollins, W H, 1904. 'On the tyranny of old ideas as illustrated by the X-light used in therapeutics', *Elect Rev* Vol 43, p120

Ron, E B, Modan, D and Preston, D L, 1989. 'Thyroid neoplasia following low dose irradiation in childhood', *Radiat Res* Vol 120, pp516–31

Rosenthal, J J, de Almeida, C E and Mendonca, A H, 1991. 'The radiological accident in Goiania: the initial remedial actions', *Health Physics* Vol 60, pp7–15

Rowland, R E, Stehney, A F and Lucas, H F, 1983. 'Dose–response relationships for radium induced bone sarcomas', *Health Physics* Vol 44, Suppl 1, pp15–31

Scott, N S, 1897. 'X-ray injuries', *Am X-ray* Vol 1, pp57–76

Stewart, A M, Webb, J W and Hewitt, D, 1958. 'A survey of childhood malignancies', *B Med J* Vol 1, p1495

Stone, R S, 1946. 'Fifty years of radiology: From Roentgen to the era of atomic power', *Western J Surg* Vol 54, p153

Taylor, L S, 1979. *Organisation for Radiation Protection. The operations of the ICRP and NCRP 1928–1974*, Report DOE/TIC-10124, US Dept of Energy, Washington, DC

Thomson, E, 1896. 'Roentgen rays act strongly on the tissues', *Elec Engr* Vol 22, p534

Thompson, S P, 1898. 'Presidential address', *Arch Roentgen Ray* Vol II, p28

Wall, B F and Hart, D, 1997. 'Revised radiation doses for typical X-ray examinations', *Brit J Radiol* Vol 70, pp437–9

Chapter 4 Benzene

ACGIH, 1946. *Transactions of the Eighth Annual Meeting, American Conference of Governmental Industrial Hygienists*, p40, Cincinnati, Ohio

ACGIH, 1948. *Transactions of the Tenth Annual Meeting, American Conference of Governmental Industrial Hygienists*, p31, Cincinnati, Ohio

ACGIH, 1957. *Transactions of the Nineteenth Annual Meeting, American Conference of Governmental Industrial Hygienists*, p47, Cincinnati, Ohio

Aksoy, M, 1977. 'Leukemia in workers due to occupational exposure to benzene', *New Istanbul Contrib Clin Sci* Vol 12, pp3–14

Aksoy, M, 1978. 'Benzene and leukaemia', *Lancet* Vol I, p441

Aksoy, M, 1987. 'Chronic lymphoid leukaemia and hairy cell leukaemia due to chronic exposure to benzene: Report of three cases', *Br J Haematol* Vol 66, pp209–11

Aksoy, M, Dincol, K, Akgun, T, Erdem, S and Dincol, G, 1971. 'Haematological effects of chronic benzene poisoning in 217 workers', *Br J Industrl Med* Vol 28, pp296–302

API, 1948. *Toxicological review: Benzene*, Department of Safety, American Petroleum Institute, New York, September

Askey, J M, 1928. 'Aplastic anemia due to benzol poisoning', *Calif West Med* Vol 29, pp262–3

Bergsagel, D E, Wong, O, Bergsagel, P L, Alexanian, R, Anderson, K, Kyle, R A and Raabe, G K, 1999. 'Benzene and multiple myeloma: Appraisal of the scientific evidence', *Blood* Vol 94, pp1174–82

Bond, G G, McLaren, E A, Baldwin, C L and Cook, R R, 1986. 'An update of mortality among workers exposed to benzene', *Br J Indust Med* Vol 43, pp685–91

Browning E, 1965. *Toxicity and metabolism of industrial solvents*, pp3–65, Elsevier Publishing Co, New York

Budinsky, R A, DeMott, R P, Wernke, M J and Schell, J D, 1999. 'An evaluation of modeled benzene exposure and dose estimates published in the Chinese National Cancer Institute collaborative epidemiology studies', *Reg Toxicol Pharm* Vol 30, pp244–58

Castleman, B I and Ziem, G E, 1988. 'Corporate influence on threshold limit values', *Am J Ind Med* Vol 13, pp531–59

Castleman, B I and Ziem, G E, 1994. 'American conference of governmental industrial hygienists: Low threshold of credibility', *Am J Ind Med* Vol 26, pp133–43

Crump, K S, 1994. 'Risk of benzene-induced leukemia: A sensitivity analysis of the Pliofilm cohort with additional follow-up and new exposure estimates', *J Tox Environ Health* Vol 42, pp219–42

DeCoufle, P, Blattner, W A and Blair, A, 1983. 'Mortality among chemical workers exposed to benzene and other agents', *Environ Res* Vol 30, pp16–25

Deschamps, F, 1995. 'Unleaded gasoline: A continuing hazard', *Occup Med* Vol 45, p55

Dolore, P and Borgomano, C, 1928. 'Acute leukemia in the course of benzene poisoning: The toxic origin of certain acute leukemias and their relationship to severe anemia', *J Med Lyon* Vol 9, pp227–33

Dosemeci, M, Yin, S-N, Linet, M et al, 1996. 'Indirect validation of benzene exposure assessment by association with benzene poisoning', *Environ Health Perspect* Vol 104, No 6, pp1343–47

Erf, L A and Rhoads, C P, 1939. 'The hematological effects of benzene (benzol) poisoning', *J Industrl Hyg Toxicol* Vol 21, pp421–35

Flandrin, G and Collado, S, 1987. 'Is male predominance (4/1) in hairy cell leukaemia related to occupational exposure to ionizing radiation, benzene and other solvents?', *Br J Haematol* Vol 67, pp119–20

Flury, F, 1928. 'Modern occupational intoxications from the aspect of pharmacology and toxicology II: Modern occupational intoxications', *Arch Exp Path Pharmakol* Vol 138, pp65–82 (Ger), cited in US Department of Health, Education and Welfare, 1974, *Occupational exposure to benzene, criteria for a recommended standard*, pp74–137, PHS, CDC, NIOSH

Goguel, A, Cavigneaux, A and Bernard, J, 1967. 'Benzene leukemia in the Paris region between 1950 and 1965: A study of 50 cases', *Nouv Rev Fr Hemato* Vol 7, pp465–80

Goldstein, B D, 1990. 'Is exposure to benzene a cause of human multiple myeloma?', *Ann NY Acad Sci* Vol 609, pp225–30

Goldstein, B D and Shalat, S L, 2000. 'The causal relation between benzene exposure and multiple myeloma', Letter to the Editor, *Blood* Vol 95, pp1512–13

Greenburg, L, 1926. 'Benzol poisoning as an industrial hazard', *Pub Health Rep* Vol 41, pp1516–39

Hayes, R B et al, 1996. 'Mortality among benzene-exposed workers in China', *Env Health Perspect* Vol 104, No 6, pp1349–52

Hayes, R B, Yin, S-N, Dosemeci, M, Li, G-L, Wacholder, S, Travis, LB, Li, C-Y, Rothman, N, Hoover, RN, Linet, MS, 1997. 'Benzene and the dose-related incidence of hematologic neoplasms in China', *J Natl Cancer Inst* Vol 89, pp1065–71

Hayes, R B et al, 1998. 'Benzene and the dose-related incidence of hematologic neoplasms in China – Response', Letter to the Editor, *J Natl Cancer Inst* Vol 90, pp470–71

Hayes, R B, Yin, S, Dosemeci, M and Linet, M, 2001 in press. Commentary: Benzene and lymphohematopoietic malignancies in China. *Am J Industrl Med*

Helmer, K J, 1944. 'Accumulated cases of chronic benzene poisoning in the rubber industry', *Acta Medica Scand* Vol 118, pp254–75

Hernberg, S, Savilahti, M, Ahlman, K and Asp, S, 1966. 'Prognostic aspects of benzene poisoning', *Br J Indust Med* Vol 23, pp204–9

Hogan, J F and Shrader, J H, 1923. 'Benzol poisoning', *Am J Pub Health* Vol 13, pp279–82

Hogstedt, B, Holmen, A, Karlsson, A, Raihle, G, Nillius, K and Vestlund, K, 1991. 'Gasoline pump mechanics had increased frequencies and sizes of micronuclei in lymphocytes stimulated by pokeweed mitogen', *Mutat Res* Vol 263, pp51–5

Hunter, F T, 1939. 'Chronic exposure to benzene (benzol) II: The clinical effects', *J Industrl Hyg Toxicol* Vol 21, pp331–54

IARC, 1974. *IARC Monographs on the evaluation of carcinogenic risk of chemicals to man: Some anti-thyroid and related substances, nitrofurans and industrial chemicals*, Vol 7, pp203–21, International Agency for Research on Cancer, World Health Organization, Lyon, France

Infante, P F, 1987. 'Benzene toxicity: Studying a subject to death', *Am J Ind Med* Vol 11, pp599–604

Infante, P F, 1992. 'Benzene and leukemia: The 0.1 ppm ACGIH proposed TLV for benzene', *Appl Occup Environ Hyg* Vol 7, pp253–62

Infante, P F, 1993. 'State of the science on the carcinogenicity of gasoline with particular reference to cohort mortality study results', *Environ Health Perspect* Supplement 101S6, pp105–10

Infante, P F, 1995a. 'Benzene and leukemia: Cell types, latency and amount of exposure associated with leukemia', in M Imbriani, S Ghittori, G Pezzagno and E Capodaglio (eds), *Update on benzene, advances in occupational medicine and rehabilitation*, pp107–20, Fondazione Salvatore Maugeri Edizioni, Pavia, Italy

Infante, P F, 1995b. 'Cancer in blue-collar workers: Who cares?' *New Solutions* Vol 5, pp52–7

Infante, P F, 1997. 'Quantitative risk from leukemia/lymphoma from occupational exposure to benzene', *The Toxicology Forum 22nd Annual Winter Meeting*, pp485–8, Toxicology Forum, Inc, Washington, DC

Infante, P F and DiStasio, M V, 1988. 'Occupational benzene exposure: Preventable deaths', *Lancet* Vol I, pp1399–400

Infante, P F, Rinsky, R A, Wagoner, J K and Young, R J, 1977a. 'Leukaemia in benzene workers', *Lancet* Vol II, pp76–8

Infante, P F, Rinsky, R A, Wagoner, J K and Young, R J, 1977b. 'Benzene and leukaemia', *Lancet* Vol II, pp867–8

Infante, P F, Schwartz, E and Cahill, R, 1990. 'Benzene in petrol: A continuing hazard', *Lancet* Vol 335, pp814–15

Ireland, B, Collins, J J, Buckley, C F and Riordan, S G, 1997. 'Cancer mortality among workers with benzene exposure', *Epid* Vol 8, pp318–20

IUD, 1980. AFL-CIO vs. American Petroleum Institute, 1980, 448 US 601, Industrial Union Department

Jakobsson, R, Ahlbom, A, Bellander, T and Lundberg, I, 1993. 'Acute myeloid leukemia among petrol station attendants', *Arch Environ Health* Vol 48, pp255–9

LeNoir and Claude, 1897. 'On a case of purpura attributed to benzene intoxication', *Bul Mem Soc Med Hop* Vol 3, pp1251–61

Lumley, M, Barker, H and Murray, J A, 1990. 'Benzene in petrol', *Lancet* Vol 336, pp1318–19

Mallory, T B, Gall, E A and Brickley, W J, 1939. 'Chronic exposure to benzene (benzol) III: The pathologic results', *J Industrl Hyg Toxicol* Vol 21, pp355–77

Maltoni, C and Scarnato, C, 1979. 'First experimental demonstration of the carcinogenic effects of benzene: Long-term bioassays on Sprague-Dawley rats by oral administration', *Med Lav* Vol 70, pp352–7

McMichael, A J, Spirtas, R, Kupper, L L and Gamble, J F, 1975. 'Solvent exposure and leukemia among rubber workers: An epidemiologic study', *J Occup Med* Vol 17, pp234–9

Naizi, G A and Fleming, A F, 1989. 'Blood dyscrasia in unofficial vendors of petrol and heavy oil and motor mechanics in Nigeria', *Tropical Doctor* Vol 19, pp55–8

Nilsson, R I, Nordlinder, R G, Tagesson, C, Walles, S and Jarvholm, B G, 1996. 'Genotoxic effects in workers exposed to low levels of benzene from gasoline', *Am J Ind Med* Vol 30

NTP, 1986. *Toxicology and carcinogenisis studies of benzene (CAS No 71-43-2) in F344/N rats and B6C3F1 mice (Gavage studies)*, NIH Publ No 86-2545, National Toxicology Program Technical Report 289, Research Triangle Park, NC

Olson, R E, 1977. Testimony before the US Department of Labor, Occupational Safety and Health Administration, Washington, DC, OSHA Docket No H-059, Exhibit No 149E

OSHA, 1977a. 'Occupational exposure to benzene: Emergency temporary standards-hearing', 3 May, Part IV, Fed Register 42, pp22516–29

OSHA, 1977b. 'Occupational exposure to benzene: Emergency temporary standards-hearing', 27 May, Part VI, Fed Register 42, pp27452–78

OSHA, 1978. 'Occupational exposure to benzene: Occupational safety and health standards', 10 February, Part II, Fed Register 43, pp5918–70

OSHA, 1987. 'Occupational exposure to benzene: Final rule', 11 September, Part II, Fed Register 52, pp34460–578

Paxton, M B, Chinchilli, V M, Brett, S M and Rodricks, J V, 1994. 'Leukemia risk associated with benzene exposure in the Pliofilm cohort: Mortality update and exposure distribution', *Risk Analysis* Vol 14, pp147–54

Rawson, R, Parker Jr, F and Jackson Jr, H, 1941. 'Industrial solvents as possible etiologic agents in myeloid metaplasia', *Science* Vol 93, pp541–2

Rinsky, R A, Smith, A B, Hornung, R, Filloon, T G, Young, R J, Okun, A H and Landrigan, P J, 1987. 'Benzene and leukemia: An epidemiologic risk assessment', *N Eng J Med* Vol 316, pp1044–50

Santessen, C G, 1897. 'Chronische vergiftungen mit steinkohlentheerbenzin: Vier Todesfalle' *Arch Hyg Bakteriol* Vol 31, pp336–76

Savitz, D A and Andrews, K W, 1996. 'Risk of myelogenous leukaemia and multiple myeloma in workers exposed to benzene', Letter to the Editor, *Occup Environ Med* Vol 53, pp357

Savitz, D A and Andrews, K W, 1997. 'Review of epidemiologic evidence on benzene and lymphatic and hematopoietic cancers', *Am J Ind Med* Vol 31, pp287–95

Schwartz, E, 1987. 'Proportionate mortality ratio analysis of automobile mechanics and gasoline service station workers in New Hampshire', *Am J Ind Med* Vol 12, pp91–9

Shu, X O, Brinton, L A, Linet, M S, Tu, J T, Zheng, W and Fraumeni, J F, 1988. 'A population-based case-control study of childhood leukemia in Shanghai', *Cancer* Vol 62, pp635–43

Tabershaw, I R and Lamm, S H, 1977. 'Benzene and leukaemia', Letter to the Editor, *Lancet* Vol II, pp867–68

Tareeff, E M, Kontchalovskaya, N M and Zorina, L A, 1963. 'Benzene leukemias', *Acta Unio Internat Contra Cancrum* Vol 19, pp751–5

Tondel, M, Persson, B and Carstensen, J, 1995. 'Myelofibrosis and benzene exposure', *Occup Med* Vol 45, pp51–2

Vigliani, E C, 1976. 'Leukemia associated with benzene exposure', *Ann NY Acad Sci* Vol 271, pp143–51

Vigliani, E C and Saita, G, 1964. 'Benzene and leukemia', *N Engl J Med* Vol 271, pp872–6

Wong, O, 1987a. 'An industry wide mortality study of chemical workers occupationally exposed to benzene I: General results', *Br J Ind Med* Vol 44, pp365–81

Wong, O, 1987b. 'An industry wide mortality study of chemical workers occupationally exposed to benzene II: Dose response analyses', *Br J Ind Med* Vol 44, pp382–95

Wong, O, 1995. 'Risk of acute myeloid leukaemia and multiple myeloma in workers exposed to benzene', *Occup Environ Med* Vol 52, pp380–4

Wong, O, 1996. 'Risk of myeloid leukaemia and multiple myeloma in workers exposed to benzene-response', Letter to the Editor, *Occup Environ Med* Vol 53, pp357–8

Wong, O, 1998. 'Re: Benzene and the dose-related incidence of hematologic neoplasms in China', Letter to the Editor, *J Natl Cancer Inst* Vol 90, pp469–70

Wong, O, 1999. 'A critique of the exposure assessment in the epidemiologic study of benzene-exposed workers in China conducted by the Chinese Academy of Preventive Medicine and the US National Cancer Institute', *Reg Toxicol Pharm* Vol 30, pp259–67

Young, R J, Rinsky, R A, Infante, P F and Wagoner, J K, 1978. 'Benzene in consumer products', *Science* Vol 199, pp248

Chapter 5 Asbestos

Acheson, E D, and Gardner, M J, 1983 'Asbestos: The Control Limit for Asbestos', Health & Safety Executive, HMSO, London

Archer, V E et al, 1973, 'Uranium Mining and Cigarette Smoking Effects in Man', *J Occ Med* Vol 15, p204

Auribault, M, 1906. 'Sur l'hygiene et la securite des ouvriers dans la filature et tissage d'amiante', in *Annual report of the French Labour Inspectorate for 1906*

Bartrip, P, 1931. 'Too little, too late? The Home Office and the asbestos industry regulations 1931', *Medical History* Vol 42, October, pp421–38

British Medical Journal, 2000. Vol 320, 20 May, p1358, at http://bmj.com/cgi/full/320/7246/1358/a

Castleman, B, 2001. Draft paper to asbestos conference at London School of Hygiene and Tropical Medicine, 5 June

Castleman, B I, 1996. *Asbestos: Medical and legal aspects*, 4th ed, Aspen Law & Business, Englewood Cliffs, NJ

Collis, E, 1911. *Annual Report of HM Chief Inspector of Factories for 1910*, HMSO, London

Cooke, W E, 1924. 'Fibrosis of the lungs due to the inhalation of asbestos dust', *British Medical Journal* Vol 2, 26 July, p147

Cooke, W E, 1927. 'Pulmonary asbestosis', *British Medical Journal* Vol 2, 3 December, pp1024–5

Dalton, A, 1979. *Asbestos: Killer dust*, British Society for Social Responsibility in Science, London

Deane, Lucy, 1898. 'Report on the health of workers in asbestos and other dusty trades', in HM Chief Inspector of Factories and Workshops, 1899, *Annual Report for 1898*, pp171–2, HMSO London (see also the Annual Reports for 1899 and 1900, p502)

Doll, R, 1955. 'Mortality from lung cancer in asbestos workers', *Brit J Industr Med* Vol 12, pp81–6

Gloyne, S R, 1935. 'Two cases of squamos carcinoma of the lung occurring in asbestosis', *Tubercle* Vol 17, pp5–10

Greenberg, M, 1993. 'Reginald Tage – a UK prophet: A postscript', *Am J Ind Med* Vol 24, pp521–4

Greenberg, M, 1994. 'Knowledge of the health hazard of asbestos prior to the Merewether and Price Report of 1930', *Social History of Medicine*, 07/03/, pp493–516

Greenberg, M, 2000. 'Re call for an international ban on asbestos: Trust me, I'm a doctor', Letter to the editor, *Am J Ind Med* Vol 37, pp232–4

Grieve, I M D, 1927. 'Asbestosis', MD thesis, University of Edinburgh

Hammond, E C, Selikoff, I J, Seidman, H, 'Asbestos exposure,cigarrette smoking and death rates,' Annals of New York Academy of Sciences, p 473–90

Health and Safety Commission, 1994–95, *Health and Safety Statistics* Vol 55, pp148–51

Heerings, H, 1999. 'Asbestos – deep in the very fibres of society', Contrast Advise study for Greenpeace Netherlands, September, Amersfoort

Heuper, W C, 1942, 'Occupational Tumours and Allied Diseases', Charles C Thomas, Springfield, Illinois

Hoffman, F L, 1918. 'Mortality from respiratory diseases in dusty trades', *Bulletin of the US Bureau of Labor Statistics* Vol 231, pp176–80

Knox, J F, 1952. 'Visits to the Thetford Mines, Asbestos, Atlas Works, Keasbey & Mattison Works, Raybestos-Manhattan Works', Report to the management of Turner Brothers Asbestos, Frames 0000 0070 1950–54 in the Chase Manhattan microfilms

Knox, J F, 1964. 'Report of a visit to the Thetford Mines, Asbestos and Montreal', Report to the management at Turner Brothers Asbestos, discovered documents marked 015039-015041

Knox J F et al, (1965) 'Cohort analysis of changes in incidence of bronchial carcinoma in a textile asbestos factory', *Annals of the NY Acad of Sciences* Vol 132, December, pp527–35

Lancet, 1967. 17 June, pp1311–12

Legge, T, 1934, *Industrial maladies*, Oxford University Press, Oxford

Lynch, K M and Smith, W A, 1935. 'Pulmonary asbestosis 111: Carcinoma of lung in asbestosis-silicosis', *Am J Cancer* Vol 24, pp56–64

Merewether, E R A, 1933. 'A memorandum on asbestosis', *Tubercle* Vol 15, pp69–81

Merewether, E R A and Price, C W, 1930. *Report on effects of asbestos dust on the lungs and dust suppression in the asbestos industry*, HMSO, London

Murray, H M, 1906. Departmental Committee on Compensation for Industrial Diseases, 1907, *Minutes of evidence*, p127, paras 4076–4104, Cd 3496, HMSO, London

Newhouse, M and Thompson, H, 1965. 'Mesothelioma of pleara and pertitoneum following exposure to asbestos in the London area', *Brit J Industr Med* pp261–9

Peto, J, 1978. 'The hygiene standard for chrysotile asbestos', *Lancet* 4 March, pp484–9

Peto, J, 1998. 'Too little, too late', interview with John Waite, BBC Radio 4, 15 October, London

Peto, J, 1999. 'The European mesothelioma epidemic', *B J Cancer* Vol 79, February, pp666–72

Roller, M and Pott, F, 1998. 'Carcinogenicity of man-made fibres in experimental animals and its relevance for classification of insulation wools', *Eur J Oncol* Vol 3, No 3, pp231–9

Scheper, G W H, 1995. 'Chronology of asbestos cancer discoveries: Experimental studies at the Saranac Laboratory', *Am J Ind Med* Vol 27, pp593–606

Seiler, H E, 1928. 'A case of pneumoconiosis', *British Medical Journal* Vol 2, p982

Selikoff, I J et al, 1964. 'Asbestos exposure and neoplasia', *J Am Med Ass* Vol 188, pp22–6

Selikoff, I and Lee, D H K, 1978. *Asbestos and disease*, Academic Press, New York

Sells, B, 1994. 'What asbestos taught me about managing risk', *Harvard Business Review* March/April, pp76–89

Simpson, F W, 1928. 'Pulmonary asbestosis in South Africa', *British Medical Journal* 1 May, pp885–7

Summers, A L, 1919. *Asbestos and the asbestos industry.* Cited in Tweedale, p5, fn10

Tweedale, G, 2000. *Magic mineral to killer dust: Turner and Newall and the asbestos hazard,* Oxford University Press, Oxford

Sunday Times, 1965. 'Urgent probe into "new" killer dust disease', 31 October, London

Wagner, J C, Sleggs, C A and Marchand, P, 1960. 'Diffuse pleural mesothelioma and asbestos exposure in the North Western Cape Province', *Brit J Indust Med* Vol 17, pp260–71

Wedler, H W, 1943. 'Über den Lungenkrebs bei Asbesttos', *Dtsch Arch Klin Med* Vol 191, pp189–209

WTO, 2000. WT/DST35/R, 18 September

WTO, 2001. WT/DS135/AB/R, 12 March

Chapter 6 PCBs

AMAP, 1997. *Arctic pollution issues: A state of the Arctic environment report,* Arctic Monitoring and Assessment Programme, Oslo, at www.amap.no/amap.htm

AMAP, 1998. 'Persistent organic pollutants' in de March et al (eds), *AMAP assessment report: Arctic pollution issues,* AMAP Secretariat, Oslo

ASCH, 1997. *A position paper of the American Council on Science and Health: Public health concerns about environmental polychlorinated biphenyls (PCBs)* (update of the 1991 report by L T Flynn and C F Kleiman), Academic Press, at www.acsh.org/publications/reports/pcupdate2.html

Aulerich, R J et al, 1986. 'Assessment of primary versus secondary toxicity of Aroclor 1254 in mink', *Arch. Environ Contam Toxicol* Vol 15, pp393–9

Bernard, A, Hermans, C, Broeckaert, F, De Poorter, G, De Cock, A and Houins, G, 1999. 'Food contamination by PCBs and dioxins', *Nature* Vol 401, pp231–2

Bernes, C, 2001. *Will time heal every wound,* Swedish Environmental Protection Agency

Boersma, E R et al, 1994. 'Cord blood levels of potentially neurotoxic pollutants (polychlorinated biphenyls, lead and cadmium) in the areas of Prague (Czech Republic) and Katowice (Poland). Comparison with reference values in The Netherlands', *Central European Journal of Public Health* Vol 2, pp73–6

Bouwman, C A, 1994. 'Modulation of vitamin K dependent blood coagulation by chlorinated biphenyls and dioxins in rats', thesis (ISBN: 90-393-0581-1), University of Utrecht, Utrecht

Bowman, R E and Heironimus, M P, 1981. 'Hypoactivity in adolescent monkeys perinatally exposed to PCBs and hyperactive as juveniles', *Neurobehav Toxicol Teratol* Vol 3, pp15–18

CBS, 1980. *PCBs in Nederland,* Centraal Bureau voor de Statistiek, Staatsuitgeverij, 's-Gravenhage

DoE, 1987. *Summary of the ministerial declaration from the International Conference of the Protection of the North Sea,* Department of the Environment, London

DoE, 1990. *Summary of the ministerial declaration from the International Conference of the Protection of the North Sea,* Department of the Environment, London

Dessens, A, Cohen-Kettenis, P, Mellenbergh, G, van de Poll, N, Koppe, J and Boer, K, 1998. 'Prenatal exposure to anticonvulsant drugs and spatial ability in adulthood', *Acta Neurobiol Exp* Vol 58, pp221–5

Drinker, C K et al, 1937. 'The problem of possible systemic effects from certain chlorinated hydrocarbons', *Journal of Industrial Hygiene and Toxicology* Vol 19 (September), pp283–311

Francis, E, 1998. 'Conspiracy of silence – how three corporate giants covered their toxic trail', at www.planetwaves.net/silence2.html (includes responses from the companies involved at www.planetwaves.net/response.html)

Fuerst, P, Fuerst, C and Wilmers, K, 1992. *Bericht über die untersuchung von Frauenmilch auf Polychlorierte Dibenzodioxine, Dibenzofurane, Biphenyle sowie organochlorpestizide 1984–1991*, Chemisches Landesuntersuchungsamt NRW, Münster

Greve, P A and Wegman, R C C, 1983. 'PCB residues in animal fats, human tissues, duplicate 24-hours diets, eel and sediments', *Proceedings of PCB seminar*, Scheveningen, The Hague, Netherlands, 28–30 September, pp54–65

Guo, L Y, 1999. 'Human health effects from PCBs and dioxin-like chemicals in the rice-oil poisonings as compared with other exposure episodes', *Organohalogen Compounds* Vol 42, pp241–3

Harada, M, 1976. 'Intra-uterine poisoning: Clinical and epidemiological studies and significance of the problem', *Bull Inst Const Med Kumamoto University* Vol 25 (Suppl), pp1–69

Hens, L, 1999. 'Dioxines en PCBs in Belgische eieren en kippen', *Milieu 1999/4*, pp220–5

Holden, A V, 1970. 'Monitoring organochlorine contamination of the marine environment by the analysis of residues in seals' in M Ruivo (ed), *Marine pollution and sea life*, pp266–72, Fishing News Books Ltd, England

Hornshaw, T C et al, 1983. 'Feeding Great Lakes fish to mink: Effects on mink and accumulation and elimination of PCBs by mink', *J Toxicol Environ Health* Vol 11, pp933–46

Huisman, M, 1996. 'Effects of early infant nutrition and perinatal exposure to PCBs and dioxins on neurological development: A study of breast-fed and formula-fed infants', dissertation (ISBN 90-3670688-2), University of Groningen, Groningen

Huisman, M, Koopman-Esseboom, C, Lanting, C I, van der Paauw, C G, Tuinstra, L G M Th, Fidler, V, Weisglas-Kuperus, N, Sauer, P J J, Boersma, E R and Touwen, B C L, 1995. 'Neurological condition in 18-month-old children perinatally exposed to polychlorinated biphenyls and dioxins', *Early Hum Dev* Vol 43, pp165–76

Jacobson, J L and Jacobson, S, 1996. 'Intellectual impairment in children exposed to polychlorinated biphenyls *in utero*', *N Engl J Med* Vol 335, No 11, pp783–9

Jacobson, J L, Jacobson, S W and Humphrey, H E, 1990. 'Effects of exposure to PCBs and related compounds on growth and activity in children', *Neurotoxicol Teratol* Vol 12, pp319–26

Jensen, S, Johnels, A G, Olsson, M and Otterlind, G, 1969. 'DDT and PCB in marine animals from Swedish waters', *Nature* Vol 224, p247

Kimburgh, R D et al, 1987. 'Human health effects of polychlorinated biphenyls (PCBs) and polybrominated biphenyls (PBBs)', *Ann Rev Pharmacol Toxicol* Vol 27, pp87–111

Koopman-Esseboom, C, 1995. 'Effects of perinatal exposure to PCBs and dioxins on early human development', dissertation, University of Rotterdam, Rotterdam

Koopman-Esseboom, C, Morse, D C, Weisglas-Kuperus, N, Lutkeschipholt, I J, van der Paauw, C G and Tuinstra, L G, 1994. 'Effects of dioxins and polychlorinated biphenyls on thyroid hormone status of pregnant women and their infants', *Pediatr Research* Vol 36, No 4, pp468–73

Koppe, J G, Pluim, H J and Olie, K, 1989. 'Breastmilk, PCBs, dioxins and vitamin K deficiency', *J Royal Soc of Med* Vol 82, pp416–20

Lanting, C I, 1999. 'Effects of perinatal PCB and dioxin exposure and early feeding on child development', dissertation (ISBN 90-3671002-2), University of Groningen, Groningen

Lanting, C I, Huisman, M, Muskiet F A J, van der Paauw, C G, Essed, C E and Boersma, E R, 1998a. 'Polychlorinated biphenyls in adipose tissue, liver and brain from nine stillborns of varying gestational ages', *Pediatr Res* Vol 44, pp1–4

Lanting, C I, Patandin, S, Fidler, V, Weisglas-Kuperus, N, Sauer, P J J, Boersma, E R and Touwen, B C L, 1998b. 'Neurological condition in 42-month-old children in relation to pre- and postnatal exposure to polychlorinated biphenyls and dioxins', *Early Hum Dev* Vol 50, pp283–92

Masuda, Y, 1994. 'The Yusho rice oil poisoning incident' in A Schecter (ed) *Dioxins and health*, pp633–59, Plenum Press, New York and London

Matthews, H B and Anderson, M W, 1975. 'Effect of chlorination on the distribution and excretion of polychlorinated biphenyls', *Drug Metab Dispos* Vol 3, No 5, pp371–80

OECD, 1973. *Decision-recommendation of the Council on Protection of the Environment by control of polychlorinated biphenyls*, C(73) 1 (Final)

OECD, 1987. *Decision-recommendation of the Council concerning further measures for the protection of the environment by control of polychlorinated biphenyls*, C(87) 2 (Final)

Oliver, B G and Niimi, A J, 1988. 'Trophodynamic analysis of polychlorinated biphenyl congeners and other chlorinated hydrocarbons in the Lake Ontario ecosystem', *Environ Sci Technol* Vol 22, pp388–97

Patandin, S, 1999. 'Effects of environmental exposure to polychlorinated biphenyls and dioxins on growth and development in young children', PhD thesis (ISBN 90-9012306-7), Erasmus University, Rotterdam

Pluim, H J, Koppe, J G, Olie, K, van der Slikke, J W, Kok, J H, Vulsma, T, van Tijn, D and de Vijlder, 1992. 'Effects of dioxins on thyroid function in newborn babies', *Lancet* Vol 339, 23 May, p1303

Schwartz, T R et al, 1987. 'Are polychlorinated biphenyl residues adequately described by Aroclor mixture equivalents? Isomer-specific principal component analysis of such residues in fish and turtles', *Environ. Sci Technol* Vol 21, pp72–6

Seegal, R F and Schantz, S L, 1994. 'Neurochemical and behavioural sequelae of exposure to dioxins and PCBs' in A Schecter (ed), *Dioxins and health*, Plenum Press, New York and London

Swedish Environmental Protection Agency, 1998. *Persistent organic pollutants: A Swedish view of an international problem*, text by Claes Bernes, Monitor 16

Theelen, R M C and Lie, A K D, 1997. 'Dioxins: Chemical analysis, exposure and risk assessment', thesis (ISBN 90-393-2012-8), University of Utrecht, Utrecht

United States Court of Appeal, 1980. *Environmental Defense Fund, Inc, petitioner, v Environmental Protection Agency, respondent, Ad Hoc Committee on Liquid Dielectrics of the Electronic Industries Association et al, Joy Manufacturing Company, Edison Electric Institute et al, and Aluminum Company of America, Intervenors*, Nos 79-1580, 79-1811 and 79-1816, United States Court of Appeals, District of Columbia Circuit, argued 6 June, decided 30 October, at www.manhattan.edu/wcb/schools/engineering/envl/wmatysti/2/files/edfcase.htm

WHO, 1999. *Dioxins and their effects on human health*, Fact Sheet No 225, World Health Organization, Geneva, at www.who.int/inf-fs/en/fact225.html

Chapter 7 Halocarbons, the ozone layer and the precautionary principle

Cagin, S and Dray, P, 1993. *Between earth and sky*, Pantheon Books, New York

Cicerone, R J, Stolarski, R S and Walters, S, 1974. *Science* Vol 185, p1165

DETR, 1999. 'Stratospheric ozone 1999', DETR Reference No 99EP0458, United Kingdom Stratospheric Ozone Review Group, Department of the Environment, Transport and the Regions

Farman, J C, Gardiner, B G and Shanklin, J D, 1985. *Nature* Vol 315, p207

Goody, R M, 1954. *The physics of the stratosphere*, Cambridge University Press, Cambridge

Houzeau, A, 1857. *Comptes Rendus Acad Sci Paris* Vol 45, p873

Lovelock, J E, Maggs, R J and Wade, R J, 1973. *Nature* Vol 241, p194

Molina, M J and Rowland, F S, 1974. *Nature* Vol 249, p810

Norrish, R G W and Neville, G H J, 1934. *J Chem Soc*, p1684

US EPA, 1987. Protection of stratospheric ozone, Fed Register 52, p47491

Weigert, F, 1907. *Ann Physik* Vol 24, p243

WMO, 1985, 1989, 1991, 1994 and 1999. *Global Ozone Research and Monitoring Project*, Reports Nos 16, 20, 25, 37 and 44, World Meteorological Organization, Geneva

Chapter 8 The DES story

Aschbacher, P W, 1976. 'Diethylstilbestrol metabolism in food-producing animals', *J Toxicol Environ Health Suppl* Vol 1, pp45–59

Bishop, P M F, Boycott, M and Zuckerman, S, 1939. 'The estrogenic properties of stilbestrol (diethylstilbestrol)', *Lancet* Vol 2, pp5–11

Brackbill, Y and Berendes, H W, 1978. 'Dangers of diethylstilbestrol: Review of a 1953 paper', Letter to the Editor, *Lancet* Vol 2, No 8088, p520

Brahams, D, 1988. 'Latent drug injury: failure of Dutch diethylstilbestrol action', *Lancet* Vol 2, No 8616, p916

Cook, J W and Dodds, E C, 1933. 'Sex hormones and cancer-producing compounds', *Nature* Vol 131, pp205–6

Dieckmann, W J, Davis, M E, Rynkiewics, L M and Pottinger, R E, 1953. 'Does the administration of diethylstilbestrol during pregnancy have therapeutic value?', *Am J Obstet Gynecol* Vol 66, No 5, pp1062–81

Direcks, A, Figueroa, S, Mintzes, B and Banta, D, 1991. Report from DES Action the Netherlands for the European Commission Programme Europe Against Cancer, p69, DES Action the Netherlands, Utrecht

Direcks, A and t'Hoen, E, 1986. 'DES: The crime continues', in K McDonnell (ed), *Adverse effects of drugs: women and the pharmaceutical industry*, pp41–9, International Organization of Consumers Unions, regional office for Asia and the Pacific, Penang

Dodds, E C, Goldberg, L, Lawson, W. and Robinson, R, 1938. 'Estrogenic activity of certain synthetic compounds', *Nature* Vol 141, pp247–8

Dodds, C, 1965. 'Stilboestrol and after', *Sci Basis Med Annu Rev 1965*, pp1–16

Dunn, T B and Green, A W, 1963. 'Cysts of the epididymis, cancer of the cervix, granular cell myoblastoma, and other lesions after estrogen injection in newborn mice', *J Nat Cancer Inst* Vol 31, No 2, pp425–55

Epelboin, S and Bulwa, S, 1993. 'Drug surveillance and reproduction: The bad example of distilbene', *Contracept Fertil Sex* Vol 21, No 9, pp658–72

Garcia–Alonso, F, Rodriguez-Pinilla, E and Martinez-Frias, M L, 1988. 'The use of diethylstilbestrol in Spain', *Medicina Clinica* Vol 91, No 11, p436

Gardner, W U, 1959. 'Carcinoma of the uterine cervix and upper vagina: Induction under experimental conditions in mice', *Ann NY Acad Sci* Vol 75, pp543–64

Geschickter, C F, 1939. 'Mammary carcinoma in the rat with metastasis induced by estrogen', *Science* Vol 89, pp35–6

Goldberg, J M and Falcone, T, 1999. 'Effect of diethylstilbestrol on reproductive function', *Fertil Steril* Vol 72, No 1, pp1–7

Greene, B R, Burrill, M W and Ivy, A C, 1939. 'Experimental intersexuality: the paradoxical effects of estrogen on the sexual development of the female rat', *The Anatomical Record* Vol 74, No 4, pp429–38

Greene, R R and Brewer, J I, 1941. 'Relation of sex hormones to tumors of the female reproductive system', *Amer J Roentgen Rad Ther* Vol 45, No 3, pp426–45

Greenwald, P, Barlow, J J, Nasca, P C and Burnett, W S, 1971. 'Vaginal cancer after maternal treatment with synthetic estrogens', *N Engl J Med* Vol 285, No 7, pp390–2

Hanselaar, A G, Van Leusen, N D, De Wilde, P C and Vooijs, G P, 1991. 'Clear cell adenocarcinoma of the vagina and cervix: A report of the Central Netherlands Registry with emphasis on early detection and prognosis', *Cancer* Vol 67, No 7, pp1971–8

Herbst, A L and Scully, R E, 1970. 'Adenocarcinoma of the vagina in adolescence. A report of 7 cases including 6 clear-cell carcinomas (so-called mesonephromas)', *Cancer* Vol 25, No 4, pp745–57

Herbst, A L, Ulfelder, H and Poskanzer, D C, 1971. 'Adenocarcinoma of the vagina: Association of maternal stilbestrol therapy with tumor appearance in young women', *N Engl J Med* Vol 284, No 15, pp878–81

Herbst, A L, Kurman, R J, Scully, R E and Poskanzer, D C, 1972. 'Clear-cell adenocarcinoma of the genital tract in young females: Registry report', *N Engl J Med* Vol 287, No 25, pp1259–64

James, W H, 1965. 'Teratogenetic properties of thalidomide', *Br Med J* October 30, 5469, p1064

Johnson, L D, Driscoll, S G, Hertig, A T, Cole, P T and Nickerson, R J, 1979. 'Vaginal adenosis in stillborns and neonates exposed to diethylstilbestrol and steroidal estrogens and progestins', *Obstet Gynecol Surv* Vol 34, No 11, pp845–6

Karnaky, K J, 1942. 'The use of stilbestrol for the treatment of threatened and habitual abortion and premature labor: A preliminary report', *South M J* Vol 35, p838

Karnaky, K J, 1945. 'Prolonged administration of diethylstilbestrol' *J Clin Endocrinol* July 1945 5, pp279–84

Kinlen, L J, Badaracco, M A, Moffett, J and Vessey, M P, 1974. 'A survey of the use of oestrogens during pregnancy in the United Kingdom and of the genito-urinary cancer mortality and incidence rates in young people in England and Wales', *J Obstet Gynaecol Br Commonw* Vol 81, No 11, pp849–55

Lacassagne, A, 1938. 'The appearance of mammary adenocarcinomas in male mice treated by a synthetic estrogenic substance', *Weekly Reports of the Society of Biology and of its Affiliates*, Vol 12, pp641–3

Laplan, B, 1948. 'Diethylstilbestrol in the treatment of idiopathic repeated abortion', *NY State J Med* Vol 48, pp2612–4

McLachlan, J A, 1993. 'Functional toxicology: A new approach to detect biologically active xenobiotics', *Environ Health Perspect* Vol 101, No 5, pp386–7

Melnick, S, Cole, P, Anderson, D and Herbst, A, 1987. 'Rates and risks of diethylstilbestrol-related clear-cell adenocarcinoma of the vagina and cervix: An update', *N Engl J Med* Vol 316, No 9, pp514–6

Miller, M, 1999. 'DES research heats up again after breast cancer finding', *J Nat Cancer Inst* Vol 91, No 16, pp1361–3

Mills, D H, 1974. 'Prenatal diethylstilbestrol and vaginal cancer in offspring', *JAMA* Vol 229, No 4, pp471–2

Newbold, R R, Hanson, R B, Jefferson, W N, Bullock, B C, Haseman, J and McLachlan, J A, 1998. 'Increased tumors but uncompromised fertility in the female descendants of mice exposed developmentally to diethylstilbestrol', *Carcinogenesis* Vol 19, No 9, pp1655–63

Noller, K L and Fish, C R, 1974. 'Diethylstilbestrol usage: Its interesting past, important present and questionable future', *Medical Clinics of North America* Vol 58, No 4, pp793–810

Palmlund, I, 1996. 'Exposure to a xenoestrogen before birth: the diethylstilbestrol experience', *J Psychosom Obstet Gynaecol* Vol 17, No 2, pp71–84

Palmlund, I, Apfel, R, Buitendijk, S, Cabau, A and Forsberg, J G, 1993. 'Effects of diethylstilbestrol (DES) medication during pregnancy: Report from a symposium at the 10th international congress of ISPOG', *J Psychosom Obstet Gynaecol* Vol 14, No 1, pp71–89

Pat Cody, DES Action, personal communication

Pons, J C, Goujard, J, Derbanne, C and Tournaire, M, 1988. 'Outcome of pregnancy in patients exposed in utero to diethylstilbestrol: Survey by the National College of French Gynecologists and Obstetricians', *J Gynecol Obstet Biol Reprod*, Paris, Vol 17, No 3, pp307–16

Robinson, D and Shettles, L, 1952. 'The use of diethylstilbestrol in threatened abortion', *Am J Obstet Gynecol* Vol 63, pp1330–3

Shimkin, M B and Grady, H G, 1941. 'Toxic and carcinogenic effects of stilbestrol in strain C3H male mice', *J Nat Cancer Inst* Vol 4, p55

Smith, A E, 1942. 'Council of pharmacy and chemistry: Diethylstilbestrol', *JAMA* Vol 119, No 8, pp632–5

Smith, O W, 1948. 'Diethylstilbestrol in the prevention and treatment of complications in pregnancy', *Am J Obstet Gynecol* Vol 56, pp821–34

Smith, O W, Smith, G v S and Hurtwitz, D, 1946. 'Increased excretion of pregnandiol in pregnancy from diethylstilbestrol with especial reference to the prevention of late pregnancy accidents', *Am J Obstet Gynecol* Vol 51, p411–5

Swan, S H, 1992. 'Pregnancy outcomes in DES daughters', in R Giusti (ed), *Report of the NIH Workshop on Long-term Effects of Exposure to Diethylstilbestrol (DES)*, pp42–9, US Department of Health and Human Services, Public Health Service, National Institutes of Health, Washington, DC

US Department of Health, Education and Welfare, 1971. Food and Drug Administration, Fed Register (21537–21538)

Wingfield, M, Donnelly, V S, Kelehan, P, Stronge, J M, Murphy, J and Boylan, P, 1992. 'DES clinic: the first six months', *Ir Med J* Vol 85, No 2, pp56–8

Chapter 9 Antimicrobials as growth promoters

Aarestrup, F M, 1995. 'Occurrence of glycopeptide resistance among *Enterococcus faecium* isolates from conventional and ecological poultry farms', *Microbiology Drug Research* Vol 1, pp255–7

Aarestrup, F M, 1998. 'Association between decreased susceptibility to a new antibiotic for treatment of human diseases, everninomycin (SCH 27899), and resistance to an antibiotic used for growth promotion in animals, avilamycin', *Microbiology Drug Research* Vol 4, pp137–41

Aarestrup, F M, Bager, F, Jensen, N E, Madsen, M and Wegener, H C, 1998. 'Surveillance of antimicrobial resistance in bacteria isolated from food animals to growth promoters and related therapeutic agents in Denmark', *APMIS* Vol 160, pp606–22

Amabile-Cuevas, C F and Chicurel, M E, 1992. 'Bacterial plasmids and gene flux', *Cell* Vol 70, pp189–99

Bates, J, Jordens, J Z and Griffiths, D T, 1994. 'Farm animals as a putative reservoir for vancomycin-resistant enterococcal infection in man', *Journal of Antimicrobial Chemotherapy* Vol 34, pp507–16

DVL, 1995. 'The effect of avoparcin used as feed additive on the occurrence of vancomycin resistant *Enterococcus faecium* in pig and poultry production', Report from the Danish Veterinary Laboratory

Fleming, A, 1929. 'On the antibacterial action of cultures of penicillin, with special reference to their use in isolation of B influenzae', *British Journal of Experimental Pathology* Vol 10, pp226–36

Government Bill, 1984/85. Regeringens proposition 1984/85:149 om lag om foder, Sweden

Klare, I, Heier, H, Claus, H, Reissbrodt and Witte, W, 1995. 'VanA-mediated high-level glycopeptide resistance in *Enterococcus faecium* from animal husbandry', *FEMS Microbiology Letters* Vol 125, pp165–72

LBS, 1977. 'Utredning avseende utnyttjandet av specialämnen såsom antibiotika/kemoterapeutika, vilka i tillväxtbefrämjande syfte inblandas i foder', Lantbruksstyrelsen, Jönköping

New York Times, 1945. 26 June, p21

SOU, 1997. 'Antimicrobial feed additives', Swedish Government Official Reports, p132

SSC, 1999. 'Opinion of the Scientific Steering Committee on antimicrobial resistance', European Commission, Directorate-General XXIV

Stokstad, E L R and Jukes, T H, 1949. 'Further observations on the animal protein factor', *Proceedings of the Society of Biological and Experimental Medicine* Vol 73, pp523–8

Swann, M M, 1969. *Report, Joint Committee on the use of Antibiotics in Animal Husbandry and Veterinary Medicine*, HMSO, London

The Copenhagen Recommendations, 1998. Report from the Invitational EU Conference on the Microbial Threat, Copenhagen, September

Walton, J R, 1988. 'Antibiotic resistance: An overview', *Veterinary Record* Vol 122, pp249–51

WHO, 1997. 'The medical impact of the use of antimicrobials in food animals', Report of a WHO meeting, Berlin

WHO, 2000. 'Global principles for the containment of antimicrobial resistance due to antimicrobial use in animals intended for food', at www.who.int/emc-documents/zoonoses/whocdscsraph20004c.html

Chapter 10 Sulphur dioxide

Ambio, 1976. Vol 5, pp200–52

Ashby, E and Anderson, M, 1981. *The politics of clean air*, Oxford University Press, London

Braekke, F (ed), 1976. *Impact of acid precipitation on forest and freshwater ecosystems in Norway*, Norges landbruksvitenskapelige forskningsråd, Oslo-Ås

Brimblecombe, P, 1987. *The big smoke: A history of air pollution in London since medieval times*, Routledge, London

Bruckmann, P, Borchert, H, Külske, S, Lacombe, R, Lenschow, P, Müller, J, and Vitze, W, 1986. *Die Smog-Periode im Januar 1985. Synoptische Darstellung der Luftbelastung in der Bundesrepublik Deutschland. Bericht des Länderausschusses für Immissionsschutz*, Ministerium für Umwelt, Düsseldorf

Coote, A T, Yates, T J S, Chakrabarti, S, Biland, D J, Riland, J P, and Butlin, R N, 1991. *UN/ECE international cooperative programme on materials, including historic and cultural monuments. Evaluation of decay to stone tablets*, Building Research Centre, Garston, Watford, UK

Council of Environmental Advisers (Rat von Sachverständigen für Umweltfragen), 1983. *Waldschäden und Luftverunreinigungen* (Forest damage and air pollution), Kohlhammer, Mainz

Drabløs, D and Tollan, A, (eds), 1980. 'Ecological impact of acid precipitation: Proceedings of an international conference', Sandefjord, Norway, 11–14 March

'Editorial', 1977. *Nature* Vol 268, p89

ECE, 1994. Protocol to the 1979 Convention on Long-range Transboundary Air Pollution on further reduction of sulphur emissions, United Nations, Geneva. Details may be found at www.ece.org

ECE and EC, 1997. *Forest Condition in Europe, Executive Report*, Federal Research Centre for Forestry and Forest Products, Hamburg, Germany

European Commission, 1999. Council Directive 1999/30/EC of 22 April 1999 relating to limit values for sulphur dioxide, nitrogen dioxide and oxides of nitrogen, particulate matter and lead in ambient air, *Off J Eur Communities* L163, 29.6.1999, pp41–60

Egnér, H, Brodin, G, and Johansson, O, 1955. 'Sampling technique and chemical examination of air and precipitation', *Kungliga Lantbrukshögskolan Ann* Vol 22, pp369–410

Hettelingh, J-P, Downing, R J, and de Smet, P A M, 1991. *Mapping critical loads for Europe*, National Institute of Public Health and Environmental Protection, Bilthoven, Netherlands

Knabe, W, 1976. *Internationale Konferenz über die Wirkung saurer Niederschläge in Telemark*, Norwegen, 14 bis 19 Juni 1976

Lykke, E, 1977. 'Europe versus itself', Letter to the Editor, *Nature* Vol 269, p372

Mason, B J, 1992. *Acid rain: Its causes and its effects on inland waters*, Clarendon Press, Oxford

Moldan, B and Schnoor, J, 1992. 'Czechoslovakia: Examining a critically ill environment', *Environmental Science and Technology*, Vol 26, pp14–21

Mylona, S, 1996. 'Sulphur dioxide emissions in Europe 1880–1991 and their effect on sulphur concentrations and depositions', *Tellus* Vol 48B, pp662–89

Nilsson, J and Grennfelt, P, 1988. 'Critical loads for suplhur and nitrogen'. Report from a workshop held at Skokloster, Sweden, 19–24 March, Nordic Council of Ministers, Copenhagen

Odén, S, 1967. *Dagens Nyheter*, 24 October, Stockholm

Odén, S, 1968. 'Nederbördens och Luftens Försurning, dess Orsaker, Förlopp och Verkan i Olika Miljöer' (The acidification of precipitation and air, causes and effects in different environments), *Statens Naturvetenskapliga Forskningsråd, Ekologikomiteen*, Bulletin No 1

OECD, 1968. *Methods for measuring air pollution*, Organisation for Economic Co-operation and Development, Paris

OECD, 1977. *The OECD programme on long range transport of air pollutants: Measurements and findings*, Organisation for Economic Co-operation and Development, Paris

OECD, 1981. *The costs and benefits of sulphur oxide control*, Organisation for Economic Co-operation and Development, Paris

Overrein, L N, Seip, H M, and Tollan, A, 1980. 'Acid precipitation: effects on forest and fish', final report of the SNSF project 1972–1980, Oslo-Ås

Stanners, D and Bordeau, P, 1995. Europe's Environment: The Dobris Assessment, European Environment Agency, Copenhagen

Skjelkvåle, B L, Wright, R F, and Henriksen, Å, 1998. Norwegian lakes show widespread recovery from acidification; results from national surveys of lakewater chemistry 1986–1997, *Hydrology and Earth System Sciences* Vol 2, pp555–62

Sweden, 1971. 'Air pollution across national boundaries: The impact on the environment of sulfur in air and precipitation', Sweden's case study for the UN conference on the human environment, Royal Ministry for Foreign Affairs, Royal Ministry of Agriculture, Stockholm

Ulrich, B, Mayer, R, and Khanna, P K, 1980. Chemical changes due to acid precipitation in a loess derived soil in Central Europe, *Soil Science* Vol 130, pp193–99

United States of America, 1970. 'Clean Air Act'

WHO, 1972. *Air quality criteria and guides for urban air pollutants*, Report of a WHO expert committee, Technical report series No 506, World Health Organization, Geneva

WHO, 1979. *Sulphur oxides and suspended particulate matter*, Environmental Health Criteria No 8, World Health Organization, Geneva

WHO, 1987. *Air quality guidelines for Europe*, WHO regional publications, European series No 23, World Health Organization, Regional Office for Europe, Copenhagen

Chapter 11 MTBE in petrol as a substitute for lead

Arthur D Little Limited, 2001. 'MTBE and the requirements for underground storage tank construction and operation in Member States, Report to the European Commission, March 2001', Ref. ENV.D.1/ETU/2000/0089R

Arvin, E, 2001. Pers comm, Department of Environment and Resources, Technical University of Denmark

ASDA (American Soap and Detergent Association, Biodegradation Subcommittee), 1965. 'Procedure for determination of biodegradability of ABS and LAS', *J Am Oil Chemists Soc* Vol 42, pp986–93

Barker, J F, Hubbard, E and Lemon, L A, 1990. 'The influence of methanol and MTBE on the fate of persistence of monoaromatic hydrocarbons in groundwater', *Proceedings of Petroleum Hydrocarbons and Organic Chemicals in Groundwater Prevention, Detection, and Restoration, 31 October–2 November*, pp113–27, American Petroleum Institute and Association of Groundwater Scientists and Engineers, Houston, Texas

Belpoggi, F, Soffritti, M and Maltoni, C, 1995. 'Methyl-tertiary butyl ether (MTBE) – a gasoline additive: causes testicular and lymphohaematopoietic cancers in rats', *Toxicol Ind Health* Vol 11, pp119–49

Belpoggi, F, Soffritti, M and Maltoni C, 1998. 'Pathological characterization of testicular tumours and lymphomas-leukemias, and of their precursors observed in Sprague-Dawley rats exposed to methyl-tertiary butyl ether (MTBE)', *Europ J Oncol* Vol 3, pp201–6

Bird, M G, Burleigh-Flayer, H D, Chun, J S, Kneiss, J J and Andrews, L S, 1997. 'Oncogenicity studies of inhaled methyl tertiary butyl ether (MTBE) in CD-1 mice and F344 rats' *J Appl Tox* Vol 17, S45-S55

BSC, 1998. *Report on carcinogenesis*, Board of Scientific Counsellors, National Toxicology Program

Borden, R C, Daniel, R A, LeBrun, L E and Davis, C W, 1997. 'Intrinsic biodegradation of MTBE and BTEX in a gasoline-contaminated aquifer', *Water Resources Research* Vol 33, No 5, pp1105–16

Blue Ribbon Panel, 1999. *Executive summary and recommendations*, Blue Ribbon Panel on Oxygenates in Gasoline, US EPA

Burleigh-Flayer, H D, Chun, J S and Kintigh, W J, 1992. 'Methyl tertiary butyl ether: Vapour inhalation oncogenicity study in CD-1 mice', Bushy Run Research Center, Export, PA, BRRC report 91N0013A, 15 October, Union Carbide Chemicals and Plastics Co, Inc, submitted to the US EPA under TSCA Section 4 Testing Consent Order 40 CFR 799.5000 with cover letter dated 29 October 1992, EPA/OPTR#42098

CAL-EPA, 1999. *Public health goal for methyl tertiary butyl ether (MTBE) in drinking water*, Pesticide and Environmental Toxicology Section, Office of Environmental Health Hazard Assessment, California Environmental Protection Agency, Sacramento, CA

Carson, R, 1962. *Silent spring*, Houghton Mifflin, Boston, MA

CEC, 1998. 'Evaluating the cost and supply of alternatives to MTBE in California's reformulated gasoline', Draft report, February 1998, California Energy Commission

Chun, J S, Burleigh-Flayer, H D and Kintigh, W J, 1992. 'Methyl tertiary butyl ether: Vapor inhalation oncogenicity study in Fischer 344 rats', Bushy Run Research Center, Export, PA, BRRC report 91N0013B, 13 November, Union Carbide Chemicals and Plastics Co, Inc, submitted to the US EPA under TSCA Section 4 Testing Consent Order 40 CFR799.5000 with cover letter dated November 1992, EPA/OPTS#42098

Couch, A and Young, T, 1998. 'Failure rate of underground storage tanks', in *Health and Environmental Assessment of MTBE* Vol 3, UC Toxics Research and Teaching Program, University of California, Davis

Crain, E F, Weiss, K B, Biijur, P E, 1994. 'An estimate of the prevalence of asthma and wheezing among inner-city children', *Pediatrics* Vol 94, pp356–62

Davis, G, 1999. Governor of the State of California, Executive Order D-5-99, 25 March 1999, at www.calepa.ca.gov/programs/MTBE/eotask.htm

Day, K J, De Peyster, A, Allgaier, B S, Luong, M and MacGregor, J A, 1998. 'Methyl t-butyl ether (MTBE): Effects on the male rat reproductive endocrine axis', Abstract #861, *Society of Toxicology: Abstracts of the 37th annual meeting* Vol 42, p174

Dekant, W, 2000. 'The mechanistic toxicology of MTBE does not support a classification as category 3 carcinogen', Expert review, Dixson-Decleve, S, 2000. Pers comm

DeWitt & Company Inc, 2000. *MTBE and oxygenates 2000 annual*, Houston, Texas

Dixson-Decleve, S, 2001. Pers comm, Environmental Consultant, Brussels office, ref to meeting of the Commission Working Group on the Classification and Labelling of Dangerous Substances, European Chemicals Bureau, Ispra, 1–17 November 2000, ECBI/76/00 08

ECETOC, 1982. 'Biodegradation methodology with emphasis on ready-biodegradibility test', Report of sub-group, European Chemical Industry Ecology and Toxicology Centre, Brussels

ENDS Environment Daily, 2000. 'EU backs MTBE despite US prohibition', Wednesday 22 March, at www.ends.co.uk/envdaily

ENDS Environment Daily, 2001, 'EU 'should take action' on MTBE risks', Wednesday 24 January, at www.ends.co.uk/envdaily

European Commission, 1967. Council Directive 67/548/EEC of 16 August 1967 on the approximation of the laws, regulations and administrative provisions relating to the classification, packaging and labelling of dangerous substances, Off J Eur Communities L196

European Commission, 1979. Council Directive 79/831/EEC of 18 September 1979 amending for the sixth time Directive 67/548/EEC on the approximation of the laws, regulations and administrative provisions relating to the classification, packaging and labelling of dangerous substances, *Off J Eur Communities* L259

European Commission, 1984. Directive 79-831, Annex V, Part C: Methods for the determination of ecotoxicity, Test methods C 3,4,5,6,7,8,9, *Off J Eur Communities* L251

European Commission, 1993. Commission Directive 93/67/EEC of 20 July 1993, laying down the principles for the assessment of risks to man and the environment of substances notified in accordance with Council Directive 67/548/EEC, *Off J Eur Communities* L277

Eweis, J B, Ergas, S J, Chang, D P and Schroeder, E D, 1998a. *Bioremediation principles*, McGraw-Hill

Eweis, J B, Watanabe, N, Schroeder, E D, Chang, D P Y and Scow, K M, 1998b. 'MTBE biodegradation in the presence of other gasoline compounds', National Ground Water Association Conference on MTBE and Perchlorate, Anaheim, CA, 3–4 June

Finnish EPA, 2001. 'Risk assessment: Tert-butyl methyl ether', CAS-No1634-04-4, EINECS-No 216-653-1, draft of January 2001; 'Risk reduction strategy: Tert-butyl methyl ether', CAS-No 1634-04-4, EINECS-No 216-653-1, draft of 5 March 2001

Hathaway, W, 1999. 'Asthma: An epidemic among Hartford's children', in *Hartford Courant* Hartford, CT

Hunter, B et al, 1999. 'Impact of small gasoline spills on groundwater', presented at the Maine Water Conference, Augusta, ME, 15 April, Maine Department of Environmental Protection, Augusta, ME

Hurt, K L, Wilson, J T, Beck, F P and Cho, J S, 1999. 'Anaerobic biodegradation of MTBE in a contaminated aquifer', In-Situ and On-Site Bioremediation Conference, San Diego, CA, 19–22 April 1999, US EPA, Ada, OK

IARC, 1999. International Agency for Research on Cancer. 'MTBE', *Chem Abstr Serv Reg* No 1634-04-4(73), p139

IPCS, 1999. 'Environmental Health Criteria 206: Methyl tertiary-butyl ether', International Programme on Chemical Safety, at www.who.int/pcs/docs/ehc_206

ISO, 1984. 'Water quality: Evaluation in an aqueous medium of the "ultimate" aerobic biodegradability of organic compounds: Method by analysis of dissolved organic carbon (DOC)', International Organization for Standardization

Jensen, M H and Arvin, E, 1990. 'Solubility and degradability of the gasoline additive MTBE and gasoline compounds in water', in F Arendt, M Hinsenveld and W J Van den Brink (eds), *Contaminated soil*, pp445–8, Kluwer, Dordrecht

Johnson, Pankow, 2000. *Environ Sci and Tech* 1 May (news section)

Joseph, P M, 1997. 'Changes in disease rates in Philidelphia following the introduction of oxygenated gasoline', Annual meeting paper 97-TA34.02, 10 June, pp1–15, Air and Waste Management Association, Pittsburg, PA

Joseph, P M, 1999. 'New hypotheses for MTBE combustion products', Annual meeting paper 99-885, 22 June, pp1–10, Air and Waste Management Association, Pittsburg, PA

Joseph, P M, 2000. 'Is urban asthma caused by methyl tertiary butyl ether (MTBE)?', *Archives of Environmental Health* Vol 55, No 1, pp69–70

Keller, A A, Fernandez, L F, Hitz, S, Kun, H, Peterson, A, Smith, B and Yoshioka, M, 1998a. 'An integral cost–benefit analysis of gasoline formulations meeting California Phase II Reformulated Gasoline Requirements', Report to the Governor of California, UC Toxic Substances Research and Training Program

Keller, A A, Froines, J, Koshland, C, Reuter, J, Suffet, I and Last, J, 1998b. 'Health and environmental assessment of MTBE, summary and recommendations', Report to the Governor of California, UC Toxic Substances Research and Training Program

Koshland, C P, Sawyer, R F, Lucas, D and Franklin, P, 1998. 'Evaluation of automotive MTBE combustion byproducts', in *Health and Environmental Assessment of MTBE* Vol 2, UC Toxic Substances Research and Training Program, University of California, Davis

Landmeyer, J E, Chapelle, F H, Bardley, P M, Pankow, J F, Church, C D and Tratnyek, P G, 1998. 'Fate of MTBE relative to benzene in a gasoline-contaminated aquifer (1993–98)', *Ground Water Monitoring Remediation* (Fall), pp93–102

Larsen, P B, 1997. *Evaluation of health hazards by exposure to MTBE and estimation of limit values in ambient air, soil and drinking water*, Institute of Toxicology of the National Food Agency of Denmark

Leighton, J, Matte, T, Findley, S, 1999. 'Asthma prevalence among school children in a Bronx community', Asthma Conference, 9 February 1999, p26, Centers for Disease Control and Prevention, Atlanta, GA

Leikauf, G D, Kline, S, Albert, R E, Baxter, C S, Bernstein, D I and Buncher, C R, 1995. 'Evaluation of a possible association of urban air toxics and asthma', *Environmental Health Perspectives* Vol 103, No 6, pp253–71

Mangione, S, Papastamelos, C, Elia, J, 1997. 'Asthma prevalence and absenteeism among innercity school children: A survey of two Philadelphia middle schools', *Am J Respir Crit Care Med* Vol 155

McBride, A D, 1996. *Outcome of asthma survey of kindergertners entering public school system in 1996*. Stamford Health Department, Stamford, CT

Mehlman, M A, 2000. 'Misclassification of carcinogenic methyl tertiary butyl ether (MTBE) by the National Toxicology Program Board: Smokescreen in, science out?', *Archives of Environmental Health* Vol 55, No 1, pp73–4

Miljø og Energiministeriet, 1998. Miljøstyrelsen: Handlingsplan for MTBE, Juni (in Danish)

Mills, E J and Stack, V T, 1954. 'Proc 8th Ind Waste Conf, Purdue Univ, Ext Ser 83:492', in R G Bond and C P Straub, 1974, *Handbook of environmental control Volume IV: Wastewater treatment and disposal*, CRC Press, Ohio

Morgenroth, E and Arvin, E, 1999. 'The European perspective to MTBE as an oxygenate in fuels', International Congress on Ecosystem Health – Managing for Ecosystem Health, Sacramento, CA, 15–20 August

Mormile, M R, Liu, S and Suflita, J M, 1994. 'Anaerobic biodegradation of gasoline oxygenates: Extrapolation of information to multiple sites and redox conditions', *Environ Sci Technol* Vol 28, pp1727–32

Moser, G J, Wolf, D C, Sar, M, Gaido, K W, Janszen, D and Goldsworthy, T L, 1998. 'Methyl tertiary butyl ether induced endocrine alterations in mice are not mediated through the estrogen receptor', *Toxicol Sci* Vol 41, pp77–87

NRC (National Research Council), 1996. *Toxicological and performance aspects of oxygenated motor vehicle fuels*, pp 75–115, National Academy Press, Washington, DC

NRC (National Research Council), 1999. *Ozone forming potential of reformulated gasoline*, pp 1–212, National Academy Press, Washington, DC

NSTC, 1997. *Interagency Assessment of Oxygenated Fuels*, Office of Science and Technology Policy, National Science and Technology Council, Washington, DC

OECD, 1970. *Pollution by detergents: Determination of the biodegradability of anionic synthetic surface active agents*, Organisation for Economic Co-operation and Development, Paris

OECD, 1981. *OECD chemicals testing programme: Expert group degradation/accumulation, final report*, Organisation for Economic Co-operation and Development, Paris; Umwelt Bundesamt, Bundesrepublik Deutschland, Berlin; Government of Japan, Tokyo (joint publication)

Østergaard, G, 2001. Pers comm

Rodriguez, R, 1997. 'MTBE in groundwater and the impact on the city of Santa Monica drinking water supply', in *Technical Papers of the 13th Annual Environmental Management and Technology Conference West, 4–6 November*

Sawyer, C N, 1960. *Chemistry for sanitary engineers*, Mcgraw Hill

Schirmer, M and Barker, J F, 1998. 'A study of long-term MTBE attenuation in the Borden aquifer, Ontario, Canada', *Ground Water Monitoring Remediation* (spring), pp113–22

Squillace, J P, Zogorski, J S, Wilber, W G and Price, C V, 1996. 'Preliminary assessment of the occurrence and possible sources of MTBE in groundwater in the United States, 1993–1994', *Env Sci Tech* Vol 30, pp1721–30

Suflita, J M and Mormile, M R, 1993. 'Anaerobic biodegradation of known and potential gasoline oxygenates in the terrestrial subsurface', *Environ Sci Technol* Vol 27, pp967–78

Swisher, R D, 1987. *Surfactant biodegradation*, Marcel Dekker Inc, New York

US EPA, 1979. 'Investigations of Biodegradability and Toxicity of Organic Compounds', EPA-600/2-79-163, US Environmental Protection Agency, Cincinnati

US EPA, 1997. 'Drinking water advisory: Consumer acceptability advice and health effects analysis on methyl tertiary butyl ether (MTBE)', EPA822-F-97-009;ODW 4304, Health and Ecological Criteria Division, Office of Science and Technology, Office of Water, US Environmental Protection Agency, Washington, DC

Williams, T M, Cattley, R C and Borghoff, S J, 2000. 'Alterations in endocrine responses in male Sprague-Dawley rats following oral administration of methyl tert butyl ether', *Toxicol Sci* Vol 54, pp168–76

Yeh, C K and Novak, J T, 1994. 'Anaerobic biodegradation of gasoline oxygenates in soils', *Water Environment Research* Vol 66, No 5, pp744–52

Chapter 12 Early warnings of chemical contamination of the Great Lakes

Broley, C L, 1958. 'Plight of the American bald eagle', *Audubon Magazine* Vol 60, pp162–71

Broley, M J, 1952. *Eagle man*, Pellegrini and Cudahy, New York

Burtraw, D and Krupnick, A, 1999. *Measuring the value of health improvements from Great Lakes cleanup*, Discussion paper 99–34, Resources for the Future, Washington, DC

Carson, R, 1962. *Silent spring*, Houghton Mifflin, Boston, MA

Chant, D W, 1969. A petition to the Ministers of Health and Welfare and of Agriculture, 25 September

Colborn, T and Clement, C (eds), 1992. *Chemically induced alterations in sexual and functional development: The wildlife/human connection*, Advances in Modern Environmental Toxicology Vol 21, Princeton Scientific Publishing, Princeton, New Jersey

Colborn, T, vom Saal, F and Short, P, 1998. *Environmental endocrine-disrupting chemicals: neural, endocrine, and behavioral effects*, Princeton Scientific, New Jersey

Cook, J W, 1964. *Review of the persistent organo-chlorine pesticides*, HMSO, London

Daly, H B, 1993. 'Laboratory rat experiments show consumption of Lake Ontario salmon causes behavioral changes: support for wildlife and human research results', *Journal of Great Lakes Research* Vol 19, pp784–8

Donahue, M J, 1999. 'The case for good government: Why a comprehensive review of the Great Lakes Water Quality Agreement is needed', *Toledo Journal of Great Lakes Law, Science and Policy* Vol 2, pp1–11

Edwards, M H, Quilliam, H R and Webb, D, 1963. 'Uninhabited island in Lake Ontario', *Audubon Field Notes* Vol 17, pp510–1

Fein, G G, Jacobson, J L, Jacobson, S W, Schwartz, P M and Dowler, J K, 1984. 'Prenatal exposure to polychlorinated biphenyls: Effects on birth size and gestational age', *Journal of Pediatrics* Vol 105, pp315–20

Fox, G A, 1991. 'Practical causal inference for ecoepidemiologists', *Journal of Toxicology and Environmental Health* Vol 33, pp359–73

Funtowicz, S and Ravetz, J, 1993. 'Science for the post-normal age', *Futures* Vol 25, pp739–55

Gilbertson, M, 1996. 'Great Lakes forensic toxicology and the implications for research and regulatory programs', *Toxicology and Industrial Health* Vol 12, pp563–71

Gilbertson, M, Morris, R D and Hunter, R A, 1976. 'Abnormal chicks and PCB residue levels in eggs of colonial birds on the lower Great Lakes (1971–1973)', *The Auk* Vol 93, pp434–42

Gilbertson, M and Reynolds, L M, 1972. 'Hexachlorobenzene (HCB) in the eggs of common terns in Hamilton Harbour, Ontario', *Bulletin of Environmental Contamination and Toxicology* Vol 7, pp371–3

Grier, J W, 1968. 'Immature bald eagle with an abnormal beak', *Bird Banding* Vol 39, pp58–9

Grier, J W, 1982. 'Ban of DDT and subsequent recovery of reproduction in bald eagles', *Science* Vol 218, pp1232–5

Hartig, J H, Zarull, M A and Law, N L, 1998. 'An ecosystem approach to Great Lakes management: Practical steps', *Journal of Great Lakes Research* Vol 24, pp739–50

Hartsough, G R, 1965. 'Great Lakes fish now suspect as mink food', *American Fur Breeder* Vol 38, pp27–35

Hickey, J J, Keith, J A and Coon, F B, 1966. 'An exploration of pesticides in a Lake Michigan ecosystem. Pesticides in the environment and their effects on wildlife', *Journal of Applied Ecology* Vol 3 (Suppl), pp141–54

Humphrey, H E B, 1983. 'Population studies of PCBs in Michigan residents' in F M D'Itri and M A Kamrin (eds), *PCBs: Human and environmental hazards*, Butterworth, Boston, MA, pp299–310

International Joint Commission, 1969. Pollution of Lake Erie, Lake Ontario and the International Section of the St Lawrence River, IJC, Ottawa and Washington

Jacobson, J L and Jacobson, S W, 1993. 'A four-year followup study of children born to consumers of Lake Michigan fish', *Journal of Great Lakes Research* Vol 19, pp776–83

Jacobson, J L and Jacobson, S W, 1996. 'Intellectual impairment in children exposed to polychlorinated biphenyls in utero', *New England Journal of Medicine* Vol 335, pp783–9

Jacobson, J L, Jacobson, S W, Fein, G G, Schwartz, P M and Dowler, J K, 1984. 'Prenatal exposure to an environmental toxin: A test of the multiple effects model', *Developmental Psychology* Vol 20, pp523–32

Jacobson, J L, Jacobson, S W and Humphrey, H E B, 1990. 'Effects of exposure to PCB and related compounds on growth and activity in children', *Neurotoxicology and Teratology* Vol 12, pp319–26

Jensen, S, 1966. 'Report of a new chemical hazard', *New Scientist* Vol 15, December, p612

Johnson, B L, Hicks, H E and DeRosa, C T, 1999. 'Key environmental human health issues in the Great Lakes and St Lawrence River basins', *Environmental Research Section A* Vol 80, ppS2–12

Johnson, B L, Hicks, H E, Jones, D E, Cibulas, W and DeRosa, C T, 1998. 'Public health implications of persistent toxic substances in the Great Lakes and St Lawrence Basins', *Journal of Great Lakes Research* Vol 24, pp698–722

Kaiser, K L E, 1974. 'Mirex: an unrecognized contaminant of fishes from Lake Ontario', *Science* Vol 185, pp523–5

Keith, J A, 1966. Reproduction in a population of herring gulls (Larus argentatus) contaminated by DDT *Journal of Applied Ecology* Vol 3 (Suppl), pp57–70

Lawless, E W, 1977. *Technology and social shock*, Rutgers University Press, New Brunswick, NJ, 616 pages

Lear, L, 1997. *Rachel Carson: Witness for nature*, Henry Holt, New York, NY

Levine, A G, 1982. *Love Canal: Science, politics and people*, Lexington Books, Toronto

Lonky, E, Reihman, J, Darvill, T, Mather, Sr, J and Daly, H, 1996. 'Neonatal behavioral assessment scale performance in humans influenced by maternal consumption of environmentally contaminated Lake Ontario fish', *Journal of Great Lakes Research* Vol 22, pp198–212

Ludwig, J P and Tomoff, C S, 1966. Reproductive success and insecticide residues in Lake Michigan herring gulls, Jack-Pine Warbler, 44, pp77–84

Monsanto, 1970. 'Monsanto cites actions taken on environmental issue', 16 July, St Louis

O'Brien, M H, 1994. 'Comment on preface to the special section on cause–effect linkages: Causality: The missing link between science and policy', *Journal of Great Lakes Research* Vol 20, pp590–2

Pekarik, C and Weseloh, D V, 1998. 'Organochlorine contaminants in herring gull eggs from the Great Lakes 1974–1995: Change point regression analysis and short-term regression', *Environmental Monitoring and Assessment* Vol 53, pp77–115

Pfister, R M, Dugan, P R and Frea, J I, 1969. 'Microparticulates: Isolation from water and identification of associated chlorinated pesticides', *Science* Vol 166, pp878–9

Ratcliffe, D A, 1972. 'The peregrine population of Great Britain in 1971', *Bird Study* Vol 19, pp117–56

Reynolds, L M, 1969. 'Polychlorobiphenyls (PCBs) and their interference with pesticide residue analysis', *Bulletin of Environmental Contamination and Toxicology* Vol 4, pp128–43

Robinson, J, 1967. 'Residues of aldrin and dieldrin in wildlife in Britain', Symposium on the science and technology of residual insecticides in food production with special reference to aldrin and dieldrin, Shell Chemical Company, 26 October

Shear, H, 1996. 'The development and use of indicators to assess the state of ecosystem health in the Great Lakes', *Ecosystem Health* Vol 2, pp241–58

Shell Chemical Company, 1967. 'Aldrin, dieldrin, endrin: A status report', Agricultural Chemicals Division

Sprunt, A I V, Robertson, Jr, W B, Postupalsky, S, Hensel, R J, Knoder, C E and Ligas, F J, 1973. 'Comparative productivity of six bald eagle populations', *Transactions of the North American Wildlife and Natural Resources Conference* Vol 38, p96

Stewart, P, Reihman, J, Lonky, E, Darvill, T and Pagano, J, 2000. 'Prenatal PCB exposure and neonatal behavioral assessment scale (NBAS) performance', *Neurotoxicology and Teratology* Vol 22, pp21–9

Stow, C A, Jackson, L J and Carpenter, S R, 1999. 'A mixed-order model to assess contaminant declines', *Environmental Monitoring and Assessment* Vol 55, pp435–44

Sudar, A and Muir, T, 1989. 'Costs and consequences of uncontrolled toxic waste sites along the Niagara River', *Water Pollution Research Journal of Canada* Vol 2, pp279–97

Swanson, T and Vighi, M, 1998. *Regulating chemical accumulation in the environment*, Cambridge University Press

US EPA, 1993. Water quality guidance for the Great Lakes system and correction: Proposed rules, Fed Register 58, pp20802–1047

US EPA, 1998. *Realizing remediation: A summary of contaminated sediment remediation activities in the Great Lakes Basin*, Great Lakes National Program Office

US EPA and NYSDEC, 2000. *Reduction of toxics loadings to the Niagara River from hazardous waste sites in the United States*, United States Environmental Protection Agency and New York State Department of Environmental Conservation

Chapter 13 Tributyltin (TBT) antifoulants

Abbott, A, Abel, P D, Arnold, D W and Milne, A, 2000. 'Cost–benefit analysis of the use of TBT: The case for a treatment approach', *The Science of the Total Environment* Vol 258, pp5–19

Abel, P D, 2000. 'TBT – towards a better way to regulate pollutants', *The Science of the Total Environment* Vol 258, pp1–4

Alzieu, C, 1998. 'Tributyltin: case study of a chronic contaminant in the coastal environment', *Ocean and Coastal Management* Vol 40, pp23–6

Alzieu, C, Sanjuan, J, Deltriel, J P and Borel, M, 1986. 'Tin contamination in Arcachon bay: Effects on oyster shell anomalies, *Marine Pollution Bulletin* Vol 17, pp494–8

Alzieu, C, Sanjuan, J, Michel, P, Borel, M and Dreno, J P, 1989. 'Monitoring and assessment of butyltins in Atlantic coastal waters', *Marine Pollution Bulletin* Vol 20, pp22–6

Ariese, F, van Hattum, B, Hopman, G, Boon, J and ten Hallers-Tjabbes, C, 1998. *Butyltin and phenyltin compounds in liver and blubber samples of sperm whales (Physeter macrocephalus) stranded in the Netherlands and Denmark*, Report W98-04, March 1998, Institute for Environmental Studies, Vrije Universiteit, Amsterdam

Bailey, S K and Davies, I M, 1988a. 'Tributyltin contamination in the Firth of Forth (1975–1987)', *The Science of the Total Environment* Vol 76, pp185–92

Bailey, S K and Davies, I M, 1988b. 'Tributyltin contamination around an oil terminal in Sullom Voe (Shetland)', *Environmental Pollution* Vol 55, pp161–72

Bailey, S K and Davies, I M, 1989. 'The effects of tributyltin on dogwhelks (*Nucella lapillus*) from Scottish coastal waters', *Journal of the Marine Biological Association*, UK Vol 69, pp335–54

Balls, P W, 1987. 'Tributyltin (TBT) in the waters of a Scottish sea loch arising from the use of antifoulant treated netting by salmon farms', *Aquaculture* Vol 65, pp227–37

Belfroid, A C, Purperhart, M and Ariese, F, 2000. 'Organotin levels in seafood', *Marine Pollution Bulletin* Vol 40, No 3, pp226–32

Blaber, S J M, 1970. 'The occurrence of penis-like outgrowth behind the right tentacle in spent females of *Nucella lapillus* (L.)', *Proceedings of the Malacological Society of London* Vol 39, pp231–3

Bouchard, N, Pelletier, E and Fournier, M, 1999. 'Effects of butyltin compounds on phagocytic activity of hemocytes from three marine bivalves', *Environmental Toxicology and Chemistry* Vol 18, No 3, pp519–22

Bryan, G W, Gibbs, P E, Hummerstone, L G and Burt, G R, 1986. 'The decline of the gastropod *Nucella lapillus* around south-west England: Evidence for the effect of tributyltin from antifouling paints', *Journal of the Marine Biological Association, UK* Vol 66, pp611–40

Bryan, G W, Gibbs, P E, Hummerstone, L G and Burt, G R, 1987. 'Copper, zinc and organotin as long-term factors governing the distribution of organisms in the Fal estuary in southwest England', *Estuaries* Vol 10, No 3, pp208–19

Cadee, G C, Boon, J P, Fischer, C V, Mensink, B P and ten Hallers-Tjabbes, C C, 1995. 'Why the whelk (*Buccinum undatum*) has become extinct in the Dutch Wadden Sea', *Netherlands Journal of Sea Research* Vol 34, No 4, pp337–9

Cardwell, R D, Kiethly, J C and Simmonds, J, 1999. 'Tributyltin in US market-bought seafood and assessment of human health risks', *Human and Ecological Risk Assessment* Vol 5, No 2, pp317–35

Clare, A S, 1998. 'Towards nontoxic antifouling', *Journal of Marine Biotechnology* Vol 6, pp3–6

Cleary, J J, 1991. 'Organotin in the marine surface microlayer and sub-surface waters of south-west England: Relation to toxicity thresholds and the UK environmental quality standard', *Marine Environmental Research* Vol 32, pp213–22

Cleary, J J, McFadzen, I R B and Peters, L D, 1993. 'Surface microlayer contamination and toxicity in the North Sea and Plymouth near-shore waters', CM 1993/E:28, International Council for the Exploration of the Sea, Marine Environment Quality Committee

Cleary, J J and Stebbing, A R D, 1987. 'Organotin in the surface microlayer and subsurface waters of southwest England', *Marine Pollution Bulletin* Vol 18, No 5, pp238–46

Dahl, B and Blanck, H, 1996. 'Toxic effects of the antifouling agent Irgarol 1051 on periphyton communities in coastal water microcosms', *Marine Pollution Bulletin* Vol 32, No 4, pp342–50

Dahllof, I, Blanck, H, Hall, P O J and Molander, S, 1999. 'Long-term effects of tri-n-butyl-tin on the function of a marine sediment system', *Marine Ecology Progress Series* Vol 188, pp1–11

Davies, I M, Bailey, S K and Harding, M J C, 1998. 'Tributyltin inputs to the North Sea from shipping activities, and potential risk of biological effects', *ICES Journal of Marine Science* Vol 55, pp34–43

Davies, I M and McKie, J C, 1987. 'Accumulation of total tin and tributyltin in the muscle tissue of farmed Atlantic salmon', *Marine Pollution Bulletin* Vol 18, No 7, pp405–7

de Mora, S J, King, N G and Miller, M C, 1989. 'Tributyltin and total tin in marine sediments: profiles and the apparent rate of TBT degradation', *Environmental Technology Letters* Vol 10, pp901–8

Ellis, D V and Pattisina, L A, 1990. 'Widespread neogastropod imposex: A biological indicator of global contamination', *Marine Pollution Bulletin* Vol 21, pp248–53

Evans, S M, 2000. 'Marine antifoulants' in C Sheppard (ed), *Seas at the millennium: An environmental evaluation, Vol III: Global issues and processes*, pp247–56, Elsevier Science Ltd, Oxford

Evans, S M, Birchenough, A C and Fletcher, H, 2000a. 'The value and validity of community-based research: TBT contamination of the North Sea', *Marine Pollution Bulletin* Vol 40, No 3, pp220–5

Evans, S M, Birchenough, A C and Brancato, M S, 2000b. 'The TBT ban: Out of the frying pan into the fire?', *Marine Pollution Bulletin* Vol 40, No 3, pp204–11

Gibbs, P E, 1993. 'A male genital defect in the dog-whelk, *Nucella lapillus* (Neogastropoda), favouring survival in a TBT-polluted area', *Journal of the Marine Biological Association*, UK Vol 73, pp667–78

Gibbs, P E, Pascoe, P L and Burt, G R, 1988. 'Sex change in the female dog-whelk, *Nucella lapillus*, induced by tributyltin from antifouling paints', *Journal of the Marine Biological Association*, UK Vol 68, pp715–31

Gibbs, P E, Bryan, G W and Pascoe, P L, 1991. 'TBT-induced imposex in the dogwhelk, *Nucella lapillus*: Geographical uniformity of the response and effects', *Marine Environmental Research* Vol 32, pp79–87

Harding, M J C, Rodger, G K, Davies, I M and Moore, J J, 1997. 'Partial recovery of the dogwhelk (*Nucella lapillus*) in Sullom Voe, Shetland from tributyltin contamination', *Marine Environmental Research* Vol 44, No 3, pp285–304

Harino, H, Fukushima, M, Yamamoto, Y, Kawai, S and Miyazaki, N, 1998a. 'Organotin compounds in water, sediment and biological samples from the Port of Osaka, Japan', *Archives of Environmental Contamination and Toxicology* Vol 35, pp558–64

Harino, H, Fukushima, M, Yamamoto, Y, Kawai, S and Miyazaki, N, 1998b. 'Contamination of butyltin and phenyltin compounds in the marine environment of Otsuchi Bay, Japan', *Environmental Pollution* Vol 101, pp209–14

Harino, H, Fukushima, M, Kawai, S and Megumi, K, 1998c. 'Measurement of butyltin contamination of water and sediment in Osaka Bay, Japan', *Applied Organometallic Chemistry* Vol 12, pp819–25

Harino, H, Fukushima, M and Kawai, S, 1999. 'Temporal trends of organotin compounds in the aquatic environment of the Port of Osaka, Japan', *Environmental Pollution* Vol 105, pp1–7

Hashimoto, S, Watanabe, M, Noda, Y, Hayashi, T, Kurita, Y, Takasu, Y and Otsuki, A, 1998. 'Concentration and distribution of butyltin compounds in a heavy tanker route in the Strait of Malacca and in Tokyo Bay', *Marine Environmental Research* Vol 45, No 2, pp169–77

Huet, M, Paulet, Y M and Glemarec, M, 1996. 'Tributyltin (TBT) pollution in the coastal waters as indicated by imposex in *Nucella lapillus*', *Marine Environmental Research* Vol 41, pp157–67

Ishizaka, T, Nemoto, S, Sasaki, K, Suzuki, T and Saito, Y, 1989. 'Simultaneous determination of tri-n-butyltin, di-n-butyltin and triphenyltin compounds in marine products', *Journal of Agriculture and Food Chemistry* Vol 37, pp1523–7

Iwata, H, Tanabe, S, Mizuno, T and Tatsukawa, R, 1995. 'High accumulation of toxic butyltins in marine mammals from Japanese coastal waters', *Environmental Science and Technology* Vol 29, pp2959–62

Kannan, K, Tanabe, S, Iwata, H and Tatsukawa, R, 1995a. 'Butyltins in muscle and liver of fish collected from certain Asian and Oceanian countries', *Environmental Pollution* Vol 90, No 3, pp279–90

Kannan, K, Tanabe, S, Tatsukawa, R and Williams, R J, 1995b. 'Butyltin residues in fish from Australia, Papua New Guinea and the Solomon Islands', *International Journal of Environmental Analytical Chemistry* Vol 61, pp263–73

Kannan, K, Yasunga, Y, Iwata, H, Ichhashi, H, Tanabe, S and Tatsukawa, R, 1995c. 'Concentrations of heavy metals, organochlorines and organotins in horseshoe crab, Tachpleus tridentatus, from Japanese coastal waters', *Archives of Environmental Contamination and Toxicology* Vol 28, pp40–7

Kannan, K, Corsolini, S, Focardi, S, Tanabe, S and Tatsukawa, R, 1996. 'Accumulation pattern of butyltin compounds in dolphin, tuna and shark collected from Italian coastal waters', *Archives of Environmental Contamination and Toxicology* Vol 31, pp19–23

Kannan, K, Senthilkumar, K, Loganathan, B G, Takahashi, S, Odell, D K and Tanabe, S, 1997. 'Elevated accumulation of tributyltin and its breakdown products in bottlenose dolphins (*Tursiops truncatus*) found stranded along the US Atlantic and Gulf coasts', *Environmental Science and Technology* Vol 31, pp296–301

Kannan, K, Guruge, K S, Thomas, N J, Tanabe, S and Giesy, J P, 1998. 'Butyltin residues in southern sea otters (*Enhydra lutris nereis*) found dead along California coastal waters', *Environmental Science and Technology* Vol 32, pp1169–75

King, N, Miller, M and de Mora, S, 1989. 'Tributyltin levels for sea water, sediment and selected marine species in coastal Northland and Auckland, New Zealand', *New Zealand Journal of Marine and Freshwater Research* Vol 23, pp287–94

Krone, C A, Burrows, D G, Brown, D W, Chan, S-L and Varanasi, U, 1989. 'Tributyltin contamination of sediment and English sole from Puget Sound', *Proceedings of Oceans '89, Vol 2: Ocean Pollution*, IEEE Publication No 89CH2780-5, pp545–9

Labare, M L, Coon, S L, Mathias, C and Weiner, R M, 1997. 'Magnification of tributyltin toxicity to oyster larvae by bioconcentration in biofilms of *Shewanella colwelliana*', *Applied and Environmental Microbiology* Vol 63, No 10, pp4107–10

Langston, W J, 1996. 'Recent developments in TBT ecotoxicology', *Toxicology and Ecotoxicology News* Vol 3, No 6, pp179–87

Langston, W J and Burt, G R, 1991. 'Bioavailability and effects of sediment-bound TBT in deposit-feeding clams, *Scrobicularia plana*', *Marine Environmental Research* Vol 32, pp61–77

Langston, W J, Burt, G R and Mingjiang, Z, 1987. 'Tin and organotin in water, sediments and benthic organisms of Poole Harbour', *Marine Pollution Bulletin* Vol 18, No 12, pp634–9

Langston, W J, Bryan, G W, Burt, G R and Pope, N D, 1994. *Effects of sediment metals on estuarine benthic organisms*, RandD Note 203, National Rivers Authority

Laughlin, R B and Linden, O, 1985. 'Fate and effects of organotin compounds', *Ambio* Vol 14, No 2, pp88–94

Laughlin, R B and Linden, O, 1987. 'Tributyltin – contemporary environmental issues', *Ambio* Vol 16, No 5, pp252–6

Law, R J, Blake, S J, Jones, B R and Rogan, E, 1998. 'Organotin compounds in liver tissue of harbour porpoises (*Phocoena phocoena*) and grey seals (*Hlichoerus grypus*) from the coastal waters of England and Wales', *Marine Pollution Bulletin* Vol 36, No 3, pp241–7

Law, R J, Blake, S J and Spurrier, C J H, 1999. 'Butyltin compounds in liver tissues of pelagic cetaceans stranded on the coasts of England and Wales', *Marine Pollution Bulletin* Vol 38, No 12, pp1258–61

Lee, R F, Valkirs, A O and Seligman, P F, 1989. 'Importance of microalgae in the biodegradation of tributyltin in estuarine waters', *Environmental Science and Technology* Vol 23, No 12, pp1515–18

Matthiessen P and Gibbs, P E, 1998. 'Critical appraisal of the evidence for tributyltin-mediated endocrine disruption in mollusks', *Environmental Toxicology and Chemistry* Vol 17, No 1, pp37–43

MEPC, 1997. Report of the 40th session of the Marine Environmental Protection Committee of the International Maritime Organization, 18–25 September 1997

MEPC, 1998. Report of the 41st session of the Marine Environmental Protection Committee of the International Maritime Organization, 30 March–3 April 1998

Michel, P and Averty, B, 1999a. 'Contamination of French coastal waters by organotin compounds: 1997 update', *Marine Pollution Bulletin* Vol 38, No 4, pp268–75

Michel, P and Averty, B, 1999b. 'Distribution and fate of tributyltin in surface and deep waters of the northwestern Mediterranean', *Environmental Science and Technology* Vol 33, pp2524–28

Minchin, D, 1995. 'Recovery of a population of the flame shell, *Lima hians*, in an Irish Bay previously contaminated with TBT', *Environmental Pollution* Vol 90, No 2, pp259–62

Minchin, D, Bauer, B, Oehlmann, J, Schulte-Oehlmann, U and Duggan, C B, 1997. 'Biological indicators used to map organotin contamination from a fishing port, Killybegs, Ireland', *Marine Pollution Bulletin* Vol 34, No 4, pp235–43

MINDEC, 1995. Ministerial Declaration of the Fourth International Conference on the Protection of the North Sea, 8–9 June, Esbjerg, Denmark

Moore, D W, Dillon, T M and Suedel, B C, 1991. 'Chronic toxicity of tributyltin to the marine polychaete worm, *Neanthes arenaceodentata*', *Aquatic Toxicology* Vol 21, pp181–98

Morcillo, Y and Porte, C, 2000. 'Evidence of endocrine disruption in clams – *Ruditapes decussata* – transplanted to a tributyltin-polluted environment', *Environmental Pollution* Vol 107, pp47–52

Nicholson, G J and Evans, S M, 1997. ' Anthropogenic impacts on the stocks of the common whelk *Buccinum undatum* (L.)', *Marine Environmental Research* Vol 44, No 3, pp305–14

OSPAR, 1998. OSPAR strategy with regard to hazardous substances, OSPAR 98/14/1 Annex 34, OSPAR Convention for the Protection of the Marine Environment of the Northeast Atlantic

PARCOM, 1987. PARCOM Recommendation 87/1 on the use of tributyl-tin compounds, 3 June, Paris Convention for the Prevention of Marine Pollution from Land-Based Sources

PARCOM, 1988. PARCOM Recommendation 88/1 on measures to reduce organotin compounds reaching the aquatic environment through docking activities, 17 June, Paris Convention for the Prevention of Marine Pollution from Land-Based Sources

Prudente, M, Ichihashi, H, Kan-atireklap, S, Watanabe, I and Tanabe, S, 1999. 'Butyltins, organochlorines and metal levels in green mussel, *Perna viridis* L. from the coastal waters of the Philippines', *Fisheries Science* Vol 65, No 3, pp441–47

Rees, H L, Waldock, R, Matthiessen, P and Pendle, M A, 1999. 'Surveys of the epibenthos of the Crouch Estuary (UK) in relation to TBT contamination', *Journal of the Marine Biological Association*, UK Vol 79, pp209–23

Ruiz, J M, Bachelet, G, Caumette, P and Donard, O F X, 1996. 'Three decades of tributyltin in the coastal environment with emphasis on Arcachon Bay, France', *Environmental Pollution* Vol 93, No 2, pp195–203

Ruiz, J M, Quintela, M and Barreiro, R, 1998. 'Ubiquitous imposex and organotin bioaccumulation in gastropods *Nucella lapillus* from Galicia (NW Spain): A possible effect of nearshore shipping', *Marine Ecology Progress Series* Vol 164, pp237–44

Santillo, D, Stringer, R, Johnston, P and Tickner, J, 1998. 'The precautionary principle: Protecting against failures of scientific method and risk assessment', *Marine Pollution Bulletin* Vol 36, No 12, pp939–50

Sarradin, P M, Astruc, A, Sabrier, R and Astruc, M, 1994. 'Survey of butyltin compounds in Arcachon Bay sediments', *Marine Pollution Bulletin* Vol 28, pp621–28

Scarlett, A, Donkin, P, Fileman, T W and Donkin, M E, 1997. 'Occurrence of the marine antifouling agent Irgarol 1051 within the Plymouth Sound locality: Implications for the green macroalga *Enteromorpha intestinalis*', *Marine Pollution Bulletin* Vol 34, No 8, pp645–51

Scarlett, A, Donkin, P, Fileman, T W, Evans, S V and Donkin, M E, 1999. 'Risk posed by the antifouling agent Irgarol 1051 to the seagrass, *Zostera marina*', *Aquatic Toxicology* Vol 45, pp159–70

Side, J, 1987. 'Organotins: Not so good relations', *Marine Pollution Bulletin* Vol 18, No 5, pp205–6

Simmonds, M, 1986. 'The case against tributyltin', *Oryx* Vol 20, No 4, pp217–20

Smith, B S, 1971. 'Sexuality of the American mud snail, *Nassarius obsoletus* (Say)', *Proceedings of the Malacological Society of London* Vol 39, pp377–8

St-Jean, S D, Courtenay, S C, Pelletier, E and St-Louis, R, 1999. 'Butyltin concentrations in sediments and blue mussels (*Mytlus edulis*) of the southern Gulf of St Lawrence, Canada', *Environmental Technology* Vol 20, pp181–9

Swennen, C, Ruttanadakul, N, Ardseungnern, S, Singh, H R, Mensick, B P and ten Hallers-Tjabbes, C C, 1997. 'Imposex in sublittoral and littoral gastropods from the gulf of Thailand and Strait of Malacca in relation to shipping', *Environmental Technology* Vol 18, pp1245–54

Tanabe, S, Prudente, M, Mizuno, T, Hasegawa, J, Iwata, H and Miyazaki, N, 1998. 'Butyltin contamination in marine mammals from north Pacific and Asian coastal waters', *Environmental Science and Technology* Vol 32, No 2, pp193–8

'TBT linked to dogwhelk decline', 1986. *Marine Pollution Bulletin* Vol 17, No 9, p390

ten Hallers-Tjabbes, C C, 1997. 'Tributyltin and policies for antifouling', *Environmental Technology* Vol 18, pp1265–8

ten Hallers-Tjabbes, C C, Kemp, J F and Boon, J P, 1994. 'Imposex in whelks (*Buccinum undatum*) from the open North Sea: Relation to shipping traffic intensities', *Marine Pollution Bulletin* Vol 28, No 5, pp311–3

Uhler, A D, Coogan, T H, Davis, K S, Durell, G S, Steinhauer, W G, Freitas, S Y and Boehm, P D, 1989. 'Findings of tributyltin, dibutyltin and monobutyltin in bivalves from selected US coastal waters', *Environmental Toxicology and Chemistry* Vol 8, pp971–9

Vos, J G, Dybing, E, Greim, H A, Ladefoged, O, Lambre, C, Tarazona, J V, Brandt, I and Vethaak, A D, 2000. 'Health effects of endocrine-disrupting chemicals on wildlife, with special reference to the European situation', *Critical Reviews in Toxicology* Vol 30, No 1, pp71–133

Wade, T L, Garcia-Romero, B and Brooks, J M, 1988a. 'Tributyltin contamination in bivalves from United States Coastal Estuaries', *Environmental Science and Technology* Vol 22, pp1488–93

Wade, T L, Garcia-Romero, B and Brooks, J M, 1988b. 'Tributyltin analyses in association with NOAA's National Status and Trends Mussel Watch Program', *Proceedings of the Oceans '88 Conference, Baltimore, Maryland, 31 October–2 November*, pp1198–201

Waldock, M J and Thain, J E, 1983. 'Shell thickening in *Crassostrea gigas*: Organotin antifouling or sediment induced?', *Marine Pollution Bulletin* Vol 14, pp411–5

Waldock, M J, Thain, J E and Waite, M E, 1987. 'The distribution and potential toxic effects of TBT in UK estuaries during 1986', *Applied Organometallic Chemistry* Vol 1, pp287–301

Waldock, M J, Waite, M E and Thain, J E, 1988. 'Inputs of TBT to the marine environment from shipping activity in the UK', *Environmental Technology Letters* Vol 9, pp999–1010

Waldock, M J, Thain, J E, Smith, D and Milton, S, 1990. 'The degradation of TBT in estuarine sediments', *Proceedings of the Third International Organotin Symposium, Monaco, 17–20 April*, International Atomic Energy Authority, pp46–8

Zabel, T F, Seager, J and Oakley, S D, 1988. *Proposed environmental quality standards for List II substances in water: Organotins*, Water Research Centre technical report TR255, Marlow, UK

Chapter 14 Hormones as growth promoters

Adkins, E K, 1975. 'Hormonal basis of sexual differentiation in the Japanese quail', *Journal of Comparative and Physiological Psychology* Vol 89, pp61–71

Aulerich, R J, Bursian, S J, Breslin, W J, Olson, B A and Ringer, R K, 1985. 'Toxicological manifestations of 2,4,5,2,4,5-2,3,6,2,3,6- and 3,4,5,4,5,-hexachlorobiphenyl and Aroclor 1254 in mink', *Journal of Toxicology and Environmental Health* Vol 15, pp63–79

Bergman, A and Olsson, M, 1985. 'Pathology of Baltic ringed seal and grey seal females with special reference to adrenocortical hyperplasia: Is environmental pollution the cause of a widely distributed disease syndrome?', *Finn. Game Research* Vol 44, pp47–62

Brown-Grant, K, Fink, G, Greig F and Murray, M A, 1975. 'Altered sexual development in male rats after oestrogen administration during the neonatal period', *Journal of Reproduction and Fertility* Vol 44, pp25–42

Bulkey, R V, 1972. 'Diethylstilbestrol in catfish feed', *Trans American Fisheries Society* Vol 101, pp537–99

Davies, J and Danzo, B J, 1981. 'Hormonally responsive areas of the reproductive system of the male guinea pig II: Effects of estrogens', *Biological Reproduction* Vol 25, pp1149–58

Delong, R L, Gilmartin, W G and Simpson, J G, 1973. 'Premature births in California sea lions: Association with high organochlorine pollutant residue levels', *Science* Vol 181, pp1168–70

European Commission, 1996. *Scientific Conference on Growth Promoters and Meat Production Proceedings*, Office for Official Publications of the EU Communities, Luxembourg

Fara, G M, Del Corvo, G, Bernuzzi, S, Bigatello, A, Di Pietro, C, Scaglioni, S and Chiumello, G, 1979. 'Epidemic of breast enlargement in an Italian school', *Lancet* Vol 11, pp295–7

Henderson, B E, Ross, R and Bernstein, L, 1988. 'Estrogens as a cause of human cancer: The Richard and Hinda Rosenthal Foundation Award lecture', *Cancer Research* Vol 48, pp246–53

Herbst, A L and Bern, H A, 1988. *Developmental effects of diethylstilbestrol (DES) in pregnancy*, Thieme-Stratton, New York

Jakes, T H, 1976. 'Diethylstilboestrol in beef production: What is the risk to the consumer?', *Preventive Medicine* Vol 5, pp438–53

JECFA/WHO, 1988. *Technical Report Series* N7/63, Geneva

Johnstone, R, Simpson, T H and Youngson, A F, 1978. 'Sex reversal in salmonid cultures', *Aquaculture* Vol 13, pp115–34

Lamming, G E, Ballarini, G, Bauliieu, E E, Brooks, P, Elias, P S, Ferrando, R, Galli, C L, Heitzman, R J, Hoffman, B, Karg, H, Meyer, H H D, Michel, G, Poulsen, E, Rico, A, van Leuwen F X R and White, D S, 1987. 'Scientific report on anabolic agents in animal production', *Veterinary Records* Vol 121, pp389–92

Loizzo, A, Gatti, G L, Macri, A, Moretti, G, Ortolani, E and Palazzesi, S, 1984. 'Italian baby food containing diethylstilboestrol three years later', *Lancet* Vol 5, pp1014–5

McMartin, K E, 1978. 'Diethylstilboestrol: A review of its toxicity and use of a growth promotant in food producing animals', *Journal of Environmental Pathological Toxicology* Vol 1, pp279–313

Mueller, G G and Kim, U H, 1978. 'Displacement of estradiol from oestrogen receptors by simple alkylphenols', *Endocrinology* Vol 102, pp1429–35

Orgebin-Crist, M C, Eller, B C and Danzo, B J, 1983. 'The effects of estradiol, tamoxifen and testosterone on the weights and histology of the epididymis and accessory sex organs of sexually immature rabbits', *Endocrinology* Vol 113, pp1703–15

Peakall, D B, 1970. 'p,p'-DDT: Effect on calcium metabolism and concentration of estradiol in blood', *Science* Vol 168, pp592–4

Perez-Comas A, 1988. 'Premature sexual development in Puerto Rico', *Boletin Asociacion Medica de Puerto Rico* Vol 80, pp85–90

Reijnders, P J H, 1986. 'Reproductive failure in common seals feeding on fish from polluted coastal waters', *Nature* Vol 324, pp456–7

Schmidely, Ph, 1993. 'Revue bibliographique quantitative sur l'utilisation des hormones anabolisantes à action steroidienne chez les ruminnants en production de viande. Performances zootechniques', *Annales de Zootechnie* Vol 42, pp333–60

Scientific Committee on Veterinary Measures Relating to Public Health, 1999. 'Assessment of potential risks to human health from hormone residues in bovine meat and meat products'

Takasugi, N, 1979. 'Development of permanently proliferated and cornified vaginal epithelium in mice treated neonatally with steroid hormones and the implication in tumorigenesis', *National Cancer Institute Research Monographs* Vol 51, pp57–66

Wilson, M E and Lasnitzki, I, 1971. 'Dihydrotestosterone found in foetal tissues of the rabbit and rat', *Endocrinology* Vol 89, pp659–68

World Trade Organization, 1997. WT/DS26/R/USA and WT/DS48/R/CAN

Zuckerman, S, 1940. 'The histogenesis of tissues sensitive to estrogens', *Biological Review* Vol 15, pp231–71

Chapter 15 'Mad cow disease'

Barclay, C, 1996. 'Bovine spongiform encephalopathy and agriculture', House of Commons Library Research Paper No 96/62, 15 May

BASES, n.d. *General introduction, national action systems and TSEs in Europe*, at www.upmf-grenoble.fr/inra/serd/BASES/

BSE Inquiry, 1999a. 'The Central Veterinary Laboratory 1985–1989', Revised factual account, No 4

BSE Inquiry, 1999b. 'The early days', Revised factual account, No 5

BSE Inquiry, 1999c. 'Slaughter and compensation', Revised factual account, No 6

BSE Inquiry, 1999d. 'Ruminant feed ban', Revised factual account, No 7

BSE Inquiry, 1999e. 'The introduction of the SBO ban', Revised factual account, No 8

BSE Inquiry, 1999f. 'Consideration of the risk from mechanically recovered meat (MRM) in 1989', draft factual account, No 14

BSE Inquiry transcript, 1998. At www.bse.org.uk

'Cash for cows', 1996. *The Economist* Vol 338, No 7959 (30 March)

Collinge, J, 1999. 'Variant Creutzfeldt-Jakob disease', *The Lancet* Vol 354, No 9175 (24 July), pp317–23

Cooke, B C, 1998. 'A brief history of the use of meat products, especially meat and bone meal in the feeds for ruminant animals', *The BSE Inquiry*, Statement No 27

Dealler, S, 1996. 'Can the spread of BSE and CJD be predicted?' in S C Ratzan (ed), *The mad cow crisis*, UCL Press, London

DTZ Pieda Consulting, 1998. 'Economic impact of BSE on the UK economy', Report to UK agricultural departments and HM Treasury

European Commission, 2000. White Paper on food safety in the European Union COM(99)719, 12 January, at http://europa.eu.int/comm/food/fs/intro/index_en.html

European Parliament, 1996. 'Replies from the Commission to questions from the Committee members', Temporary Committee of Inquiry into BSE, Doc_PE 218.980, 18 September

European Parliament, 1997. 'Report on alleged contravention or maladministration in the implementation of Community law in relation to BSE, Part B, Work of the Committee of Inquiry and basic data', Doc_EN\RR\319\319055 A4-0020/97A, 7 February

Farmers Weekly Interactive Service, 1999. At www.fwi.co.uk (accessed 26 April)

Hansard, 1990. 8 June

House of Commons, 1999. *BSE: The cost of a crisis*, Select Committee on Public Accounts, 24th report, HC 790, HMSO, London

House of Commons Agriculture Committee, 1990. 'Bovine spongiform encephalopathy (BSE)', Fifth report, 10 July

House of Commons Agriculture and Health Select Committees, 1996. 'Bovine spongiform encephalopathy (BSE) and Creutzfeldt-Jakob disease (CJD): Recent developments', Minutes of evidence, HC-331

Kimberlin, R H, Cole, S and Walker, C A, 1987. 'Temporary and permanent modifications to a single strain of mouse scrapie on transmission to rats and hamsters', *Journal of General Virology* Vol 68, pp1875–81

Martin, W B, 1998. 'Involvement with scrapie as scientific director of the Moredun Research Institute', The BSE Inquiry, Statement No 5

Minute, 1988. Minute from the private secretary of Mr MacGregor to the private secretary of Mr Thompson, dated 29 February 1988, BSE Inquiry Document No YB 88/2.29/4.1

Nature, 1990. 24 May, p278

New Scientist, 1996. 30 March, p4

Panorama, 1996. BBC Television, broadcast 17 June

Phillips et al, 2000. *The BSE Inquiry report: Evidence and supporting papers of the inquiry into the emergence and identification of bovine spongiform encephalopathy (BSE) and variant Creutzfeldt-Jakob disease (vCJD) and the action taken in response to it up to 20 March 1996*, The Stationery Office, London

Radio Times, 1992. Keith Meldrum, quoted in issue of 31 May

RCEP, 1979. 'Agriculture and pollution', Seventh report, Royal Commission on Environmental Pollution

Chapter 16 Twelve late lessons

Ashford, N, 1984. 'Alternatives to cost–benefit analysis in regulatory decisions', *Annals of the New York Academy of Sciences* Vol 363, April

Ashford, N, 1991. 'An innovation-based strategy for the environment and for the workplace' in A Finkel and D Golding (eds), *Worst things first: the debate over risk-based national environmental priorities*, Resources for the Future, Washington, DC

Copeland et al, 1977. 'Bias due to misclassification in the estimate of relative risk', *American Journal of Epidemiology* Vol 105, pp488–95

Dowlatabadi, H and Rotmans, J, 2000. 'Integrated assessment', Special issue of *Integrated Assessment* Vol 1, No 3, Battzer Science Publishers

EEA (European Environment Agency), forthcoming 2002. 'An EEA response to late lessons from early warnings: Some implications for policymakers and the public', European Environment Agency, Copenhagen

EFIEA (European Forum for Integrated Environmental Assessment), 2000. 'Integrated environmental assessment in European Environment Agency reporting', Report of the EEA/EFIEA special session, Copenhagen/Amsterdam

Hanley, N and Spash, C, 1993. *Cost–benefit analysis and the environment*, Edward Elgar, London

Harding, R and Fisher, E (eds), 1999. *Perspectives on the precautionary principle*, The Federation Press, Sydney

HELCOM, 1996. 'Third periodic assessment of the state of the marine environment of the Baltic Sea 1989–1993, Executive summary', *Baltic Sea Environment Proceedings* 64 A

IEGMP (Independent Expert Group on Mobile Phones), 2000. *Mobile phones and health* (The Stewart Report), Chilton, United Kingdom, at www.iegmp.org.uk/IEGMPtxt.htm (accessed 16 May 2001)

Kourilsky, P and Viney, G, 1999. 'Le principe de précaution', Rapport au Premier ministre, France

Krohn, W and Weyer, J, 1994. 'Society as a laboratory: The social risks of experimental research', *Science and Public Policy* Vol 21, pp173–83

Levy, A and Derby, B, 2000. 'Report on consumer focus groups on biotechnology', US Food and Drug Administration, Center for Food Safety and Applied Nutrition, Office of Scientific Analysis and Support, Division of Market Studies, Washington, DC and Paper presented to session on 'Public attitudes to agricultural biotechnologies', Annual Meeting of the Society for the Social Studies of Science (4S), University of Vienna, 30 September

Ministry for the Environment (New Zealand), 2001. Resource Management Act, text and background discussion, at www.mfe.govt.nz/management/rma/rma11.htm (accessed 17 May)

National Oceans Office, 2001. Australia's oceans policy home page, at www.oceans.gov.au/aop/main.htm (accessed 26 April)

NRC (US National Research Council), 1996. 'Understanding risk', Report of an ad hoc working party chaired by H Feinberg, summary at www.riskworld.com/Nreports/1996/risk_rpt/html/nr6aa045.htm (accessed 17 May 2001)

O'Brien, M, 2000. *Making better environmental decisions: an alternative to risk assessment*, MIT Press, Cambridge, MA

Omen, G S, Kessler, A C, Anderson, N T et al, 1997. *Framework for environmental health risk management*, US Presidential/Congressional Commission on Risk Assessment and Risk Management, Final report, Vol 1, Environmental Protection Agency, Washington

O'Riordan and Cameron, 1994. *Interpreting the precautionary principle*, Cameron May, London

O'Riordan, Cameron and Jordan, 2001. *Reinterpreting the precautionary principle*, Cameron May, London

Phillips et al, 2000. *Return to an order of the Honourable the House of Commons dated October 2000 for the Report, evidence and supporting papers of the Inquiry into the emergence and identification of bovine spongiform encephalopathy (BSE) and variant Creutzfeldt-Jakob disease (vCJD) and the action taken in response to it up to 20 March 1996*, The Stationery Office, London, at www.bse.org.uk/index.htm (accessed 16 May 2001)

Popper, K R, 1962. *The open society and its enemies*, Vol 1, Chapter 5, fourth edition, Routledge & Kegan Paul, London

Raffensberger, C and Tickner, J (eds), 1999. *Protecting public health and the environment: Implementing the precautionary principle*, Island Press, Washington, DC

Renn O, Webler, T and Kastenholz, H, 1996. 'Procedural and substantive fairness in landfill siting: A Swiss case study', *Risk, Health, Safety and Environment* Vol 7, No 2 (Spring 1996), pp95–8, Franklin Pierce Law Center, Concord, NH

Rip, A, Misa, T and Schot, J, 1996. *Managing technology in society*, Pinter, London

RCEP, 1998. *Setting environmental standards*, 21st Report of the Royal Commission on Environmental Pollution, Cm 4053, HMSO, London, summary at www.rcep.org.uk/reports2.html#21 (accessed 16 May 2001)

RMNO, 2000, 'Willingly and Knowingly: The roles of knowledge about nature and the environment in policy processes', *Advisory Council for Research on Spatial Planning, Nature and the Environment*, Lemma Publishers, Utrecht

Stirling, A, 1999. 'On science, and precaution in the management of technological risk', Final summary report, Technological Risk and the Management of Uncertainty project, European Scientific Technology Observatory, EC Forward Studies Unit, Brussels, cited in European Commission, 2000. Communication from the Commission on the precautionary principle, COM(2000)1, Brussels

Stirling, A and Mayer, S, 1999. 'Rethinking risk: A pilot multi-criteria mapping of a genetically modified crop in agricultural systems in the UK', SPRU, University of Sussex

Tickner, J A, 2000. 'Precaution in practice: A framework for implementing the precautionary principle', Dissertation prepared for the Department of Work Environment, University of Massachusetts, Lowell, MA

Underwood, T, 1999. 'Precautionary principles require changes in thinking about and planning environmental sampling' in R Harding and E Fisher (eds), *Perspectives on the precautionary principle*, pp254–66, The Federation Press, Sydney

van den Berg, N, Dutilh, C and Huppes, G, 1995. *Beginning LCA: A guide into environmental life cycle assessment*, CML/Unilever/Novem/RIVM

van Dommeln, 1997. *Coping with deliberate release: The limits of risk assessment*, International Centre for Human and Public Affairs, Tilburg/Buenos Aires

von Hayek, F, 1978. *New studies in philosophy, politics, economics and the history of ideas*, Chicago University Press

WBGU, 2000. *Welt im Wandel: Handlungsstrategien zur Bewältigung globaler Umweltrisiken* (World in transition: strategies for managing global environmental risks), Jahresgutachten 1998 (Annual report 1998), Springer, Berlin

Wynne, B, 1992. 'Uncertainty and environmental learning: Reconceiving science and policy in the preventive paradigm', *Global Environmental Change* Vol 6, pp111–27

Wynne, B, 2001. 'Managing and communicating scientific uncertainty in public policy', Harvard University Conference on Biotechnology and Global Governance: Crisis and Opportunity, Kennedy School of Government, April

Wynne, B, Marris, C, Simmons, P, De Marchi, B, Pellizoni, L, Renn, O, Klinke, A, Lemkow, L, Sentmarti, R and Carceras, J, 2000. 'Public attitudes to agricultural biotechnologies in Europe', Final report of project PABE, 1997–2000, DG Research, European Commission, Brussels

Wynne, B et al, 2001. *Wising up*, Lancaster University

Index

Page references in *italics* refer to figures, tables and boxes